The Territorial Status of the Falkland Islands (Malvinas): Past and Present

Rudolf Dolzer

Oceana Publications Inc
New York * London * Rome

Library of Congress Catalog in Publication Data

Dolzer, Rudolf

The Territorial Status of the Falkland Islands(Malvinas): Past and Present

CIP: 92-064018

ISBN: 0-379-20155-0

10 0 0176582

Manufactured in the United States of America on acid-free paper.

Acknowledgments

I gratefully acknowledge the assistance provided in the preparation of this book by Dr. Peter Macalister-Smith, Max Planck Institute for Comparative Public Law and International Law, Heidelberg. My sincere thanks are also owed to the staff members of my department at the University of Mannheim.

Autumn 1992   Rudolf Dolzer

Table of Contents

I.   Introduction

The first scholarly monograph on the international legal
status of the Falkland Islands (Malvinas) was probably the
thesis written by a certain Isaac Areco who in 1885 published
his doctoral study entitled "Titulos de la República
Argentina a la Soberania y Possessión de las Islas Malvinas"
("Titles of the Argentine Republic to the Sovereignty and
Possession of the Malvinas Islands")[1]. Since then,
publications on the same subject have continued to appear,
albeit at irregular intervals. What emerges from a survey of
the literature, amounting now to hundreds of articles and
dozens of books, is that the dispute over the Falklands
(Malvinas) is almost exclusively a dispute over the law
applicable.

As to the underlying facts, it would appear that the
truth about the discovery of the Falklands (Malvinas), which
consist of two main islands and 200 smaller surrounding
islands having a total area of some 5000 square miles[2], is
clouded with uncertainty, and is unlikely ever to be clearly
revealed. However, legal evaluation of the territorial status
of the Islands will not require special emphasis to be placed
upon the relevant facts of discovery, inasmuch as these have
not in the event given rise to declarations or actions which
resulted in any change of legal status. Both Argentina and
the United Kingdom have in the past made reference to the
discovery of the Islands, as they judge it, but the legal
case of each state does not depend upon this historical
aspect[3]. With regard to the subsequent developments on the
Falklands (Malvinas), it is apparent that not all authors
base their legal analysis upon the same facts when addressing
the takeover of the Islands by the United Kingdom in 1832 to

---

1   I. Areco, Titulos de la República Argentina a la
     Soberania y Possesión de las Islas Malvinas (1885).

2   As to the geographic situation of the islands, see
     Annex 2.

3   See infra p. 16 ff.

1833. However, a closer scrutiny shows that there is no real dispute in this respect either. Reports were drawn up at the time by the main protagonists in the events which took place, and comparison reveals no substantial differences in the nature or the sequence of the relevant actions[4]. No reasons exist to doubt the accuracy of these parallel statements. Moreover, Argentina and the United Kingdom do not disagree about the factual history of the Islands in the period after 1833.

Thus, the dispute is characterised by its classical legal nature. To a considerable extent, the rules in dispute involve the history of international law, i.e. they are no longer valid in relation to actions which occur today[5]. As will be discussed below, however, the rules of intertemporal law as generally accepted in international law require that, in principle, historical events be judged in the light of the law as it stood at the time rather than as it stands today. For this reason, a thorough discussion of the status of the Falklands (Malvinas) as it has evolved historically is bound to require recourse to libraries holding collections on the history of international law and on the international law that was valid in the past. The matter becomes all the more complex as the relevant rules on war, peace and the acquisition of territory were never entirely without ambiguity in the 19th century, either in practice or in legal theory.

The legal nature of the dispute holds consequences for the manner in which the issue can or rather must be treated. Only a chronologically-based approach to the various sequences of actions concerning the Islands will satisfy proper methodological requirements. Each new step and period will have to be related to the previous developments and to the previous status as governed by the law then applicable.

---

4   See infra, p. 103.
5   See infra, p. 111.

In other words, studies with a limited historical focus are
in danger of missing the relevant starting point. Therefore,
the subject matter does not, in principle, lend itself to
cursory treatment, although after the 1982 war a large number
of short articles appeared. Moreover, analysis must be
governed by rigorous attention to legal discipline rather
than political or historical insights. The blending of
historical and contemporary legal aspects in a full study of
the issue practically will not allow for a sound assessment
in the absence of a strict examination of the various complex
and highly technical legal rules that must be applied. While
it is not true that these rules are only accessible to study
and analysis by members of the legal profession, the danger
that experts with no legal training may be overwhelmed by the
technicalities involved cannot be overlooked. Several
articles and monographs published by non-lawyers after 1982
bear witness to this observation.

As to the more comprehensive legal studies, it is not
surprising that most have been written by authors of
Argentine nationality. The above-mentioned dissertation by
Areco was followed by a study by the famous Carlos Calvo
(1887)[6] and by books by J. Moreno (1938)[7], Gomez Langenheim
(1939)[8], Hidalgo Nieto (1947)[9], Caillet-Bois (1948)[10],

---

[6]   C. Calvo, Différend entre les Etats-Unis et la
       République Argentine au sujet du droit du pêche, in: Le
       droit international théorique et pratique, Vol. 1
       (1887), p. 489; idem, Discussions entre l'Angleterre et
       la République au sujet de l'occupation des îles
       Malouines, ibid., p. 417; as Calvo was of Argentine
       nationality, his French studies are listed here.

[7]   J. Moreno, Nuestras Malvinas (1938); 7th Ed. (1956).

[8]   Gomez Langenheim, Elementos para la historia de
       nuestras islas Malvinas, Vol. 2 (1939).

[9]   M. Hidalgo Nieto, La cuestión de las Malvinas,
       Contribución al estudio de las relaciones hispano
       inglesas en el siglo XVIII (1947).

[10]   R. Caillet-Bois, Las islas Malvinas, Una Tierra
       argentina (1948).

Moncayo (1959)[11] and F. Vieyra (1984)[12]. While these authors focused on the legal issues, many other studies were not characterised by a clear distinction between political preference and legal analysis. Special reference must be made in this context to the three volumes published by J. Muñoz Aspiri in 1966 under the title "Historia completa de las Malvinas". These volumes have rarely been cited and have gone virtually unnoticed on the international plane; nevertheless, this compilation on the history of the Falkland Islands (Malvinas), covering more than 1600 pages, contains a series of documents and statements which are hardly accessible otherwise. Thus, this work deserves attention even though it also reproduces a large number of documents which are legally entirely irrelevant.

Judging from their publications, British international legal experts have shown a remarkable lack of interest in the problem of the Falklands (Malvinas). So far, the only broadly-based study written by a prominent international lawyer is the article published by Waldock in the British Year Book of International Law in 1948[13], which refrains, however, from taking a clear position with regard to the essential questions raised in the article. Remarkably, neither in the United Kingdom nor abroad has any particular attention been paid in the discussion of the legal issues to the dissertation written in Cambridge by Wilfred Down as early as 1926[14]. Apparently, the study by Down has only been acquired by very few libraries. For a simple reason, it would have deserved greater attention: It appears that Down is the only author who has had access to the relevant files of the

---

11   G. Moncayo, Aspect juridiques de la controverse sur les Iles Malouines (1959).

12   F. Vieyra, Las Islas Malvinas y el Derecho Internacional (1984).

13   C. H. M. Waldock, Disputed Sovereignty in the Falkland Islands Dependencies, BYIL, Vol. 25 (1948), p. 311.

14   W. Down, The Occupation of the Falkland Islands and the Question of Sovereignty (1927); Down's work is mentioned by Caillet-Bois (note 10), p. 440.

various ministries involved in London and who presents his arguments in the context of long citations drawn from these files.

Subsequent to the studies by Waldock and Down, no British expert in international law has dealt with the issue of the Falklands (Malvinas) in a comprehensive manner. Following the Argentine invasion of the Islands in 1982, the United Kingdom government established a commission under the chairmanship of Lord Franks in order to determine the developments leading up to the events in 1982. Remarkably, international legal aspects were not discussed in the Franks report[15]. Later on, hearings were held on the subject in the Foreign Affairs Committee of the House of Commons. Concerning the legal issue of sovereignty, James Fawcett[16] and Michael Akehurst[17] discussed the relevant questions; but, in the context of these hearings, Akehurst only developed the relevant questions without attempting to draw any specific conclusions. The legal issues were also addressed by two non-lawyers, P. Beck and M. Deas[18]. A memorandum prepared by the Foreign Office, dated 1982, is reprinted below as an annex[19]. In 1988, Beck published a monograph entitled "The Falkland Islands as an International Problem", drawing upon previous articles written from a political science perspective. *Inter alia,* Beck discusses the differences in the legal positions between London and Buenos Aires. The book is also valuable as it presents the developments on the diplomatic level between 1982 and 1987. From a legal point of view, the discussion of

---

15   Falkland Islands Review, Report of a Committee of Privy Counsellors (Cmnd. 8787) January 1983.

16   J. Fawcett, in: House of Commons, Foreign Affairs Committee, Session 1982-83, Falkland Islands, Minutes of Evidence, Monday 17 January 1983, p. 139.

17   M. Akehurst, in: House of Commons, Foreign Affairs Committee, Session 1982-83, Falkland Islands, Appendices to the Minutes of Evidence, p. 440.

18   House of Commons (note 16), p. 109 (P. Beck), p. 131 (M. Deas).

19   See below Annex 2, p. 217.

the British legal position on pages 49 to 55 of Beck's
monograph contains the most interesting references. Having
apparently reviewed internal British files, Beck presents the
substance of internal memoranda written in the Foreign Office
in London in 1910, 1928 and 1946[20]. The relevant pages are
reprinted below as an annex[21].

Since it remains true that no prominent British
international lawyer has presented a comprehensive study of
the legal status of the Islands, the historical work by the
American historian Julius Goebel, "The Struggle for the
Falkland Islands" (1927), remains the source most often
quoted in the literature on the Falklands (Malvinas)[22].
Indeed, the research done by Goebel concerning the early
history of the Islands must be considered a definitive
treatment of the relevant facts and developments, and it does
not appear that any further light has been shed on this issue
since the publication of Goebel's book. Even though Goebel
was not a lawyer, his book has significantly contributed to
the study of individual facets of the history of
international law, in particular with regard to the rules
concerning the acquisition of territory. Nevertheless, Goebel
did not argue from a strictly legal point of view, and
presumably did not intend to do so, especially with regard to
the evaluation of the secret promise allegedly made in 1771
by Spain in discussions with Britain.

In 1982, Goebel's study was reprinted by Yale University
Press with the addition of a preface and an introduction
which deal with legal issues but do not go into details of

---

20   According to P. Beck, the Foreign Office prepared
       memoranda on the status of the Islands, for
       international purposes, in 1910 (FO 371/824;
       44753/10549; cited by Beck, id., note 34), 1928 (FO
       371/12735, A 2070/128/2, cited by Beck, id., note 45),
       and 1946 (cited by Beck, id., without file number).

21   See below, Annex 2, p. 217).

22   J. Goebel, The Struggle for the Falkland Islands
       (1927).

legal history or legal doctrine[23]. In 1983, Raphael Perl of
the Library of Congress presented an impressive compilation
of relevant documents, amounting to more than 1500 pages,
preceded by an analysis which is, however, not aimed
especially at the discussion of legal issues in a technical
sense[24]. In 1988, Lowell Gustafson, a professor of political
science, published a study entitled "The Sovereignty Dispute
of the Falklands (Malvinas)". The value of the book lies
mainly in its broad discussion of the political developments
leading up to the war in 1982. From a legal point of view,
this study has not made any independent contribution, and it
does not avoid contradictory statements[25].

Among the publications in the French language, the study
by the Argentine author Groussac, published in 1910 with the
sub-title "Nouvel exposé d'un vieux litige"[26], seems to have
been the first. More than four decades later, Pop followed
with a dissertation[27]. The most important recent study is
that written by G. Cohen Jonathan and published in 1972 in
the Annuaire Français de Droit International[28]. In 1987, the
Latin Union in Paris organised a colloquium on the legal
issues of the Falkland Islands (Malvinas); the contributions
were published in 1988 under the title "La question des
Malouines". Again, the sovereignty issue was most extensively
discussed by G. Cohen Jonathan.

In the German language, two monographs were published in

---

23   J. Goebel (note 22), (ed. 1982), p. VI.

24   R. Perl, The Falkland Islands Dispute in International
      Law and Politics (1983), p. 1.

25   On p. 31, the author seems to argue that Argentina has
      no territorial title to the Islands; however, on p. 37,
      reference is made to "Argentina's superior historical
      claim". On the whole, the treatment of the legal issues
      in the book suffers from a lack of appreciation of
      technical points of law.

26   P. Groussac, Les îles Malouines (1910).

27   C. Pop, L'affaire des îles Falkland (1952).

28   G. Cohen Jonathan, Les Iles Falklands (Malouines) AFDI,

the late 1970s. The study by Weber entitled ""Falkland-
Islands" oder "Malvinas"?"[29] (1977) was followed, one year
later, by a dissertation by Hillekamps under the title "Der
Streit um die Falklandinseln"[30].

In fact, the issue of sovereignty over the Falkland
Islands (Malvinas) is not central or is not even discussed in
most recent publications. Contributions aimed at political
analysis have addressed the role of the United Nations in the
conflict[31], the viewpoints of the United Kingdom[32] and
Argentina[33], the attitude of Latin America[34], of the United

---

Vol. 18 (1972), p. 235.

29   H. Weber, "Falkland-Islands" oder "Malvinas"? (1977).

30   B. Hillekamps, Der Streit um die Falklandinseln (1978).

31   A. Parsons, The Falklands Crisis in the United Nations,
     31 March-14 June 1982, International Affairs 59,
     (1983), p. 169-178; V. Caracciolo, La Falkland-Malvine
     alle Nazioni Unite (1960-1983) Riv.di
     Stud.Polit.Internaz. 51, (1984), p. 263-291; F.
     Sánchez/ Pablo A., La crisis de las Malvinas ante las
     Naciones Unidas, Rev. de Estud. Internac. 5, (1984), p.
     923-953; L. Forlati,(ed), Crisi Falkland-Malvinas e
     organizzazione internazionale, Padoue (1985); E. de la
     Guardia, La cuestión de las Islas Malvinas en las
     Naciones Unidas, Anuario Juridico Interamericano
     (1986), p. 97-140.

32   P. Beck, Britain's Falklands Future, The Round Table
     (1984), p. 139-152; A. Parsons, The Future of the
     Falklands: A View from Britain, International Relations
     9, (1987), p.131-139; G. Robson, The Falklands
     Election-Absentee ownership issue heats up politics,
     The Parliamentarian 71, (1990), p. 112-113.

33   M. Kohen, Alternativas para la solución del conflicto
     por las Islas Malvinas, Rev. de Estud. Internac. 7
     (1986), p. 1145-1163.

34   R. Dupuy, L'impossible agression: les Malouines entre
     l'O.N.U. et l'O.E.A., AFDI 28 (1982), p. 337-353; S.
     Rubin, The Falklands (Malvinas), International Law and
     the OAS, AJIL Vol. 76 (1982), p. 594-595; G. Connell-
     Smith, Latin America and the Falklands Conflict, Yb. of
     World Aff. (1984), p. 73-88; A. Schacht, Reacción de la
     América latina y el tercer mundo en relación con el
     problema de las Islas Malvinas Decisiones de los
     gobiernos y los organismos latinoamericanos, Anuario
     Argentino de Derecho Internac. 2 (1984-1986), p. 35-52.

States[35] and of Europe[36], geopolitical implications[37] and the possibilities for alternatives to the current situation[38]. Also, the military conflict itself, its history and the diplomacy surrounding and following the war have been the subject of further studies[39]. As to legally-oriented studies,

35   D. Acevedo, The US Measures against Argentina resulting from the Malvinas Conflict, AJIL 78 (1984), p. 323-344; V. Popov, The United States and the Falklands Crisis, International Affairs (Moscow) (1988), p. 121-130.

36   J. Dewost, La Communauté, le Dix et les "sanctions" contre l'Argentine-De la crise iranienne à la crise des Malouines, AFDI 28, (1982), p. 215-232; M. Panebianco, Regolamenti comunitari di cooperazione politica per il mantenimento della pace e della sicurezza internazionale ne conflitto Falkland-Malvinas, Riv. di Diritto Eur. 23, (1983), p. 289-324; G. Edwards, Europe and the Falkland Islands Crisis 1982, J. of Common Market Stud. 22, (1984), p. 295-313.

37   A. Asseff, Chile, Magallanes y Las Malvinas, Ceinar 8, (1982), p. 29-49; W. Wagner, Der Konflikt um die Falkland-Inseln - Ein Streit um die hergebrachte Weltordnung, Europa Archiv Vol. 37 (1982), p. 509-516; C. Joyner, Anglo-Argentine Rivalry after the Falklands/Malvinas War: Laws, Geopolitics and the Antarctic Connection, Lawyer of the Americas 15, (1984), p. 467-502; P. Beck, The Falkland Islands as an international problem, London (1988).

38   P. Beck, Britain's Falklands Future, The Round Table (1984), p. 139-152; P. Beck, The Future of the Falkland Islands: a Solution made in Hongkong?, Internat. Affairs (London) 61, (1985),p. 643-660; M. Kohen, Alternativas para la solucion del conflicto por las Islas Malvinas, Rev.de Estud.Internac. 7, (1986), p. 1145-1163; M. Kohen, La alternativa jurisdiccional en la disputa sobre las Islas Malvinas, Rivista di Studi Politici Internaz. 55 (1988), p.395-424.

39   F.S. Northedge, The Falkland Islands: Origins of the British Involvement, International Relations 7, (1982), p. 2167-2189; J. Pearce, The Falkland Islands Dispute, The World Today Vol. 38 (1982), p. 161-165; F. Hoffmann, Sovereignty in dispute: the Falklands/Malvinas 1493-1982 (1984); J. Meister, Der Krieg um die Falkland-Inseln 1982. Geschichtliche Hintergründe, Strategie und Taktik der Kriegsführung, politisch-wirtschaftliche Perspektive, Osnabrück (1984); C. Moneta, The Malvinas Conflict: Some Elements for an Analysis of the Argentinian Military Regime's Decision-making Process (1976-1983), Verf. und Recht in Übersee 17, (1984), p. 457-473; J. Boltersdorf, Krisen und Krisenkontrolle in den internationalen Beziehungen am Beispiel des Falkland-Konflikts von 1982, Berlin

the application of the laws of war to the conflict was
reviewed in several articles[40]; the question of the maritime
zones surrounding the Islands[41] has been of major interest in
the light of the practicalities of the situation as it
evolved after 1982; and such issues as the legality of

(1985); A. Coll, (ed), The Falkland War: lessons for
strategy, diplomacy and international law, (1985); M.
Hastings, The battle for the Falklands, London (1986);
C. Alvarez, Las Islas Falkland o Malvinas su historia,
la controversia Argentino-Británica y le guerra
consiguente, Santiago de Chile (1987); C. Bluth, The
British Resort to Force in the Falkland/Malvinas
Conflict 1982, J. of Peace Research 24, (1987), p. 5-
20; V. Gamba, The Falklands/Malvinas War: a model for
north-south crisis prevention, (1987); D. Sanders,
Government Popularity and the Falklands War: A
Reassessment, British J. of Political Science 17
(1987), p. 281-313; G. Lowell, The Sovereignty Dispute
over the Falkland (Malvinas) Islands (1988); The
Unnecessary War: Proceedings of the Belgrano Enquiry
November 7/8 (1986), the Belgrano Action Group,
Nottingham (1988); M. Charlton, The Little Platoon:
Diplomacy and the Falklands Dispute, Oxford (1989); D.
Kinnay, National interest, national honor: the
diplomacy of the Falkland crisis, N.Y. (1989); R. Moro,
The history of the South Atlantic conflict: the war for
the Malvinas, N.Y. (1989); L. Freedman, Signals of war:
the Falklands Conflict of 1982, London (1990).

40   L.C. Green, The Falklands, the Law and the War, The
Yearbook of World Affairs (1984), p. 89-119; W. J.
Fenrick, Legal Aspects of the Falklands Naval Conflict,
Rev. de Droit Penal Mil. et de Droit de la Guerre 24,
(1985), p. 241-268; L. Green, The Rule of Law and the
Use of Force-The Falklands and Grenada, Archiv des
Völkerrechts 24, (1986), p.173-195; A. Zuppi, El
fracaso de la negociación internacional ante la
renuncia al uso de la fuerza. Reflexiones en relacion
al conflicto anglo-argentino, Derecho 124 (1987), p.
845-852.

41   R.P. Barston/P.W. Birnie, The Falkland Islands/Islas
Malvinas Conflict: A Question of Zones, Marine Policy 7
(1983), p. 14-24; G. W. Jewkes, Falkland Islands:
Declaration on the Conservation of Fish Stocks and on
Maritime Jurisdiction around the Falkland Islands,
Internat. J. of Estuarine and Coastal L. 2, (1987),
p.97-100; M. Kohen, La declaración britanica de una
zona de pesca alrededor de Malvinas, Revista Juridica
Argentina La Ley (1987) p. 940-948; C. Symmons, The
Maritime Zones Around the Falkland Islands, ICLQ 37,
(1988), p. 283-324.

sanctions[42] in response to the use of force and the relevance
of special conventions such as the Treaty of Tlatelolco[43]
have also been analysed.

After the Argentine invasion of the Falklands (Malvinas)
in 1982, the number of publications addressing the legal
status of the Islands increased dramatically[44]. It is

---

42   J. Dewost, La Communauté, le Dix et les "sanctions"
      contre l'Argentine - De la crise iranienne à la crise
      des Malouines, AFDI 28, (1982), p. 215-232; M.
      Panebianco, Regolamenti comunitari di cooperazione
      politica per il mantenimento della pace e della
      sicurezza internazionale nel conflitto Falkland-
      Malvinas, Riv.di Diritto Eur. 23, (1983), p. 289-324;
      E. David, Les sanctions économiques prises contre
      l'Argentine dans l'affaire des Malouines, Rev.Belge de
      Droit Internat. 18, (1984-85), p. 150-165.

43   H. Gros Espiell, El conflicto bélico de las Malvinas,
      las armas nucleares y el tratado de Tlatelolco, Riv. di
      Studi Politici Internaz. 52, (1985), p. 63-80.

44   D. Blumenwitz, Falkland oder Malvinas? Der britisch-
      argentinische Streit über die Inselgruppe im
      Südatlantik aus der Sicht des Völkerrechts, Zeitschrift
      für Politik, Vol. 29 (1982), p. 318-330; A. B. Bologna,
      Los derechos argentinos sobre las islas Malvinas,
      Revista de Estudios Internacionales, Vol. 3 (1982), p.
      799-814; J. E. S. Fawcett, The Falklands and the Law,
      The World Today, Vol. 38 (1982), p. 203-206; F. Hassan,
      The Sovereignty Dispute Over the Falklands, Virginia
      Journal of International Law, Vol. 23 (1982), p. 53-71;
      C. Rousseau, Argentine et Grand-Bretagne, Revue
      Générale de Droit International Public, Vol. 86 (1982),
      p. 724-773; A. Schwed, Territorial Claims as a
      Limitation to the Right of Self-Determination in the
      Context of the Falkland Islands Dispute, Fordham
      International Law Journal, Vol. 6 (1982/83), p. 443-
      471; H. Weber, Der Streit um die Falklandinseln
      (Malwinen) als Völkerrechtsproblem, Vereinte Nationen,
      Vol. 30 (1982), p. 77-81; A. B. Bologna, Los derechos
      de Inglaterra sobre las islas Malvinas, Revista de
      Estudios Internacionales, Vol. 4 (1983), p. 775-783; D.
      C. Dicke, Der Streit um die Falklandinseln oder
      Malvinen. Festschrift Scupin (1983), p. 429-440; J.
      Fisch, The Falkland Islands in the European Treaty
      System 1493-1833, German Yearbook of International Law,
      Vol. 26 (1983), p. 105-124; H. Fox, Legal Issues in the
      Falkland Islands Confrontation 1982, International
      Relations, Vol. 7 (1983), p. 2454-2475; T. M. Franck,
      Dulce et Decorum Est: The Strategic Role of Legal
      Principles in the Falklands War, AJIL Vol. 77 (1983),
      p. 109-124; D. W. Greig, Sovereignty and the Falkland

legitimate under these circumstances to ask whether a new
monograph will add anything to the existing state of
knowledge. However, as soon as one turns from a quantitative
evaluation of the literature to the qualitative aspects, and
in particular to a comparison of the conclusions reached so
far, the impression cannot be gained that the discussion has
led, for the time being, to any provisional result. Along
with the conciseness of presentation, the methods of inquiry
and the results of the many recent studies are extremely
divergent. While the contours of international law may in
certain areas be less precise than those of legal norms in
the national context, the differences in the conclusions
reached in the literature concerning the Falklands (Malvinas)
can only be described as extraordinarily wide.

Islands Crisis, Australian Yearbook of International
Law, Vol. 8 (1983). p. 20-70; A. F. J. Hope,
Sovereignty and Decolonization for the Malvinas
(Falkland) Islands, Boston College International and
Comparative Law Review, Vol. 6 (1983), p. 391-446; J.
M. Lindsey, Conquest: A Legal and Historical Analysis
of the Root of United Kingdom Title in the Falkland
Islands, Texas International Law Journal, Vol. 18
(1983), p. 11-35; B. M. Mueller, The Falkland Islands:
Will the Real Owner Please Stand Up, Notre Dame Law
Review, Vol. 58 (1983), p. 616-634; M. Pinto,
Argentina's Rights to the Falkland/Malvinas Islands,
Texas International Law Journal, Vol. 18 (1983), p. 1-
10; A. Randelzhofer, Der Falkland-Konflikt und seine
Bewertung nach geltendem Völkerrecht, Europa Archiv,
Jg. 38 (1983), p. 685-694; W. M. Reisman, The Struggle
for the Falklands, Yale Law Journal, Vol. 93 (1983), p.
287-317; M. A. Sánchez, Self-Determination and the
Falkland Islands Dispute, Columbia Journal of
Transnational Law, Vol. 21 (1983), p. 557-584; N. J.
Watkins, Disputed Sovereignty in the Falkland Islands:
The Argentina-Great Britain Conflict of 1982, Florida
State University Law Review, Vol. 11 (1983), p. 649-
676; H. Gros Espiell, El Caso de las Malvinas y el
derecho a la libre determinación de los pueblos,
Anuario Hispano-Luso-Americano de Derecho
Internacional, Vol. 7 (1984), p. 27-41; M. Schröder,
Der Kampf um die Falkland-Inseln - Völkerrechtliche und
europarechtliche Aspekte, German Yearbook of
International Law, Vol. 27 (1984), p. 334-366; J. F.
Gravelle, The Falkland (Malvinas) Islands: An
International Law Analysis of the Dispute between
Argentina and Great Britain, Military Law Review, Vol.
107 (1985), p. 5-69.

It is also worth noting that some authors have questioned whether, or to what extent, the issue of sovereignty with regard to the Falkland Islands (Malvinas) can be resolved by reference to the categories and norms generally recognised in international law. For instance, Greig seems to indicate that the matters under discussion lie in the border area of different conceptions of the nature of international law[45]. Fawcett goes a step further[46]; against the background of a certain inclination, often found in Anglo-American jurisprudence and legal scholarship, to identify and equate rules of law with decisions reached by courts and tribunals, Fawcett concludes that a clear-cut answer to the issue of sovereignty cannot be given due to the lack of a binding decision by a third party, and that therefore both states concerned retain the right to insist upon their own legal point of view. While this conclusion is correct so far as it goes, it would nevertheless be unconvincing for Fawcett thereby to imply that any attempt to objectively assess the legal questions involved would be devoid of purpose or justification. Ultimately, Fawcett's argument carries with it the danger of reducing international law to principles applied and decided upon by courts and thus of relegating entire libraries of scholarly writing to the category of

---

45   D. Greig, Sovereignty and the Falkland Islands Crisis, Australian Yearbook of International Law, Vol. 8 (1983), p. 20.

46   Fawcett, (note 14), p. 139: "I would like to say that in a situation like this, as in much of international relations, law is really a question of tactics. The idea that there is a certain solution or that the law is certain on any one side or in respect of any one position is, as often in national law, not the case. There is no certainty. Moreover, unless you have a binding decision - and the record is not brilliant as to how far the judgements of the International Court can be said to be binding - or you perhaps have a treaty that governs the problem, I think it is impossible to say that the law is more than a matter of diplomacy. It is a question of advancing arguments which are politically reasonable and convincing. That is what will in the end prevail. Under the role, so to speak, of law, that is the situation for international law in a situation like this."

useless products of academic occupational therapy. Of course, academic juridical analysis cannot claim an ultimate validity, even though every effort at objectivity must be made. With regard to the territorial rights to the Falkland Islands (Malvinas), the need for further enquiry must be all the more urgent, inasmuch as the essential issues touch upon questions which so far have not been fully discussed or have not been decided upon by courts or tribunals and have not arisen in territorial disputes in other parts in the world in precisely the same manner.

As to the scope and intentions of the present work, no effort is made here to discuss or to assess all the periods and actions which are especially important from historical or political points of view. Instead, the work deliberately aims at highlighting those few facts and periods which it is essential to take into account from the perspective of an international legal study on the territorial issue of sovereignty.

Important dates concerning the Falkland Islands (Malvinas) may be found in a memorandum of the United States State Department, reprinted below as annex 1. The reader who is interested in further historical or political details of specific periods or actions is referred to the existing monographs in the Spanish language and to the study by Goebel. The development of the political relations between Britain and Argentina in the past century has been presented in a comprehensive manner by Ferns[47]. The natural characteristics of the Islands were described in a vivid manner by Boysen in 1924[48].

A series of documents is reprinted in the annexes to this study. Comparison with the volumes by Muñoz Azpiri and Perl

---

47   H. Ferns, Britain and Argentina in the Nineteenth
      Century (1960).

48   V. Boysen, The Falkland Islands (1924).

will show that there exists a much larger quantity of notes,
declarations and documents relating to the Islands. The
selection of documents reprinted here was made with primary
regard to the importance of the document from the point of
view of international legal analysis. In a few instances,
documents are reprinted which are not of direct legal
relevance but which nevertheless illuminate the context of
the legal issues or which have not received sufficient
attention in the past.

II.   The development of territorial status

1.   The status of the Islands in the period before 1764

The continuing legal dispute over the Falkland Islands (Malvinas) has its origins in the early colonial period of the Latin-American subcontinent. Both England and Argentina have in the past based their claims to territorial sovereignty over the Islands on legal and factual arguments which involve documents and developments of the 15th and 16th centuries. Argentina considers her claim to be reinforced by her succession to the rights of Spain, which Pope Alexander VI conferred on the Spanish Court in the year 1493 in the bull *Inter Caetera*[49]. The United Kingdom, while denying the legal relevance of this document for the present situation, has in the past supported her claim to the Islands by reference to the discovery of the Islands by the English seafarers Davis and Hawkins in 1592 and 1594[50]. Argentina in turn rejects these arguments, claiming that the Spaniard Amerigo Vespucci had discovered the Islands earlier than the English voyagers[51]. The question as to the facts of the discovery are rendered even more complex because French seafarers firmly believed that they had first seen and set

---

49   See, for instance, the statement by Argentina before the United Nations (Subcommittee III of the Special Committee on the Situation with Regard to the Implementation of the Declaration on the Granting of Independence to Colonial Countries and Peoples) on September 9, 1964, printed in: R. Perl, The Falkland Islands Dispute in International Law and Politics (1983), p. 351.

50   Cf. the position taken by England in the communications with Argentina in the years 1829 and 1832 (reprinted in Annex 21, p. 263).

51   See the Argentine statement, cited in footnote 49, p. 353.

foot on the Islands[52].

As mentioned previously, Julius Goebel has presented what
is still the most comprehensive study of the early history of
the Islands[53]. Goebel concluded that none of the states
concerned had provided clear proof that its nationals
discovered the Islands first. The difficulties which arise in
establishing the relevant factual details presumably explain
why, today, neither the United Kingdom nor Argentina place
any special emphasis in their legal arguments on developments
previous to the 18th century. Argentina still regularly
refers to rights derived from the Papal bull, but the major
thrust of the Argentine case is concerned with developments
in the period after 1760[54]. In memoranda dated 1829 and 1832,
Britain based her claim to the Islands on her rights as
discoverer[55]. In 1982, the representative of the Foreign
Office expressed the opinion before the Foreign Affairs
Committee of the House of Commons that the facts were not
clear for the early part of the history[56]; consequently, it
was said, the British government has at no point based its

---

52   J. Goebel, The Struggle for the Falkland Islands
      (1927), p. 1 - 46. See also L. Muñoz Azpiri, Historia
      Completa de las Malvinas, vol. 1 (1966), p. 23, 31; in
      the same collection, the question of discovery is
      discussed in a text edited by Z. Becu ("Los derechos
      argentinos sobre las Islas Malvinas"), vol. 1, p. 298;
      M. Pondal, Derechos de la Argentinia a las islas
      Malvinas pasados en autores inglesas, vol. 3 (1966), p.
      257. More recently, F. Northedge, The Falkland Islands:
      Origins of the British Involvement, International
      Relations, vol. 7 (1982), p. 2167, 2174; G. Marsico/G.
      Conetti, L'Evoluzione della Controversia e il Problema
      della Sovranita, in: N. Ronzitti (ed.), La Questione
      delle Falkland - Malvinas nel Diritto Internazionale
      (1984), p. 5 ff., 32 ff.

53   Goebel, (note 52), p. 1 - 46.

54   See the statement made in 1964 (note 49).

55   See note 50, above.

56   Memorandum by the Foreign and Commonwealth Office, in:
      House of Commons, Foreign Affairs Committee, Session
      1982 - 83, Falkland Islands, Minutes of Evidence,
      Monday 17 January 1983, (reprinted here in Annex 2, p.
      217.

claim exclusively on the right of discovery.

A short review of the period before 1764 is, nevertheless, worthwhile in order to gain a full picture of the historical developments. In examining the legal basis of the claims presented in relation to this period, the question must first be raised as to the legal relevance of Papal bulls, in particular with reference to their universal effects on states which did not at the time consider themselves subject to the jurisdiction of the Pope[57]. Von der Heydte correctly referred to the wording of the bulls and concluded that these were meant only to legalise and recognise a certain situation, but were not intended to render inapplicable the requirement of effective occupation of the territory in question[58]. In cases in which bulls were issued prior to the occupation of territory, the state privileged by the bull could, according to this view, only acquire a *jus ad occupationem*[59].

A further consideration must be added in the same context. The Argentine opinion concerning the legal effects of the bull *Inter Caetera* for the subsequent historical developments is necessarily based upon the assumption of the binding effect of the bull *erga omnes*. It will not be

---

57   As to the more recent comments, see, for instance, D. Greig, Sovereignty and the Falkland Islands Crisis, Australian Yearbook of International Law, vol. 8 (1983), p. 20, 21; J. Fisch, The Falkland Islands in the European Treaty System, German Yearbook of International Law, vol. 26 (1983), p. 105, 106. Earlier discussions are found in: H. M. Waldock, Disputed Sovereignty in the Falkland Islands Dependencies, British Year Book of International Law, vol. 25 (1948), p. 311, 321; A. Truyol y Serra, The Discovery of the New World and International Law, Toledo Law Review 1971, p. 305, 310; M. Lindley, The Acquisition and Government of Backward Territory in International Law (1926), p. 124 ff., all with further references.

58   A. von der Heydte, Discovery, Symbolic Annexation and Virtual Effectiveness in International Law, AJIL vol. 29 (1935), p. 499, 450, citing Fuglsang, Der Streit um die Insel Palmas (1931), p. 83.

disputed that the Pope enjoyed, even during the latter part
of the Middle Ages, extensive rights over church and state
and that the modern structure of international law, based
upon a legal order among states of equal rank, developed only
after the dissolution of the medieval order founded upon the
rights of the Pope. England, however, had objected to the
binding effect of the Papal bulls at a very early stage[60].
The absence of universal recognition of the legal effect of
the bull hardly leaves room for the opinion that English
rights, in particular, had been curtailed by Papal decisions.
No instance is known in which a state considered territorial
decisions of the Pope as binding while not at the same time
recognising a general supremacy of the Pope in religous and
secular matters. As to the relationship between England and
Argentina, it is immaterial to what extent the direct
addressees and beneficiaries of the Pope, Spain and Portugal,
were affected in their legal rights by the bull. Against this
background, the conclusion is warranted that the rights of
Spain and Argentina contained in the bull were not opposable
to England.

Even if one were to disagree and to assume that the Pope,
in the year 1493, enjoyed a universally binding jurisdiction
regarding all territorial matters, one would still have to
take into account the fact that it was not less than 274
years after the bull had been issued that the Spanish for the
first time occupied the Islands in the year 1767[61]. According
to the principles of intertemporal law, the legal
significance of this period for a claim of acquisition of the
Islands would have to be raised[62]. In particular, a

---

59   See below p. 23.

60   C.F. Waldock (note 57), with further references.

61   See below p. 44.

62   Concerning the principles of intertemporal law, see
      generally the Reports by M. Sörensen, in: AnnIDI, vol.
      55 (1973), p. 1, 50, 85; as well as the Resolution of
      the Institut in Annuaire, vol. 56 (1975), p. 339; T.
      Elias, The Doctrine of Intertemporal Law, AJIL, vol. 74
      (1980), p. 285.

satisfactory answer would have to address the principle of effectiveness[63] as recognised during the relevant period. An abstract discussion of this kind is not found in the literature of that time. One sector of state practice in that period, however, did concern rules on the acquisition of territory which addressed the principle of effectiveness of the law as it then stood. Reference is made here to the legal effect of symbolic acts which express the will to effect acquisition without simultaneous factual occupation of the territory claimed.

Even though such symbolic acts of territorial acquisition were quite common during the period in question, legal commentators on that practice have not reached a uniform evaluation of their legal significance. Arthur S. Keller, Oliver J. Lissitzyn and Frederick J. Mann examined this matter extensively in their study entitled "Creation of Rights of Sovereignty through Symbolic Acts 1400-1800", published in 1938. These authors carefully reviewed the legal forms by which states, in the period after 1400, expressed their determination to have recognised and to claim a certain territory[64].

A common practice of the times was to set up the sign of the cross on the territory discovered and to celebrate a mass. Also, the insignia of the sovereign or ruler on behalf of whom the discoverer acted were sometimes left on the territory. The raising of the flag was also seen as one form of claiming the territory. The three authors mentioned were of the opinion that acts of this sort had already led to the acquisition of the territory. Von der Heydte did not share this view of the legal effects of symbolic acts. He assumed that such symbolic acts only led to an inchoate right of the

---

63   With regard to the principle of effectiveness, see more recently K. Doehring, Effectiveness, EPIL, Instalment 7 (1984), p. 70.

64   A. Keller, O. Lissitzyn, F. J. Mann, Creation of Rights of Sovereignty through Symbolic Acts 1400 - 1900

state concerned which in turn led to a territorial acquisition only by subsequent effective occupation of the territory[65].

It seems that von der Heydte had the better case. Keller, Lissitzyn and Mann in no way addressed the arguments raised by von der Heydte; this is surprising inasmuch as von der Heydte's position was not novel[66]. It is true that the three authors may have based their view upon the wording of individual instructions given to discoverers for their voyages made on behalf of their rulers; some of these documents indeed expressed the position that the acquisition of territory had already been achieved by symbolic acts. It cannot be overlooked, however, that this point of view served the interests of the rulers concerned, particularly in view of the fact that it was difficult to know in advance how fast and under what circumstances a subsequent occupation would take place. The fact alone that the discoverers undertook their symbolic acts on the basis of their instructions does not answer the question whether these acts led to an inchoate right to or to a full acquisition of the territory. Of decisive importance is state practice in those special cases in which symbolic acts were not followed within an appropriate time by effective occupation. Only the assessment of this particular constellation allows conclusions to be drawn regarding the constitutive effect of symbolic acts, on the one hand, and the legal significance of actual occupation for the acquisition of territory, on the other hand.

Keller, Lissitzyn and Mann themselves discussed two relevant historical cases in point[67]. A dispute between England and Portugal arose after 1561 with regard to the rights of the territory today called Guinea. Portugal based her claims on the rights of discovery and symbolic acts of

---

(1938), p. 148.

65   Von der Heydte (note 58).

66   See Lindley (note 57), p. 136, with further references.

acquisition, whereas England vehemently objected to the view that these acts could legally amount to the acquisition of territory. England called upon the Portuguese to prove in detail that fortresses had in fact been established in the relevant area on behalf of Portugal and that the natives had recognised the Portuguese territorial rights by payments of tribute.

The second relevant case concerns a dispute between England and France over the island of St. Lucia in the Caribbean. In the treaty of Aix-La-Chapelle (1748) a mixed Anglo-French commission was charged to decide this dispute. While France was able to show that the first settlements had been established in 1643 by French nationals, England referred to the fact that an Englishman had discovered the islands in 1606 and claimed the islands for England by way of symbolic acts. England also pointed to similar acts of other Englishmen in the year 1626. Keller, Lissitzyn and Mann attempted to show on the basis of the position of the French members of the commission that their view of the assessment of symbolic acts was the correct one[68]. The French members of the commission only objected to the factual arguments relied on by England, without denying their legal relevance. However, the authors did not address the fact that England, in the view of the French members of the commission, had lost her rights due to the undisputed dissolution of the English settlement. Contrary to the opinion of Mann, Keller and Lissitzyn, the French understanding of the situation speaks against the view that symbolic acts were of permanent constitutive significance for the acquisition of territory. The period between the time of the loss of the English rights due to the dissolution of the settlement and the first occupation of the islands by France was at most seventeen years. As France was of the opinion that a dissolution of the English settlement had led to the loss of the territory after

---

67   Keller et al. (note 64), p. 148.
68   Ibid.

such a short period, this would seem to indicate that France attributed decisive importance to the concept of effective occupation. One will thus have to conclude that in those instances in which symbolic acts of occupation were not followed by effective occupation, or by permanent effective occupation, the states interested in fact claimed that they had acquired the territory, but that these claims were strictly objected to by third states and were therefore not recognised legally.

A survey of general state practice in the 16th and 17th centuries indicates that in virtually all cases effective occupation immediately followed the symbolic acts in question[69]. Practice of this kind will have to be considered as the most relevant criterion for establishing the preconditions of territorial acquisition according to the views of that time. Ultimately, the question of the legal significance of symbolic acts in ascertaining the status of unoccupied territory does not have to be decided in the limited context of an inquiry concerning the Falkland Islands (Malvinas). Neither of the two sides concerned has shown or has asserted that symbolic acts were undertaken on their behalf in the 16th and 17th centuries on these Islands.

Against the background of this review of state practice, it is not surprising that the claim of a constitutive effect of symbolic acts is not supported by legal doctrine. An examination of the state practice of the period leads to the conclusion that discovery alone did not suffice for the acquisition of territory[70]. The Falkland Islands (Malvinas)

---

69   Von der Heydte (note 58), p. 452.

70   In the dispute over the Mollucan Islands between Portugal and Spain, Spain took the position that the acquisition of territory necessarily required effective occupation; see the views on state practice of H. Weber, "Falkland Islands" or "Malvinas"? (1977), p. 56 ff.; generally with regard to the legal consequences of discovery also J. Moore, International Law, vol. 1 (1906), p. 258 ff.; Bleiber, Die Entdeckung als Rechtstitel für den Gebietserwerb (1933); also Lindley

were first occupied in 1764 with the intention of
incorporating them into the territory of an existing state.
It was only at this point that the Islands began to form the
immediate object of the expansive territorial interests of
the European colonial powers[71].

In the light of Spanish colonial policy and territorial
expansions in the southern part of the Latin-American
subcontinent in the 17th and 18th centuries, it might have
been expected that Spain would have been inclined to broaden
her territorial rights on the continent at some point by
acquiring the Falkland Islands (Malvinas). Given the
closeness of the Islands to the mainland and the relatively
modest efforts required to occupy them, it is difficult to
understand today that Spain tolerated their uninhabited
status. One possible explanation for the passive Spanish
attitude relates to the fact that Spain considered her
interests to be securely covered by treaty arrangements[72].
The treaty of Utrecht of 1703 had frozen the territorial
status of America with the consent of all concerned[73]. The

(note 57), p. 139 ff.

[71]   The conclusion by the International Court of Justice in
the dispute concerning the Minquiers and Ecrehos and
the relevance of previous developments might also be
applied to the Falkland Islands (Malvinas): "What is of
decisive importance, in the opinion of the Court, is
not indirect presumptions deduced from events in the
Middle Ages, but the evidence which relates directly to
the possession of the Ecrehos and Minquiers group." ICJ
Reports 1953, p. 47, 57.

[72]   See particularly Goebel (note 52), p. 174 ff.

[73]   See also the wording of the treaty of Utrecht, which
does not contain any specific language concerning a
renunciation by England to acquire the uninhabited
Falkland Islands (Malvinas); the relevant clause reads:
"(I)t is by Common Consent established as a chief and
fundamental Rule, that the Exercise of Navigation and
Commerce to the Spanish West Indies should remain in
the samestate it was in the Time of the aforesaid King
Charles II. That therefore this Rule may hereafter be
observ'd with inviolable Faith, and in a manner never
to be broken, and thereby all Causes of Distrust and
Suspicion concerning that Matter may be prevented and
remov'd, it is especially agreed and concluded, that no

treaty conferred on Spain the exclusive right to occupy both parts of the American continent. However this right was modified by the simultaneous recognition, on the part of Spain, of the rights of the English Crown with regard to existing settlements in the West Indies and on the North American continent.

2. The occupation of the Islands by France in 1764

The treaty of Utrecht of 1703 was subsequently reconfirmed[74]. Nevertheless it may appear doubtful whether Spain could have derived any rights from these treaties in the period after 1750; the frequency with which the parties had violated treaty provisions seems to indicate that the treaty had been set aside by implicit conduct[75]. Fisch has drawn attention to the fact that the Falklands (Malvinas) were not mentioned explicitly in any of the treaties between England and Spain before 1770, and this may raise additional doubts as to whether any of these treaties related to the status of the Islands[76].

Licence, nor any Permission at all, shall at any time be given, either to the French, or to any Nation whatever, in any Name, or under any pretence, directly or indirectly to sail to, traffick in, or introduce Negroes, Goods, Merchandizes, or any things whatsoever, into the Dominions subject to the Crown of Spain in America...". See also Greig (note 57), p. 36.

74   See for details A. Hope, Sovereignty and Decolonization of the Malvinas (Falkland) Islands, Boston College International and Comparative Law Review, vol. 6 (1983), p. 391, 408; W. Reisman, The Struggle for the Falklands, Yale Law Journal, vol. 93 (1983), p. 287, 290.

75   See Reisman (note 74), p. 290.

76   J. Fisch, The Falkland Islands in the European Treaty System 1493 - 1833, German Yearbook of International Law, vol. 26 (1983), p. 105; Fisch refers to the

The fact that France, rather than Spain or England, occupied the Islands for the first time was a consequence of the changes which had arisen out of the Seven Years War (1756-1763). In the treaty of Paris (1763) France had to renounce the major part of her colonial possessions on the American continent. The question of suitable new settlements arose subsequently for those French persons who had to withdraw from the American territories as a consequence of these arrangements. Some of the settlers concerned determined soon after their return to France to found a new colony on the Falkland Islands (Malvinas)[77].

Shortly after the conclusion of the Paris treaty, Louis Bougainville, an officer who had returned from the Canadian colonies, began his first voyage with the intention of occupying the Falklands (Malvinas)[78]. The French Crown approved and supported the expedition. The then foreign minister Choiseul was keen to open up new trade routes and therefore gave his assent to the expedition and its objectives. Bougainville assumed the costs of the voyage largely out of his own pocket, in part supported by relatives. Some of these relatives joined the expedition of two ships, *L'Aigle* and *Le Sphinx*, as did several other families which had returned from Canada. Several members of the expedition came from the fishing village of St. Malo in Britanny. Seafarers from the same village had already devoted special attention to the Falklands (Malvinas) and had named the Islands, after their home, "Les Malouines". After about 100 days of voyage, the two ships arrived at their destination. No suitable place to anchor was found on the Western Island. So the expedition landed in the Berkeley Sound on the Eastern Island.

The party's first task after arriving was to establish a small fortress, named St. Louis. Some cottages were built

---

treaties of 1604, 1630, 1667, 1670 and 1713.

77   See Goebel (note 52), p. 225.

nearby. The work lasted for about two months. When it was
largely finished, Bougainville formally claimed the Islands
on April 5, 1764, on behalf of King Louis XV of France[79].
Shortly thereafter, Bougainville returned to France, while
the new settlement was maintained and expanded by the
remainder of the expedition. France issued a public
declaration on August 3, 1764, after the return of
Bougainville to Paris, formally announcing the occupation of
and the claim to the Islands[80]. In January 1765, Bougainville
returned to the Islands for a short period. In the summer of
1765 more settlers arrived from France with new equipment and
supplies. The colony then consisted of about 150 persons.

The status of the Islands at the end of the year 1765 has
to be assessed against this factual background. The selection
of this point in time seems to be relevant from the
perspective of international law in two respects. It has to
be assumed, firstly, that the initial phase of the
establishment and of the consolidation of the French colony
had been finalised by the end of 1765. Secondly, this moment
in time deserves special attention because shortly
thereafter, in February 1766, a British expedition reached
the Falkland Islands (Malvinas), with the aim of taking
possession of them. Several statements made subsequently by
Britain seemed to assume that France had not yet acquired the
Islands at the end of 1765, and that Britain acquired
sovereign rights over the Islands in the following months or,
in the alternative, reconfirmed rights previously acquired.
As has been shown above, however, Britain did not have any

78   See Goebel, (note 52), p. 225 ff.
79   See Annex 7, below p. 199. - Bougainville described the
     circumstances of the occupation of the Islands in his
     book "Voyage autour du Monde" in 1771. The part
     concerning the Falkland Islands (Malvinas) is reprinted
     by Munoz Azpiri (note 52), vol. 1, p. 243; see also the
     data referred to in vol. 2, p. 10. The relevant facts
     are also reported by B. Hillekamps, Der Streit um die
     Falklandinseln (1978), p. 70; Weber (note 29), p. 166.
80   The French declaration is reprinted as Annex 8 below,
     p. 240.

rights over the Islands before 1765. An objective analysis, therefore, has only to decide whether Britain acquired such rights for the first time in 1766. Thus, from the point of view of the British case, the period between 1765 and 1766 is of direct importance. In this respect, the status of the Islands at the end of 1765 must be carefully ascertained.

Did France acquire the Islands as of the end of 1765? Did the landing of the French settlers in March 1764, the formal occupation, the establishment of a fortress and several cottages, and the official French declaration as well as the expansion of the colonies in the year 1765 to about 150 inhabitants, suffice for acquisition of the Islands according to the international rules applicable during the period in question?

The starting points for this discussion will have to be the fact that the Falkland Islands (Malvinas) were uninhabited in 1765 and the fact that France was the only state, at the end of 1765, which had undertaken activities on the Islands. Also, it must be recognised that the rules on the acquisition of territory were not interpreted and applied in the past on a level of high abstraction. Brownlie[81] has emphasised as much as Charles de Visscher[82] that judicial decisions have generally not been based on abstract classifications of types of territorial acquisition (such as effective occupation, discovery, prescriptive acquisition, etc.). The task of the courts has rather consisted in weighing the relative strength of the competing territorial claims in order to ascertain which state has established the relatively stronger position[83]. This approach of the

---

81   I. Brownlie, Principles of Public International Law (4th. ed. 1990), p. 131 f.

82   Charles De Visscher, Les effectivités du droit international public (1967), p. 101 ff.

83   See also G. Schwarzenberger, International Law (3rd. ed. 1957), p. 290; also Y. Blum, Historic Titles in International Law (1965), p. 222; Waldock (note 57), p. 336.

tribunals has developed because, in practice, various categories of territorial acquisition may exist side by side and the competing claims may also be based on the same category of territorial acquisition.

With regard to the British claim, it has been pointed out in this respect that British activities only started at the end of the year 1765. One will have to assume that France already enjoyed the better rights due to the consolidated settlement which she had established. One might object that the beginning of activities by Britain prevented a consolidation of the French territorial claim and that the territorial issue therefore remained open. Such an argument would have to assume, however, that the process of territorial acquisition by France had not been concluded in 1765. In view of the progress made in the colonisation of the Islands by France and in view of the formal claim made by France, one will have to conclude, nevertheless, that the Islands, being previously uninhabited, had definitely been acquired already by France at the end of 1765[84]. The fact that the British authorities were possibly not aware of the French activities when the plans to acquire the Islands were made in London will have no effect upon this legal assessment. The rules on the acquisition of territory attribute constitutive significance to the relevant objective situation; in the case of *terra nullius*, notification of the acquisition of territory or approval by third states is not required as a precondition for the acquisition of the territory[85].

---

[84]   Concerning the preconditions of the acquisition of uninhabited islands, see below p. 33 ff.

[85]   See for details Lindley (note 57), p. 293. Treaties concluded later were concerned with specific regions and had no retroactive effect (see for instance the Act of Berlin of 1885).

3.   The uniform international legal status of the Islands

It is of importance to determine the geographical extent of the rights acquired by France. The French settlements were established only on the Eastern Island, raising the question of the status of the large Western Island and the approximately 200 smaller islands in the surrounding area.

Generally speaking, the determination of an acquisition of territory and the delimitation of acquired territory belong to the most difficult issues concerning the rules on acquisition of territory. The manner, for instance, in which England derived claims out of the first occupation of North America in 1497 illustrates the legal issues involved. Keller, Lissitzyn and Mann refer to a memorandum of the English Court of 1667 which stated: "The King's title to Acadia, Canada, and counties adjacent is derived from the time that Sebastian Cabot took possession of that continent, and it is confessed in French maps that the gulf and river of Canada were first discovered by the English."[86]

This claim of the English Crown was based upon a single expedition of Cabot in the year 1497, during which, presumably, he landed on one island lying before the North American continent, from where he declared the occupation of the land, without having any details concerning its extent, and subsequently raised the English flag. On the other hand, it is also known that England, upon the occupation of West Spitsbergen in 1615, marked the territory acquired by a series of signs of the cross on which the royal coat of arms was displayed; these signs were established at a distance of a few leagues[87]. Apparently, the English were concerned that the Dutch intended to occupy the same territory and secured

---

86   Keller et al. (note 64), p. 54.
87   Ibid., p. 83.

their claim by marking their territory in this particular
manner. In the literature, Bartolus had already taken the
position in 1547 that generalisations are hardly possible and
that the individual nature of the circumstances is decisive.
Max Huber repeated this point of view in his famous decision
on the Palmas Islands[88]. Nevertheless, it is indispensible to
assess individual aspects against the background of the more
abstract principles concerned, or at least against the
background of a broad legal concept relating to the
acquisition of territory. In the absence of any broad
principle of this kind, a legal determination would be
impossible.

The commentators have indeed pointed out basic criteria
of the kind just mentioned. Von der Heydte refers, as others
do, to the principle of effectiveness: a state is only
entitled to claim an area to the extent it is willing and
able to guarantee respect for the rules of international
law[89]. In fact, von der Heydte stretches this point even
further and assumes quite generally that establishment of a
public order is a precondition for the acquisition of
territory. The same concept seems to underlie Max Huber's
determination in the Palmas case, according to which the
exercise of the rights of the sovereign "must make itself
felt throughout the territory"[90].

In this context, however, it is also important not to
replace the specific understanding of the determination of
competing claims of several states entirely by generally
phrased, abstract categories of international law. The
Permanent Court of International Justice emphasised this
necessity of reference to the specific aspects of the
individual case in the Greenland case[91]; it will not be

---

88   RIAA, vol. 2 (1949), p. 829, 854.

89   Von der Heydte (note 58), p. 465.

90   RIAA, vol. 2 (1949), p. 867.

91   "It is impossible to read the records of the decisions

overlooked, however, that the determination of the relative
weight of the respective claims does not eliminate the
necessity to observe the minimum requirements concerning the
acquisition of territory by a state. Brownlie points out in
this context that according to a widespread opinion in the
case of uninhabited and distant territories even a slight
activity of the state will suffice[92]. He adds, however, that
these requirements of acquisition of territory cannot be
considered especially strict in the case of weaker states,
for otherwise the relevant rules would favour the more
powerful states. Brownlie draws attention in this context to
the principles of state responsibility, as distinct from the
norms concerning the acquisition of territory, and he argues
that the violation of minimum standards of domestic order has
to be assessed on the basis of the rules on state
responsibility.

As to specific issues concerning acquisition of islands,
the principle of contiguity is mentioned frequently[93]. In
this context, as well, generalisations have to be avoided.
Most authors do not consider that the principles of
contiguity are alone sufficient to confer an independent
title to territory. In the Palmas decision, Max Huber
carefully pointed to the problems of interpretation and
application of the principle in practice[94]. In the light of
the facts, however, the Eastern Greenland case is more

---

in cases as to territorial sovereignty without
observing that in many cases the tribunal has been
satisfied with very little in the way of the actual
exercise of sovereign rights, provided that the
otherstate could not make out a superior claim. This is
particularly true in the case of claims to sovereignty
over areas in thinly populated or unsettled countries",
PCIJ A/B 53, p. 46.

[92]   Brownlie (note 81), p. 141 f.

[93]   See for a comprehensive examination D. Schenk,
Kontiguität als Erwerbstitel im Völkerrecht (1978), as
to previous state practice, J. Moore, A Digest of
International Law, vol. 1 (1906), p. 264 ff. See also
Waldock (note 57), p. 41.

[94]   RIAA, vol. 2 (1949), p. 854; see also Schenk, (note

relevant for the discussion of these questions than the Palmas case. The Permanent Court of International Justice had to decide whether the irregular, sometimes sporadic activities of Denmark on the territory of Greenland could form the basis of acquisition of the entire area of Greenland[95]. The Court answered in the affirmative. The decision should best be understood in the sense that, in the view of the Court, Greenland forms a territorial unit. It is beyond dispute that this concept of a territorial unit is not subject to an easy and abstract definition. Nevertheless, the geographic form of a territory will frequently be the starting point.

For the purpose of addressing the status of the Falkland Islands (Malvinas) as of 1765, it is immaterial to what extent the population of the area and other factors such as permanence of the population, the duration of the established legal order or the political organisation concerned will be of relevance. At least prima facie, the geographic form of the Falklands (Malvinas) will support the existence of a geographic unit. If account is taken of the size of the territories which various other states have claimed on the basis of a single act without protest by third states[96], the total extent of the Falkland Islands (Malvinas) has to be considered as a relatively small geographic unit.

Akehurst has raised the issue as to the possibility of separating the Islands for the purpose of territorial acquisition, but without attempting to give an answer[97]. Also, in 1842 the government of Argentina addressed the possibility of a separate legal status of Eastern Island and Western Island[98], as did an internal British memorandum of

93), p. 114.

95   PCIJ A/B 53.

96   Cf. generally Keller et al. (note 64).

97   M. Akehurst, in: House of Commons (note 16), p. 139.

98   Compare the text of the Argentine note of February 19, 1842, reprinted in: Munoz Azpiri (note 52), vol. 2, p.

1832[99]. Ultimately, these considerations are unconvincing. The independent relevance of the criterion of a geographic unit is confirmed by a series of declarations and memoranda produced by the governments of France, Spain, Britain and Argentina. None of these governments differentiated with regard to the Eastern and the Western Island in the context of acquisition or occupation of the Islands. All statements refer to the Malouines, the Malvinas, or the Falkland Islands.

State practice which attributes uniform status to all the Islands from the perspective of international law therefore shows that the Islands have to be considered as a geographic unit in the sense mentioned above[100]. The only period in which different orders and powers existed on the Eastern and Western Islands was the time between the arrival of the British on the Western Island in the year 1766 and their departure in 1770. However, attention has to be paid in this context to the fact that the negotiations initiated after the departure of the British as well as the stipulations in the treaty of 1771 were made on the basis of the unequivocal assumption of a common status of the Islands. If the parties to the dispute had seriously considered the possibility of separate status of the Eastern and Western Islands, the factual situation between 1766 and 1770 would have led them to express this point of view, in one way or another, in the ensuing negotiations. In the light of the constant practice between 1764 and 1833 one will not be inclined to attach decisive importance to the British memorandum of 1832 or the

185.

99   Letter of the Secretary of the Admiralty and the Colonial Department of August 4, 1832, cited by W. Down, The Occupation of the Falkland Islands and the Question of Sovereignty (1927), p. 148; a similar view had already been expressed by Prime Minister Wellington in a note of July 25, 1829, ibid., p. 119.

100   In the case of Minquiers and Ecrehos, ICJ Reports 1953, p. 67, the Court simply pointed to the Unity of the Islands: "... le groupe est traité comme partie intégrante du fief des Iles de la Manche..."; see also

Argentine statement of 1848. When Argentina drafted the memorandum of 1848, the possibility of a separate status as a kind of subsidiary argument supporting her minimum rights may well have been considered. After 1848, Argentina never again made reference to a separate status of the Islands. Thus, in view of the fact that all states which had occupied the Islands considered the Falklands (Malvinas) to enjoy a common status, this point of view must today also be considered as reflecting the contemporary international status of the Islands[101].

4.   The legal position of Britain: 1766 - 1770

So far, only the activities of France in the period between February 1764 and the end of 1765 have been discussed. During this period, however, Britain was also striving to acquire the Islands. For almost two decades, British colonial policy had been directed towards the Falkland Islands (Malvinas). From a strategic point of view, the Islands had to be considered as especially important in the light of Britain's running dispute with Spain about the freedom of navigation in the Caribbean and in the Pacific Ocean. As early as 1748, a British expedition under Admiral Anson with six ships had explored the southern coastal areas of the Latin-American subcontinent in the search for a suitable base. Portugal, the colonial power in Brasil, did not support British efforts to compete with the Spanish navigation rights in the Pacific. Thus, Anson considered that from the point of view of Britain, the acquisition of the Falkland Islands (Malvinas) would be an important step in the dispute over navigation rights in the Pacific Ocean[102]. The

---

Schenk (note 44), p. 114.

101   For the same view Weber (note 29), p. 64.

102   The ideas and plans of Anson are described in a book by William Walter, Voyage around the World, vol. 1 (1748), p. 153 of the edition of 1753; reprinted by Munoz

closeness of the Falklands (Malvinas) to Cape Horn, the central strategic point, attributed further importance to the Islands from the point of view of Britain.

After his return, Anson submitted plans for an expedition to be arranged which would lay claim to the Islands. The king immediately approved the idea in principle. However, it was not overlooked in London that the implementation of such a plan was bound to lead to an escalation of the rivalry with Spain for dominance in the southern Pacific. The aspect was important for Britian at that time because the Crown was generally inclined to maintain the satisfactory political relations with Spain and to improve them. The two states had previously concluded a treaty of friendship, and negotiations for a treaty to settle commercial relations were about to begin. Under these circumstances, the British Crown decided that the most suitable way of pursuing Anson's plans was to discuss the project with Madrid. As Spain immediately objected during these talks to the establishment of a British settlement on the Islands, London subsequently restricted further consultations with the Spanish to a project for a scientific expedition. The Court in Madrid was also emphatically opposed to such a limited project, and London subsequently abandoned the original plans altogether in the light of the rigid attitude taken by Spain[103].

As to the legal evaluation of the status of the Islands during that period, it is of special importance to recognise that neither of the two parties made reference in their discussions to any existing rights. Britain was prepared to make the scientific exploration of the Islands dependent on approval by Spain. Mention may be made in this context of

---

Azpiri (page 4), vol. 2, p. 9 f. (reprinted here as Annex 4). With regard to Anson's plans and reactions from Madrid see also Munoz Azpiri, vol. 1, p. 53; with regard to further deliberations in London see also the letter by the Duke of Bedford of April 24, 1750 (reprinted here as Annex 5, p. 237).

103   See also Goebel (note 22), p. 198.

commitments undertaken by England in the treaty of Utrecht[104]. Whatever the substance of these commitments around 1750 may have been, the British conduct after the return of Anson can only be understood to imply that Britain did not consider that she had previously acquired any rights with regard to the Islands. On the other hand, it is also important to note that Spain also did not, at least not explicitly, refer to any Spanish rights concerning the Islands. It is true that Spain referred in the negotiations to her knowledge of the Islands; but, as revealed by the protocols of the negotiations, this reference was at no point followed by mention of any existing rights of Spain[105]. It might be suggested that these discussions in the year 1749 had taken place in a context of friendly relations and that reference to legal arguments should not be expected with in such a framework. However, it is doubtful whether such a point of view can be upheld. Legal arguments would probably have been advanced without hesitation if one of the two parties had considered that such arguments existed to support its political position. Thus, these first negotiations concerning the Islands clearly indicate that around 1750 the Falklands (Malvinas) were regarded as *terra nullius*[106].

The period of friendly relations between Britain and Spain came to an end in 1762 when Spain joined France against Britain in the Seven Years War (1756 - 1763). As a result of this war, only Britain and Spain competed for expansions on the American continent after 1763. Britain never recognised the Spanish claim to exclusive rights in Latin America. In

---

104   See above p. 27.

105   Goebel (note 22), p. 199.

106   Duro, Armada Espanola, vol. 8 (1910), cited by Down (note 14), p. 15, reports that a shipowner in Spain had arranged for a map of the Islands in 1763. Initially the Spanish government had approved the plans of this shipowner to send a ship and declare the rights of Spain on the Islands. Due to financial difficulties, the plan was not implemented. This incident also indicates that Spain considered the Islands to be terra nullius during that period.

the treaty arrangements made in 1763 Britain acquired new rights, and her rights in the Bay of Honduras were explicitly recognised. Under these circumstances, acquisition of the Falkland Islands (Malvinas) was considered to be a further move against the Spanish claim to monopoly rights. As Lord Egmont considered, in 1765, not unlike Anson in 1748: "This station .... is undoubtedly the Key to the whole Pacific Ocean. The Island must command the ports of trade of Chili, Peru, Panama, Acapulco, and in one word all the Spanish territory upon that sea. It will render all our expeditions to those parts most lucrative to ourselves, most fatal to Spain and no longer formidable, tedious, or uncertain in a future war".[107]

By this point in time, the British had already given some emphasis to their plans to acquire the Islands. On June 21, 1764, an expedition consisting of two British ships set course for the Falkland Islands (Malvinas), charged to find a suitable place for British settlements on the Islands. The precise time of landing of these ships cannot be clearly determined today. However, it can be safely assumed that they reached the Islands at the end of January in 1765. The leader of the expedition, Byron, formally took possession of the Islands: "Of this harbor and all the neighbouring Islands, I took possession for his Majesty, King George the Third, of Great Britain, by the name of Falkland's Islands."[108] Concerning the extent of the claim, it should be noted that the British laid claim to the harbour "and all the neighbouring Islands". Byron had landed on the Eastern Island. There is nothing to indicate that Byron had knowledge at this time of the existing French settlements on the neighbouring island.

News of the declaration of possession made by Byron

---

107   Cited by Down (note 14), p. 26.

108   Goebel (note 22), p. 232; see also Weber (note 29), p. 11; Hillekamps (note 30), p. 72; Munoz Azpiri (note 52), vol. 1, p. 65.

reached the British Court through a communication of Byron's on June 21, 1765. Byron also informed the Court that he had not found any indication of a foreign population on the Islands. In the light of this news, the British government decided immediately to strengthen the British presence on the Islands. Three further ships were sent, reaching Port Egmont, on Eastern Island, on January 8, 1766. An immediate start was made to establish a fortress. A communication from London dated March 17, 1766, received in the autumn of the same year, informed the leader of the expedition, McBride, about the presence of French settlers. McBride subsequently explored the Eastern Island and found the French settlements. Without further ado, McBride called upon the French to explain the legal basis of their settlement. The French governor cited instructions of his king, referred to the British as aggressors and prepared for the defence of his settlement[109]. McBride visited the French settlement, called upon the French to depart, and himself returned to England in January 1767. Already in May 1766, Britain had officially been informed that France had ceded the Islands to Spain.

The legal aspects of this cession will have to be discussed, but first it must be considered how and to what extent the French rights concerning the Islands had been impaired by the British activities described. The British conduct deserves special attention from two points of view. First, the British actions reconfirmed that London regarded the Islands as a single geographic unit. Secondly, it has to be pointed out that the wording of the instructions for the leader of the expedition took account of the possibility of foreign settlers: McBride was supposed to call for a departure of such settlers from the Islands, but he was not ordered to use force[110]. The latter fact does not, however,

---

109   See also Goebel (note 22), p. 239.

110   The text is reprinted in Goebel, p. 234; Hope (note 44), p. 409, assumes that the English kept their settlements of 1765/66 secret inasmuch as they believed that they were made in violation of the arrangements.

permit the strict conclusion that Britain did not regard herself as having any legal basis for the use of force. Against the background of the political tensions prevailing between Britain and France during this period, it is not unreasonable to assume that Britain did not act with the conviction that she possessed a firm legal basis for military actions to force the French from the Islands.

An objective assessment of the activities in question has to start from the fact that France acquired the Islands in 1764. It is not possible today to point to the precise time at which the British learned about the French activities. As the acquisition of territory does not, however, depend upon the notification and knowledge of third states[111], the determination of the precise time is immaterial from the point of view of international law. The question of occupation by conquest is not posed in this phase in view of the British conduct. Under these circumstances it is clear that the British actions did not change the territorial status of the Islands[112].

Thus, France retained her territorial rights. On October 4, 1766, France ceded these rights to Spain. As early as September 17, 1766, Paris informed London that France would cede the rights to the Islands in the light of the treaty of Utrecht. Paris took the position that Britain had recognised the treaty of Utrecht as binding in 1749[113]. Madrid subsequently declared that the British actions on the Islands had to be considered as a violation of Spanish rights during a time of peace[114].

If this is correct, it would explain why the instructions were phrased so carefully.

111   See above, p. 27.

112   See Weber (note 29), p. 63; Hillekamps (note 30), p. 77.

113   Goebel (note 22), p. 250.

114   Goebel, p. 253.

At this point, special attention must be paid to the evaluation of the legal situation by the Court in London. Britain did not issue any formal declaration. However, the Earl of Egmont, First Lord of the Admiralty, had addressed the issue in a letter to a member of the foreign office, Grafton[115]. In his letter of July 20, 1765, Egmont had based the British rights on the discovery of the Islands by English seafarers during the reigns of Queen Elizabeth and King Charles II. As pointed out above, this position was weak and could not be upheld objectively. Also, Egmont's thesis was incompatible with the British conduct in the year 1749.

5.   The acquisition of the Islands by Spain in 1766

As mentioned above, a change in the status of the Islands occurred as early as 1766. Soon after learning of the French activities on the Islands, the Spanish ambassador in Paris requested the dissolution of the French settlement. From a political point of view, Spain argued that the French actions might lead the British Crown to undertake similar steps. From the legal perspective, Madrid referred to the territorial proximity of the Islands. Spain considered that she had a right to the Islands on this geographical basis. France gave in to the request made by Madrid. In the treaty concluded on October 4, 1766, France even conceded that she had acquired the Islands unlawfully ("ses établissements illégitimes dans les Iles Malouines appartenant à sa Majesté Catholique")[116]; nevertheless, France received a considerable sum for the foundation and construction of the settlement. The treaty did not spell out the reason why the occupation of the Islands should have been illegal; statements made by the French foreign minister in discussions with London seem to indicate

---

115   Down (note 14), p. 26.

116   A declaration by Bougainville, approved by France and accepted by Spain, is reprinted, infra p. 201, as annex

that reference was made to the rights of Spain contained in the treaty of Utrecht[117].

The validity of the cession of the Islands was not affected by the question whether or not the French legal position was correct. Of decisive importance is that France had previously been in possession of the Islands, that Spain and France agreed upon the transfer of sovereignty, that Spain immediately exercised her sovereign rights, and that France subsequently never considered the treaty to be void. Under these circumstances, the motives of France in transferring the Islands were immaterial so far as the conclusion of the treaty and its legal consequences were concerned. Incidentally, Britain herself never argued that the convention between France and Spain was legally defective. It is also worth remembering in this context that Britain and France were equally bound by the treaty of Utrecht[118]. If the acquisition of the Islands violated the terms of the treaty, the same reasoning would have applied to Britain. In consequence, the treaty of Utrecht cannot be said, in any way, to point to an acquisition of the Islands by Britain in the year 1765 or 1766. On April 1, 1767, France transferred the Islands in a formal and valid act to Spain[119].

The intense diplomatic activities of Britain, France and Spain in the following months and years did not affect the status of the Islands and need not be described here in any detail. In these discussions, Britain seems to have considered the possibility, at the end of 1766, of submitting the dispute over the Islands to an arbitral tribunal. It is not clear whether Spain reacted in any way to this suggestion. The British initiative concerned not only the Falkland Islands (Malvinas) but also another, unrelated

9.

117   See Goebel (note 22), p. 244.
118   See supra pp. 27, 43.

dispute[120].

On December 29, 1766, the Spanish government drew the attention of its commander-in-chief in Buenos Aires to the existence of a British settlement on the Islands. Initial efforts to locate the settlement failed. Madrid, however, was firmly convinced of the existence of the settlement and issued further specific instructions to the commander on February 25, 1768. The British were to be requested to leave the Islands, and the request was to be enforced, if need be, by the use of force[121].

6.   The conflict between Spain and Britain in 1770

An armed conflict with Britain arose in June 1770[122]. Both local commanders had called on the other side to vacate their settlements. The British captain had set an ultimatum to the Spanish in February 1770. The Spanish response spoke of an "absolute violation of existing treaties" on the part of the British; in turn, London referred to the legal rights of the British as discoverers and settlers. On June 9, 1770, a Spanish officer called upon the British settlers to leave the Islands and to capitulate within 15 minutes. As the British did not follow this request, the Spanish ships landed and opened fire. The Spanish forces were clearly superior, and in a short time they forced the British to surrender and to lower their flag.

---

119   See Weber (note 9), p. 62.

120   See Goebel (note 22), p. 254.

121   Ibid., p. 271. A letter by Captain Hunt, dated December 10, 1769, seems to contain the first legal analysis on the part of Britain with regard to the Islands during that period; it is reprinted below, as annex 10, p. 242.

122   See generally Goebel (note 22), p. 271.

The lengthy negotiations that followed concerned
basically four different subjects: the Spanish request for an
apology from Britain with regard to the ultimatum of February
1770; the British request for an apology from Spain for the
use of force in June 1770; the question of the legal status
of the Islands; and the further presence of Britain and Spain
on the Islands[123]. Spain attempted to avoid a serious crisis
in relations with Britain by pretending that the Spanish
commander had acted without corresponding instructions from
Madrid. The British argued that they also had excluded the
use of force in their instructions and had intended to leave
the solution of the dispute to the authorities concerned.
Britain called for an expression of disavowal by the Spanish
of the Spanish action on the Islands and for the restoration
of the state of affairs that had prevailed before June 9,
1770. Madrid referred to the illegality of the British
settlement in the light of the existing treaty. In view of
the opposing positions, Britain, France and Spain were faced
with an immediate outbreak of hostilities in the dispute over
the Islands.

The Spanish King Charles III took the decisive
initiative, following a British proposal, which ultimately
led to the peaceful settlement of the dispute. Charles
proposed a restoration of the state of affairs before June 9;
in addition, the two states were to agree to abandon their
settlements on the Islands totally in the future and thus to
avoid further conflicts[124]. However, Madrid did not consider
abandoning her rights on the Islands. Spain even insisted for
some while that Britain should distance herself from the acts
taken by commander Hunt in February 1770. British negotiators
seemed to indicate for a while that London would be prepared
to leave the Islands if an acceptable solution to the ongoing
crisis could be found[125]. Remarkably, the legal aspects of

---

123   Ibid., p. 271 ff.
124   Ibid., p. 291.
125   Goebel (note 22), p. 310 f.

the status of the Islands were apparently always taken into account in a series of diplomatic initiatives, negotiations and proposals over the coming months. Gradually, it appeared that neither Spain nor Britain was willing to make any concessions in a treaty on the future status of the Islands[126]. In any case, London was not willing to agree to a proposal which would have resulted in a recognition or strengthening of the Spanish rights.

After almost five months of negotiations, a settlement was finally reached on January 22, 1771. Formally, Spain issued a declaration, followed by a subsequent declaration by Britain, which made reference to the Spanish act[127]. In substance, the Spanish declaration disapproved of the use of force by the Spanish commander in June 1770, declared the Spanish willingness to restore the *status quo*, and explicitly reserved the Spanish legal position[128]. The British declaration consisted in essence of the statement that Britain considered the Spanish declaration and its implementation as sufficient satisfaction for the injury suffered[129]. It is conspicuous that the British declaration in no way addressed or referred to the Spanish reservation of rights.

The wording of the declarations deserves special attention in view of the lengthy negotiations that had accompanied their drafting and the careful assessment made of the implications for the respective legal positions by the two parties. It will not be overlooked that the British

---

126   Ibid., p. 328.

127   Ibid., p. 359; Hope (note 44), p. 410, note 48, correctly points out that the heading reads in the French version "Acceptation de la Grandbretagne", and that the translation "Counter-declaration" is not precise on this point.

128   Goebel (note 22), p. 359; the declaration is reprinted in annex 11, p. 203.

129   The British declaration is reprinted in annex 11, p. 203.

declaration spoke of "a satisfaction for the injury done to his Britannic Majesty". Apparently, this formula was chosen so as not to express the recognition of British territorial rights by Spain, and without expression of any such claim on the part of Britain. The same endeavour will be observed in the geographic designation of the localities. The place at which force was used is referred to in the Spanish declaration as "the island commonly called the Great Malouine, and by the English Falkland Islands"; similarly, a few sentences later, reference is made to "the Great Malouine at the port called Egmont". The British declaration avoids addressing the Islands by name and at two points speaks of "Port Egmont" ("of the port and fort of Port Egmont", and "the expedition against Port Egmont").

Conspicuous wording was also chosen in the passage expressing the Spanish reservation of rights. Initially, the obligation "to restore to his Britannic Majesty the possession of the port and fort called Egmont" is mentioned; similar wording is found in the British declaration ("dispossessing him [the King of Great Britain] of the port and fort of Port Egmont"). In the formulation of the reservation on the part of Spain, reference is made to the sovereign rights to the "Malouine islands, otherwise called Falkland's Islands". On the whole, an examination of the terminology shows that Britain at no point mentioned the name of the Islands while Spain addressed them as the Malouine Islands, albeit with the addition "otherwise called Falkland's Islands". While Spain explicitly reserved her rights, Britain consistently avoided any hint of a territorial claim.

The use of the term "possession" is also of interest in this context. Both the British and the Spanish declarations chose this term for the designation of the British settlements at the time of the conflict with Spain. According to general international usage, the term does not imply the existence of sovereign rights; different British terminology subsequently used in the Interpretation Act of 1889 has not been followed on the international level. Remarkably, the formulation of the Spanish reservation on this point is entirely unequivocal and uses the terms "right of sovereignty". Thus, the Spanish declaration is based on the terms "possession" and "right of sovereignty", contrasting both of them, whereas against this background the declaration by London uses the term "possession" for the designation of the British legal position. Also, Spain refers, in the central passage, to the Falkland Islands (Malvinas) as a legal unit, while the British position nowhere indicates that the Islands should be treated separately from a legal point of view[130]. In conclusion, therefore, it has to be observed that Spain explicitly reserved her rights to the Islands while Britain at no point addressed the issue of sovereignty.

In the assessment of the status of the Islands subsequent to the declarations of the two parties it is beyond doubt, in the light of the careful drafting, that Spain did not abandon any rights which she had previously possessed. Britain neither acquired any rights, nor claimed any territorial rights. Following the identification of the legal position prior to the conflict, described above[131], the declaration of 1771 must be considered as an indirect confirmation of the territorial rights of Spain. Obviously, further developments in the future were not thereby excluded.

One may be inclined to speculate extensively with regard to a "secret promise" made by Britain to leave the islands subsequently, as Goebel suspected[132]. Goebel's reconstruction

---

130   See supra p. 38 ff.

131   See infra p. 53 ff.

132   Goebel (note 22), pp. 316 - 363. See generally also R. Caillet-Bois, Una Tierra Argentina, Las Islas Malvinas (1945), p. 132; M. Hidalgo Nieto, La cuestión de las Malvinas, Contribución al estudio de las relaciones hispano-inglesas en el Siglo XVIII (1947); O. Gil Munilla, Malvinas, El Conflicto Anglo-Español de 1770,

of the course of negotiations seems to support his conclusion about the existence of such an arrangement. Moreover, the existence of such a promise would be entirely consistent with the wording of the declarations of 1770. The absence of any claim on the part of Britain would be entirely compatible with a promise to leave the Islands at a later point. Nevertheless, in a legal study of the status of the Islands it would appear inappropriate to rely upon the existence of such a promise. No one has supplied adequate proof of the existence of a promise. In addition, Goebel himself is at pains to point out that in the negotiations the British Crown always emphasised that the Spanish would have to rely upon the word given by the British with regard to future conduct. This fact itself can be seen as evidence of Britain's reluctance to accept a binding legal committment rather than a political statement of intention. Goebel himself points out that the British authorities insisted that they had made no assurances - "neither officially nor confidentially"[133].

The public declarations reveal no hint of a relevant promise made by Britain, and it has so far not been proved that any such promise was ever given. Thus, it will have to be assumed that, while Britain may have given a political declaration, no legally binding commitment was made. Against this background, and from a legal point of view, it is immaterial whether there are good reasons which speak in favour of the existence of such a political promise, or not.

A comprehensive analysis of the solution of the dispute on the basis of the two declarations must also turn to the issue why Spain was prepared to grant a satisfaction even though she took for granted the existence of her territorial

---

Anuario de Estudios Americanos, Vol. 4 (1948); J. Torre Revello, La Promesa secreta y el Convenio Anglo-Español sobre las Malvinas de 1771 (1952); Zoraquin Becu, Inglaterra Prometto Abandonar Las Malvinas (1983); Hillekamps (note 30), p. 87; Reisman (note 44), p. 297; Greig (note 44), p. 29.

133   Goebel (note 22), p. 362.

rights to the Islands. It has to be realised in this context that Spain was seriously concerned about the negative effects upon relations with the Court in London once the news of the battle with the British settlers and its outcome had reached Madrid. Also, the rules then recognised with regard to conduct in times of peace have to be considered: Spain had taken military measures against Britain without prior warning and without efforts to settle the dispute by way of diplomacy. The norms of law applicable during times of peace did not permit such conduct[134]. Presumably, this was the legal basis for the satisfaction granted by Spain.

In conclusion, it appears that the Spanish declaration of 1771 and the British counter-declaration did not lead to a change in the territorial status of the Islands; the Islands remained within the territorial domain of Spain. Nevertheless, Spain granted Britain the right to occupy the Western Island and thus contributed to a legal situation which, after the resettlement by the British on this Island, was not entirely clear. Moreover, no time limit was set on the right of the British to occupy the Islands in the wording of the declaration. Were these facts opposed to the assumption that the Islands remained Spanish? Legally speaking, the Spanish declaration can well be construed to indicate that Spain conceded to Britain the right to settle on the Spanish Islands for an unlimited period as a measure of satisfaction for the illegal conduct on the Islands in 1770. In view of the clear and unequivocal wording of the Spanish reservation, this interpretation seems to be correct. However, it will not be overlooked that this evaluation would have been considerably weakened had the British maintained the Islands and continued to assert their own claims. If this had been the case, the question of a separate legal status of the two Islands would indeed have been raised. However, the subsequent course of events does not make it necessary to pursue these issues.

---

134   See Down (note 14), p. 51.

As to the period between 1771 and 1774, new developments occured which might have had an effect upon the legal status of the Islands. In the British Parliament, a lengthy debate addressed the situation as it stood after the declarations of Madrid and London. The opposition raised doubts as to whether the wording of the declarations sufficiently expressed the British legal position. In response, the government maintained that both sides had reserved their legal positions[135]. Further negotiations between Britian and Spain took place in order to ensure implementation of the agreement. Goebel makes reference to a discussion between Earl Rochford, then Secretary of State for the Northern Department, and the Spanish ambassador; in these discussions, Rochford took the position that the Islands had not been acquired by discovery, but by way of effective occupation, and that therefore France had acquired the Islands in 1764[136]. In the further exchanges, the question of the British promise was raised again, and the Spanish ambassador repeated the argument that this promise was of a binding quality[137]; internal Spanish documents, however, do not necessarily express the same point of view[138]. In any case, Port Egmont was returned to Britain in a formal ceremony on September 15, 1771.[139]

7.   The British departure from the Islands in 1774

Almost three years later, on June 11, 1774, the British government informed its ambassador in Madrid of Britain's intention to leave the Falkland Islands (Malvinas); the

---

135   See Goebel (note 22), p. 370.
136   Goebel (note 22), p. 388.
137   Ibid., p. 393.
138   Ibid., p. 400, 406.
139   The wording of the evacuation order by the Spanish King is reprinted in Muñoz Azpiri (note 52), Vol. 2, p. 39.

letter explains that considerations of economy on the part of
the navy were responsible for this plan[140]. On May 20, 1774,
the plan was carried out and the British troops left the
Islands. However, Britain did not fail to simultaneously
manifest a continuing claim to the Islands. Before leaving
the Islands, a plaque made of lead was affixed by the British
troops on a wooden cottage, bearing an inscription to the
effect that the rights to the Falkland Islands (Malvinas)
belonged exclusively to His Britannic Majesty[141].

It is not appropriate at this point to evaluate the
dissolution of the British settlement and the simultaneous
manifestation of *animus possidendi* by way of the inscription
on the plaque; subsequent developments on the Islands after
1774 shed additional light on the legal situation and
facilitate its evaluation[142].

8.   Factual developments and the legal status of the
      Islands after 1774

The plaque set up by the British, which was supposed to
document the claim of sovereign rights, remained in place
only for about a year. In 1775 a Spanish officer, acting upon
instructions, moved the plate and shipped it to Buenos
Aires[143]. The plate remained there until 1806 when it was
found by the British General Beresford after British troops
had moved into Buenos Aires. He transported it back to
England. When the Colonial Office searched for it in 1832,
the plaque could no longer be found.

---

140   Down (note 14), p. 74.
141   The text of the plaque is reprinted as annex 12, p.
      205; cf. for the relevant factual circumstances Hope
      (note 44), p. 406.
142   See for details infra p. 57 ff.
143   Cf. generally Down (note 14), p. 79.

In 1776, the Spanish formally incorporated the Islands into the jurisdiction of a newly created office of the vice-regent in Buenos Aires. In the following year, Madrid ordered the removal of all settlements left by the British in Port Egmont. Spain also assumed the costs of stationing a small contingent of soldiers on the Western Island, which the British had left.

The Spanish settlement on the Falklands (Malvinas) remained small. Its main purpose was to keep foreigners away from the Islands on a permanent basis[144]. Rich stocks of whale and seal in the waters surrounding the Islands attracted American whalers, and the Islands were occasionally used as a base for their activities. It is of special interest to note the way in which the Spanish and British governments reacted to the news that, allegedly, British fishermen also came to the Islands. Spain protested in 1775 and Britain responded by pointing out that the ships concerned must have been American[145]. Indirectly, the answer provides reconfirmation that Britain and Spain considered the Islands to be part of Spanish territory at that time. However, there are also reports according to which British fishermen took rest on the Islands while searching for whales; between 1784 and 1790, seven British ships appeared to have landed on the Islands[146].

In 1780, a Spanish company received permission from the Crown in Madrid to fish waters near the Islands; later on, the Crown took charge of the company. Even then, British fishermen occasionally landed on the Islands in order to convert blubber into oil. In Art. VI of the Nootka Sound Convention, Britain secured these rights for her

---

144   The situation is described by Down (note 14), p. 80.

145   Ibid., p. 83. In 1790, in a written order the Spanish commander requested a British ship to leave the Islands: the text of the order is reprinted in Muñoz Azpiri (note 52), Vol. 2, p. 17; the answer is reprinted on page 18.

fishermen[147]; Spain agreed that British ships retained the right to "land on the coast and Islands (on the east and west coast of South America) for the purposes of fishery, as well as to establish cottages and other settlements temporarily, without pursuing other objectives". In the first sentence of Art. VI, Britain agreed not to establish settlements on the coast and islands owned by Spain. The arrangement ensured that a landing on the coast and islands in no way was to establish sovereign rights. With regard to the Falkland Islands (Malvinas), this meant that the Spanish territorial rights were not in any way affected by the activities of the British fishermen. Even though the Nootka Sound Convention dramatically expanded British shipping rights and opened up access to the Pacific, the British Crown abstained in the following decades from establishing a base on the Islands, in accordance with the Convention.

For the period between 1806 and 1811, the factual situation on the Islands cannot be fully reconstructed today. In 1806, Governor Martinez apparently left the Islands together with their population, after having been informed that the city of Buenos Aires had been taken over by Britain. However, the Spanish forces reconquered the city. It is not clear whether and if so when Martinez returned to the Falkland Islands (Malvinas). In the following years, Spain sent armed ships once a year to the Islands in order to prevent the establishment of foreign settlements. By the year 1811, eleven governors appointed by Madrid had resided on the Islands[148]. In the wake of the revolutionary developments in Spain at that time, the settlement was then totally

---

146   Down (note 14), p. 86.

147   See on the Convention infra p. 60 ff.

148   See Goebel (note 22), p. 424; Muñoz Azpiri (note 52), Vol. 1, p. 88, 355; see also J. Torre Revello, Las Islas Malvinas bajo la Soberania española, Vol 3, p. 471. Also, I. Areco, Titulos de la República Argentina a la Soberania y Posesión de las Islas Malvinas (1885), p. 44.

abandonded[149]

Thus, almost half a century came to an end during which Spanish foreign policy had attributed special importance to the Islands. The "Spanish Epoch" on the Falkland Islands (Malvinas) was terminated at the same time as the Spanish colonies on the Latin American continent collapsed. Between 1776 and 1811, Britian apparently never raised any protest against the Spanish presence on the Islands. In turn, Spain never raised any claim after 1811, even though she had never formally terminated her rights[150]. Britain renewed her claim in 1828, fifty four years after her forces had left Port Egmont.

In view of these historical developments, how did the territorial status of the Islands develop after 1774? Before 1771, Britain had not acquired any territorial rights to the Islands; even after the Spanish declaration, the right of Britain to occupy the Eastern Island without limitation of time could not be considered as a sovereign right, even though it was clear that an element of uncertainty and open-endedness of the further development of territorial status had thereby been created. After 1774, half a century followed during which Britain chose not to manifest any territorial interests at all. By 1776 the British plaque had been removed by the Spanish. In view of the extensive activities of fishermen in the waters surrounding the Islands, there is no basis for assuming that Britain was not aware of the fact that after 1774 Spain had claimed the Islands and had established not only the settlement on the eastern part but also another on the western; the Spanish protest against the British settlement in 1775 also has to be taken into account. Britain accepted all these developments without any objection.

---

149   The Spanish retreat is described in a letter by a Spanish civil servant, reprinted in Muñoz Azpiri (note 52), Vol. 2, p. 47.

150   See for details infra p. 62 ff.

It is relevant in this context to refer to the rules which govern the abandonment of territorial rights[151]. It is beyond doubt that abandonment of territorial rights on the basis of a voluntary decision is possible. Due to the fact that state practice has known only a few cases of territorial abandonment, the commentators have not paid much attention to the related problems. An abandonment clearly has to be assumed once a state evacuates its possessions and declares that it thereby abandons the territory. The legal situation is more complex in a case where the abandonment of the possession is not accompanied by a corresponding declaration; and it is even more complex, as was the case of the British conduct in 1774, when factual departure from the land takes place against the background of a positive declaration of continuing will to retain sovereign rights. Under such circumstances, the question of the significance of effective occupation is again raised, especially in the case of distant territories. From the perspective of a logical structure and systematic coherence of the law, it must be assumed that similar factors and criteria are relevant in this case to those which operate in the context of the rules on territorial acquisition. In the case of distant territories it must be questioned whether the temporary exercise of sovereign rights suffices for the continued existence of the rights; a crucial question in this context will relate to the length of the period during which sovereign rights can be held without a manifestation of sovereign activities. However it will appear, here again, that generalisations on the rules concerning the existence of territorial rights will only be of limited value in the solution of specific poblems.

In the case of the British claim to the Falkland Islands (Malvinas), regard must be paid to the following facts: that before 1771 Britain enjoyed no territorial rights, that Britian had not acquired such rights in 1771, did not protest against the Spanish reservation of territorial rights in

---

151   See Lindley (note 57), p. 48 ff.

1771, and also did not protest in the period between 1775 and 1828 against the establishment of settlements and the manifestation of sovereign claims by Spain and Argentinia. No lengthy explanation is needed in order to point out that under such circumstances the symbolic act of the fixing of a plaque should be assessed other than in the case of an uninhabited island which is claimed neither prior to the act nor subsequently by a third state. In the context of a situation which is legally not entirely clear, the symbolic manifestation of the will to possess will not secure the same result as the effective exercise of sovereign rights; this is particularly the case when a claim is not objected to by a third state. As these were clearly the circumstances on the Falkland Islands (Malvinas) after 1774, there is no need here to discuss in any detail the relevance of symbolic acts in the context of territorial acquisition or the abandonment of territory. In conclusion, the departure of the British from the Islands in 1774 and the subsequent silence of London in the following 54 years will have to be interpreted as an abandonment of the British claim. Under the circumstances, the leaving of the plaque will have no independent legal significance *vis à vis* the facts discussed above[152]. It is not without interest that during the time under discussion here Britian herself took the position that the silence of a government upon the establishment of a settlement by a third state had immediate legal consequences for the status of the territory concerned[153].

---

152   Cf. G. Cohen Jonathan, Les Iles Falkland (Malouines), AFDI Vol. 18 (1972), p. 235, 238; Weber (note 29), p. 67; Hillekamps (note 30), p. 95.

153   In a proceeding under Article IV of the treaty of Ghent of 1794 ("Title to Islands in Passamaquodoly Bay"), Britain claimed in 1817: "The United States ... remained silent spectators of the settlements and improvements ... upon these islands ... during a period of more than thirty years ..." and added: "... (this) will justly furnish an argument, that the United States have no claim at this day to any of those islands"; cited by J. Moore, International Adjudications, Vol. 6 (1933), p. 213.

The question as to Spanish territorial rights after 1774 has to be evaluated against the background of this legal situation. No other state maintained a settlement on the Islands, Spain destroyed the British settlement without any protest, and Spain herself maintained her own settlements on both of the large islands. Large populations of whales and seals continued to attract foreign fishermen to the waters surrounding the Islands. Spain undertook to keep these boats away from the shores of the Islands, but it appears that these efforts were not always successful.

The question as to whether this level of Spanish activities secured the continued existence of rights will have to be answered in the affirmative in view of the situation of the Islands and in the absence of activities of third states. This conclusion must be reached in view of the minimum activities required under international law in the context of distant territories for the acquisition and the continued existence of sovereign rights.

9.   The legal significance of the Nootka Sound Convention
       (1790)

In discussion of the period after 1774, the literature frequently addresses the significance of the so-called Nootka Sound Convention[154]. Britain and Spain signed this agreement in 1790 in order to settle a dispute over the right of Britain to establish a settlement on the Pacific coast of America. By this time, the Spanish naval forces had already

154   Concerning the Nootka Sound question, see the
       comprehensive analysis by W. Manning, The Nootka Sound
       Controversy, Report of the American Historical
       Association (1904), p. 279; Goebel (note 22), p. 425;
       R. Caillet-Bois, La controversia del Nootka Sound y el
       Rio de la Plata, Humanidades, Vol. 20 (1929), p. 341;
       more recently, see, e. g., Hillekamps (note 30), p.
       162; F. Vieyra, Las Islas Malvinas y el Derecho

lost some of their power. Madrid had no choice but to abandon the system of previous treaties which had conferred on Spain exclusive rights of navigation in the Pacific Ocean and in the seas to the east and west of Latin America. In the Nootka Sound Convention the right to sail these seas was conceded to Britain.

In relation to the Falkland Islands (Malvinas), the Convention is of interest inasmuch as Spain was strong enough to insist on a clause according to which Britain would not in future establish any settlements in the area of the eastern and western parts of South America and the surrounding islands. Clearly, no change in the existing status of the Falkland Islands (Malvinas) was intended by the parties, as the Convention only addressed the future conduct of Britain. Nevertheless, the British commitment made in the treaty raises the issue of the further status of the Islands. It is beyond doubt that the Falkland Islands (Malvinas) were geographically within the province of the Convention. The subject of discussion concerns the argument that the Convention had influence upon the legal dispute between Argentina and Britain which arose subsequently. The parties to the treaty in 1790 were Britain and Spain. The object of the agreement was the determination and the delimitation of the political spheres of influence between these two countries. It is appropriate to view the Convention as a political treaty between the two major powers, designed to establish a new foundation for bilateral relations in the light of their geographic situation and their political and military strength. The political nature of the Convention is irreconcilable with the proposition that Argentina, as the legal successor of Spain, could have derived any rights from the treaty. The political situation as it developed after the fall of the Spanish colonial empire in Latin America was entirely different from the one that existed in 1790. Therefore, it will have to be concluded that the Nootka Sound

---

Internacional (1984), p. 65; Fisch (note 44), p. 120.

Convention influenced neither the legal situation in the year 1790 nor the subsequent development of the territorial status of the Falkland Islands (Malvinas).

10.   The status of the Islands between 1811 and 1820

In the chronological sequence of activities on the Islands, the question arises whether Spain lost her rights when the Spanish forces decided to leave the Islands pursuant to an order of the government in the year 1811. It is appropriate in this context to consider briefly the further developments. After the declaration of independence by the Argentine provinces in the year 1816 and the establishment of the Republic of Argentina, the new Argentine government sent out a frigate to the Islands and formally took possession of them. The captain of the Argentine ship met with around 50 foreign ships and issued orders prohibiting fishing and hunting on the Islands. In 1823, Buenos Aires appointed the first Argentine governor who was temporarily successful in enforcing the fishing and hunting regulations. The first attempt to settle the Islands after the establishment of Argentina took place in the same year, but it was discontinued in 1824. The second attempt, two years later, was more successful, and in 1828 the Argentine government conferred exclusive fishery rights upon the leader of the new settlement.

It is against this background that the question of the status of the Islands in the period after 1811 has to be raised. It is of interest to remember that the Islands were claimed at this point only by Spain, in contrast to the situation in 1774. The British conduct between 1774 and 1811 shows that a British claim no longer existed after 1811. No other conclusion can be drawn from the complete lack of any manifestation of sovereignty when confronted with the

positive Spanish exercise of sovereign rights in this period
of 37 years. Thus, one has to take for granted a situation in
1811 in which only one state had a claim to the Islands.

Under these circumstances, the general rules concerning
the loss of territory which were valid in state practice for
distant territories not subject to competing claims had to
find application. Regard must be paid to the fact that Spain
did not manifest any will to abandon her rights at the time
of departure from the Islands; on the contrary, the Spanish
Cortes expressed its intention to resettle the Islands later
on under changed circumstances[155]. Under the circumstances, a
temporary departure from the territory will not be considered
as a ground for a loss of territorial rights; in any case, a
change in the status of the Islands cannot be assumed for the
immediate period after 1811[156]. The short span of years
between the departure from the Islands by the Spaniards and
the declaration of independence by the Argentine Republic in
1816 therefore did not lead to a loss of territorial rights
on the part of Spain.

The creation of the Argentine state raises the new issue
whether the Islands became a part of Argentina in 1816 on the
basis of the principle of *uti possidetis*. In essence, this
principle indicates that the borders existing in colonial
periods between states or administrative units of the
colonies continued to exist after the process of independence
among the newly established political units[157]. Legal effects

---

155   For a discussion of the declaration of the Cortes in
       1811, see Hillekamps (note 30), p. 99. Concerning the
       further development of the Spanish rights, see infra p.
       65 ff.

156   See also Weber (note 29), p. 71.

157   Cf. E. Jiménez de Aréchaga, Boundaries in Latin
       America: *uti possidetis* Doctrine, in: EPIL, Instalment
       6 (1983), p. 45, with further citation. Concerning the
       application of the principle to the situation of the
       Islands in 1816, see, e. g., Cohen Jonathan (note 28),
       p. 239; Weber (note 29), p. 107; Hillekamps (note 30),

may emanate from the principle in relation to newly
established territorial units or between a new territorial
unit and a third state. In the first context, the principle
stabilises the existing borders; in the second relationship,
the principle operates so as to avoid new colonisations in
the territory in question by third states, by establishing
the sovereign rights of the new unit within the borders
previously recognised. However, the question concerning the
acquisition of the Falkland Islands (Malvinas) by Argentina
did not fall into either of these two categories. As Spain
had retained her territorial rights until 1816, and as no new
ground for a loss of territory had emerged, the pertinent
constellation of events did not involve the avoidance of a
new colonial settlement subsequent to a loss of territorial
rights by a previous colonial power.

Of greater relevance was the distance between the
Falkland Islands (Malvinas) and the Latin-American
subcontinent, as well as the absence of a necessary
territorial unity between the continent and the Islands. The
principle of *uti possidetis* does not imply that a state
created in the wake of a process of decolonisation will
necessarily acquire the same territorial rights as the
previous colonial power, without regard to the geographic
territorial unity of the colonial empire, and the occupation
of the territory in question by the newly created state.
State practice does not provide evidence of such an
understanding of the principle of *uti possidetis* in the
relationship between the colonial power and the newly created
state[158]. In consequence, it has to be concluded that
Argentina did not acquire the Islands in 1816 automatically
after independence, without regard to the principle of
effective occupation[159]. Spanish territorial rights over the

---

p. 114; Hope (note 44), p. 418.

158   In view of this special context, there is no need to
       discuss at this point the relevance of the principle
       outside of Latin America.

159   This conclusion is also supported by the wording of the

Islands continued.

11.   The status of the Islands from 1820 to 1832

a) Continued existence of the Spanish rights?

In the year 1820, Spain attempted to take formal possession of the Islands. At this point, Argentina sent a frigate, with special instructions to acquire possession of the Islands. Accordingly, the captain raised the Argentine flag and informed about 50 ships of different nationalities, lying off the coast, of the new legal situation and simultaneously declared that Argentine laws would from then on apply on the Islands[160]. Spanish authorities were no longer present on the Islands at the time, nor did Spain raise any protest against the Argentine activities. Spain had left the Islands a decade previously. Argentine independence had been declared four years before, and any active resistance on the part of Spain against the new state had long ceased. In the period concerned, a voyage between the Spanish coast and the Islands would have taken more than a

---

declaration, issued by Argentina in 1820 on the occasion of the formal occupation of the Islands. Cf. infra note 160. The language chosen by Argentina in 1820 appears to indicate that the authorities in Buenos Aires themselves assumed that the Islands were acquired for the first time at this point.

160   The Argentine declaration of November 9, 1820, is reprinted below as annex 13, p. 206. The formalities of the occupation of the Islands by Argentina are described in a document reprinted in BFSP, Vol. 20 (1832/33), p. 422. A letter of notification of the Islands, published on June 8, 1821, in an American newspaper, addressed to an American captain, is reprinted in Muñoz Azpiri (note 52), Vol. 2, p. 47; according to this letter, commander Jewett notified foreign governments on November 9, 1820, about the occupation. Concerning the situation on the Islands in 1820, see also the letter by Vernet, BFSP, Vol. 20 (1832/33), p. 369, 419; see also the discussion in Hope (note 44), p. 413.

month. Given these special circumstances, it will have to be
assumed that the Spanish claim to the Islands no longer had
any effects in relation to a third state which might have
raised a new claim. Such a finding presupposes that, in
between the normal existence of territorial rights on the one
hand and the loss of territory due to the absence of the
manifestation of sovereign activity or sovereign rights on
the other hand, a period of transition may occur during which
the loss of the rights on the part of the old sovereign has
not yet clearly occured while at the same time the raising of
a claim by a third state cannot be considered as a violation
of the rights of the previous sovereign. It would appear that
just such a situation of territorial instability
characterised the status of the Islands in 1820.

Under the circumstances, Spain had the choice, subsequent
to the activities on the part of Argentina by which sovereign
rights were asserted, either to enforce her existing claim
and to consolidate it or to abandon it. As Spain in no way
reacted to the activities on the Islands and did not even
raise any protest, it will have to be assumed that Madrid had
lost any specific interests in the exercise of sovereign
rights on the Islands and, therefore, that these could no
longer be considered as part of the Spanish state. The fact
that Spain did not recognise Argentina at this point in time
does not speak against such a conclusion[161]. As the Islands
do not form a territorial unit with the continent, and as the
lack of recognition of Argentina by Spain had no influence
upon the legal status of Argentina as an independent subject
of international law, with all resulting consequences, it
cannot be assumed that the Spanish silence was necessarily
conditioned by the lack of recognition of the Argentine
government. In no way was Spain hindered from expressing her
legal point of view in the context of a protest against the
Argentine activities on the Islands. The subsequent conduct
of Spain lends additional support to these considerations in

---

161   See also infra p. 73 ff.

view of the lack of a Spanish will to exercise sovereign rights on the Islands. When the dispute over the Islands between Argentina and Britain arose in 1828 and thereafter, Madrid never raised any protest. As Spain refrained from any expression of sovereign rights and remained completely silent in regard to all activities on the Islands after 1811, it would not appear to be justified to assume that, after 1820, Spanish rights were infringed upon. Had Spain decided, in 1820 or in the following decades, to claim any territorial rights the legal situation would have been much more complex than it was in reality. Under the circumstances it has to be concluded that no Spanish rights for the period after 1820 have to be taken into account in an assessment of the activities of Argentina and Britain.

b) Argentine measures in 1820

The efforts of Argentina to acquire the Islands in the period between 1820 and 1832 have to be evaluated against this background. For two principal reasons, the status of the Islands at the end of 1832 has to be considered as a crucial matter which requires close examination. First of all, the legal positions of Britain and of Argentina clearly differ on this point. Moreover, a comprehensive assessment of the British actions in 1833 would appear to depend on a clear identification of the legal status prevailing at the time immediately prior to these actions.

As mentioned above, the relevant conduct on the part of Argentina in the period between 1820 and 1832 consisted of a series of activities. The rules on the acquisition of territory do not call for an individual assessment of the specific actions. The only relevant question pertains to the status of the Islands in the year 1832, in particular with regard to Argentina's claim to have acquired territorial

rights on the basis of activities on the Islands. The
Argentine measures in the period mentioned thus have to be
ascertained and evaluated in their entirety.

It is beyond doubt that the measures taken by Argentina
in November 1820[162] satisfied the requirements of formal
possession of territory. In particular, the public expression
of the will to extend Argentine law to the Islands is
sufficient evidence that Argentina claimed sovereign rights.
The fact remains, however, that an Argentine settlement was
not established on the Islands for the time being.

c)   Argentine measures in 1823

The next manifestation of the Argentine claim appears in
the records for the year 1823[163]. Argentina appointed a
governor for the Islands at that time, and there is evidence
that foreign fishermen landing on the Islands respected and
followed the Argentine orders concerning fishery rights in
the following years. It is clear that in 1823 Argentina
conferred a concession to use a part of the land on the
Eastern Island upon two persons, and that certain fishery
rights and a right to manage certain livestock on the Islands
were also conferred[164]. It is also clear, however, that the
three ships which the concessionaires had sent to the Islands
returned to the mainland in 1824; the reasons for this
development cannot be ascertained today.

---

162   See supra p. 67.

163   Cf. Goebel (note 22), p. 434.

164   See for the wording of the documents Muñoz Azpiri (note
      52), Vol. 2, p. 47; see also decree of August 18, 1823,
      reprinted as annex 14, infra p. 252.

d)   Argentine measures from 1826 to 1832

The concession was not formally discontinued, and in January 1826 one of the two concessionaires, Louis Vernet, personally assumed command of a new crew of about 100 persons, who were charged with the establishment of a settlement[165]. Before long, Vernet made a request to the government in Buenos Aires for virtually exclusive fishery rights. Vernet referred not only to his own capabilities but also to the general advantages which would accrue to the country from a fisheries venture in the future. Vernet's application was granted in 1828; the pertinent decision also referred to the Eastern Island. However, the decision was subject to the condition that Vernet establish a settlement within three years and notify the government of the fulfillment of this condition. The decision of the government was adopted in the form of a public order[166] which stated, *inter alia*, that Argentina had granted the request in order to strengthen the Argentine fishing fleet.

The establishment of the settlement by Vernet proceeded speedily in the following months. This development in turn encouraged Buenos Aires to issue an order which established a new administrative framework for the Islands[167]. Together with other islands near Cape Horn in the southern Atlantic, the Falkland Islands (Malvinas) from now on were part of the jurisdiction of a "military and political governor", with seat on the Eastern Island. The governor was mainly charged to enforce Argentine law, in general, and the rules regarding the catching of seals, in particular. According to the order, a small military unit was to be stationed at the seat of the

---

165   See the extensive description by Vernet, reprinted in BFSP, Vol. 20 (1832/33), p. 369.

166   The wording of the decree of January 5, 1828, is reprinted infra, annex 16, p. 254.

167   The wording of the decree of June 10, 1829, is reprinted as annex 18, infra p. 218.

governor[168]. Remarkably, the order also spelt out the basis for the claim of sovereign rights on the part of Argentina.

On August 30, 1829, Louis Vernet assumed the office of "military and political governor". In his new capacity, Vernet called upon foreign fishers to cease the hunting of seals in the areas surrounding the Islands[169]; apparently, the previous orders issued in 1820 had not been respected after 1826. The British protest against the Argentine measures will be discussed below. Subsequently, Vernet, as governor, threatened to apply criminial sanctions in cases of disregard of the Argentine orders[170]. According to a British report, about 50 men, women and children lived on the Eastern Island; the Western Island apparently was not inhabited[171]. These figures are consistent with those contained in a report of April 1829 which counted altogether 103 members of the Argentine settlement[172]. A third contemporary report speaks of "about 70 persons"[173]. Meanwhile, Vernet had established a house in Port Soledad which contained a library with Spanish, German and English literature[174].

In the following months, the settlement prospered and no special incidents ocurred. At the end of July 1831, the dispute concerning the U.S.S. *Lexington* arose, raising problems for the first time between Argentina and the United States of America concerning the status of the Islands[175].

---

168   Cf. Goebel (note 22), p. 437.

169   See the text in Muñoz Azpiri (note 52), Vol. 2, p. 74; the circular was published on October 16, 1830, in an Argentine newspaper.

170   The text of a circular by Vernet is reprinted as annex 22, infra p. 224.

171   See Down (note 14), p. 115.

172   Ibid., p. 116.

173   Ibid., p. 127; according to a report by Vernet, reprinted in Muñoz Azpiri (note 52), Vol. 3, p. 211, about 120 persons lived on the Islands in May 1829.

174   See Down (note 14), p. 128.

175   Cf. for the details of lengthy statements by the

The United States had recognised Argentina in 1823[176]. The dispute arose in 1831 after the Argentine governor on the Islands had seized two United States ships which had disregarded the Argentine fishery orders in spite of a special warning. One of the two ships was soon released as the captain had promised to return subsequently to the Islands for the purpose of clarification of his responsibility. The second ship, however, together with the crew, was brought immediately to Buenos Aires for the preparation of criminal charges.

These Argentine measures led to a protest by the consul of the United States in Buenos Aires. Argentina rejected the protest with reference to both the formal position of the consul and Argentina's existing territorial rights. By chance, the U.S.S. *Lexington*, a United States ship, reached the Argentine coast at this point. The United States consul in Buenos Aires discussed the situation with the captain of the *Lexington*, issued an ultimatum and threatened the Argentine government to send the *Lexington* to the Islands in order to protect American citizens. The commander of the *Lexington* demanded the conviction of the Argentine governor on the Islands for piracy and robbery.

It is of interest that on the day of the ultimatum's expiry on December 9, 1831, the British representative in Buenos Aires addressed a formal communication to the United States consul in which he spelt out the view that the territorial rights to the Islands belonged to Britain and not to Argentina. Argentina disregarded the ultimatum, and the *Lexington* reached the Falkland Islands (Malvinas) on December 28, 1831. The captain of the *Lexington* and his crew destroyed or seized all the arms on the Islands and burnt all the

---

governments of the United States and Argentina, the documents reprinted in BFSP, Vol. 20 (1830/32), pp. 311-441; see also Muñoz Azpiri (note 52), Vol. 1, p. 92, Vol. 2, p. 77.

176   See Weber (note 29), p. 24; Hillekamps (note 30), p. 99.

powder. The captain ordered that all buildings be destroyed, took possession of some seal furs and put under arrest nearly all the inhabitants of the Islands. The *Lexington* left the Islands with seven Argentine citizens as prisoners.

Attention has to be paid to the circumstances under which these Argentine captives were subsequently released. The captain of the *Lexington* had chosen not to return to Buenos Aires and instead sailed to Montevideo in the newly-founded state of Uruguay. From there, he informed the Argentine government that the prisoners would be released under one condition. The Argentine government was to immediately confirm that the prisoners had followed Argentine orders when they had seized the United States ships. Buenos Aires did not hesitate to make such a declaration, without any reservation, and the prisoners were at once allowed to return to Argentina.

As could be expected, these exchanges led to a series of reactions in Buenos Aires and in Washington. Argentina called for satisfaction from the United States for the illegal conduct which had resulted from the instructions of the United States consul. Even before the actions taken by the captain of the *Lexington*, United States President Jackson had informed the United States Congress on December 6, 1831, that a United States ship had been seized on the Falkland Islands (Malvinas) by a group of bandits claiming to act on behalf of the government in Buenos Aires[177].

In January 1832 the government in Washington sent a special emissary who was supposed to represent the interests of the United States in Buenos Aires. The instructions given to this emissary clearly assumed that the government in Washington considered the actions of the Argentine governor on the Falkland Islands (Malvinas) to be acts of piracy. For

---

177   Cf. Goebel (note 22), p. 446.

two reasons, Washington assumed that the Argentine order of 1829 was null and void: the order had been signed by a governor who soon thereafter had been dismissed from office, and it had also not been published.

The legal position thus assumed by Washington was incorrect when considered from an objective point of view. The order had in fact been published, and it has never been doubted that the legal effects of a governmental measure are not dependent upon the subsequent political fate of the officer who signed the act in question. Moreover, the United States insisted only upon the fishery rights of United States nationals, claiming on the basis of historical developments that these rights could not be considered to depend upon any actions of the territorial sovereign of the Islands. In contrast, Argentina pointed to her rights as sovereign of the Islands. Thus, the United States called for reparation of the damage which the Argentine measures against the United States ships had created, while Buenos Aires in turn made the same claim against Washington because of the actions of the U.S.S. *Lexington*. The details of the extensive correspondence which ensued between the two states are beyond the scope of this study[178]. Argentina subsequently proposed a settlement of the dispute with the participation of a third state, but without a positive response from the United States. At no time did the United States claim territorial rights to the Islands in the dispute with Argentina.

e)   Legal significance of the Argentine activities

Having in view the factual developments referred to above, it must now be considered whether the Argentine activities in the period between 1820 and 1832 established a

---

178   See supra note 175.

rightful claim to the Islands. The starting point for the
legal discussion will have to be that, according to the law
of the times, a *terra nullius* was acquired by the state
which effectively occupied the territory; it was generally
assumed that effective occupation required both the will to
occupy and the factual possession of the land[179].

There is no doubt that Argentina had expressed *animus
possidendi* by the formal act of the year 1820 and by the
subsequent governmental activities which reconfirmed the
Argentine will to claim sovereign rights. The further
question arises as to whether the Argentine measures also
satisfied the preconditions for the acquisition of the
Islands from a factual point of view. In the discussion of
this issue, the decisions of international tribunals cannot
be left out of consideration; this is true in particular for
the decisions in the disputes over Las Palmas[180], Clipperton
Island[181], Eastern Greenland[182], and the Minquiers and
Ecrehos[183]. Brownlie has reviewed these decisions and has
pointed out, correctly, that the previous conception of the
necessity for full and comprehensive settlement and
possession of a territory can no longer be considered as a
precondition of effective occupation today[184]. This is
certainly true for uninhabited territories. The context again
clearly suggests that a general discussion of issues of
territorial acquisition without special regard to the
circumstances of the individual case is only of limited
value.

It is a legitimate question, against the background as
set out by Brownlie, whether the term "effective occupation"

179   See for details I. Brownlie, Principles of Public
      International Law, fourth edition (1990), p. 138.

180   RIAA, Vol. 2 (1949), p. 829.

181   RIAA, Vol. 2 (1949), p. 1105.

182   PCIJ, A/B 53.

183   ICJ Reports 1953, p. 47.

should not be replaced by the concept of "a sufficient degree of governmental activity". In any case, the concept of effective occupation must not be understood in the same manner as it was earlier, with regard to uninhabited territories; the modern concept comes close to a standpoint according to which symbolic acts and a clear and unequivocal will to acquire the land suffice for acquisition in cases of uninhabited territories[185].

The case most directly in point is the decision concerning Clipperton Island. A review of the details will show that the legal issues in this case and those relevant for the Falkland Islands (Malvinas) are parallel in important respects[186]. For present purposes, the interpretation of the concept of "effective possession" by the court is of immediate interest. The Clipperton tribunal was faced with the question whether France had acquired the Island on the basis of the following facts: firstly, an officer of the French navy had claimed the Island by an oral declaration made on behalf of France, pursuant to an order of the French minister in charge of the navy; secondly, notes on the geographical situation of the Island were made aboard the ship; thirdly, some members of the crew stayed on the Island for less than three days; and fourthly, this act was notified to the government in Hawaii and a corresponding notice was published in a local newspaper in Honolulu. Prior to all these actions, France had granted a concession to exploit guano, which, however, had not been made use of. Until the year 1897, no further French acts supported the French claim to sovereignty. In 1897, France requested an explanation from the United States of the legal significance which the United States attributed to the exploitation of guano by three of her nationals; these three persons had also raised the American flag on the Island when they had recognised a French

---

184   See Brownlie (note 179), p. 141.
185   Cf. supra p. 34 ff.
186   Infra p. 76 ff.

ship on the high seas. The United States subsequently
informed France that she had no territorial claims. The
dispute between Mexico and France which led to the arbitral
tribunal arose when Mexico claimed the Island in the same
year and ordered that the Mexican flag be raised there.

In the event, the arbitrator decided that an acquisition
of Clipperton Island by Mexico in the year 1897 had been
prevented by the fact that France had previously successfully
claimed the Island. Remarkably, the arbitrator decided that
the date of acquisition of the territory was December 13,
1857. The award stated that the establishment of the organs
of government cannot be considered as a necessary component
of effective occupation in the case of uninhabited islands.
The appearance on an island of a representative of
governmental authority coupled with the *animus possidendi* was
held to be sufficient for the acquisition of uninhabited
territory not claimed by a third party. The establishment of
governmental authority was considered as a requirement for
the acquisition of African territories according to the Act
of Berlin of 1885, but this requirement was not part of
general international law with regard to the acquisition of
territory.

On the whole, the arbitral award spelt out that a public
manifestation of the act of taking possession suffices in
case of uninhabited territories. The decisive elements
consist of the exercise of governmental powers, as expressing
the will of possession, together with the exclusion of third
parties.

It is not without interest to examine the situation of
the Falkland Islands (Malvinas) in the year 1832 in the light
of the Clipperton award. To what extent was the situation of
the two islands comparable in the critical periods? Without
difficulty, parallels can be demonstrated. In both cases, the
islands were situated far from governmentally organised
territory, no permanent settlements existed at the time of

the taking of possession, and the islands were claimed by only one state at the critical point in time. A difference may be recognised in the fact that Clipperton was not suitable for permanent settlement. The Falkland Islands (Malvinas) were not hostile to the same extent to the erection of buildings and the acquisition of resources; however, in the light of the climatic conditions prevailing on the Falkland Islands (Malvinas), the differences are of a relative nature.

In view of the parallels and the peculiarities of the two situations, an attempt to apply the principle spelt out in the Clipperton award to the situation existing in the Falkland Islands (Malvinas) in the year 1832 would have to accomodate not only the relativity of preconditions for a territorial acquisition in accordance with the geographic situation of the territory in question, but also the existence of previous claims and the aspect of use by governmental organs. In cases where islands are distant from other territory or are more or less unsuitable for human habitation, the requirement of effective occupation is correspondingly reduced to the necessity of symbolic acts expressing the will to claim the islands. Conversely, the measure of governmental activity required for the acquisition of territory is higher where the territory in question is inhabited, is close to densely populated areas and is particularly suitable for human occupation. On such a scale of factors relevant for the acquisition of territory, the Falkland Islands (Malvinas) must be considered closer to the lower end, as territory easily acquired, than to those areas the acquisition of which requires effective factual occupation and a number of governmental acts.

The Argentine activities on the Falkland Islands (Malvinas) between 1820 and 1832, as described above, have to be assessed against this background of legal requirements for the acquisition of territory. In view of the formal act of occupation, the continued territorial claim, the number of governmental acts pertaining to the Islands and the factual occupation by about 100 persons in the period after 1826, it will have to be concluded that the Argentine activities were sufficient for legal acquisition of the territory.

A specific argument which may be opposed to this conclusion requires consideration in view of the attention often given in scholarly literature to the Palmas award, in which the question arose. The award indicated that from the legal acquisition of territory devolves, on the one hand, the right to exclude other states from the territory; but that, on the other hand, such acquisition also establishes the duty on the part of the acquiring state to protect the general rights of third states, and in particular their nationals, on the territory acquired[187]. It is not clear from the reasons given in the award whether this requirement has independent significance for the acquisition of territory. If the award is understood to imply that a state has to observe the general rules of international law after acquisition of a territory, there can be no dispute about this position. Brownlie has correctly pointed out in this context that a violation of these obligations will not have any consequences for the status of the territory on which the violation has occurred; rather, the rules on state responsibility find application[188]. However, if the relevant passage in the Palmas award must be understood so as to imply that a state acquires territory only at the moment when it has established a governmental organization which directly guarantees the existence and observance of the rights of third states and persons, such an understanding would be isolated and would not find any support in state practice or in other awards.

It appears that the more recent literature generally assumes that the preconditions for the acquisition of

---

187   RIAA, Vol. 2 (1949), p. 839.
188   Brownlie (note 179), p. 144.

territory cannot be determined in a schematic manner, and that, in particular, the special situation prevailing in the case of distant territories has to be taken into account. Moreover, there are good reasons to assume that the Palmas award should not be understood so as to imply that the peculiarities of distant territories are irrelevant for the purpose of acquisition of territory; the award specifically recognises this principle in another passage[189]. The state practice concerning the acquisition and the maintenance of sovereign rights in desert areas, in the Arctic and in the Antarctic is uniform in the sense that the special qualities of these regions have to be considered in the case of territorial acquisition, and that the rules concerning effective occupation can only be applied in a modified manner in such areas[190]. In summary, these considerations also support the conclusion that Argentina developed a degree of activities on the Falkland Islands (Malvinas) between 1820 and 1832 which was sufficient to meet the criteria required for the acquisition of the Islands.

So far, no attention has been paid here to the fact that Britain protested against the Argentine activities in 1829, both maintaining British territorial rights to the Islands,

---

189   The decision reads, p. 867: "The acts of indirect or direct display of Netherlands' sovereignty at Palmas (or Miangas) especially in the eighteenth and early nineteenth centuries are not numerous, and there are considerable gaps in the evidence of continuous display. But apart from the consideration that the manifestations of sovereignty over a small and distant island, inhabited only by natives, connot be expected to be frequent, it is not necessary that the display of sovereignty should go back to a very far distant period. It may suffice that such display existed in 1898, and had already existed as continuous and peaceful before that date long enough to enable any Power who might have considered herself as possessing sovereignty over the island, of having a claim to sovereignty, to have, according to local conditions, a reasonable possibility for ascertaining the existence of a state of things contrary to her real or alleged rights."

190   See for details Lindley (note 57), p. 158.

and denying the acquisition of the Islands by Argentina[191].
The British communication of protest drew attention to the
fact that the British claim was based on discovery, on
subsequent occupation and on the resettlement of the Islands
in the year 1771. At the same time it was argued that the
withdrawal from the Islands in 1774 did not lead to a loss of
territorial rights due to the fact that Britain had left a
plaque on the Islands, and that no intention to abandon the
Islands had existed. The British arguments were not
substantiated in the protest. The actions to which the
British document refers have been discussed above. It has
been shown that, in relation to the Argentine claim, no
rights of Britain existed on the basis of the legal
foundations spelt out by Britain in 1829.

The British note of protest ignored the legal
consequences of a discovery, the factual situation concerning
the discovery of the Falkland Islands (Malvinas), the
existence of French and Spanish rights after 1764, as well as
the reservation of rights on the part of Spain in 1771.
Reference was made only to acts on the part of Britian. One
may speculate about the approach taken in the protest,
considering that Britain was fully aware of the relevant
governmental acts of France, Spain and Argentina. Ultimately,
the motives on the part of London in drawing up the note in
this way are without significance from the perspective of
international law, and there is therefore no need to discuss
them here. It only remains to be pointed out that the British
protest was based on a view of the status of the Islands
which could not be upheld against the generally recognised
rules of international law. In consequence, the British
protest could in no way hinder, change or eliminate the
Argentine rights[192]. In 1833, Britian based a renewed protest

---

191   The text of the English protest of November 19, 1829,
      is reprinted in BFSP, Vol. 20 (1832/33), p. 346.

192   The same principle is reflected in the decision of the
      International Court of Justice, in the case of
      Minquiers and Ecrehos, ICJ Reports 1953, p. 47, 66.

upon the communication of 1829 and justified the
"resettlement of the Islands" in the light of the activities
mentioned in the protest of 1829. Necessarily, the evaluation
of the protest of 1829 will be of legal significance for the
assessment of the reasoning which led to the British acts in
1833.

The question must be raised at this point whether
Argentina was legally in a position, between 1820 and 1833,
to acquire new territory. In his monograph on the Falkland
Islands (Malvinas), Hermann Weber assumed that this was not
the case[193]. The argument deserves attention because it is of
central importance for Weber's analysis and for his
conclusions. Ultimately, Weber assumed that Britain acquired
the Islands in 1833 and in the following years in view of the
weak governmental situation of Argentina between 1820 and
1833. Weber drew attention in this context to the lack of a
broad international recognition of the new Argentine state;
factually, reference was made to the internal weaknesses of
Argentina during the relevant period. In particular, Weber
assumed that the process of emergence of independence of
Argentina as a state had not been concluded due to the fact
that Spain did not consider the secession to have been
completed at the time[194]. Thus, Weber arrived at the
conclusion that Argentina had acquired an inchoate right to
the Islands in 1832, but had not perfected it so as to become
the territorial sovereign; the inchoate right, according to
this point of view, was eradicated by Britain's exercise of
territorial rights after 1833 "factually, continuously and
since the end of the century undisputed"[195].

Weber did not fail to note that Britain had recognised
the government in Buenos Aires in 1825 as a *de facto*
government; he refered in this context to a "recognised *de*

---

193   Weber (note 29), p. 76.
194   Ibid., p. 100.
195   Ibid., p. 101.

facto government with limited competences"[196]. This qualification must be taken in context with Weber's opinion that the secession of Argentina did not influence the powers of Spain "as owner of the territory and as the government legitimised to issue declarations under international law with regard to territorial issues of the Crown"[197]. The treaty of friendship between Argentina and Britain concluded in 1825 was not mentioned by Weber at all in this context. Weber considered that the formal occupation of the Islands by Argentina in 1820 and the subsequent sovereign acts carried out until the year 1832 were expressions of a limited territorial sovereignty and were legitimate because they seemed justified by the existing power situation at the time[198]. With regard to the further developments, Weber argued that the silence of Spain in view of the exercise of territorial rights by Britian immediately led to the acquisition of the group of islands by Britain[199]; according to this point of view, the Argentine protests were capable of destroying Britain's assumption of the Islands as *terrae nullius*, but they could not effect the definitive acquisition of the Islands after a period of years in which governmental power was exercised uninterrupted and in an effective manner[200].

On the whole, it must be pointed out, Weber's arguments were not presented in a clear and concise manner. In their substance, they were tied to the assumption that Spain maintained her sovereign rights over the Islands despite the secession of Argentina after 1820 and that therefore Argentina was only in a position to acquire inchoate title to the Islands. *In abstracto*, Weber did not cite any precedents for his singular construction of the legal situation after

---

196   Ibid., p. 86; the treaty of February 2, 1825, is
        reprinted infra as annex 15, p. 253.

197   Ibid., p. 76.

198   Ibid., p. 85.

199   Ibid., p. 98.

1820. Nor did he cite any scholarly opinion which reaches the same result as with regard to the Falkland Islands (Malvinas). In particular, Weber failed to explain why the acquisition of the Islands by Argentina was subject to the approval of Madrid after 1816. The central legal error in Weber's argument must be his opinion that a state created after a process of secession is, in his view, unable to acquire territory until the mother state has formally approved the secession. Weber disregarded the fact that the beginning and the end of the process of secession are determined according to objective criteria, and consequently the subjective opinion of the former state has no decisive weight in international relations in relation to the factual process of secession[201].

Moreover, in this context as well, Weber flatly disregarded the legal significance of the recognition of Argentina by Britain in the year 1823 and the treaty of friendship concluded by the two states in 1825[202]. The treaty shows that Britain assumed as early as 1825 that the new state on the La Plata was fully capable of acting on the international level. Against this background, it cannot be maintained, in particular in the relationship between Britain and Argentina, that the status of Argentina in 1832 was one of a *de facto* state with limited competences. In conclusion, Weber's construction is not convincing when regarded in the light of the general norms of international law relating to the position of states created after a process of secession and in the light of the treaty concluded between Britain and Argentina.

Finally, Weber's analysis was not consistent within its own terms. On the basis of the inchoate right which he

---

200   Ibid., p. 99.

201   Brownlie (note 179), p. 88 ff.

202   The text of the treaty is reprinted in BFSP, Vol. 12 (1824/25), p. 29.

assumed, he asserted that Argentina was in a position to
prevent the original acquisition of rights by third states;
it is hardly surprising to note that this point of view is
probably derived from German civil law doctrine concerning
inchoate rights, which does not find any counterpart in
international law. At a late stage, however, Weber did
conclude that an original acquisition of the Islands by
Britain had occurred, without explaining the consistency of
this opinion with the existence of the inchoate right in any
manner. Weber's construction of an inchoate right is without
any systematic basis and is not convincing from the
perspective of international law doctrine. In many other
parts, Weber's arguments were entirely plausible. However, in
view of the significance of Weber's construction of inchoate
rights for the conclusions of his study, this aspect has
required special scrutiny here.

Prior to a discussion of the British measures taken in
1833, it will now have to be considered whether Argentina
lost her territorial rights due to the developments in the
years 1831 to 1832. Initial attention has been paid to the
Lexington affair above[203]. After the *Lexington* incident,
governor Vernet had left the Islands in order to discuss and
justify his conduct comprehensively in Buenos Aires[204]. Also,
a large percentage of the population returned to the mainland
after the destruction of the dwellings by captain Duncan.
Only a few persons remained on the Islands; their number
remains unclear. It has to be noted that the government in
Buenos Aires appointed a new "civil and military commander"
for the Falkland Islands (Malvinas) on an interim basis on
September 10, 1832[205]. Vernet's successor had reached the
Islands already in the autumn of 1832. At the same time, a

---

203   See supra p. 70 ff.

204   See also the report by Vernet, in BFSP, Vol. 20
      (1832/33), p. 369.

205   See the text of the order of the government of
      September 18, 1832, in: Muñoz Azpiri (note 52), Vol. 2,
      p. 85.

number of prisoners were moved to the Islands from Argentine prisons[206]. As early as 1829, some prisoners had been sentenced in Buenos Aires and were supposed to serve in prisons on the Falkland Islands (Malvinas) at a later point[207]. Apparently, a prison constructed to hold prisoners from the mainland had existed already during the Spanish reign on the Islands[208]. It has been said that this prison existed until the year 1813.

In 1832, the transport of the prisoners was carried out on the warship *Sarandí*, and some family members of the prisoners were also on board. The warship remained permanently stationed at the Islands and was at the disposal of the governor. Vernet's affairs as concessionaire were now taken care of by a representative[209].

Britain protested against the appointment of the new governor almost immediately, on September 28, 1832[210]. The note of protest did not contain any explanation of the basis for the alleged British rights; however, reference was made to the protest raised in 1829. As discussed above, this protest had no legal foundation and could have had no legal consequences[211]; in turn, the protest made by London in 1832 could also not affect any territorial rights of Argentina.

The Argentine legal position was demonstrated not only by the appointment of the new interim governor, but also by instructions from Buenos Aires according to which the Argentine representatives on the Islands were ordered to keep off or to remove all foreign ships from the coastal waters of

---

206   Down (note 14), p. 150.

207   Ibid., p. 110.

208   Ibid., p. 113.

209   See the report by Vernet, supra note 204.

210   Down (note 14), p. 156.

211   Supra p. 79 ff.

the Islands[212]. The *Lexington* affair notwithstanding, no exception was made for ships from the United States. In accordance with this order, a United States ship was forceably removed from the Islands by the Argentines in November 1832. The ship returned to Uruguay.

A notable situation arose on the Islands when the new interim governor was murdered on November 30, 1832, by seven prisoners who had recently been transferred from Buenos Aires[213]. Subsequently, Pinedo, the captain of the *Sarandí*, being the highest officer present, assumed the power of command on the Islands. With the help of the crew of a French ship, Pinedo arrested the mutineers on the Islands; they were returned to Buenos Aires, sentenced and executed. On December 20, 1832, three weeks after the murder of the governor, the British warship *Clio* reached Port Egmont to announce the British claim to the Islands and to enforce it. At this point, the Argentine colony consisted of only about 25 persons.

Did the actions on the Islands in the years 1831 to 1832 lead to a loss of Argentine territorial rights? The conduct of Argentina leaves no doubt, at any point, that no dereliction was intended. The appointment of an interim governor after the *Lexington* affair, the permanent stationing of a warship on the Islands, and the instruction relating to foreign ships on the Islands were unmistakable signs of a continued will of possession. Therefore the only question is whether the development of the situation on the Islands in the period between the *Lexington* affair and the arrival of the *Clio* amounted objectively to a loss of Argentine territorial rights. For this span of about 18 months, it is of significance that an acquisition of the Islands had occurred previously, that Argentina continued to express the will of possession, that the Islands were continuously under

---

212   Down (note 14), p. 152.
213   Ibid., p. 153.

the jurisdiction of a governor who was mostly present on the Islands, that even after the attack by the *Lexington* some settlers remained on the Islands, and that at the end of 1832 about 25 persons remained on the Islands.

A review of state practice and an examination of relevant arbitral awards does not suggest any argument which would support the thesis that Argentina had lost her territorial rights under these specific circumstances. In view of the primary significance of the manifestation of sovereign rights in distant territories, as opposed to effective occupation in the sense of factual settlement, the manifest will of Argentina must be considered more important than the occupation of the Islands[214]. The crisis on the Islands, caused by acts of force by a foreign power in the year 1832, lasted only for 18 months. The conduct of Argentina in the following years clearly indicates that the will to re-establish the settlement existed also after the attack by captain Duncan. Finally, it will have to be noted that even short periods of total lack of sovereign manifestation have not led to a loss of existing territorial rights as long as no intention of dereliction on the part of the territorial sovereign could be assumed[215]. Against the background of this legal situation, it will have to be concluded that factual developments during the 18 months concerned did not change the territorial status of the Islands.[216]

12.   The events leading to the British actions on the

---

214   Supra p. 73 ff.

215   For details see Blum (note 83), p. 111.

216   See also Hillekamps (note 30), p. 121; Hope (note 44), p. 423 (note 95); Greig (note 44) fails to discuss clearly the status of the Islands in 1832; on p. 59 he refers to the "uncertain status of the islands in the period from 1811 - 1833". Correspondingly, Greig does not, in a subsequent remark, address the issue of partial annexation.

Falkland Islands (Malvinas) in 1832 to 1833: The state
of information and the decision-making process in
London from 1829

In the chequered colonial history of the Falkland Islands
(Malvinas), the British actions in the years 1832 and 1833
ushered in the last chapter, which has now extended over more
than 150 years. Thus, the situation today is the immediate
consequence of those actions. It is evident that legal
evaluation of the actions taken in the years 1832 to 1833 has
had a decisive impact upon the further development of the
territorial status of the Islands[217]. It is hence appropriate
to review the British decisions of that time with particular
care.

The internal aspects of the state of information and the
process of decision-making in London have no immediate
influence upon the situation under international law, which
is determined only by actions of an external nature.
Nevertheless, a close relationship between the internal
developments and the external measures will be recognised.
Indirectly, the discussion of the internal process of
decision-making can even provide insights which may assist an
assessment of the international legal situation.

For the period under discussion, Down assembled in his
dissertation of 1926 the relevant policy decisions concerning
the Falkland Islands (Malvinas) on the basis of files of the
foreign office, the colonial office and the admiralty

---

217   While the United Kingdom argued before 1936 that her
      rights were based upon actions in the period before
      1833, she has changed her position and has since argued
      that the Islands were acquired in 1833 and thereafter;
      see P. Beck, The Anglo-Argentine Dispute over Title to
      the Falkland Islands: Changing British Perceptions on
      Sovereignty since 1910, in: Millennium, Journal of
      International Studies, Vol. 12 (1983), p. 6, 15.

office[218]. Under the coordination of Prime Minister
Wellington, these ministries participated in the relevant
decision-making. The following discussion is based largely
upon the official documents cited, often at length, by Down.

The first nine years of the exercise of sovereign rights
by Argentina on the Falkland Islands (Malvinas) after 1820
did not lead to any reactions in London, and apparently did
not lead to any internal discussions in the ministries
concerned. The first known British document of the period
which addresses the situation on the Islands is a letter by
Parish, the British representative in Buenos Aires, addressed
to the foreign minister Aberdeen and dated March 15, 1829.

Parish had represented Britain in Argentina since 1824,
and he had also carried out the negotiations which, in 1825,
had led to the conclusion of the treaty of friendship between
the two states[219]. The relations between Buenos Aires and
London during that time were in general quite close; the
early recognition of the new state on the La Plata river by
the British Crown was largely influenced by the British
policy against Spain and the negative attitude of London
toward the political order which had been designed and
developed by the continental powers of Europe in the Congress
of Vienna in 1814 within the framework of the Holy Alliance.
It may by presumed that the explanation for the British
silence with regard to the question of the Falklands
(Malvinas) between 1820 and 1829 will have to be sought and
viewed in the light of this broad political context and the
corresponding desire on the part of London to cooperate with
the new state. However, the British motives have apparently
never been spelt out. It is not without interest that the
subject of the Falklands (Malvinas) was not discussed in any
way by Britian during the negotiations on the treaty of 1825.
There is no reason to assume that Britain had not been aware

---

218   Down (note 14), p. 141 ff.
219   See supra, p. 83.

of the Argentine activities on the Islands after 1820. The official Argentine measures were also published. Moreover, British ships kept sailing to the Islands, and the crews kept reporting their information on the development of the settlements back to Britain. According to Down, reports of the foreign office in London indicate that in the period between June 1826 and May 1827 thirteen British ships landed on the Falkland Islands (Malvinas)[220].

The letter written by Parish in March 1829 drew the attention of the British foreign office to the plan to establish a prison on the Islands by Argentina[221]. Parish also mentioned that Argentina had in the past granted privileges to those persons who had been willing to establish settlements for the purpose of hunting seal and wild cattle. Conspicuously, Parish spoke only of temporary settlements. It is not clear what objective facts would have justified this qualification. It cannot be excluded that Parish indeed considered that his description of the situation was correct. However, Parish had failed to send any reports to London concerning previous sovereign acts by Argentina, and possibly the letter of March 1829 was an attempt to conceal his failure by referring only to temporary settlements that had been made earlier. It may already be noted here in this regard that a later report made by a British minister in the year 1832 was also not entirely correct from an objective point of view[222], but the letter of 1832 formed the basis of the decision taken in London to assume power on the Islands.

The letter of March 1829 also stated that Argentina claimed rights, even though, as Parish considered, Britain had never formally abandoned her own traditional claims. Parish drew attention to the fact that Britain had secured freedom of navigation in the Pacific since the dispute with

---

220   Down (note 14), p. 233.
221   See Down (note 14), p. 110.
222   See infra p. 100.

Spain and that, therefore, the Islands had then become more important from the point of view of Britain. Moreover, in accordance with a report by a knowledgeable British naval officer, it would have had to be presumed that the Islands were not as uninhabitable as had earlier been assumed.

The letter sent by Parish to the foreign office did not remain the only cause for an increase in the attention paid by Britain to the Falkland Islands (Malvinas). Apparently by coincidence, the two other ministries concerned also received information in the first part of 1829 which drew their attention to the Islands. The colonial office received from a member of parliament a letter written by lieutenant Langdon on April 12, 1829[223]; Langdon had already underlined the importance of the Islands at an earlier point. As captain of a commercial ship, he had rounded Cape Horn five times, and he now pointed to the necessity of establishing a base for the merchant navy on the Islands[224]. He considered that the Islands were better suited than any other place on the Cape Horn route for the storage and collection of food and for the repair of damaged ships. According to Langdon, the increasing importance of this route required stronger efforts on the part of London in this context. From a financial point of view, a base on the Islands was quite feasible as a team of a hundred men would suffice for the establishment of a colony. Langdon's letter also emphasised the value of the Islands for agriculture and the raising of livestock. Curiously enough, the third letter written in the first half of the year 1829 also referred to the latter aspect; this was all the more remarkable as the communication was addressed to the

---

223   See the text of the letter in Muñoz Azpiri (note 52), Vol. 2, p. 65; a further letter written by Langdon on June 16, 1829, is reprinted on p. 60, followed by further correspondence on the part of Langdon on p. 84. See also the letter by Beckington to Peel, dated June 11, 1829, ibid., p. 68.

224   Down (note 14), p. 112.

admiralty by a certain admiral Ortay[225].

Apparently, the effect of these three reports on the significance of the Islands was to impress the authorities in London. In addition, British attention was increased by a communication from Parish dated April 25, 1829, in which he pointed out that in 1829 Argentina had conferred privileges upon Vernet on the Islands[226].

In this situation, all three ministries concerned expressed their interest in redefining the British policy toward the Falkland Islands (Malvinas), albeit in different ways. The question of sovereignty was addressed as early as June 5, 1829 by a high representative of the foreign office in a private and confidential letter to the secretary for colonial affairs[227]; apparently, the latter had directed a memorandum to the foreign office on this point. Remarkably, the communication from the foreign office avoided taking a definite position. Essentially, its author was content to present the British and the Spanish claims as formulated between 1770 and 1774. Subsequent relevant developments were ignored. The foreign office was in this respect much more reserved in its judgment than a representative of the admiralty who had previously spoken out in favour of pressing British territorial claims ("Remember they are virtually ours...") and had added: "The people of Buenos Aires can have no pretensions whatever to them."[228] Less than three weeks later, on July 23, 1829, the colonial office added its own point of view in a circular letter. The gist of the position taken by the colonial office was that it was time either to enforce the British claim to the Islands or to abandon them fully. The colonial office left no doubt that it supported the first alternative in order to promote the interests of

---

225   Ibid., p. 115.
226   Ibid., p. 116.
227   Ibid., p. 117.
228   Ibid., p. 115.

the merchant navy, while also indicating that general
considerations of policy pointed in the same direction. The
letter was accompanied by a remarkable legal analysis of the
status of the Islands which is reprinted below[229].

After discussing the dispute with Spain it was noted that
the British settlements had been given up in 1774; cautiously
it was added: "it is apprehended that the same right (of
sovereignty), although it has not since been exercised, has
not, nevertheless, been abrogated by disuse". In contrast to
the foreign office, the colonial office did point out that
Spain had taken possession of the Islands after 1774 and had
sent prisoners to the Islands. The various Argentine
activities and claims were clearly presented. The relevant
passage was introduced with the following statement: "By the
last Accounts from the same quarter it would seem that the
Government of Buenos Aires assumed the power of disposing of
these islands." However, the legal analysis ended with a
description of the Argentine intentions and activities. There
was no effort whatsoever to assess the British claim of 1774
in the light of subsequent activities and claims of Spain and
Argentina. Thus, the analysis was incomplete at the central
point.

The importance attached to the matter by the colonial
office is evident from the fact that the office also sent its
analysis to Prime Minister Wellington. The latter answered
three days later, on July 25, 1829[230]. At the beginning of
his discussion, Wellington unmistakeably drew attention to
the weaknesses of the legal analysis of the colonial office
in the following short passage: "I have perused the enclosed
papers respecting the Falkland Islands. It is not at all
clear to me that we have ever possessed the sovereignty over
all these islands. The Convention certainly goes no further
than to restore us Port Cummont (sic!), which we abandoned

---

229   Annex 19, p. 259.
230   See Down (note 14), p. 119; Wellington's letter is

nearly sixty years ago." The recommendation issued by Wellington, however, was entirely incompatible with this legal analysis. The prime minister advised that Argentina be informed that Britain had a claim to the Islands and therefore would not tolerate any Argentine settlements.

Apparently, Wellington was unaware of the fact that the legal adviser to the king had already been asked on June 9 to prepare a memorandum on the legal status of the Islands[231]. This memorandum was signed on July 28, only three days after Wellington had written his own advice. The memorandum is reprinted below[232]. The royal advocate reached the opposite conclusion to Wellington and, after a short discussion, stated that Britain did have territorial rights over the Islands. He argued that Britain had discovered and occupied the Islands, and that the British departure from the Islands in 1774 had not led to a loss of territorial rights. Therefore, Argentina had not been in a position to acquire sovereign rights. On the whole, the content of this short paper is best characterised as a series of legal assertions, none of which are in any way substantiated in their essential points.

As would be expected, the subsequent British attitude reflected the advice of the prime minister. Thus, the first phase of the decision-making process with regard to a new definition of policy toward the Falkland Islands (Malvinas) after a period of silence of 55 years came to an end. Two weeks after the advice rendered by Wellington, foreign secretary Aberdeen instructed Parish to inform the Argentine government of the British claim to the Islands and to point out that Britain would not remain indifferent toward governmental acts of Argentina on the Islands[233]. However, Parish was not authorised to raise a formal protest. As

---

reprinted as annex 17, p. 216.

231   Down (note 14), p. 179.

232   Annex 20, p. 260.

pointed out in the letter, a final decision on the new policy
which London would follow had not been taken; it remained
open "whether it shall be thought proper to resume possession
of a settlement which had been relinquished for a time,
although never abandoned". The abstract wording ("... of a
settlement...") seems to indicate that the doubts about
Britain's right to occupy the Islands, which the prime
minister had expressed in his communication, still remained.
The same context may supply clarification of the meaning of
the following sentence with regard to general developments on
the Islands: "The question is one of much delicacy, involving
important consequences and demanding therefore the most
mature deliberation."

The specific instructions contained in this letter were
never carried out. When the letter arrived in Buenos Aires on
October 26, 1829, the factual situation had already changed,
and Parish considered that a different response was
required[234]. The new element consisted of the Argentine
decree of June 10 which had indirectly confirmed the
Argentine claim. Parish had informed London about this new
development in a letter dated September 17, 1829, and in
response received new instructions, on November 18, to
protest formally against the Argentine position[235].
Accordingly, Parish protested in Buenos Aires on November
19[236]. As was discussed above, this protest could not affect
the rights of Argentina[237]. It is conspicuous that the
substance of the protest was patterned on the colonial office
memorandum, addressed only actions and developments up to the
year 1774 and only discussed British rights. Thus, the
external position taken by London did not in any way reflect
Wellington's doubts as to whether Britain had acquired

---

233   Down (note 14), p. 121.
234   Ibid., p. 123.
235   Supra p. 79.
236   The protest is reprinted below as annex 20, p. 260.
237   Supra p. 80.

territorial rights in 1774 or at an earlier point. No words
in the protest speak of the activities of Spain and Argentina
after 1774. However, London was well aware of these
developments, as is revealed by the memorandum of the
colonial office of July 2, 1829.

When the protest of November 19, 1829 is considered in
the light of the decisions taken in London in the previous
months, it becomes apparent that Britain was interested in
possession of the Islands for economic and political reasons;
it is also clear that the decision makers were well aware of
the weaknesses of their legal position. The internal
consideration given to the subject in London had clearly
revealed these weak points, to which no satisfactory answers
could be found. In the end, the remaining serious legal
doubts were not considered as weighty as the political
interests. Thus, the protest of November 19 had to be
formulated so as to express a legal position adopted by
Britain which was consistent neither with the objective legal
situation nor with the information available to the British
authorities.

After the British protest had been filed on November 19,
1829 there was a standstill in the dispute for two years.
Argentina took note of the protest, but did not in any way
respond. In Britain, Aberdeen had meanwhile been replaced by
Palmerston as foreign secretary. It is not clear whether the
process of intense deliberations, which had been announced by
Aberdeen, proceeded in an active way after 1829. In London,
renewed attention was drawn to the Islands after Vernet sold
land there in October 1831. Remarkably, the British
lieutenant Langdon was the buyer; this was the same Langdon
who had written the letter in 1829 emphasising the value of
the Islands and reporting on the Argentine activities. Vernet
also authorised Langdon to sell other lands on the Islands to
Englishmen, but he did not fail to emphasise that Argentine
territorial rights had to be recognised. In a letter to the
colonial office in London dated January 20, 1832, Langdon

again referred to the increased importance of the Islands,
without referring to the transactions of land in which he had
taken part[238]. At the same time Langdon indicated that Vernet
had hinted to him that no objections would be raised if
Britain were to occupy the Islands. Nothing indicates that
Vernet had in this respect spoken as the representative of
Buenos Aires; moreover, it is not at all clear how such a
statement on the part of Vernet was compatible with his
demand that eventual new British settlers would have to
respect the rights of Argentina. Under these circumstances,
no decisive importance can be attached to these remarks of
Langdon.

On December 31, 1831, after the *Lexington* had left for
the Falkland Islands (Malvinas), Fox, the British minister in
Buenos Aires, wrote to London to report on his efforts to
bring Argentina to resind all sovereign acts taken since June
1829[239]. However, it was not this communication but the
letter written by Langdon which caused London to give renewed
attention to the Islands. The colonial office had passed on
Langdon's letter to the foreign office on February 25, 1832.
As the concessions which were mentioned in Langdon's letter
had been granted in October 1831, the colonial office
correctly assumed in its accompanying letter that the British
protest of 1829 had not led to a change in the Argentine
position. The letter therefore suggested that Britain should
request Argentina to withdraw the appointment of the new
governor[240]. Following this proposal the foreign office
issued corresponding instructions to Fox, who was in
Argentina, on March 22, 1832. However, the instructions
crossed with the letter sent by Fox dated December 31, 1831,
which reported that governor Vernet had imprisoned seafarers
from the United States; it appears that this letter by Fox
arrived in London only on April 18, 1832.

---

238   Down (note 14), p. 142.
239   Ibid., p. 147.
240   For details see Down (note 14), p. 143.

Fox received the instructions of the foreign office dated March 22 on May 21, 1832. He assumed correctly that the foreign office had not been informed, when the letter was written, of the dispute between Argentina and the United States. For this reason, Fox decided not to address the foreign ministry in Buenos Aires immediately, but instead to send a new report to London, dated May 31, 1832, in which he explained why he had not carried out the instructions of March 22. Meanwhile, Fox had also obtained knowledge of the actions of the *Lexington* on the Islands. The new situation on the Islands was described by Fox as follows: "Mr. Vernet's Government and Colony at the Falkland Islands have in fact ceased to exist, and there is not the least chance that either he, or anyone belonging to him will ever return thither"[241]. Fox also explained that revolutionary movements in Argentina had led to two changes of government in 1829, that no communication existed between the Islands and the government, and that the new government "probably had forgotten" the Islands[242].

The conclusions drawn by Fox in the second part of his letter have to be explained against the background of British fears that the United States might claim the Islands. In order to avoid any dispute between Britain and the United States, Fox believed it was inappropriate to raise any claims on behalf of Britain in Buenos Aires at this point. Before Fox wrote his letter, London felt that there was cause for renewed consideration of the subject[243]. On March 16, 1832, a British admiral had reported a conspicuously high number of warships at anchor in Rio de Janeiro, and that a relationship between the arrival of these ships and the dispute between the United States and Britain concerning the Falkland Islands (Malvinas) had to be considered. In the light of this new information, the admiralty had asked the foreign office as

---

241   Ibid., pp. 145-146.
242   Ibid., p. 146.
243   Ibid., p. 147.

early as May 7, 1832, for a legal opinion concerning the
issue of sovereignty[244]. Curiously enough, this request only
related to treaty commitments made by Britain in relation to
Spain. It is not entirely clear, in view of the extensive
discussion of the legal situation in the various ministries
in 1829[245], in particular the denial of any rights on the
part of Argentina by the admiralty, why the legal issue was
raised anew.

In retrospect it is apparent that the request by the
admiralty, particularly in conjunction with the report by Fox
from Buenos Aires of May 31, 1832, ushered in the last phase
of the decision-making process in London before the Islands
were taken over by the British. As early as August 4,
immediately after receipt of the letter from Fox, the
admiralty informed the colonial office of its intention to
send ships to Port Egmont on the way back from Cape Horn "and
assert our sovereignty to that Island at least"[246]. Possibly
this careful approach reflected the doubts which Wellington
had expressed, in 1829, that British territorial rights may
have existed with regard to Port Egmont, but not in relation
to the entire group of islands. Any such doubts, however,
were not reflected in the decision to assume power on all the
islands which was communicated by the foreign office to the
admiralty on August 30, 1832[247]; the letter contained
instructions to the effect that a British ship was to land in
Port Egmont "... for the acting at the said Islands (the
Falkland Islands (Malvinas)) as in a possession belonging to
the Crown of Great Britain".

Apparently, the words "... as in a possession ..." were
chosen in order to avoid taking a clear legal position on the
situation. On the following day, August 31, 1832, the

---

244   Ibid., p. 147.
245   Supra p. 92 ff.
246   Down (note 14), p. 148.
247   Ibid., p. 148.

admiralty responded that the orders necessary for the implementation of the plan had been given[248]. Ten days later, on September 10, 1832, Buenos Aires appointed a new interim governor for the Islands. At this moment in time, the British minister in Argentina, Fox, was not yet aware of the decision taken in London to assume power on the Islands. Under these circumstances, Fox decided on September 28 to raise a formal protest, without having been specifically instructed at this point by London to do so[249]. Fox referred to the British protest of the year 1829, emphasised British claims and insisted that no other country was entitled to issue governmental acts on the Islands. Three days later, the foreign ministry in Buenos Aires responded to the protest, declaring that Argentina maintained her territorial rights to the Islands[250].

On September 4, 1832, the authorities in London addressed a letter to Fox informing him of the decision to assume power on the Islands. For reasons that have not been clarified, this letter never reached Buenos Aires. Fox was assigned to a new position by the foreign office in October 1832. Lacking the relevant information, his successor Gore was as much surprised by the British actions at the end of the year 1832 as was the Argentine government. The forcible measures taken by Britain were carried out in December 1832 and in January 1833. The orders of the captain of the *Clio*, J. Onslow, are reprinted below[251].

The manner in which the order was implemented will be discussed later. Initially, it is worth considering whether the decision-making process in London, as described above, may assist in an evaluation of the British takeover from the perspective of international law. Firstly, it needs to be

---

248   Ibid., p. 148.
249   Ibid., p. 151.
250   Ibid., p. 151.
251   Annex 23, infra p. 225.

established whether legal aspects had played any role from
the point of view of Britain, and, if this was the case, the
manner in which Britain had assessed the situation should be
examined.

It is clear that the decision-making process in London
had taken account of the legal aspects of the situation in
all phases of the developments between 1829 and 1832.
Correspondingly, it has to be assumed that the legal status
of the Islands was of significance from the point of view of
British policy toward the Islands. Several statements
including that of 1829 by Prime Minister Wellington and the
order of the foreign office to Parish of August 8, 1829,
indicate that the legal aspects were not only noted by
London, but also that they were considered essential in the
process of decision-making. Following on this observation,
the further question has to be raised as to the motives which
caused Britain only to protest in 1829 while three years
later London was prepared to resort to the use of force in
order to acquire the Islands. The considerations relating to
navigation, strategy and economics which accorded a special
value to the Islands from the point of view of Britain were
just as valid in 1829 as in 1832; in any case, the decision-
making process as reflected in the internal files and
documents does not point to any new factors which surfaced
after 1829.

The only new development which could be mentioned here
was the *Lexington* affair of 1832, and its consequences on the
Islands. It may well be speculated that the British decision
to take over the Islands was made during a weak phase of the
Argentine presence on the Islands, in the wake of the affair,
and at the same time was intended to prevent the United
States from acting more speedily and from claiming the
Islands ahead of Britain. In the light of the overall
developments in London which preceded the crucial decision,
it is reasonable to assume that these factors influenced the
British thinking.

From a legal point of view it is more important to consider in detail the letter written by Fox in which he described the effects of the *Lexington* affair, including the objective situation on the Islands, and in which the Argentine position toward the Islands was described in a manner which indicated that, in this respect as well, a change had occurred. Objectively, the report made by Fox was not correct inasmuch as it stated that Argentina had abandoned the settlement on the Islands[252]; it was true that some settlers had left the Islands, but others remained. Even more important, Fox created the impression, in two places in his report, that Argentina had abandoned her claim to the Islands. In any case, this was the impression which an unbiased observer in London would have received both in view of the statement that "not a least chance" existed for the return of the Argentine settlers and in the light of the speculation by Fox that the Islands had been entirely forgotten in Buenos Aires. Thus, it may be assumed that Britain was aware of the earlier activities and claims of Argentina at the time when the decision to assume power on the Islands was made at the beginning of August 1832, but it is also true that London had to assume that Argentina had abandoned these claims in the wake of the *Lexington* affair.

From the perspective of Britain, the central new factor at the beginning of August 1832 thus consisted in the change of the factual and the legal situation on the Islands. The special interests of Britain in possessing the Islands existed in 1832 just as in 1829, but meanwhile the evaluation of the legal situation had changed. According to the information available in Britain, Argentina had abandoned her claims while simultaneously there was concern that the United States would raise claims in the near future. From this perspective it may easily be explained why Britain immediately decided to acquire the Islands after receipt of the report sent by Fox. The task was now to pre-empt any

---

252   See supra p. 98.

plans on the part of the United States, and possibly even on the part of France, and so to use the existing opportunities to promote the national interest.

It thus turns out that the authorities in London reached their decision to assume power on the Islands against the background of information which had indicated that the Islands were *terra nullius* and, consequently, London believed that no legal obstacles existed to the British assumption of power on the Islands; in other words, the decision was made in London *bona fide*. The peculiar element in this situation was that the pertinent information was objectivly wrong. Thus, the far-reaching consequences of the letter containing the misinformation sent by Fox become apparent.

It is worthy of mention that Fox attempted, in a letter of October 15, 1832, to justify his incorrect evaluation of the Argentine position; he informed London that the appointment of a new interim governor, in direct contradiction to his former assessment of the situation, was nothing else than "a silly show of defiance to the Americans"[253]. However, the dice had been cast in London at this point, and the *Clio* was on her way to the Islands.

13.   The taking of power by Britain in 1832 to 1833

The circumstances under which Britain assumed power on the Islands in 1832 to 1833 are described both in a report made by captain Onslow of the *Clio*[254] and in a report by the Argentine government prepared on the basis of a communication by captain Pinedo[255]. In all essential points, these two

---

253   Down (note 14), p. 150.
254   Ibid., p. 155.
255   BFSP, Vol. 20 (1832/33), p. 1194; the instructions of
        Onslow from Baker in accordance with the orders of

descriptions tell the same story. Thus, it can be assumed that the existing record of the process by which Britain assumed power in 1823 to 1833 is reliable and correct.

On December 20, 1832, the *Clio* reached Port Egmont on the Western Island and there found the ruins of the settlement which the British had left in 1774. In this place, captain Onslow ordered that the following inscription be carved into a wooden plank: "Visited by H.B.M.: sloop *Clio*, for the purpose of exercising the right of Sovereignty over these Islands. 23rd December 1832." Onslow stayed on Western Island with his crew from December 20 to 30. His crew searched the neighbouring coasts for a distance of about 60 miles in the hope of finding human settlements. When none was found, Onslow decided on December 30 to explore the Western Island and not to wait for a second British ship, the *Tyne* under captain Hope, which was expected to reach the Islands in the following days. As Onslow had not met with any resistance on Western Island or the surrounding territory during the first ten days, he considered that the assistance of the *Tyne* was not needed. In a bottle, Onslow left a message addressed to Hope saying that he had left for Berkely Sound on the Western Island "where he expected to find inhabitants if there were any in the Islands".[256]

On January 2, 1833, the *Clio* landed on the Western Island. There, Onslow found the Argentine settlement with about 40 persons, including 25 men, and the *Sarandí*. On the same day, Onslow met with Pinedo. The latter stated that he held the power of command both on land and at sea. In the further course of the discussion, Onslow revealed his mission, drew the attention of Pinedo to the territorial rights of Britain to the Islands and demanded that Pinedo lower the Argentine flag and leave the Islands together with

London are reprinted in Muñoz Azpiri (note 52), Vol. 2, p. 87. The report written by Onslow on January 19, 1833, concerning the details of the takeover, addressed to Baker, is reprinted in the same Vol. on p. 101.

his crew and all belongings[257]. Pinedo protested against
Onslow's demand and requested a version in writing; Onslow
responded by providing the same[258].

According to Onslow's report, Pinedo agreed on January 2
to meet Onslow's requirements. Pinedo indicated, however,
that he wished to await the instructions of his government in
Buenos Aires before taking a decision. Later, Pinedo reported
that, on the same day, he made an attempt to meet for a
second time with Onslow and to inform him that he intended to
resist the implementation of Onslow's plans, if necessary by
force; this attempt failed as Onslow no longer wished to
receive the Argentine delegation. Given this state of
affairs, Pinedo concluded that every effort at resistance
against the measures planned by Onslow was bound to fail, and
he therefore discarded any thought of an exchange of force
with the British. On January 3, Pinedo visited the *Clio* in
the early morning and protested once more; he requested

---

256   Down (note 14), p. 155.

257   "I acquainted him civilly with the object of my
       mission, and requested him to embark his force and haul
       down his flag on shore, he being in a possession
       belonging to the Crown of Great Britain. At first he
       acquiesced, provided I would put the same in writing,
       which I did (a) ... On the morning of the third instant
       at 5 a.m. he visited me, to request me to allow the
       Buenos Ayrean flag to be kept flying on shore till
       Saturday the 5th, when we would finally set sail,
       taking with him the force and such of the settlers as
       expressed a desire to leave the Island. I told him his
       request was inadmissible, and that he must consider he
       was in a port belonging to Great Britain. Finding he
       wavered, and was reluctant to strike his flag, I
       immediately landed, hoisted the Union and caused it to
       be lowered, sending it with a civil message on board
       the national schooner. It is to be observed that while
       the schooner of war was at sea, the soldiers mutinied
       and shot their commander: and from all I could learn
       from the commander of the schooner, great
       insubordination existed in the settlement, which
       paralysed the settlers, and had we not arrived might
       have led to worse consequences, as there were a great
       many bad characters who left in the national schooner."
       The report is reprinted in Down (note 14), p. 156.

258   See the wording in annex 24, infra p. 266.

Onslow to grant two extra days before his departure was due.
Onslow denied the request, with a reference to the British
rights. In the course of the exchange, Onslow, according to
Pinedo's report, referred to the strength of his crew and the
possibility of a further reinforcement of his troops within a
very short time.

"In this state of affairs, after having endeavoured in
vain to surmount the difficulties which, in his opinion,
would render the most desparate resistance unavailing, he
became thoroughly convinced of it; and at 6 o'clock on the
morning of the 3rd, he went personally on board the Sloop
Clio, and, for the last time, protested to her Commander
against the violation he was about to commit. Captain Onslow
replied to him in the sense of the latter part of the
subjoined Note, assuring him that he could not defer the
execution of the Orders he had received to take possession of
the Malvinas; that he could see what Force he had, and that
he was in momentary expectations of more; and that he,
Commandant Pinedo, could therefore act as he might think fit.
Commandant Pinedo immediately withdrew, declaring that Great
Britain was responsible for the insult, and violation of the
dignity and rights of the Republic, which were thus
inconsistently and disrespectfully trampled upon, by force:
that it was his intention to depart, but that he would not
strike the Flag on shore."[259]

Under these circumstances, Pinedo was no longer prepared
to simply lower the Argentine flag. Onslow responded
immediately and landed with the crew of three boats on the
Island. His first act was to hoist the British flag, which
has flown there ever since. Subsequently, Onslow ordered the
Argentine flag to be lowered and sent to Pinedo. Pinedo
departed from this situation on January 15, 1833, after
appointing a provisional successor in command and requesting
both him and the remaining force not to lower the Argentine

259   BFSP, Vol. 20 (1832/33), p. 1196 (report of the

flag. Down was of the opinion that Onslow and his crew were much superior to the Argentine force, and that resistance on the part of Pinedo would accordingly have been "obviously useless"[260]. About twenty five men left the Islands together with Pinedo. Fourteen men, three women and one child from the Argentine settlement remained on the Islands with the consent of Onslow[261].

Onslow departed from the Islands on January 10, 1833, and handed over command on behalf of the British Crown to an Irish settler in the Argentine colony who had been on the Islands since 1826. Shortly thereafter, the *Tyne* arrived, and on March 1, the *Beagle* reached the Islands on its famous expedition. In the summer of 1833, a mutiny with several deaths occurred on the Islands; at this time there was no effective command there[262]. From January 7, 1834, onwards, a permanent representative of the British Crown has been in residence on the Islands[263].

14.   Legal evaluation of the taking of power by Britain

Following the above presentation of the facts of the British takeover, it is of importance for an assessment of the British assumption of power and its effect on the status

---

Argentine government), emphasis added.

260   Down (note 14), p. 157. Subsequently, Pinedo became subject to disciplinary measures because of his conduct during the departure from the Islands. The documents on these disciplinary proceedings are reprinted in Muñoz Azpiri (note 52), Vol. 1, p. 429 ff.; Pinedo's statements are found on p. 487 ff.

261   Ibid., p. 157.

262   See Down (note 14), p. 162; Weber (note 29), p. 32; J. Lindsey, Conquest: A Legal and Historical Analysis of the Route of United Kingdom Title in the Falkland Islands, Texas International Law Journal, Vol. 18 (1983), p. 11, 27.

263   Down (note 14), p. 164.

of the Islands to discuss whether the loss of power on the part of Argentina may be characterised as voluntary or whether it has to be concluded that Argentina lost her factual command on the Islands as a result of the use of force or the threat of force. Argentina has stated that the British actions must be considered as an exercise of force[264], while Britain has referred to the fact that not a single shot was fired during the takeover of the Islands and that therefore there is no basis to assume that force was used[265]. From the point of view of international law, this dispute may be taken to indicate that, according to the British position, the rules governing the acquisition of a territory without a sovereign have to be applied, whereas, according to the Argentine position, the rules governing the acquisition of territory by the use of force, that is by conquest, have to be applied.

As a starting point in the evaluation of the different positions, the instructions of Onslow will have to be considered; according to these he was to force troops stationed on the Islands to leave ("and if, after this command any further hesitation or resistance be attempted, you are to compel them to depart...")[266]. According to Onslow's own report, and the description given by Pinedo, Onslow certainly did not leave the impression that Pinedo had any choice regarding the question of staying on the Islands. Onslow's ultimatum to leave the Islands, his reference to his superior force, and the lowering of the Argentine flag made it clear that Onslow would have been prepared, in accordance with his instructions, to use force to compel the Argentines to leave the Islands. In these circumstances, Pinedo reached his decision to leave the Islands; Onslow's report leaves no doubt that the interpretation of all the circumstances on the

---

264   See the Argentine Memorandum of 1964 (note 49), p. 363.
265   See the Memorandum of the Foreign Office of 1983 (note 56), p. 146.
266   See supra p. 100, and annex 23, p. 265.

part of Pinedo was correct.

If it be asked whether the sequence of events described can be taken to indicate a voluntary abandonment of the Islands or an enforced departure, it must be replied that the Argentine departure took place under the threat of the use of force. The fact that no shot was fired does not change this assessment. The credible threat of the use of force is treated in international law, in its legal effects, in the same manner as the use of force itself. If the weaker party avoids the use of force after a corresponding threat has been made, and decides not to offer any resistance, no disadvantage will arise to that party simply because the actions taken did not lead to an armed confrontation.

As to the further evaluation of the British actions, the relevant considerations indicate that Britain did not acquire the Islands in 1833 as *terra nullius*. The representatives of Argentina had to leave the Islands as a consequence of the application of force, within the meaning of the rules governing the acquisition of territory, and this use of force by Britain was the only way for the British to assume power on the Islands. Therefore, the rules governing conquest of foreign territory have to be applied to the actions taken in 1832 to 1833[267]. The special component in the situation which thus arose resulted from the fact that the decision-makers in London had assumed *bona fide* that at the relevant moment in time the Islands did not belong to any state. This situation had occurred due to the incorrect report made by Fox to the foreign office in the summer of 1832, based on Fox's personal assessment which had not been authorised by Argentina, and due to the lack of prompt communication between Buenos Aires and London at that point. The legal consequences of the British actions under these peculiar circumstances will now be discussed in detail.

---

267   See Hillekamps (note 30), p. 123; a similar view is
      expressed by Weber (note 29), p. 88.

A legal assessment of the British measures can be undertaken in relation to various aspects of the situation. It may be asked from a procedural point of view whether Britain was under an obligation to have recourse to consultations and to negotiations with Argentina before the threat of the use of force was made. Another point concerns the issue whether the actual use of force under the given circumstances was in violation of rules of international law. In the context of the present study, however, the central issue relates to the effect of the British measures upon the sovereign rights of Argentina to the Islands. Given the specific focus of this study, it may be asked whether a discussion of this latter issue alone would not suffice. However, the presentation of the issues will be more transparent if the procedural aspects and the question of the legality of the use of force are discussed separately at first, and then the central issue of sovereignty can be examined against the background of the conclusions reached in the preliminary discussion.

It may be useful to delineate the basic characteristics of the problem thus raised, initially without having regard to the specific details. In the legal literature, at least some authors seem to have assumed that all questions arising in the context of the use of force were excluded from the application of international law due to the lack of a general prohibition of the use of force. This point of view has considerable weight as the principles of application of the rules of intertemporal law are certainly also relevant to the British actions in 1832 to 1833 on the Falkland Islands (Malvinas). Frequently, the fundamental progress which international law has made in relation to the use of force in the present century seems to serve as the background for this point of view. The Kellogg-Briand Pact of 1928 and the prohibition of the use of force in Art. 2(4) of the United Nations Charter must indeed be considered as milestones in the preservation of peace in the conduct of international

relations[268]. However, the recognition of this fact should
not be allowed to obscure the further discussion whether and
to what extent the development of international law in the
19th century reflected the existence of certain rules
concerning the use of force which prepared the ground for
modern development, or even to a certain extent operated in a
similar manner to the modern law itself. The discussion of
the details of these questions will show, in any case, that
the issue of the development of international law relating to
the use of force was first raised earlier than 1928[269]. It is
not relevant in this context to decide the general issue
whether the development of international law in the 19th
century should be considered from the perspective of the
traditional legal concept of the *bellum justum* or from the
point of view of the ushering in of the 20th century. It will
have to be recognised, however, that the tendency in state
practice and legal doctrine in the 19th century to disregard
issues concerning the preservation of peace must be
considered, from a historical point of view, as a unique
development. Neither in earlier periods nor thereafter did
the law confer on states such a broad range of discretion.
These general remarks do not of course provide any detailed
answers. Initially, nevertheless, the general problem of the
relationship between the use of force and international law
in the 19th century deserves attention.

A further point needs to be discussed in this context. It
might be imagined that the number of wars during the 19th
century leaves no doubt that the prohibition of the use of
force did not exist in the state practice of that time and
thus could not place any restrictions upon the use of force
by an individual state. Such an assessment, however, deserves
careful scrutiny. If the number of wars between 1945 and the
present is compared with those between 1850 and 1900, the

---

268   See S. H. Wehberg, L'interdiction du recours à la
       force, RdC Vol. 78 (1951 I), p. 1; A. Randelzhofer, Use
       of Force, in: EPIL, Instalment 4 (1982), p. 265.

269   Cf. supra p. 125 ff.

result is not particularly favourable for the period after the Second World War. The matter deserves attention in this context because it is directly relevant to the question of the normative nature of international law and its relative independence *vis à vis* factual developments in the context of the laws of war. In spite of the significant number of wars and situations of armed hostility after 1945, neither any pronouncements by states nor a review of legal literature will produce convincing arguments to the effect that the prohibition of the use of force as laid down in Art. 2(4) of the United Nations Charter has been set aside by state practice after 1945.

This assessment in no way overlooks the fact that the practical effectiveness of international law tends to be limited with regard to the observance of rules relating to the use of force. The point is that the normative effect of international law cannot be simply denied even in a phase of state practice which is partially inconsistent with the law. Of course, a discrepancy between legal norms on the one hand and empirical realities on the other hand will lead to tensions in the system of international law. The principle of effectiveness indicates that the rules of international law are based upon the assumption that they themselves must be corrected in certain factual situations in order not to operate in an illusory manner without regard to reality. Of course, it is obvious that international law does not automatically recognise as lawful all situations existing in reality. The dilemma of legal order is found in the establishment of the appropriate balance between a static normative order and the real forces operating in practice in the individual case, taking into consideration all relevant circumstances applicable to the specific legal issue. This is true both for legal developments in the 19th century and for the development of the law after 1945.

a) Procedural obligations: exhaustion of peaceful
means of dispute settlement

In his study entitled "Force in Peace", Albert Hindmarsh
showed that a state was under an obligation, according to the
law valid in the 19th century, to exhaust peaceful means of
settling a dispute before resorting to the use of force. "It
is generally conceded that states should exhaust regular
diplomatic and judicial means before resort to
coercion..."[270]. Reference to one relevant incident in
British state practice may suffice. The British government
used force against Greece in 1850 without previous
consultations after a British national had been treated
illegally by the Greek authorities. Subsequently, the house
of lords passed a resolution which deplored the fact that
Britain had resorted to the use of force without first
attempting to settle the dispute in a peaceful manner; the
wording suggested that the house of lords considered the
British measures to be in violation of international law[271].

The initial question that may be asked in this context is
whether or not the relevant procedural rules had been
observed by Britain in the case of the Falkland Islands
(Malvinas) when Britain made her protests in 1829 and 1832.
It might be considered that these acts amounted to gestures
which suffciently spelt out the British point of view. It
will have to be doubted, however, whether a written protest
can be considered to amount to an attempt to settle a dispute
in a peaceful manner before resort to the use of force, in
the absence of any offer of consultation or negotiation. The
purpose of a process of peaceful settlement consists in the
clarification of the different standpoints in a more or less
formalised procedure during which opinions are exchanged and
differences can be narrowed down or eliminated. A written

---

270   A. Hindmarsh, Force in Peace (1933), p. 59.

271   See Hansard, Debates (3rd series), CXI, p. 1321, 1400
      (1850); see R. Phillimore, International Law, Vol. 3
      (1885), p. 41.

protest will in general not have these effects. It is also clear that no duty to settle a dispute could have existed if the Islands were not subject to the jurisdiction of any state.

It is not an easy task to assess the consequences in ralation to the duty to exhaust peaceful means of settlement which arose from the fact that London had not properly evaluated the objective legal situation at the time when the decision to take power on the Islands was made. No case is known in which a legal problem occuring in such circumstances was discussed in the 19th century. Thus, one may at best speculate in retrospect. Perhaps, the most appropriate solution might have been to assume a duty to negotiate starting at the point at which Britain was informed from the report of captain Onslow that, contrary to the report of Fox, Argentina had not abandoned her rights to the Islands. As will be shown, Britain several times refused to commence negotiations following diplomatic protests made by Argentina[272].

Under these circumstances, it may be appropriate to examine whether a violation of the procedural rule to exhaust peaceful means of settlement could have had any effect on the question of the acquisition of territory. Further consideration of this matter will be deferred, however, until other aspects posed by the British use of force have been discussed.

b) The legality of the use of force by Britain

There is no reason to doubt that the principles of intertemporal law have to be applied to the question of the legality of the use of force by Britain in the years 1832 to

272   Cf. infra p. 142 ff.

1833. Thus, it is indispensable to turn to the law as it
stood during the time in question. It has often been repeated
that the international law doctrine of that period had not
developed precise terms and categories for the discussion,
evaluation and classification of war; von Holtzendorff, for
instance, emphasised this point in his study published in
1872[273]. No independent assessment of the relevant historical
problems will be attempted here; instead, existing studies
will be relied upon.

At first glance it may be imagined that the lack of
specificity of the rules of international law regarding the
phenomenon of war and the use of force essentially reflected
the helplessness of the law when confronted by power, echoed
by a corresponding acceptance of all forms of the use of
force on the part of the legal order. However, a closer
scrutiny indicates that more subtle issues of international
law peculiar to the international legal system of the 19th
century found expression in this context. At the beginning of
the 19th century, considerations of natural justice had lost
much of their earlier influence upon the rules of
international law[274]; the sweeping away of the concept of the
just war, which had prevailed for centuries, found expression
in the context of the laws of war. The former conceptions of
law gave way to a strong emphasis on the principle of
sovereignty. Thus, according to this new perspective, the use
of force could be understood as the highest form of
expression of state sovereignty in its manifestation in
international relations; because of its tensions and
contradictions with the positivistic emphasis on the will of
the state, the concept of natural law was no longer suitable,

---

273   F. von Holtzendorff, Eroberungen und Eroberungsrecht
       (1872), p. 19.

274   See H. Wehberg, Krieg und Eroberung im Wandel des
       Völkerrechts (1953), p. 88; generally U. Scheuner,
       Naturrechtliche Strömungen im heutigen Völkerrecht,
       ZaöRV Vol. 13 (1950/51), p. 556, also reprinted in: U.
       Scheuner, Schriften zum Völkerrecht, ed. by C.
       Tomuschat (1984), p. 99.

from this point of view, for determining the substance and the boundaries of the laws of war.

It must not be overlooked, however, that the emphasis on sovereignty as the new foundation of international law in the 19th century met with inherent limitations in the legal evaluation of war. A "right to war" could only be understood as the highest expression of freedom on the part of the state from the isolated perspective of one single state. The fact that the exercise of this right affects or may even destroy the sovereign will of the enemy illustrates that emphasis on a *jus ad bellum* tends to deny the very concept of sovereignty from the point of view of the international community[275]. Neither state practice nor legal doctrine found a convincing answer to the solution of this dilemma in the 19th century.

One approach to the problem was often seen in the characterisation of war as a phenomenon not capable of being made subject to the rules of law[276]. A survey of specific issues of the laws of war from the point of view of the 19th century illustrates, however, that this approach had significant limitations. Thus it must be noted that specific concepts which recognise and limit the right to war, such as the right to self-preservation, the right to self-defence, the legal position of neutral states and the rules relating to humanitarian intervention were especially emphasised in the 19th century or were only developed during that period[277]. What need would have been served in the legal order by the concept of self-defence if every form of the use

---

275   Generally in regard to the development of international law during this period S. Verosta, History of the Law of Nations, 1648 to 1815, in: EPIL, Instalment 7 (1984), p. 160.

276   Specifically with regard to the development of the laws of war after 1750, see Moore, Digest (note 44), Vol. 1, p. 291.

277   See also the historical discussions in K. Partsch, Self-Defence, in: EPIL, Instalment 4 (1982), p. 212; U. Beyerlin, Humanitarian Intervention, in: EPIL, Instalment 3 (1982), p. 211.

of force were justified under all circumstances? Why did Britain refer in the famous *Caroline* case[278] to a narrow conception of this right, and why was this approach followed by the United States in principle? For which reasons did states develop and observe special rules on the admissibility of humanitarian intervention in the 19th century instead of basing their acts upon a general unlimited right to the use of force? There is no need here to discuss these questions in detail. They are only posed in order to illustrate the fact that the international legal order of the 19th century cannot be fully appreciated in all its facets when every limitation of the right to use force is denied without reservation. With regard to the Falkland Islands (Malvinas), a further question may be raised in this context. Why has the United Kingdom so far never argued that the Islands were acquired in 1832 to 1833 on the basis of the use of force against Argentina?

Returning to the special situation of the assumption of power on the Falkland Islands (Malvinas) in 1832 to 1833, a closer examination of the subject shows that a general discussion of the foundations of the laws of war as defined at the time is not necessary. The reason therefor relates to the specific definition of the concept of war in the 19th century. In their extensive studies, Hindmarsh[279], Bowett[280] and Brownlie[281] have shown that the concept of war in the 19th century was characterised by the subjective perspectives of the parties concerned. A state of war existed between two parties if and when one of the states concerned declared that this was the case. The legal significance of this situation has to be assessed in conjunction with another aspect of the laws of war. The preconditions for and the consequences of

---

278   For a recent discussion of the *Caroline* case, see W. Meng, The Caroline, in: EPIL, Instalment 3 (1982), p. 81, with further references.

279   Hindmarsh (note 270), p. 90.

280   D. Bowett, Self-Defence in International Law (1958), p. 118.

281   J. Brownlie, International Law and the Use of Force by

acts of war were judged according to norms that were different to those applied to hostilities during times of peace; in various respects, the rights of states were limited to a considerably greater degree than in war by the rules of international law applicable during times of peace.

The paradoxical element that characterises this legal situation, if judged under standards of law applicable today, cannot be overlooked. Where there are no significant limitations upon the state to set aside the rules of law applicable in times of peace by declaring war, then a differentiation between war and peace as well as the respective norms involved assumes an artifical character[282]. It is only possible to speculate as to why this distinction was, nevertheless, recognised in the 19th century and was observed in practice. Certainly it may be of importance to realise that the lack of a differentiation between war and peace would immediately have endangered the existence of a number of rules of international law which had arisen in the 17th and 18th centuries. Had the differentiation between war and peace not been upheld, each state would have been at liberty, in the case of a violation of these norms, to avoid any consequences simply by referring to the freedoms conferred by the rules governing in time of war. In spite of the emphasis placed upon the concept of sovereignty, such a drastic limitation of the development of international law was apparently not in the interests of the international community. A state which declared the existence of war, and thus the applicability of the rules of war, had to take into account the fact that freedoms thus established were accompanied by certain disadvantages, in particular the suspension of existing treaties and the rights which the laws of war conferred upon the enemy. The internal contradictions inherent in the treatment of the laws of war are not removed by these considerations, but they help to explain their

---

States (1963), p. 26.

282   See Bowett (note 280), p. 118; Brownlie (note 281), p. 26; Hindmarsh (note 270), p. 96.

historical development. From a contemporary point of view, however, the power of persuasion of such an explanation is ultimately immaterial. The principles of intertemporal law require no more and no less than the determination and application of the law valid at the time.

Neither Britain nor Argentina have ever declared that they were in a state of war in 1832 to 1833. Argentina has more often referred to the principles applicable during times of peace[283]. Britain would not admit the existence of a state of war as she considered that the Islands were not in the jurisdiction of any sovereign power and the representatives of Argentina were consequently not recognised; in this context, the incorrect assessment made by Fox, the British minister, also had its legal effects.

Under these circumstances everything suggests that it will have to be accepted that the British measures taken were subject to the principles of the international law governing times of peace as they applied in the 19th century. The relevant legal discussions in the literature are to be found under the concept of "hostilities short of war"[284]. Brownlie, in particular, has reviewed the pertinent state practice of the 19th century and he has concluded that the use of force during times of peace either required a specific justification or, in any case, had to be limited in its objectives: "The absence of any admission that a state of war existed indicated that the action might be intended as a reprisal or justified intervention. And even if there were no obvious justification for reprisal or intervention, its absence nearly always signified the use of force for a limited purpose, either to settle a grievance or to punish wrongdoers or to provide warning or preventive action. In

---

283   Brownlie (note 231),p. 26; Bowett (note 230), p. 118.
284   See Bowett (note 230), p. 117; Brownlie (note 231), p. 28; Hindmarsh (note 220), p. 38.

such a case there is no intention to conquer or annex."[285]

The presentation and summary of state practice by C. Bluntschli published in 1872[286] largely coincides with this result. Thus, Bluntschli stated on the one hand: "Not only the protection of recognised and existing rights, but also the unjustified hinderance of the further necessery development of laws and the progressive development of the legal order can give rise to war"[287]. On the same page, Bluntschli continued, however: "The mere interest of a state in itself does not justify war." The following reason was quoted: "The very fact that war is accompanied necessarily by the use of force explains why only legal considerations, but not mere considerations of expedience (interests) are suitable to justify war."[288]

More recently, Verosta has summarised this state of the law in a concise manner: "The following rules which were to remain valid throughout the period 1648 to 1815 were contained in the terms of the Peace of Westphalia to govern the cardinal problems of international relations and international law: Treaties were to be observed (*pacta sunt servanda*); a conflict concerning the new peace order was to be settled by peaceful means, i.e. negotiations, conciliation and mediation, or arbitration; the injured state could take up arms against the transgressor in order to restore its rights and was to be accorded the military support of the other Treaty partners in such a justified war to obtain redress; a war initiated without just cause was illegal and the Treaty states were to confront the disturber of the peace jointly. These principles conformed with the then prevailing doctrine of the *bellum justum*, whereby "justum", does not mean "just" in the moral sense but "legal", according to the

---

285   Brownlie (note 281), p. 40.
286   C. Bluntschli, Das moderne Völkerrecht der
       civilisierten Staaten (1872).
287   Ibid., p. 290.

law of nations and treaties in force. The policy of even
absolute and self-confident monarchs always included alleged
legal claims to certain areas which they wished to acquire,
but in the European system of states sovereigns had no
automatic right to wage war. If the "legal" claim was seen as
a mere pretext, interested states intervened as mediators,
often quite forcefully".[289]

From a terminological point of view, the effort to
systematise state practice relating to the use of force
within a generally recognised scheme was never entirely
successful. In English terminology, "intervention" and
"necessity" were the broadest categories employed, comprising
all other terms for the use of force during peacetime. State
practice appears to have provided two different grounds for
justification of these two categories. On the one hand, the
enforcement of rights not recognised or affected has been
discussed. On the other hand, intervention and necessity have
been justified on the basis of the preservation of the
security of the state, including, occasionally, significant
changes of the *status quo* without any direct proof of the
impact upon the state[290].

Against the background of these concepts, it is clear
that the British measures cannot be considered from an
objective point of view as a case of enforcement of existing
rights, as Britain did not possess any such rights to the
Islands; the separate question of enforcement of a right that
was wrongly considered to exist will have to be discussed
later[291]. If it be asked, from an objective point of view,
whether the situation on the Islands in 1832 to 1833 amounted
to a threat to British security or involved a negative impact
upon British security relative to the *status quo*, it must be

---

288   Ibid.
289   Verosta (note 275), p. 160, 161.
290   See Brownlie (note 281), p. 47; Hindmarsh (note 270).
291   See infra p. 123 ff.

recalled that no change in the international legal status of the Islands had occurred during the relevant period. Argentina had acquired the Islands years before. The developments on the Islands in the summer of 1832 were of a purely internal character and in no way affected in a negative manner the geopolitical interests of Britain.

An assessment of the objective situation on the Islands at the end of 1832 therefore indicates that at the time Britain was not in a position to refer to any factor which could have justified the use of force in a time of peace.

This result has sense and meaning in the legal system applicable at the time, under which certain acts of a hostile nature were considered to be lawful even during peacetimes but when certain limitations also existed on the lawful use of force. In disputes of a particular legal or political difficulty, some types of use of force were allowed, although pure aggression was not admitted from a legal point of view during peacetime. The definition of disputes in which the use of force was allowed was broad, and also vaguely circumscribed, but it was not entirely meaningless. In the case at hand, the legality of the British measures ultimately cannot be upheld because Argentina had not given the least cause for the use of force. If the legal or the factual situation had been of a different nature, Britain would certainly have pointed to this fact in 1833 or later. The authorities in London kept referring to the argument that the Islands were not subject to any jurisdiction, even after they had received the report of captain Onslow which in effect indicated the continued existence of Argentine rights. A stronger argument with legal relevance was not available from the British viewpoint.

In view of the factual and legal situation it may be asked whether Britain should not have based her further actions on the new information received in the report by captain Onslow. In fact, it appears that Onslow's report indeed gave occasion for a renewed consideration of the legal situation. A memorandum prepared in London in 1835 by the legal adviser of the Crown addressed the question whether the Islands fell under the jurisdiction of the British Crown in 1833. Apparently, the memorandum assumed that the Islands did not belong to Britain prior to 1833. The relevant passage of the memorandum reads: "...it is submitted that after the possession taken by Commodore Onslow the Settlement in Berkeley Sound became a part of and within the Dominions of His Majesty and thus these individuals (altho' Foreigners and originally settled there under a Foreign Dominion) being resident within the King's Dominion and therefore entitled to the King's protection and owing allegiance to him became subjects of His Majesty within the meaning of the Statute."[292]

The discussion so far has been based upon the objective legal situation of the Islands. No attention has been paid to the fact that Fox had given wrong information in his report, whether on purpose or not. In the light of the report written by Fox the British authorities would have or must have been aware that a new situation had developed on the Islands in which other maritime powers, be it the United States or France, might be able to acquire the Islands as *terra nullius* and thus establish themselves for the first time after the fall of the Spanish colonial empire in an important strategic part of the southern Atlantic as competing maritime powers. It is not without interest to assess this situation within the framework of the categories of possible justification of military force during peacetime. If the situation which was presumed by the British authorities to exist had in fact existed, it would not have been unreasonable to take the position that a significant change of the *status quo* to the

---

292   See R. Ware, The Case of Antonio Rivero and Sovereignty over the Falkland Islands, The Historical Journal, Vol. 27 (1984), p. 961; concerning the role of the law officers, see I. Edwards, The Law Officers of the Crown (1964).

detriment of Britain would have permitted the use of force. From this perspective, the British conduct with regard to the Falkland Islands (Malvinas) both in 1829 and in 1832 to 1833 illustrates and reconfirms the system of limited justifications for the use of force during peacetime then applicable. When informed of the acquisition of the Islands by Argentina in 1829, Britain did not go beyond the filing of a protest, and no coercion was used; the decision to apply military force was only taken in London in 1832 when Britain was concerned that her global maritime power was threatened in the Atlantic.

What is the legal relevance of the fact that the ground for a justification of the use of military force, as assumed by Britain, did not in fact exist? Presumably, a meaningful answer can only be given on the basis of the generally recognised principle that a wrong assessment of the facts must be held against the party which controlled the sphere where the mistake occurred[293]. In the case at hand, Britain was responsible for the actions of Fox and the report which led to the decision to use force. In addition, it must be borne in mind that Britain was subsequently in a position to revise her decisions on the basis of the reports of the facts delivered by Onslow; then, however, Britain was no longer prepared to withdraw from the Islands as a consequence. Under these circumstances it will have to be concluded that at the time of taking the decision to use force Britain acted unlawfully from an objective point of view but that the actions were lawful in the light of the information existing in London, and that the reasons for the wrong assessment of the factual and legal situation must be attributed to a British official and therefore cannot be regarded as a ground for a justification of acts in relation to Argentina.

---

293   See Blum (note 83), p. 147.

c)   The legality of the annexation, 1832 to 1833

A discussion of the legal effects of the factual
assumption of power on the Islands by Britain must not only
address the question of the use of force with regard to a
delimitation between the laws of war and the laws of peace,
but also must examine this question in the light of the
general rules applicable to annexations and the relevant
preconditions according to the law that was current at the
time.

The legal regime of annexation was one of the fundamental
issues of international law in the 19th century. The subject
was discussed several times in monographs; reference may be
made, for instance, to the studies of von Holtzendorff
(1872)[294], and Heimburger (1888)[295], as well as Basdevant
(1901)[296], Schätzel (1920)[297], MacMahon (1940)[298] and
Brownlie (1963)[299]. No general consensus on all details of
the relevant legal order can be said to have emerged from
these studies.

For the purposes of this discussion it should be pointed
out that a number of territorial changes took place in the
19th century as a consequence of war or of military actions.
The aspect of the acquisition of colonial territories
inhabited by an indigenous population will not be pursued
here because it did not arise with regard to the Falkland
Islands (Malvinas). In accordance with legal doctrine, state
practice in the 19th century shows that the use of force for
the purpose of the acquisition of foreign territory was

---

294   Von Holtzendorff (note 223).

295   K. Heimburger, Der Erwerb der Gebietshoheit (1988).

296   J. Basdevant, La Revolution Française et le Droit de la
      Guerre continentale (1901).

297   W. Schätzel, Die Annexion im Völkerrecht (1920).

298   M. McMahon, Conquest and Modern International Law
      (1940).

299   Brownlie (note 281).

basically not prohibited by the international law of the time. In principle, international law admitted not only war as such, but also war as a means for the acquisition of territory.

At this point, some consideration of the foundations of the legal order will be useful, with particular attention to the ambivalence of the situation that arose from the toleration of war by the legal order, on the one hand, and the emphasis placed on the sovereign freedom of all states, including those affected by a war, on the other hand. In this context, it is essential to recognise that the law applicable at the time distinguished between the factual conduct of war on a given territory and sovereignty over that territory. Thus, Karl Pölitz states in his five-volume study published in 1828: "Belligerent occupation *(occupatio bellica)* refers to the possession of real property of the enemy and sovereignty over the land controlled. But the fact of conquest is essentially different from the right to conquest; because the latter would include, instead of the possession and use, the acquisition of the objects conquered as a matter of property right. According to the natural order of international law, however, the latter right will only be conferred upon that party which conducts a just war against an unjust enemy who rejects the peace offered and denies the compensation required."[300]

This legal construction found expression in particular in the legal evaluation of a belligerent occupation. The occupying state assumed sovereign rights, but the sovereignty of the state occupied was considered not as terminated, but only as suspended. The classic study written by Philippson places this development in the following context: "In the earlier days - say, to the middle of the eighteenth century - an invader claimed that as soon as territory or property of

---

300   K. Pölitz, Die Staatswissenschaften im Lichte unserer Zeit, 5. Teil (2. Aufl. 1828), S. 226.

the enemy fell into his hands it became his absolutely, and he was entitled to dispose of it as he pleased. But gradually mitigations were introduced; and such limitations were imposed on the severe practice and wide pretension of belligerents as to cause the earlier theory to be abandoned. The growing conception of nationality, territorial sovereignty, and State independence, together with the advocacy of jurists and publicists, and the pronouncements of judical tribunals all contributed to bring about this amelioration."[301]

The quotation illustrates that the independent will of the state occupied retained legal relevance in spite of the legal toleration of war. The international legal order developed along these lines with a view to preserving state sovereignty, as can be seen from a review of state practice in the 19th century.

For present purposes, the specific rules on occupation are less important than the principles underlying the rules applicable after termination of war. To what extent was the will of the state that lost the war of legal significance? Under the law applicable, the cases of total annexation of the enemy and of partial annexation of foreign territory had to be distinguished. In the case of a total annexation, the law applicable at the time solved the problem in favour of the victorious power on the basis that the will of the occupied state had been extinguished by the total annexation and therefore could no longer affect the further development of territorial status. In the case of a partial annexation, the problem had to be seen in a different context. As the will of the losing state continued to exist, the assumption of the extinction of its existence was not available. Therefore, the will of the losing state necessarily had to be taken into account, and legal construction of the transfer of

---

301   C. Philippson, Termination of War and Treaties of Peace (1916), p. 29.

territory had to recognise this continued will. As a
consequence of these systematic considerations, a transfer of
a part of a territory required a corresponding expression of
the will of the losing state. Practically, this meant that a
partial annexation required the consent of the losing state
expressed in a peace treaty.

The internal structure of this systematic treatment of
annexation is not devoid of logic. It may be objected that
the system suffers from a fundamental contradiction inasmuch
as it allows the dissolution of a state without its consent
while in the less drastic case of partial annexation this
consent is required. Along these lines it may be argued that
no system can be considered to be meaningful which does not
allow a state with superior military power to annex part of
foreign territory without consent of the enemy after an
initial military success, but nevertheless permits a war to
be carried on to the point of total extinction of the enemy
and subsequently permits the victor to claim the entire
territory. In terms of the concept of strict power politics,
these considerations are indeed convincing. However, if the
central concern of international legal rules relates to state
sovereignty, the system described does not appear as self-
contradictory. Ultimately, it is not a question of logic
whether normative effects can emanate from such a system.
Only the review of state practice and of legal doctrine will
clarify the question of what position was legally acceptable
in the 19th century. For this reason, the practical
development of the law and the corresponding views of the
commentators will be described in detail.

d)   Partial annexation in the legal doctrine of the 19th
      century

The position taken by Grotius (1538-1645) was dominated
by concepts of Roman law. No distinction between full

annexation and partial annexation can be found in his discussion; transfer of ownership and of sovereignty occurred, according to his view, once the territory was occupied and a former owner was no longer in a position to have access to the land owing to permanent fortresses[302].

A certain development in this perspective became apparent in the writings of Samuel Pufendorf (1632-1694); it appears that he assumed that the exercise of force in itself cannot be considered as providing a title to land but that a treaty between the states concerned was required[303].

The views of Vattel (1714-1767) are based on the right of conquest, but he also tied his view to the ideas of Pufendorf and stated without reservation that ownership of land, not yet clearly distinguished from sovereignty, can only be acquired on the basis of a treaty or as a consequence of the total subjugation and extinction of the enemy: "Real property – lands, towns, provinces – become the property of the enemy who takes possession of them; but it is only by the treaty of peace, or by the entire subjection and extinction of the State to which those towns and provinces belong, that the acquisition is completed and the ownership rendered permanent and absolute.

A third party cannot, therefore, obtain secure possession of a conquered town or province until the sovereign from whom it has been taken has either renounced it by the treaty of peace or lost his sovereignty over it by final and absolute submission to the conqueror."[304]

---

302   H. Grotius, De Jure Belli ac Pacis, Vol. 3 (1625).

303   S. Pufendorf, De Jure Naturae et Gentium, Libro Octo, Vol. II, 1688, here cited in the English translation by C. and W. Oldfather (1934), p. 1085.

304   E. de Vattel, The Law of Nations or the Principles of Natural Law, here cited in the English translation by Charles Fenwick (1916), p. 308; on this point, see also the decision of the United States Supreme Court in U.S. et al. v. Huckabee, 16 Wallace 434 (1872).

In his work "Outline of a System of European International Law" ("Grundriß eines Systems des europäischen Völkerrechts") Saalfeld stated in 1809 that a conqueror acquires ownership rights as sovereign on a temporary basis, and that the final acquisition is subject to the consent of the former sovereign[305].

A similar view is found in the treatise by Schmalz, "The European International Law in 18 Books" ("Das europäische Völkerrecht in 18 Büchern"), published in 1817: "A conquest is recognised by the law only in peace when the former sovereign cedes the province to the conqueror. No legal significance is attached to former dispositions of the victor concerning the province or its belongings and domaines. The right is created by the cession alone; conquest confers mere possession. And even if other powers recognise this possession, it remains true that other powers cannot grant any right which they do not themselves possess."[306]

In his treatise entitled "Droit des Gens Modernes de l'Europe", published in 1819, Jean-Louis Klüber considered that the right of booty is limited by the purpose of a war and he also assumed that a definitive transfer of the property of a sovereign depends upon the expression of agreement in a peace treaty:

"Les biens immeubles de l'ennemi, ainsi que la souveraineté des provinces qui lui sont soumises, peuvent également être occupés par ce qu'on appelle la conquête a) (occupatio bellica). Dans les provinces ainsi conquises, le conquérant prend la place de l'ancien gouvernement, dans l'exercice des droits de souveraineté, et dans la jouissance des propriétés de son ennemi b). Cependant ce n'est point le fait de la conquête qui donne le droit de s'attribuer la

---

305   F. Saalfeld, Grundriß eines Systems des europäischen Völkerrechts (1809), p. 90, 92.

306   T. Schmalz, Das europäische Völkerrecht in 18 Büchern (1817), p. 267.

propriété des choses occupées, ou la souveraineté du pays c).
Ce droit n'appartient, selon le droit des gens naturel, qu'au
belligérant en juste cause ..., et seulement en tant que le
but de la guerre l'exige. La conquête n'est pour lui qu'un
moyen de réaliser son droit, ou de se procurer ce qu'un juge
commun, s'il y en avait un, aurait adjugé à la juste cause.
Il peut se prévaloir de son droit, sans qu'une protestation
quelconque, soit du souverain ennemi ou de quelqu'un de sa
famille, soit de ses protecteurs, amis, alliés ou sujets,
puisse avoir aucun effet contraire .... Selon les principes
aujourd'hui suivis en Europe, la seule perte de la possession
par le sort des armes, ne peut éteindre la propriété. Il s'en
suit que le conquérant, quoiqu' exerçant les droits de
souveraineté et jouissant des propriétés de son ennemi, ne
peut pas se les approprier, ni en disposer en faveur d'un
tiers, à moins qu'un traité de paix ne lui en ait conféré le
droit."[307]

Nine years later, Pölitz took the same position in his
textbook: "Even though the conqueror acquires the possession
and the enjoyment and the territorial rights in the land
conquered, these principles establish that he may not treat
these acquisitions as his property or dispose of them in
favour of a third party as long as no cession exists in a
peace treaty."[308]

The same function of the peace treaty was referred to
generally by G. F. de Martens in his study entitled "Précis
du Droit des Gens Modernes de l'Europe 1831": "A proprement
parler, tout ce qui a donné lieu à la guerre devrait être
décidé par la paix, ainsi que ce qui, discuté dans le cours
de la guerre (b), pourrait laisser un germe de nouvelles
mésintelligences, que la paix doit couper, si on ne veut pas

---

307   J.-L. Klüber, Droits des Gens Moderne de l'Europe
       (1819), Vol. 1, p. 401.
308   Pölitz (note 300), p. 227.

qu'elle soit plâtrée."[309]

Rayneval emphatically endorsed this point of view in 1832: "La propriété réelle et incommutable ne peut être établie que par un traité de paix. Alors seulement tous les droits comme toutes les charges de l'ancien possesseur sont transmis au nouveau; ainsi toutes les créances non personnelles passent à celui-ci, et il est chargé de toutes les dettes. Il doit en général maintenir l'ancien ordre de choses, à moins que la conduite des habitans, ou des raisons d'état majeures ne le déterminent à faire des changements, dans la forme de l'administration."[310]

In his often-cited study "Contemporary European International Law" ("Das Europäische Völkerrecht der Gegenwart"), published in 1848, Heffter highlighted the principle that in the case of a lack of agreement by treaty, only the total subjugation of the enemy in war could lead to a definitive territorial change: "So long as the territorial power is still in a position to continue the war and to change the fortunes of war, the invading enemy does not immediately replace the existing government power by taking possession of its territory or part of it. The victor can only assume governmental powers and enter into a governmental relationship, albeit one of usurpation, with the conquered people once a complete defeat of the enemy *(debellatio)* has occurred which renders impossible any further resistance ... Until this point, only a factual seizure of the rights and of the wealth of the governmental power, meanwhile suspended, can take place."[311]

The next major international law treatise published in

---

309   G.F. de Martens, Précis du Droit des Gens Moderne (1831), Vol. 2, p. 298.

310   G. Rayneval, Institutions du Droit de la Nature et des Gens, Vol. 2 (1832), p. 91.

311   A. Heffter, Das Europäische Völkerrecht der Gegenwart (1848), p. 229.

the German-speaking world appeared twenty four years later.
In the relevant passage of his important work, Bluntschli
explained, fully consistent with the earlier commentators:
"Even though the conquest of a part of a foreign territory
will initially occur in war through the use of force, it
nevertheless forms the legal basis for the governmental power
over the area conquered and will be considered as a lawful
acquisition to the extent that, on the basis of a peace
treaty or without one, the end of resistance and the
recognition on the part of the politically legitimised
population the continuation of the new governmental bond
appears to be a necessity."[312]

Among French authors, reference may be made here to the
presentation of the legal situation in the "Traité de Droit
International Public" published in 1885 by Pradier-Fodéré:
"La théorie enseigne, en effet, que tant que l'une des
Puissances en guerre n'est pas définitivement vaincue et
qu'elle peut prendre les armes, l'état des choses existant à
son égard ne doit être regardé que comme transitoire ou
usurpé; elle enseigne même que la prise de possession ne sera
qu'un fait reposant sur la force et non sur le droit, tant
que les populations soumises ne se seront pas assez
assimilées à la nation victorieuse pour former avec elle une
seule nation. Ce que les publicistes exigent, en un mot, pour
que l'occupation militaire, la prise de possession, se
transforment en une acquisition de la propriété, c'est qu'un
traité, ou, à défaut, la reconnaissance par la population des
changements survenus, ait démontré la nécessité du nouvel
ordre des choses."[313]

---

312   Bluntschli (note 286), p. 175.
313   A. Pradier-Fodéré, Traité de Droit International
      Public, Vol. 2 (1885), p. 393.

e)   Partial annexation in 19th century state practice

A review of the legal forms of territorial acquisition of
parts of the territory of states defeated in war shows that
in nearly all cases the change in status was based upon a
treaty; as to the details of the practice, reference can be
made, in particular, to the extensive study by Philippson of
1916[314]. Here, only three cases will be briefly discussed to
highlight the problem of partial annexation in the period
before the Covenant of the League of Nations introduced
significant limitations on the right to go to war.

The legal concepts recognised in the 19th century found
expression in the legal positions adopted by Chile and
Bolivia after Chile had occupied part of the west of the
Bolivian coast in 1879 in the wake of a war [315]. In 1866 and
1874, Chile had recognised the sovereignty of Bolivia in the
areas occupied in 1879, following earlier disputes. The
decision to occupy part of Bolivia was taken in 1879 in
response to the fact that Bolivia had not respected the
territorial rights guaranteed by her to Chile in the earlier
arrangements. The two states concluded a truce in 1884 after
the military defeat of Chile in 1880. *Inter alia*, it was
agreed that Chile would continue to exercise governmental
powers in the areas occupied until the conclusion of a final
peace treaty ("... continuará gobernanda..."). This treaty
was entered into only in 1904. Meanwhile, certain problems
had arisen between the parties because of the interpretation
of the rights which had been accorded to Chile in the truce
arrangements of 1880. For present purposes, it is most
interesting to note that in this dispute Chile agreed with
the Bolivian position that no rights of sovereignty were to
be exercised by Chile in the occupied territories. In the
peace treaty of 1904, the occupied areas were explicitly
designated, in Art. II, as areas of occupation; in the

---

314   Philippson (note 301), passim.
315   For details see G. Lang, Boliviens Streben nach freiem

treaty, Chile agreed to various important concessions in
response to the cession of the occupied territory.

A similar position was taken by Chile in relation to Peru
in the question concerning Tacna-Arica[316]. In 1880 Chile had
occupied the Peruvian provinces of Tacna and Arica. In 1883,
Chile and Peru agreed in Art. III of a peace treaty that the
provinces would remain in the possession of Chile until a
referendum had been held ("... continuará poseido por
Chile..."). In 1900, Chile clearly confirmed that she had not
acquired full sovereign rights over the territories. Five
years later, however, Chile made reference to full, albeit
not definitive, sovereignty. A solution to this territorial
dispute was agreed upon only in the treaty of Lima concluded
in 1929, according to which Tacna remained with Peru while
Chile acquired Arica. Chile's conduct presumably can only be
understood on the basis of the assumption that she never
claimed a right to annexation of the territories; this is
particularly remarkable inasmuch as the exercise of her
rights in these territories extended over a period of 49
years.

After 1908, the question of the legal rules governing
partial annexations arose in the dispute between Bosnia and
Herzogovina[317]. According to Art. 25 of the Final Act of the
Congress of Berlin of July 1878, the two Turkish provinces
"... were occupied and administered by Austria-Hungary ...".
In October 1908, the emperor of Austria-Hungary decided "to
extend the rights of my sovereignty to Bosnia and Herzegowina
...". Not only Turkey, but also other states considered these

---

Zugang zum Meer (1966).

316   See C. Jane, The Question of Tacna-Arica, Transactions
of the Grotius Society, Vol. 15 (1930), p. 93; Lang, p.
46.

317   For details see D. Koyitek, L'annexion de la Bosnie et
de l'Herzegovine et le droit international public
(1910); N. Wurmbrand, Die rechtliche Stellung Bosniens
und der Herzegowina (1915); G. Zimmer, Gewaltsame
territoriale Veränderungen und ihre völkerrechtliche
Legitimation (1971), p. 111.

measures to be in violation of international law, but no strict separation of treaty law and customary law can be detected in the arguments that were brought forward. Also, Vienna indicated in the following months that a final legal solution would depend upon the consent of Turkey. A corresponding treaty was concluded in 1909 in which Turkey recognised the existing state of affairs, while Austria-Hungary also agreed to considerable concessions in relation to Turkey. Thus, Austria-Hungary failed in the attempt to unilaterally enforce her claim.

In view of the fact that the British measures on the Falkland Islands (Malvinas) occurred in 1832 to 1833, it is of interest to observe that the necessity for recognition in a treaty of a partial annexation had already been emphasised in a decision by the United States Chief Justice Marshall in 1825. "The usage of the world is, if a nation be not entirely subdued, to consider the holding of conquered territory as a mere military occupation until its fate shall be determined at the treaty of peace. If it be ceded by the treaty, the acquisition is confirmed, and the ceded territory becomes a part of the nation to which it is annexed; either on the terms stipulated in the treaty of cession or on such as its new master shall impose."[318]

A survey of the extensive state practice of the 19th century confirms that this judicial pronouncement was not an isolated pronouncement made by a state official not directly involved in international relations; it correctly reflects the legal opinion of states as evidenced in international relations. In view of the uniformity of state practice one must consider individual opinions to the contrary as legal

---

[318] The American and Ocean Insurance Companies v. 356 Bales of Cotton, 1 Peters 510 (1828), p. 536. A similar decision by a French court, rendered in 1818, is reported by H. Taylor, A Treatise on Public International Law (1902), p. 587; the same author discusses the less consistent English jurisprudence on this point.

constructs of a right to conquest which do not sufficiently take into account the central dimension of the concept of sovereignty in international legal practice during the relevant period[319].

The broad study of legal practice by Schätzel shows that the cónquest of Massaua was, in addition to that of the Falkland Islands (Malvinas), the only case in the 19th century in which a state attempted to acquire part of a foreign territory by the use of force without a corresponding treaty[320]. Massaua, situated on the western coast of the Red Sea, was occupied by Italy in 1885, even though the territory had belonged to Turkey and a Turkish governor remained there in 1885, together with some soldiers. An interesting parallel arose in the conduct of Italy to that of Britain after 1833. Italy also asserted that the Turkish territorial claim had ceased to exist due to dereliction[321]. Given the facts of the case, it might have been expected that Italy would have referred to a right to annexation if she had considered that such an argument could have been upheld legally. However, Italy never mentioned any such right and instead argued on the basis of relinquished territory. This is a further expression of the legal opinion prevalent in the 19th century according to which no right existed to unilateral annexation of a foreign territory.

As to the general issue of the independence of the law when concerned with factual situations relating to territorial claims, it is worth noting that in none of the many arbitral proceedings on territorial issues has a state argued that the simple presence of its representatives and its will to exercise governmental power were sufficient to

---

319   See the bibliographic references in: Schätzel (note 297) and McMahon (note 298).

320   Schätzel (note 297), passim.

321   See W. Schätzel, Massaua, Wörterbuch des Völkerrechts und der Diplomatie, ed. by K. Strupp, Vol. 2 (1925), p. 17.

lead to a territorial change in spite of the existence of earlier rights on the part of a third state. Such an argument might well have been conceivable in the Eastern Greenland case[322], the Clipperton case[323] or in the the Chamizal decision[324]. The fact that no such argument was ever presented must be taken as a demonstration of the autonomy of the law when confronted by factual situations in the 19th century.

In conclusion, a survey of 19th century practice clearly supplies a positive answer to the question whether the acquisition of a part of a foreign territory required the consent of the state concerned[325]. In view of the law applicable at the time and its emphasis on the free sovereign will of each state, this conclusion is not without an internal logic and it also appears to conform to the systematic conceptions prevalent at the time. The fact that other solutions would have been conceivable is irrelevant in view of the principle of intertemporal law for the determination of the law valid at the time.

For the sake of completeness, it may be mentioned that Belgian courts reached the same conclusion on the basis of section III of the Regulations respecting the Laws and Customs of War on Land annexed to the Hague Conventions of 1899 and 1907. The Belgian court of cassation stated in 1947, in the context of the legal situation of parts of Belgium after their annexation by Germany subsequent to the invasion by German troops in 1940: "The annexation by one state of part of the territory of another state which remains an international person cannot produce the legal effects of an

---

322   PCIJ, A/B 53.

323   RIAA Vol. 2 (1949), p. 1105.

324   AJIL Vol. 5 (1911), p. 782.

325   See Verosta (note 275), p. 166: "Acquisition of territory required the approval of the former sovereign. Conquest as such conferred no legal title. Cession only became legally valid after the conclusion

annexation unless it was effected with the co-operation or the agreement of the state whose territory has been dismembered. That principle of international law is embodied in several international Regulations and Agreements, such as Section III of the Regulations respecting the Laws and Customs of War on Land annexed to the Hague Conventions of July 29, 1899, and of October 18, 1907, entitled 'Military Authority over the Territory of the Hostile State'; and Article 10 of the Covenant of the League of Nations signed at Versailles on June 28, 1919."[326]

Once again, it becomes apparent that a legal acquisition of part of a territory without the consent of the sovereign concerned cannot have taken place under the law as it stood in 1832 to 1833. Thus, it is also irrelevant to seek to determine the legal consequences, according to the law applicable, of the fact that the British actions occurred in a time of peace and without prior warning. The practice of limited purposes of actions taken during peacetime, not directed at territorial change, and a requirement of a confirmation of the loss of territory by a state defeated in war, demonstrates the conformity of the system based upon the respect of the autonomous will of a state which could only be ignored in the wake of its total subjugation. The British measures taken on the Falkland Islands (Malvinas) could not lead to a change of sovereignty within the framework of such a legal order, neither under the law of peace nor under the laws of war. Britain assumed *de facto* territorial rights: Sovereignty remained with Argentina. London did not seek a confirmation of the change in the status of the Islands or a treaty to acquire sovereignty over the Islands due to the

---

of a treaty, usually a peace treaty".

326   Bindels v. Administrations des Finances, Annual Digest and Reports of Public International Law Cases (H. Lauterpacht, ed), Year 1947, p. 45, 49; the same position is found in Deneffe v. Administration des Finances, ibid., Year 1948, p. 60; concerning the legal rules currently applicable see M. Bothe, Occupation, Belligerent, EPIL, Instalment 4 (1982), p. 64.

fact that the British authorities had erroneously assumed that the Islands were *terra nullius* at the time of the takeover, and this position was maintained even when the British authorities became aware of the true situation.

15.   The legal status of the Islands after 1833: preliminary issues

The United Kingdom has exercised *de facto* sovereign rights over the Falkland Islands (Malvinas) since 1833. The contemporary legal status of the Islands cannot be ascertained alone on the basis of the facts that power was assumed by the British with the illegal use of force, and that no peace treaty confirming British sovereignty has been concluded in the past 150 years and more. International law recognises in principle, as do national legal systems, that the passing of time may have an effect upon the continued existence of a legal right[327]. In the analysis of the current legal situation, the central difficulty is that international legal practice in the modern period knows of no other case, besides the problem of the Falkland Islands (Malvinas), in which a state has partially annexed foreign territory and in which the affected state has continued to insist on the illegality of the situation thus created up to the present day.

An initial methodological remark is appropriate in relation to the unique quality of the legal configuration encountered here. There is no need to emphasise that the uniqueness of a legal issue does not give rise to an

---

327   See, for instance, the statement of the arbitral award in the Grisbadarna dispute: "... it is a settled principle of the law of nations that a state of things which actually exists and has existed for a long time should be changed as little as possible." RIAA, Vol. 11 (1961), p. 147, 161.

assumption that the problem is outside of the operation of
rules of law. The lack of precedents may well make it more
difficult to establish the law than otherwise, but the
applicability of those legal principles within which the
problem falls will not thereby become impossible. The concept
of a living legal order implies that new and even unique
issues will not fall outside the scope of the law.

Specifically with regard to the problem of the Falkland
Islands (Malvinas), a further methodological issue has to be
addressed in this context. The principle of *quieta non movere*
must be taken into account in the discussion of a situation
which has existed *de facto* for over 150 years; the structural
elements of international law as manifested concretely in the
principle of effectiveness require that the factual context
not be ignored. The manner in which the principle of
effectiveness can be harmonised with the notion of
international law as a legal order will be discussed below in
detail[328]. The point which seems to arise here at first sight
is the following. Would there not be grave consequences for
the further development of international relations,
unacceptable from the point of view of legal policy, if a *de
facto* situation lasting for 150 years would have to be
designated as illegal under international law? Would not such
a result require the existing political landscape to be
turned upside-down in many regions of the world?

Greig, for instance, has recently posed these questions.
Indeed, he has concluded that the non-recognition of a
factual situation by the legal system would necessarily lead
to serious consequences in many other cases and would
ultimately threaten the function of international law as an
instrument designed to establish and to secure order[329].

---

328   Cf. infra p. 159 ff.

329   "To allow such a title to be challenged would amount to
       acknowledging that many territorial adjustments
       achieved *de facto* rather than *de jure* could similarly

Empirically, however, this argument is untenable. The specific constellation of a long-lasting partial annexion opposed by the sovereign from the very beginning exists today only with regard to the Falkland Islands (Malvinas). In all cases which may otherwise be comparable, the sovereign has expressed its consent either explicitly or tacitly, or at least has tolerated the situation. This point certainly does not lead to a final determination of the legal issue under consideration, but it had to be mentioned, initially, from the perspective of a conception of the law with exclusive emphasis on stability and order.

16.   The Argentine reaction to the assumption of power by Britain

As will be shown below, the conduct of a state subsequent to the development of an adverse territorial situation is of particular importance for the further development of territorial status. A number of decisions by international tribunals bears this out. The conduct of Argentina since 1832 to 1833 must therefore be discussed.

When Argentina became aware of the takeover of power by Great Britain, she protested immediately on January 22, 1833[330]. The note of protest was communicated to the British representative in Buenos Aires. A second protest followed on June 17, 1833, this time handed over by the Argentine minister plenipotentiary in London[331]. As Argentina was not satisfied with the negative British response contained in the

---

be questioned." Greig (note 44), p. 59; the same position is taken in the memorandum by the United Kingdom of April 28, 1982, written to the President of the Security Council of the United Nations, reprinted in Perl (note 24), p. 650.

330   Reprinted infra as **annex 25, p.** 268.

331   Reprinted infra as **annex 26, p.** 269.

letter of January 8, 1834[332], the Argentine arguments were
presented again in a letter dated December 29, 1834[333]. This
exchange had no influence upon the British attitude toward
the Islands. After seven years, the next protest was raised
on December 18, 1841[334], underlined by two further notes of
February 19, 1842[335], and March 10, 1842[336]. This renewed
attempt by Argentina to bring about a change was apparently
not caused by any specific incidents. After another seven
years, on July 31, 1849, Argentina protested when English
newspapers reported that the government in London had stated
in response to a question by a member of parliament that the
dispute over the Islands had come to an end, and that it
therefore should not again become the subject of a new
exchange of views[337]. Argentina contested this interpretation
of the situation unmistakeably and insisted upon the
correctness of her legal position. In the response dated
August 8, 1849, Britain confirmed her awareness of the
Argentine position at all times, but still emphasised the
legalitiy of her own conduct[338].

After this failure by Argentina to bring about a further
review of the situation of the Falkland Islands (Malvinas),
35 years went by before the contradictory viewpoints were
exchanged again in 1884. The starting point for this new
controversy was the fact that a map had been published at the
time in Argentina with the support of governmental
authorities. On this map, the Falkland Islands (Malvinas)
appeared as a part of Argentina. Britain attempted to prevent

---

332   Infra p. 270, annex 27.

333   Infra p. 282, annex 28.

334   Infra p. 285, annex 29; the reply by Britain is found
       in Muñoz Azpiri (note 52), Vol. 2, p. 183.

335   Ibid., p. 185.

336   Ibid., p. 189; see the British reply of March 15, 1852,
       ibid., p. 191.

337   Infra p. 288, as annex 30.

338   Infra p. 290, as annex 31.

publication of the map[339]. Argentina maintained her previous legal position[340]. In this situation Argentina proposed "to solve the dispute by peaceful means and in the legal forms which civilised states today consider as appropriate for the settlement of disputes of this kind"[341]. Britain responded simply with the opinion that the dispute was ended and should not be taken up again[342].

In 1888 Argentina renewed her proposal to settle the dispute by referring it to an arbitral tribunal, but the proposal was not taken up.[343]. Following this exchange, Argentina again filed a protest and expressed regret "about the silence with which the British government had responded to the Argentine proposals to settle the matter by an arbitral tribunal"[344]. The next formal protest was presented by Argentina in 1908[345]. It appears that this note led the foreign office in London to review the legal situation on the

---

339   Reprinted in Muñoz Azpiri (note 52), p. 204.

340   See the note by Argentina of January 2, 1885, infra annex 32, p. 291. and the reply by Britain of November 14, 1887, annex 32, p. 291.

341   See infra, annex 34, p. 295. According to Greig (note 44), p. 66, Argentina had invited Britain as early as 1844 to submit the case to an arbitral tribunal. Greig reports that Britain categorically rejected this proposal "for the reason that His Majesty's Government are not in any circumstances prepared to envisage the possibility of such an arbitration going against them." The source quoted by Greig is H. Godwin, Memorandum on The Falkland Islands and Dependencies, Public Record Office, FO 371/22 499, p. 143. - I have had no access to this document.

342   Reprinted by Muñoz Azpiri (note 52), Vol. 2, p. 352.

343   Ibid., p. 360; reprinted here as annex 34, p. 295; see also the Argentine protest of January 1, 1888, ibid., p. 354.

344   Ibid., p. 360; on May 4, 1887, Argentina filed a protest with the United States because of the *Lexington* affair; this document is 71 pages long, see Muñoz Azpiri (note 52), Vol. 2., p. 360.

345   See Hope (note 44), p. 434.

basis of an internal legal memorandum[346].

Between the two world wars, the dispute over the Islands continued without any change of attitude on the part of Argentina. In this period, the controversy was discussed several times in international bodies. In a multilateral context, Argentina protested against the continuing situation for the first time, in 1919, with regard to an agreement concerning international radio communication[347]. A formal protest to Britain followed in this matter in 1925[348]. A year earlier, Argentina had presented her legal position in the context of agreements to prevent the spreading of infectious diseases, this time *vis à vis* Belgium[349]. Buenos Aires also set forth its concern about the legal status of the Islands in 1933 within the framework of the Universal Postal Union[350]. All these initiatives on the international level indicated without any doubt that Argentina was not satisfied with the existing state of affairs and had not abandoned her efforts to change the situation. Argentina also re-insisted on her legal position when centenary commemorative postage stamps were issued by Britain on the occasion of 100 years of presence on the Islands[351]. In domestic legislation, Argentina's point of view was expressed in questions of

---

346   Concerning the dates see Beck (note 20).

347   C. Dias Cisneros, La Soberania de la República Argentina en las Malvinas ante el Derecho Internacional, Annuales de la Faculdad de Sciencias Jurídicad y Sociales, La Plata (1951), p. 7, 121 (cited by Hope (note 44), p. 434). See also Muñoz Azpiri (note 52), Vol. 2, p. 367.

348   Reprinted in: Muñoz Azpiri, Vol 2., p. 365.

349   Ibid., p. 368.

350   The Argentine memoranda are reprinted in Muñoz Azpiri (note 52), Vol. 2, p. 372, 375. Concerning the position of Argentina in the International Postal Union see E. Premoli, Las Malvinas y el Correo argentino, ibid., p. 382.

351   See the correspondence in Muñoz Azpiri, Vol. 2, p. 394; also P. Beck, Argentinia's Philatelic Annexation of the Falklands, History Today, Vol. 33 (1933), p. 39.

nationality of the Island's inhabitants[352].

In 1948, Britain offered Argentina an opportunity to
settle the dispute over the so-called Falkland Islands
(Malvinas) Dependencies, being the group of islands situated
to the south of the Falkland Islands (Malvinas), by
submitting it to the International Court of Justice[353]. This
proposal had been preceded by renewed evaluation of the legal
status of the Falklands (Malvinas) by the foreign office in
London[354]. During the same period, H. Waldock published his
study of the Islands in the British Year Book of
International Law[355]. Contrary to the view expressed by J.
Fawcett in 1982[356], the British proposal in 1948 to settle
the dispute by judicial means did not extend to the Falklands
(Malvinas) themselves. This was one reason why Argentina took
a negative attitude when the United Kingdom unilaterally
submitted the dispute over the Falkland Islands (Malvinas)
Dependencies to the Court[357]. In this context it may be noted
that the United Kingdom had issued a declaration under
Article 36 of the statute of the International Court of
Justice. However, the United Kingdom limited the temporal
application of the declaration so as, in effect, to exclude
the dispute over the Falkland Islands (Malvinas). Whether

352   Concerning questions of nationality law, see the
      decision of the Argentine Federal Court in Rio Gallegos
      of 1941, reprinted in ILR, Vol. 8 (1941), p. 130; also
      Chroniques des faits internationaux Argentine et Grand-
      Bretagne, RGDIP, Vol. 69 (1965), p. 111. As to
      questions of the nationality of inhabitants of the
      Falkland Islands (Malvinas), see also the documents in
      Muñoz Azpiri (note 4), Vol 2, p. 370, 393. Generally,
      see I. Arce, Las Islas Malvinas (1950), p. 120;
      Hillekamps (note 30), p. 139.

353   See the documents in Muñoz Azpiri, Vol. 2, p. 438.

354   See Beck (note 20), p. 17.

355   Waldock (note 57).

356   J.E.S. Fawcett, Legal Aspects, in: The Falkland Islands
      Dispute, Chatham House Special (April 1982), p. 6.

357   See the note by Argentina of May 4, 1955, ICJ
      Pleadings, Antarctica Cases (1956), p. 91. See also the
      correspondence between the two governments of 1954,

this restriction was made specifically in view of the dispute over the Falklands (Malvinas) is not clear[358]. Argentina presented her legal position before the United Nations several times[359]. Detailed legal arguments are found, in particular, in the statement which the then ambassador J. Ruda delivered in 1964[360].

It is worth mentioning in the present context that resolution 2065 (XX) of the United Nations General Assembly, adopted by a majority on December 16, 1965, noted the existence of a dispute between Argentina and the United Kingdom. The resolution appeared to imply that the international community did not take any side in favour of one or the other party in the territorial dispute. The United Nations General Assembly also referred to resolution 2065 (XX) after the unlawful attempt by Argentina to incorporate the Islands into Argentine territory by the use of force in 1982[361].

17.   Subsequent legitimation of the British takeover?

The question of the subsequent legitimation of an illegal

Muñoz Azpiri (note 52), Vol. 2, p. 436.

358   See Greig (note 44), p. 66.

359   As to the development of the discussions on the Falkland Islands (Malvinas) in the United Nations between 1946 and 1963 E. Ros, Las islas Malvinas y las Naciones Unidas: Como se planteo el problema en Nueva York, reprinted in Muñoz Azpiri (page 4), Vol. 3, p. 423 ff.; also Weber (note 29), p. 40; Hope (note 44), p. 436. Specifically with regard to the ambivalent position of the United States on this point N. Petersen, Background of the Falkland Islands Crisis, Department of State Bulletin, Vol. 82 (1982), p. 88. See also the documentation in: Malvinas, Georgias y Sandwich del sur, ed. by Consejo Argentino para las Relaciones Internacionales (1983).

360   See annex 3, infra p. 182.

361   See UNGA Res. 37/09, November 9, 1982.

acquisition of territory belongs to those basic problems of
international law which have not been resolved despite long-
standing discussion. From the contemporary point of view, the
prohibition of the use of force, being a norm of general
international law, must be considered as the central norm
relevant to the acquisition of territory[362]. The lack of such
a prohibition in the legal order of the 19th century and the
non-existence of universal international organisations
concerned with war and peace together contributed to bring
about a legal situation which was hardly susceptible to the
rendering of precise statements about the consequences of
unlawful partial annexations. Also, as has often been pointed
out, the doctrine of international law dealt with the
relevant issues on the basis of categories which were not
clearly defined and which often reflected subjective
preferences of the authors involved rather than the reality
of state practice; this was true both for those authors with
pacific tendencies and for those who were not prepared to
accept any limits whatsoever on the use of force and its
consequences.

As to the state practice of the 19th century, it is
difficult to draw any specific conclusions. Partial unlawful
annexations were rare, and foreign ministries had no reason
to clearly state their legal views. It is worth mentioning,
however, that in a remarkable number of cases states were
prepared to submit their territorial disputes for settlement
to arbitral tribunals[363]. On a general level, this suggests
that the dominant international attitude in the 19th century
was not characterised by the view that international law was
basically irrelevant in territorial issues. In view of the
lack of a uniform general state practice, the pertinent
arbitral awards should be given special weight in the
determination of the law then applicable. The fact that the

---

362   See generally W. Meng, Stimson Doctrine, in: EPIL,
       Instalment 4 (1982), p. 230 with further references.

363   See the list of cases in A. Stuyt, Survey of
       International Arbitrations 1794 - 1970 (Vol. 2 1972).

decisions in question were widely recognised by the states concerned as being in conformity with the law and were subsequently observed will have to be considered as strong evidence for the proposition that the law as determined by the arbitral tribunals reflected the general legal convictions of the times.

A survey of the extensive legal literature relating to subsequent legitimation following the illegal acquisition of territory reveals at least five different conceptual approaches[364]. One approach is that an initial legal deficiency can be corrected if the international community approves of the relevant acts retrospectively. This point of view was developed in particular by Heimburger in his study "The Acquisition of Territorial Sovereignty" ("Der Erwerb der Gebietshoheit") published in 1888. The conceptual foundations of this point of view were refined by Schätzel in his monograph "Annexation in International Law" ("Die Annexion im Völkerrecht") published in 1920. The writings of Hersch Lauterpacht on this subject have their roots in the same conception[365].

Another approach attempts to relate the questions under consideration to the general categories relevant for the formation of international legal rules, and to reach a solution on the basis of principles concerning the development of customary law; with various nuances, the notions of acquiescence and prescription are central to this approach. The studies by Pinto[366], Sperduti[367], Blum[368] and

---

364   See for a comprehensive discussion G. Zimmer, Gewaltsame territoriale Veränderungen und ihre völkerrechtliche Legitimation (1971).

365   H. Lauterpacht, Recognition in International Law (1948).

366   R. Pinto, La prescription en droit international public, RdC Vol. 87 I (1955), p. 387.

367   G. Sperduti, Prescrizione, consuetudine e acquiescenza in diritto internazionale, Rivista di diritto internazionale, Vol. 44 (1961), p. 10.

Barberis[369] may be attributed to this school of thinking,
differences in detail notwithstanding.

Schwarzenberger[370] and Charles De Visscher[371] base their
discussions of the subject on another terminology. Even
though their substantive approach has similarities with the
conceptions mentioned above. Both authors prefer to employ
the expression historic consolidation.

Authors such as M. Sorensen[372], Verykios[373], Berber[374]
and Cavaré[375] are inclined to base their views less upon
general state practice and legal conviction than upon the
relevance of the existing factual legal situation. A close
scrutiny of their views shows, however, that there is no
uniform position among these authors concerning the
acquisition of territory on the basis of the rules of
prescription. In part, the adherents of this school of
thinking require the explicit consent of the former
sovereign, while others consider that such consent is no
longer necessary after the passing of a certain period of
time, usually not specified; the latter exponents primarily

---

368   Blum (note 83).

369   J.A. Barberis, La prescripción adquisitiva y la
      costumbre en el derecho internacional, Revue de droit
      international, de sciences diplomatiques et politiques,
      Vol. 45 (1967), p. 233.

370   G. Schwarzenberger, The Fundamental Principles of
      International Law, RdC Vol. 87 I (1955), p. 258; ibid.,
      Title to Territory: Response to a Challenge, AJIL Vol.
      51 (1957), p. 308.

371   De Visscher (note 82).

372   M. Sorensen, La prescription en droit international,
      Acta Scandinavia Iuris Gentium, Nordisk Tidsskrift for
      International Ret, Vol. 3 (1932), p. 145.

373   Verykios, La prescription en droit international public
      (1934).

374   F. Berber, Lehrbuch des Völkerrechts, Vol. 1 (1960), p.
      346.

375   L. Cavaré, Droit international public positif, Vol. 1
      (2nd ed. 1961), p. 602.

refer to the principle of effectiveness[376].

For the purposes of this study, it is not necessary to discuss and to review extensively all the opinions set forth in the literature. The legal assessment of the British measures taken in 1832 to 1833 and the continuous protests by the Argentine government since that time narrow down the issue to the question whether a continuous practice of protest, or other measures, on the part of the former sovereign will stand in the way of the transfer of sovereignty; in the case of an affirmative answer, the further question is posed whether the Argentine conduct after 1832 to 1833 satisfies the requirements necessary for the existence of protests or other measures under international law.

Irrespective of the fundamental positions adopted, the authors mentioned above have also addressed this narrow issue, as have a number of other writers who were concerned with the same problem in shorter studies. Initially, it should again be pointed out that the relevant resolutions of the General Assembly of the United Nations do not express any clear legal position on one side or the other in the dispute between Argentina and the United Kingdom; thus, it cannot be assumed, within the doctrine espoused by Schätzel and Lauterpacht, that a legal consolidation of the situation existing in 1832 to 1833 has taken place as a result of an unequivocal approval by the international community. Consequently, it will only have to be discussed whether a legitimation has occurred in some other manner.

The views of the commentators in this respect may be divided roughly into three groups. On the one hand, authors such as Brownlie[377], Hyde[378], Jennings[379], Lauterpacht[380],

---

376   See K. Doehring, Effectiveness, in: EPIL, Instalment 7
       (1984), p. 70 with further references.
377   Brownlie (note 179), p. 153 ff.

Reuter[381], Sorensen[382], Wengler[383] and Verdross[384] are inclined to conclude that a factual situation of an illegal character does not lose its illegality in the course of time so long as the sovereign explicitly protests against the situation. In clear contrast to this position are those opinions according to which *de facto* sovereignty which has existed for a long period will at some point acquire the stamp of legality; Charpentier[385], von der Heydte[386] and Charles de Visscher[387] have expressed opinions consistent with such an approach.

In between these two positions, another group of authors holds that a factual situation in itself has no legal relevance, while also insisting that a formal protest of the sovereign will as such not suffice to conserve the original legal situation. Blum[388], D.H.N. Johnson[389], Pinto[390] and Suy[391] are of this opinion. With various nuances, these authors insist that the sovereign concerned must make avail

378   C. Hyde, International Law, Chiefly as Interpreted and Applied by the United States, Vol. 1 (2nd ed. 1947), p. 307.

379   R. Jennings, The Acquisition of Territory in International Law (1963), p. 22.

380   Lauterpacht (note 365).

381   P. Reuter, Droit International Public (3rd ed. 1968), p. 152.

382   M. Sorensen, Principes de droit international public, RdC Vol. 101 III (1960), p. 147.

383   W. Wengler, Völkerrecht, Vol. 2 (1964), p. 981.

384   A. Verdross, Völkerrecht (5th ed. 1964), p. 287 f.

385   I. Charpentier, La reconnaissance internationale et l'évolution du droit des gens (1956).

386   A. von der Heydte, Völkerrecht, Vol. 1 (1958), p. 255.

387   De Visscher (note 82), p. 25 ff.

388   Blum (note 83), p. 162.

389   D.H.N. Johnson, Acquisitive Prescriptions in International Law, BYIL, Vol. 27 (1950), p. 332, 345.

390   Pinto (note 366), p. 387, 416.

391   E. Suy, Les actes juridiques unilatéraux en droit international public (1962), p. 47, especially p. 72.

of further means at its disposal, such as an offer to
negotiate or the resort to judicial settlement, in order to
preserve its rights. More recently, Doehring has taken the
same position[392].

With specific regard to the issue of the Falkland Islands
(Malvinas), a review of the legal literature indicates that
those opinions which refer to legal developments in the 19th
century are generally based upon the view that conquest
provided a lawful title to territory, albeit mostly without
taking into account the issue of illegal partial annexations.
For the purposes of the present discussion, only those
opinions will be considered relevant which explicitly address
the consequences of illegal conduct. An adequate answer to
the problem under review can only be expected in the light of
a discussion concentrated on the cases of unlawful partial
annexation during the 19th century and of annexations based
upon acts violating the prohibition of the use of force as it
existed at the time. More general discussions of the rules of
lawful acquisition of territory are immaterial for present
purposes. The specific nature of the question thus defined is
of particular importance in the assessment of opinions which
are inclined to give priority to the existence of a factual
situation over a long period and to disregard the legal
situation as it existed at a previous time.

---

392   "In international law the principle of prescription is
       recognized, a principle stemming from municipal law and
       evaluated as a general principle of law. Thus, for
       instance, the right of jurisdiction over a territory
       cannot be questioned after a long period of effective
       exercise, even if the lawfulness of the jurisdiction
       may be doubtful at the time of its establishment. It
       must, however, be emphasized that such prescription can
       only be considered to create a legal title if the
       possession has been exercised effectively and in an
       uninterrupted manner during the period concerned. The
       fact alone that other States emphatically protest
       against the taking of possession could hinder the legal
       validity of the prescriptions. Those protests, however,
       must be accompanied by other effective measures;
       otherwise their legal effect may be doubtful"; Doehring
       (note 376), p. 73.

As to the opinion which requires more than a formal
protest for the preservation of existing rights, in the
context of the Falkland Islands (Malvinas) it may be asked
what concrete measures were available and were to be expected
from Argentina. Certainly, Argentina had no chance of
applying military measures against Britain in the 19th
century. The offer to initiate friendly negotiations was
repeated again and again in the Argentine notes of protest.
In addition, Buenos Aires proposed in 1884 to 1885 to settle
the issue by arbitration[393]. Following the establishment of
international organisations, Argentina submitted the dispute,
to the extent it was relevant for the work of such
organisations, to the appropriate fora[394]. Since 1946, the
dispute over the Falkland Islands (Malvinas) has been on the
agenda of the United Nations at the request of Argentina.
Unilateral military actions on the part of Argentina are
prohibited by Article 2(4) of the United Nations Charter.
Inasmuch as binding pronouncements of the United Nations
Security Council would be possible in this context, the
United Kingdom, as a permanent member, has always held the
right to veto any such acts.

The British attitude in relation to all the initiatives
undertaken by Argentina since 1833 has been consistent and
clear. Britian has considered the dispute over the
sovereignty of the Islands to have been ended and
correspondingly has never submitted or accepted any proposal
for the settlement of the dispute by a third party. In view
of this peculiarity of the British point of view and the
existing political, military and economic superiority of the
United Kingdom, it might be asked what further measures
Argentina could have employed in order to emphasise her legal
position more firmly. In the Chamizal Award, discussed in

---

393   Supra p. 144.

394   Generally with regard to the legal relevance for
      resolutions of international organisations concering
      territorial disputes after 1919, see Lauterpacht (note
      365), p. 150.

detail below[395], the competent commission indicated that no disadvantage may arise for a state which expresses its legal position by means of legal arguments rather than the use of force. Indeed, it is inherent in the very concept of law that no different perspective could be allowed. It is no response in this context to suggest that the lack of a legal order regulating the maintenance of peace and security as well as the resort to the use of force in the 19th century provided an excuse to accord priority to the use of force in relation to lawful conduct. The argument would be untenable inasmuch as the taking of power by Britain and its maintenance despite subsequent knowledge of the true legal situation amounted to a violation of the *lex lata* at the time.

The additional question might be raised as to whether the Argentine protests were formulated clearly enough and were delivered frequently enough. A review of the Argentine protests, beginning with the one delivered by Moreno in 1834[396], reveals that political rhetoric against Britain was avoided in most cases. Indeed, very often, strictly legal arguments were presented, sometimes even couched in the form of legal treatises, and these documents leave no room for doubt with regard to their message.

The longest period without an Argentine protest was the time between 1849 and 1884. During this period, Argentina did not in any way indicate a change in attitude. In this context, it must be taken into account that in 1849 Britain had clearly insisted that the dispute over the Islands had been closed once and for ever, and this opinion had been expressed to Argentina in an unmistakable manner[397]. Also, it must be noted that Britain had at no point based her title before 1884 upon prescription, having continuously insisted

---

395   Infra p. 161 ff.
396   See supra p. 142 ff.
397   See supra p. 143.

that the Islands had been acquired in 1832 to 1833[398]. A
schematic consideration of the requirement to protest
repeatedly would not be tenable from the point of view of
legal doctrine without regard to these specific aspects[399].
Moreover, one specific aspect which must not be overlooked in
this context was pointed out by Argentina in her protests of
1842 and 1849. The regular repetition of a protest despite
the lack of any change in the factual or the legal situation
cannot be an absolute requirement, taking into consideration
the dignity of the state concerned, as long as the other
state has not indicated that it is prepared to change its
previous attitude in some way[400]. Finally, it will be
remembered that, although the period of time necessary for
prescription to operate, if this institution can be regarded
as recognised, has not been generally determined,
occasionally a period of 50 years has been proposed, for
example in the settlement between Great Britain and the
United States in the dispute over British Guyana and
Venezuela[401]; from this perspective as well, the passing of
the period of 35 years without repetition of a protest cannot
be considered in itself to lead to loss of title.

It is also of interest in this context to draw attention
to those patterns of argument which appear repeatedly in
international jurisprudence with regard to territorial

---

398   See, for instance, the statements by Britain of January
      8, 1834 (reprinted in Perl, note 49, p. 323) and of
      February 15, 1842 (reprinted in Muñoz Azpiri (note 52),
      Vol. 2, p. 183) and of January 8, 1885 (reprinted in
      Muñoz Azpiri, Vol. 2, p. 230).

399   The requirement to assess the legal relevance of
      protests in the light of the special circumstances of
      the case is emphasised in Blum (note 83), p. 153, 165.

400   See the wording of the British statements, supra note
      348. Generally, see, I. MacGibbon, Some Observations on
      the Part of Protest in International Law, BYIL Vol. 30
      (1954), p. 293, 306, 310; ibid., Customary Law and
      Acquiescence, BYIL Vol. 33 (1958), p. 115.

401   "Adverse holding or prescription during a period of 50
      years shall make a good title". See the wording in BFSP
      Vol. 89 (1896/97), p. 57; see Johnson (note 389), p.

issues. In a broad sense, the principle of consensus plays a role in nearly all of the relevant decisions. Courts and tribunals have noted the absence of protests in the decision on the border dispute in Alaska between the United States and Britain[402], in the award in the border dispute between Britain and Brazil[403], in the Bulama award[404], in the decision on Delagoa Bay[405], in the Grisbadarna award[406], in the Palmas Island decision[407], in the award concerning the border dispute between Columbia and Venzuela[408], in the decision on the Bay of Fonseca[409], and in the Walvis Bay award[410].

The importance of the absence of protests in territorial disputes was recognised by the International Court of Justice in the Right of Passage case[411], and in the Temple of Preah Vihear case[412]. Neither of these judgments addressed the

332, 340.

402   Cmnd. 1877 (1904), p. 49, 79.

403   RIAA, Vol. 11, p. 21, 22.

404   La Pradelle/Politis, Recueil des arbitrages internationaux, Vol. 2 (1923), p. 612.

405   RIAA, Vol. 11, p. 21, 22.

406   Ibid., p. 155, 161.

407   RIAA, Vol. 2, p. 829, 868.

408   RIAA, Vol. 1, p. 223, 280.

409   AJIL, Vol. 11 (1917), p. 674, 705.

410   RIAA, Vol. 11, p. 267, 307.

411   ICJ Reports 1960, p. 6, 39.

412   ICJ Reports 1962, p. 6, 39. Greig (note 44), p. 45, appears to assume that the application of the reasoning of this decision to the Falklands (Malvinas) speaks in favour of an acquisition of the Islands by Britain. However, Greig overlooks totally that in the case of the Temple a practice of Cambodia and Thailand existed which was accepted by both sides for more than 50 years without any protest; it is precisely on this point that the conduct of Argentina in the case of the Falklands (Malvinas) differs from the Temple case. In this context, a clear definition of the terms acquiescence and prescription is important, and the distinction between the two has to be observed. See, on this point, Blum (note 83), p. 59; generally Suy (note 391), p. 63,

question of the acquisition of territory by the use of force; nevertheless, various references concerning the lack of protest may be noted in the present context. The Court implied in the two judgments that questions of territorial acquisitions must not be assessed exclusively from the point of view of a factual situation. The emphasis placed by the Court on the lack of any expression of will on the part of the states affected may be viewed as amounting only to an indirect confirmation of the relevance of protests. On the whole, however, these decisions indicate that the international legal order could not be regarded as having developed in a manner which would have attributed absolute priority to the factual situation in relation to the will expressed by the states affected. As Blum has shown[413], no tribunal has so far decided a territorial dispute on the basis of prescription, and indeed most decisions do not take any notice whatsoever of this concept.

As an intermediate conclusion, it may be pointed out that Argentina retained her sovereign rights from the perspective not only of those commentators who consider the filing of protests as a suitable means to preserve existing rights and responsibilities, but also from the point of view of those who require, in addition to protests, such measures as are at the disposal of the sovereign concerned. It remains to be discussed whether the loss of territory by Argentina may be supposed from the point of view of those other commentators, who consider that the passing of time will in itself lead to a destruction of title without any possibility on the part of the previous sovereign to conserve the *status quo*[414]. If such an opinion were correct, the passage of more than 150 years would certainly lead to the transfer of sovereignty. Thus, it is of importance to examine whether this construction of the law can indeed be regarded as correct.

Pinto (note 366), with further references.
413   Blum (note 83), p. 20.
414   Supra p. 169 f.

Specific doctrinal explanations are not to be found in the writings of the authors concerned. Presumably, the opinion of these authors is based upon the desire to adapt international legal rules to reality, as reflected in the principle of effectiveness. Thus, a primary test is whether the principle of effectiveness as recognised in international law supports or requires such an assessment of the passage of time. The starting point for this inquiry will be that the principle of effectiveness has to be considered as the sum of individual norms which can be understood as expressing the necessity to adapt legal rules to reality in the specific context in which they operate. Individual aspects of the recognition of states, of nationality law, or of the law of international organisations reflect the need for an effective international legal order. However, the principle of effectiveness must not be understood so as to attribute legal significance to every empirical situation.

"Generally, effectiveness is not a justification *per se* but must be seen in connection with a comprehensive view of the legal situation. Effectiveness is only legally relevant in so far as the legal system permits it. Effectiveness alone as a consequence of a mere factual event does not create rights."[415]

Methodologically, this construction of the principle of effectiveness requires special caution to be exercised against an attempt to deduce a legal norm directly from the principle of effectiveness in cases where the concrete manifestation of the principle is not logically required or at least may not be regarded as advisable from the point of view of international practice. Thus, the proponents of the doctrine of the legal significance of factual situations in the context of the acquisition of territorial title must accept the burdon of proof and show that a modification of the norms generally recognised for the acquisition of

---

415   Doehring (note 376), p. 70.

territory by the principle of effectiveness is required. No logical principle of law exists according to which the factual situation is predominant in all circumstances in relation to the rules of law which normally operate. The relevance of special situations and interests in the light of the legal position of the inhabitants of the territory concerned cannot be discussed simply with reference to the principles of logic; their legal relevance will have to be discussed in detail[416].

Ultimately, therefore, it will have to be assumed that the relevance of a factual situation in relation to generally recognised norms concerning the acquisition of territory depends upon international legal practice. Again, the specific doctrinal context and the consequences with respect to the proof of relevant state practice have to be emphasised: Inasmuch as the acquisition of territory was governed in 1832 to 1833 by specific norms of law, the question remains whether these special norms must be ignored in view of the length of time which has since passed. If it is not possible to show such an effect of the passage of time on the basis of the structure of the norms concerned or of international practice, the applicability of the norms governing in 1832 to 1833 remains intact.

In this context, reference must be made to factors which have been discussed above, especially with regard to the dispute between Chile and Bolivia after 1870 and the status of Herzogovina and Bosnia at the beginning of this century[417]. As demonstrated above, the factual situation in both cases was not considered sufficient in itself to establish legal status in the absence of additional legal factors, in particular the consent of the sovereign concerned. Aside from these two individual cases, the consistent legal practice of the 19th century in recognising

---

416   Infra p. 173 ff.
417   Supra p 135 f.

changes in the status of territory after armed hostilities
not on the basis of unilateral statements but only as a
consequence of relevant treaties must be considered. This
legal practice is inconsistent with an assumption that the
príinciple of effectiveness means that the factual exercise of
sovereign rights in a case of the continued existence of the
previous sovereign requires the transfer of sovereignty to
the factual sovereign.

It appears that so far only one tribunal has had to rule
upon the principle here under consideration. In the dispute
concerning the so-called Chamizal frontier territory situated
on the Rio Grande, between Mexico and the United States, the
legal setting of the case was in general not comparable to
the issue of the status of the Falklands (Malvinas), but the
tribunal did have to rule on the relationship between a rule
of law concerning acquisition of territory and the passing of
time[418]. In view of the uniqueness of this decision, rendered
in 1911, it deserves special attention.

The territorial dispute had its origin in the application
and interpretation of treaties concluded between the United
States and Mexico in 1848 and 1853, under which the Rio
Grande was to be considered as the border in the relevant
area between the two states. In the view of the tribunal,
which was composed of a chairman of Canadian nationality, one
member nominated by Mexico, and another by the United States,
these treaties did not answer the question as to whether a
change in the course of the river would lead to a change of
the border along the new line of the river, or whether the
mid-point of the river as it had been in 1848 and 1853 would
remain the border. According to the view of the majority of
the tribunal, a third convention concluded by the two states
in 1884 had to be construed so as to imply that the border
was to follow the changing bed of the river. In the view of

---

418   The decision is reprinted in RIAA Vol. 11 (1962), p.
       309.

the majority, this third convention had to be taken into account in the interpretation of the first two treaties. However, changes of the border would only arise if the changes in the bed of the river were the result of a slow and gradual erosion. The majority concluded that such a process of erosion had not taken place and thus concluded that the border in the Chamizal area had not changed since 1848.

In reality, the bed of the river had changed to the considerable disadvantage of Mexico after 1853, due to rapid erosions, which according to the tribunal were irrelevant in view of its interpretation of the 1884 convention. Under these circumstances, the question of the "legalisation" of an illegal factual situation was raised because the United States had pleaded before the tribunal that the middle of the river as it stood in 1911 was in any case bound to form the border, as a consequence of the factual exercise of sovereign rights in the relevant area in the period between 1853 and 1911. It was argued that the United States had exercised *de facto* sovereignty at all times since 1848 in the area which the changing bed of the river had created after 1848 on the northern side. According to this opinion, the rules of prescription had to be considered under the circumstances as conferring a separate title to territory in favour of the United States as the latter had been in *de facto* possession of the territory under dispute for 60 years.

The tribunal's decision did not follow the legal reasoning of the United States. Although the members of the commission were not all in agreement on some aspects of the case, there was a unanimity of opinion on the question of prescription. In the relevant passage, the tribunal referred to three aspects which spoke against the opinion presented by the United States. The initial remarks in the opinion pointed out that it was immaterial whether the general rules of international law recognise the principle of prescription. According to the unanimous view of the tribunal, the factual

preconditions for the acquisition of territory on the basis
of prescription did not exist in the event, since the United
States had not been in "undisturbed, uninterrupted and
unchallenged possession" in the area in dispute. The
commission found that these conditions did not exist because
the legal status of the Chamizal had been the subject of
requests and diplomatic notes on the part of Mexico to the
United States since 1856.

Apparently, although not explicitly, the commission
considered that the Mexican activities before 1884 were
inconsistent with the assumption of unchallenged possession
on the part of the United States before 1884. In the second
stage of the argument, the tribunal pointed out that the very
treaty of 1884 established that the parties had not
considered that the territory had changed its status on the
basis of the principle of prescription, and instead they had
intended to settle the problem in the treaty itself. In the
third part, the tribunal returned to the factual and legal
situation in the period before 1884 and pointed to the
requirement of undisturbed possession as a precondition for
the operation of prescription, concluding that this
requirement had not been met. In this context, the tribunal
recognised that in 1874 Mexico had considered establishing a
customs post in the disputed territory but had refrained from
doing so in view of the likelihood that such an activity
would have led to the use of force on the part of the United
States. In this context, the tribunal explained: "It is clear
from the circumstances related in this affidavit that however
much the Mexicans may have desired to take physical
possession of the district, the result of any attempt to do
so would have provoked scenes of violence, *and the Republic
of Mexico cannot be blamed for resorting to the milder forms
of protest contained in its diplomatic correspondence*. In
private law, the interruption of prescription is effected by
a suit, but in dealings between nations this is of course
impossible, unless and until an international tribunal is

established for such purpose. In the present case, the
Mexican claim was asserted before the International Boundary
Commission within a reasonable time after it commenced to
exercise its functions, and prior to that date the Mexican
Government *had done all that could be reasonably required of
it by way of protest against the alleged encroachment*. Under
these circumstances the commissioners have no difficulty in
coming to the conclusion that the plea of prescription should
be dismissed."[419]

To what extent does the legal context allow these
considerations to be applied to the situation prevailing on
the Falklands (Malvinas) after 1832 to 1833? It might be
argued that the Chamizal decision has no bearing inasmuch as
it concerned a dispute for territory determined by treaties,
while the problem of the Falklands (Malvinas) concerns the
application of the norms of general international law.
Indeed, the legal status of the Chamizal had been subject to
treaty as early as 1848 to 1853, at the beginning of the
period relevant for the decision of the tribunal. In view of
the legal context it might be considered that the
determination of a border by agreement at the beginning of a
long-lasting dispute will not give rise to a special legal
situation from the point of view of the legimitate
expectations of the parties, as opposed to a situation in
which the general norms concerning acquisition of territory
apply. Ultimately, however, such an argument would appear to
be artificial and unconvincing.

In the specific setting of the Chamizal case, the
applicable norms of treaty law were not formulated more
precisely than the general rules concerning acquisition of
territory. The tribunal specifically referred in its decision
to the ambiguity of the treaties concerned. More important, a
general objection to a differentiation between territory
acquired on the basis of a treaty and territory acquired by

---

419   Ibid., p. 329; emphasis added.

unilateral acts must be pointed out. International law does
not recognise any distinction in the legal status of
territories on the basis of the type of acquisition. The
modus acquirendi does not generally bear upon the status of
the territory once the acquisition has taken place. Thus, no
importance can be attached to the fact that the dispute
concerning the Chamizal had its origin in a consensual
arrangement. The decisive point was, therefore, that the
United States had pleaded that the territory had been
acquired on the basis of the factual exercise of sovereign
rights.

As to the general significance of the Chamizal decision,
what importance should be attached to the fact that a new
treaty was concluded in 1884 which, according to the
tribunal, had to be applied in a retroactive manner? If the
tribunal had considered that the treaty alone was decisive,
there would have been no point in examining the conduct of
the parties between 1848 and 1884. It will be noted in this
context that the treaties concerned applied to a section of
the boundary which was much longer than the Chamizal itself.
The decision must be assessed against this background. In the
context of its statements on prescription, the tribunal
considered whether the factual situation in the Chamizal area
led to a separate legal regime which was no longer determined
by the treaty concluded in 1884. Thus, the subject of the
decision was, in this respect, the question whether the
Chamizal was governed by a regime established by a special
title rather than a treaty applicable to the whole boundary
concerned. The attention paid by the tribunal to the specific
question of prescription can only be understood from this
perspective. Within this framework it is clear that the
tribunal examined the preconditions for a title based upon
prescription for the period before 1884. Thus, it appears
that the discussion of the elements of prescription was not
dependent upon the treaty regime created in 1848, 1853 and
1884. Rather, the general rules governing prescription as

applicable to the factual situation in the period between 1853 and 1884 were of much greater relevance from the point of view of the tribunal.

In its award, the tribunal concluded that a subsequent legalisation of a defective acquisition of territory will not take place if the affected sovereign makes clear its opposition to the factual situation, so long as the power of the sovereign does not allow for a unilateral enforcement of its legal claim and as long as the sovereign concerned undertakes all measures reasonably to be expected for preserving its rights[420].

In the light of these conclusions, the relevance of the pronouncements made in the Chamizal decision for the general problem of the subsequent legalisation of a defective title becomes apparent. The unanimous position taken by the members of the tribunal reinforces, in the context of the facts of the case, the view already derived from state practice that, according to the rules of international law applicable in the 19th century, the acquisition of a part of a foreign territory against the will of the sovereign affected was not possible solely on the basis of factual possession.

In this context it is worth drawing attention to the British position as expressed before the International Court of Justice in the dispute with Norway concerning fishery rights in Norwegian costal areas. Norway had argued in the proceedings that she had acquired certain rights on the basis of the expression of an uninterrupted claim and the exercise of the corresponding rights. Britain opposed this argument with reference to the fact that she had protested against the

---

420   See also Cohen Jonathan (note 28), p. 235, 243;
       Hillekamps (note 30), p. 145; Hope (note 44), p. 427;
       generally Vieyra (note 12), p. 153. Superficial and
       unconvincing discussions are found in Reisman (note
       44), p. 287, 303, and F. Hassan, The Sovereignty
       Dispute over the Falkland Islands, Virginia Journal of
       International Law, Vo. 23 (1982), p. 53, 67.

unilateral claim of rights on the part of Norway and had
instituted other measures against the Norwegian conduct.
Britain based her argument upon the assumption that the
filing of a protest hinders the loss or acquisition of a
right when additional measures are taken which support the
protest: "The protest of a single State ... is effective to
prevent the establishment of a prescriptive title precisely
to the extent that the State takes all necessary and
reasonable steps to prosecute the available means of
redressing the infringements of its rights."[421]

Clearly, this argument reflects the assumption that
protest can, in principle, prevent the acquisition of
territorial rights, if certain other conditions are met. The
British position also made it clear that protest in itself
will not preserve a legal position; further measures are
needed for the protest to be effective. More specifically,
this opinion considers a protest to be effective if all the
measures are taken by a state that are at its disposal, in
order to retain its legal position; as to the nature of such
additional measures, the British argument referred to the
"necessary and reasonable steps". The nature of the measures
required was also addressed in this context by Britain:
reference was made to the unequivocal expression of a protest
in the context of diplomatic negotiations, to the
establishment of a *modus vivendi* and to willingness to submit
the dispute to an international judicial body. Having in view
the position taken by Argentina with regard to the Falklands
(Malvinas), it will be noted that Britain did not consider
the use of force to be a necessary condition for an effective
protest intended to preserve a legal position. Thus, the
concept of reasonable steps operates to form the general
framework for further determination of an effective protest
according to the British argument. As to the period
concerned, it will be noted that the beginning of the dispute
between Britian and Norway did not fall within the period in

_____

421   ICJ Pleadings, Vol. 2 (1951), p. 653.

which the comprehensive prohibition of the use of force was generally accepted; the same is true for the dispute over the Falklands (Malvinas).

The historical background of the dispute between Britain and Norway is not material in the present context. The point is to evaluate the conduct of Argentina in the light of the criteria accepted by Britain in the dispute before the International Court of Justice with regard to the existence of an effective protest. According to the British argument advanced here, Argentina had taken all necessary steps. Buenos Aires not only presented its position clearly in diplomatic negotiations, and maintained its legal position so far as was possible under the circumstances, taking into account the limited opportunities for establishing a *modus vivendi*, but also submitted a proposal to settle the dispute by judicial means. The fact that the proceedings between Norway and Britain concerned fishery rights, whereas the dispute over the Falklands (Malvinas) is of a territorial nature, is not of importance in determining the criteria by which an effective protest can be established. There is no reason to differentiate in this respect between fishery rights and territorial issues. In conclusion, therefore, it appears that the British line of argument reconfirms the generally accepted position with regard to the legal framework of the concept of prescription, in particular with regard to protests and other appropriate measures intended to prevent a change of legal status.

Finally, the question remains whether the long period of British *de facto* sovereignty over 150 years in itself requires the above considerations and the results so far reached to be modified[422]. Ultimately, a positive answer could only be based on the view that protests against an illegal situation have to be assessed in a different manner in the case of long-lasting situations than in developments

---

422   See the short discussion of the issue by Reisman (note

which occur over a short period of time. In view of the fundamental rationale for the concept of the protest, such a temporal perspective does not seem appropriate. With regard to the attitude of a state which exercises *de facto* sovereignty over a long period, in violation of the rights of the sovereign, the question is thus posed whether the international legal order countenances a reward for the state which responds to the illegal situation, despite continuous protest, with the simple argument that the process of acquisition of territory has led to the creation of a definitive situation.

It will not be easily granted that the rules of international law, being part of a legal order, can respond in such a manner to an insistence upon the continued existence of an illegal situation. The premises upon which the concept of international law has been based are not inconsistent with the idea that territorial issues may under certain circumstances not be finally resolved over a longer period of time[423]. In the modern context, there is no doubt that the rules protecting an existing territorial situation against the use of force must also apply to a situation in which the definitive territorial status of an area is in dispute[424]. However, if violations of the law are not to be promoted and rewarded, the inescapable conclusion is that international law does not lend such a stamp of legality, even over longer periods, and that the quest to provide

---

44), p. 303.

[423] See generally A. Verdross/B. Simma/R. Geiger, Territoriale Souveränität und Gebietshoheit (1980). These authors have shown convincingly that practice, in particular treaty practice, knows of a variety of cases in which the power exercising governmental rights has not been identical for longer periods with the sovereign; see also the discussion in J.H.W. Verzijl, International Law in Historical Perspective: Part III, State Territory (1970), Chapter IV.

[424] See J.A. Frowein, Das *de facto*-Regime im Völkerrecht, Eine Untersuchung zur Rechtsstellung "nichtanerkannter Staaten" und ähnlicher Gebilde (Beiträge zum ausländischen öffentlichen Recht und Völkerrecht, Vol.

mechanisms to restore legitimate rights will be given precedence.

The subject of peaceful change is of particular relevance in the context of long-lasting illegal situations, but it will have to be admitted that the development of international law has so far not given rise to satisfactory solutions of this problem[425]. The more extensive discussion of this fundamental issue of contemporary international law does not form the subject of the present inquiry. The point to be made here is that it would not be an appropriate response to the problem of peaceful change in the context of modern international law if it were assumed that, with the passing of time, long-lasting illegal situations would necessarily lose their illegality on the basis of a legal concept placing exclusive reliance upon the factual situation. From the point of view of legal logic, differentiations made in accordance with the legality of the initial acquisition of power and the subsequent conduct of the sovereign states concerned are in no way excluded. The fundamental principles of territorial sovereignty, the unity of the legal system in the context of an applicable prohibition of the use of force, the rules on the preservation of peace and the norms concerning the acquisition of territory are all factors which indicate that such differentiations are not only possible but are in conformity with the system of international law.

The question of peaceful change can also be viewed in the wider context of the requirement of *bona fides* in the case of negotiations between the two parties concerned. In accordance with the resolutions of the United Nations General Assembly, Argentina and the United Kingdom have several times started negotiations on a future legal status of the Islands[426]. The

---

46) (1968), p. 35.

425   See W. Grewe, Peaceful Change, in: EPIL, Instalment 7 (1984), p. 378 with further references.

426   G. Edwards, Europe and the Falkland Islands Crisis

question as to whether both parties have acted *bona fides* in these talks may be a subsequent field of study based upon full access to the files of the foreign offices concerned. Beyond doubt, Argentina violated the principle of fair negotiations when relying on the use of force in 1982. In the light of the information so far available, however, it cannot be excluded that the United Kingdom continued the ongoing negotiations after an internal parliamentary debate in December 1980 without seriously aiming at a solution which would have been mutually acceptable[427]. If the relevant files of the British foreign office ever show that this was indeed the case, the Argentine violation of the prohibition of the use of force would have been preceded on the part of the United Kingdom by violation of the principle of *bona fides* in the conduct of bilateral negotiations. There is no need here to consider the issue in detail, because neither the violation of the prohibition of the use of force nor the violation of the principle of *bona fides*, if indeed the latter occured, would have any bearing upon the question of the present territorial status of the Islands.

In view of the lack of obligatory and effective modes of peaceful settlement of disputes, the issue of peaceful change will require additional efforts on the part of the international community in order to establish and to strengthen mechanisms which are designed to allow appropriate peaceful change. To ignore this problem by weakening lawful positions in the case of illegal situations cannot be considered an acceptable alternative from any perspective.

1982, Journal of Common Market Studies, Vol. 22 (1984), p. 295: J. Pearce, The Falkland Islands Negotiations, 1965 - 1982, in: The Falkland Islands Disputes: International Dimensions, Chatham House Special, p. 1 ff.; M. Pinto, Argentina's Rights to the Falkland/Malvinas Islands, Texas International Law Journal, Vol. 18 (1983), p. 1, 6 ff.; P. Beck, Cooperative Confrontation in the Falkland Islands Dispute: The Anglo-Argentine Search for a Way Forward: 1968 - 1981, Journal of Interamerican Studies and World Affairs, Vol. 24 (1982), p. 37.

427   See for details Edwards (note 426), p. 296.

This is particularly true in the areas where the law has to respond to the illegal use of force and to the conduct of states which insist upon international recognition of the factual situations thus created.

III.   The application of the right to self-determination and
        the current status of the Falkland Islands (Malvinas)

The United Kingdom is of the opinion that the current
population of the Falkland Islands (Malvinas) enjoys the
right to self-determination; this right is supposed to exist
irrespective of the question of the territorial status of the
Islands[428]. There is no doubt that the majority of the
current population has no desire to change the current legal
status of the Islands or their rights within the United
Kingdom. According to the British position, the current
factual situation on the Falklands (Malvinas) could also be
legally upheld on the basis of the right to self-
determination even if Argentina were to have a title to the
Islands from a territorial point of view.

Argentina has contested this British interpretation of
the right to self-determination and considers that the
Argentine territorial title is not impaired in any way by the
principle of self-determination. From the point of view of
Buenos Aires, the right to self-determination finds no
application under the particular circumstances prevailing on
the Falkand Islands (Malvinas). Moreover, according to the
view of Argentina, the present population cannot be
considered as a people which would be the proper subject of
such a right[429].

The relevance of the norms of self-determination may now
be reviewed in the light of the above conclusions as to the
territorial title[430]. It will be assumed at the outset that

---

428   As to the British position, see, for instance, UN Doc.
       S/14 988 and S/15 007.

429   The Argentine position is found in UNGA A/37/553.

430   Cf. Cohen Jonathan (note 28), p. 247; H. Fox, Legal
       Issues in the Falkland Islands Confrontation 1982,
       International Relations, Vol. 7 (1983), p. 244; Hope
       (note 44), p. 443; Hillekamps (note 30), p. 46, 166;
       Weber (note 29), p. 110; D. Dunnett, Self-Determination
       and the Falklands, International Affairs, Vo. 59

the existence of the right to self-determination as a
principle of contemporary international law is beyond doubt
today. The reference to this right in Articles 1 and 55 of
the United Nations Charter, the recognition of the right in
resolutions of the United Nations General Assembly, the
acceptance of the right in the human rights covenants of the
United Nations, the affirmative judgment of the International
Court of Justice in the advisory opinion concerning the
Western Sahara[431], as well as the inclusion of the right in
the Final Act of the Conference on Security and Co-operation
in Europe provide, in their entirety, sufficient evidence for
the existence of the right in international law as it stands
today[432]. The question whether this right is limited to
situations in which colonial or colonial types of domination
exist, in the sense of the so-called "salt water theory"[433],
does not require any discussion at this initial stage.

In the light of the factual situation now prevailing on
the Islands and the above conclusions concerning the abstract
Argentine title to the Islands, what is the correct legal
framework within which the right to self-determination has to
be applied? Is there an exclusive relationship between the
right to self-determination and the right to territorial
integrity? As a general matter, how can these two fundamental
principles of international law be reconciled?

As a starting point, it may be noted that the right to

(1983), p. 415; M. Sanchez, Self-Determination and the
Falkland Islands Dispute, Columbia Journal of
Transnational Law, Vol. 21 (1983), p. 557; A. Schwed,
Territorial Claims as a Limitation to the Right of
Self-Determination in the Context of the Falkland
Islands Dispute; Fordham Journal of International Law,
Vol. 6 (1983), p. 443; M. Jovane, Le Falkland/Malvinas:
Autodeterminazione o Decolonizzazione?, in: Ronzitti
(ed.) (note 52), p. 87.

431   See infra p. 181 f.

432   See generally D. Thürer, Self-Determination, in: EPIL,
Instalment 8 (1985), p. 470.

433   Ibid., p. 473.

self-determination has presumably been recognised as a principle of law only since 1945, even though in the previous period the principle had found some expression on the political level and had even been applied to some extent. The development of the principle as a legal principle has taken place within the legal order created by the United Nations. The fact that the principle has mainly been applied and developed by United Nations organs found expression when the International Court of Justice referred to the relevant resolution of the United Nations General Assembly in the Western Sahara advisory opinion. In a broader sense, the application of the principle of self-determination relates to an area of the law within which the effects of resolutions of the General Assembly are more far-reaching than the power of recommendation laid down for the Assembly in Article 11 of the United Nations Charter and extend into the sphere of the creation of law.

It is not material in this context to examine the doctrinal foundation of rights created within the framework of the United Nations General Assembly, or their limitations. It must be noted, however, that analysis and definition of the right to self-determination depends upon an examination of the practice of the organs of the United Nations. Necessarily, resolution 1514 (XV) of the United Nations General Assembly will have to be addressed in this context; this resolution was adopted by consensus in 1960 and gave for the first time the specific contours to the right to self-determination that have been recognised consistently in the subsequent practice of the United Nations. Paragraph 2 of the resolution unmistakably laid down the right to self-determination: "All peoples have the right to self-determination; by virtue of that they freely determine their political status and freely pursue their economic, social and cultural development."

For present purposes, paragraph 2 should be read in conjunction with paragraph 6: "Any attempt aimed at the partial or total disruption of the national and territorial integrity of a country is incompatible with the purposes and principles of the Charter of the United Nations."

Prima facie, a certain antinomy between paragraph 2 and paragraph 6 cannot be overlooked, and a legal interpretation of resolution 1514 (XV) faces the difficult task of reconciling the two areas of law. The potential conflict between the right to self-determination and the right to territorial integrity can only be avoided by a construction which allows a separate area of application for both principles. The wording of resolution 1514 does not point to any specific manner of interpretation which would lead to a corresponding result. In any case, a construction of one principle without due regard to the other would have to be considered as inconsistent with the purpose and with the wording of resolution 1514.

The application of the right to self-determination must be based upon the view that a differentiation is necessary between the period before the initial exercise of the right to self-determination and the period after[434]. In the first phase, it will have to be assumed that the people concerned have an unqualified right to self-determination, with precedence over the right of the state concerned to preserve its territorial integrity. In the second phase, subsequent to the initial exercise of the right to self-determination, the principle of territorial integrity will operate so as to allow only the assumption of a latent existence of the right to self-determination; the right is reactivated only if the organs of the state concerned in effect deny the separate identity of the people concerned. Such aspects as the prohibition of the use of a particular language, of cultural activities, or restriction of the freedom of integration or non-integration must be assessed when considering whether or not a revival of the right to self-determination can be

---

434   UNGA Res. 2625 (XXV), October 24, 1970.

justified. Such a synthesis of the two principles is
consistent with the wording of resolution 1514 (XV) and is
not contradicted by state practice.

With regard to the current situation on the Falkland
Islands (Malvinas), the applicability of the principle of
self-determination will have to be reviewed, in addition to
the definition of the "people". In particular, it must be
considered whether the underlying personal basis for the
right to self-determination can also be said to exist if a
part of an existing state is annexed unlawfully, and if the
previous population is expelled and replaced in the territory
in question by nationals of the annexing state. It must also
be asked whether such a constellation has to be discussed
from the point of view of the applicability of the right to
self-determination or from the vantage point of the notion of
a people. In view of the logical priority of the problem of
general applicability of the right to self-determination, it
appears appropriate to address initially the normative scope
of the right to self-determination as applied to the
circumstances of the Falkland Islands (Malvinas) rather than
to scrutinise one particular element neccesary for a positive
affirmation of the right.

From the point of view of legal policy, conflicting
aspects of the subject can be discerned. In favour of the
pre-eminence of the right to self-determination it may be
pointed out that a dependence of this right upon territorial
issues would be bound to lead to unstable situations,
inasmuch as territorial issues tend to be complex and often
are not easily susceptible to a legal evaluation by
international organs such as the United Nations General
Assembly. Even though the right to self-determination is
subject to various interpretations at its periphery, in many
cases its application may present fewer difficulties than
historically-based territorial issues. On the other hand, in
favour of a higher ranking of the territorial issue it may be
argued that such an approach avoids the problem of rewarding

unlawful annexation and thus reinforces the principle of respect for domestic sovereignty from the point of view of the state affected by an annexation.

In the examination of these issues, the intertemporal dimension of the problem must not be overlooked. If it be assumed, as is generally the case, that the right to self-determination found legal recognition only in 1945 through the adoption of the United Nations Charter, it has to be concluded, in view of the results reached above, that the *nudum jus* of Argentine sovereignty existed before 1945. Thus, the problem is narrowed down to the question whether the violation of the principle of territorial integrity by an illegal use of force before 1945, as determined by the principles of intertemporal law, can be rectified on the basis of the right to self-determination as applied after 1945.

From this point of view it is appropriate to ask initially whether a violation of the prohibition of the use of force may legitimise a situation resulting from a violation in the period after 1945. Which rules apply in the period after 1945 if a state violates the right of a people to self-determination by expelling the existing population and creates a new basis for the future application of the right to self-determination in factual terms by moving its own nationals to the area annexed? The question must not be confused with the issue of enforcing a legally recognised right to self-determination in an individual setting. As to the question posed, is it possible within the system of the contemporary international legal order to assert that the double violation of both the prohibition of the use of force and the right to self-determination will in effect lead to a reversal of the legal situation at the expense of the state affected by the annexation and to a creation of a new right of self-determination in favour of the imported population? The systematic coherence of the rules relating to the prohibition of the use of force and the principle of territorial sovereignty suggests that a positive answer to this question may be excluded. The prohibition of the use of force, as a norm of *jus cogens*, and the necessity for a corresponding sanction within the decentralised system of international law speak clearly in favour of attributing a higher ranking to the preservation of peace and to the principle of respect for territorial integrity[435].

If it is true that a violation of the prohibition of the use of force in the period after 1945 cannot undermine the right to self-determination, then in the light of the previous conclusions concerning the status of the Falklands (Malvinas) the further question arises whether the same considerations apply if the violation occurred before 1945 in relation to a rule of law proscribing the use of force as applicable at the time. The additional peculiar element to be considered here relates to the fact that the population on the Falklands (Malvinas) came to the Islands following the illegal use of force at the behest of the state using force, and before the right to self-determination acquired the status of a rule of law.

In answering the question posed, the *ratio* of the right to self-determination has to be considered in its historical and contemporary contexts. Historically, the right to self-determination was conceived so as to legally prevent the domination of weaker and smaller peoples. Essentially, the concept operates so as to render unlawful the use of force and to establish a legal order opposed to the recognition of facts arising in the wake of such unlawful conduct. Systematically, it follows that it would be inappropriate to recognise a chronological differentiation in the context of the operation of the principle of self-determination and to attribute greater legal significance to the principle in the context of violations of rules regarding the use of force in

---

435   See generally Randelzhofer (note 268), p. 265.

the period before 1945 than to such a violation after 1945. On the basis of these considerations it may be concluded that the right to self-determination is by definition not applicable in those cases in which the right of a people or of a group similar to a people is involved when the latter was moved into an area by the state using force subsequent to the illegal expulsion of the previous population.

It might be argued that such a result cannot be maintained in view of the insecurity which it produces. From a systematic point of view, such an argument has no basis in the principles of international law. It has never been argued seriously that all territorial disputes existing in 1945 have been frozen in order to establish a legal order exclusively dedicated to the preservation of legal certainty. Correspondingly, the argument that territorial disputes have to be ignored in the context of discussions of the scope of the right to self-determination must also fail. The response of contemporary international law to the relevant problems consists in upholding the prohibition of the use of force, not in ignoring the norms related to the principle of territorial integrity. As to the Falklands (Malvinas), this means that the norms of self-determination neither require nor permit a revision of the territorial attribution of the Islands to Argentina.

The question remains whether this conclusion is compatible with the recognition of individual rights associated with the right to self-determination, in other words with appropriate protection of the present population in the annexed territory. The conception of the right to self-determination, as referred to above, is relevant in this context as well. In conjunction with the prohibition of arbitrary mass expulsions, the right to self-determination operates so as to prevent the current population from losing its cultural identity subsequent to its integration in the new state concerned. From a historical perspective, it will

be recalled that the territorial changes ordered by the
victor states at the end of the First World War were
accompanied by a detailed regulation of the rights of the
minorities thus created.

The systematic discussion of the relationship between the
right to self-determination and the principle of territorial
integrity remains to be reviewed in the light of the practice
of the organs of the United Nations. As pointed out above,
this practice cannot be overlooked in establishing the proper
understanding of the right to self-determination[436]. The
International Court of Justice addressed the general issues
involved in its advisory opinion on the status of the Western
Sahara in 1975[437]. The Court was requested to determine
whether legal ties had existed between the Western Sahara and
Morocco or Mauritania at the end of the 19th century. The
question had apparently been posed to the Court under the
assumption that such ties would be relevant for the future
status of the Sahara in the light of a claim of self-
determination by the Saharouis. In the event, the Court
denied the existence of any legal ties, and therefore did not
have to address a general relationship between the right to
self-determination and the principle of territorial
integrity. The Court seemed to indicate, however, that under
special circumstances the right to self-determination can be
affected by other relevant legal factors. Thus, the Court
pointed out that territorial claims prevail over the right to
self-determination if the population in question cannot be
characterised as a people within the meaning of the right to
self-determination or if an inquiry into the will of the
people does not appear to be necessary.

The remarks made by the Court do not allow concise legal
consequences to be drawn concerning the limits of the right

---

436   Supra p. 173 ff.
437   ICJ Reports 1975, p. 12.

to self-determination. In principle, however, the
considerations referred to by the Court reinforce the
position that situations are conceivable in which
historically-based territorial claims are opposed to the
existence of a right to self-determination with respect to a
certain territory; in other words, that the right to self-
determination cannot be construed as enjoying absolute
priority in relation to other relevant principles of
international law.

In the practice of the United Nations General Assembly,
the resolutions concerning the status of Gibraltar are worth
considering in this context[438]. The Assembly has stated in
two resolutions, not adopted unanimously, that the status of
Gibraltar is not dependent upon the will of the present
population (see resolution 2231 (XXI) and 2353 (XXII)). Under
the treaty of Utrecht of 1713, the United Kingdom exercises
sovereign rights over Gibraltar, while it is also stipulated
that the Spanish interests will prevail over those of third
states in case of a change in the status of Gibraltar.
According to the United Nations General Assembly, the rights
thus reserved for Spain are opposed to the development of a
right to self-determination in favour of the present
population.

Any attempt to apply this position of the United Nations
General Assembly to the situation of the Falkland Islands
(Malvinas) will have to take into account considerable
differences between Gibraltar and the Falklands (Malvinas).
In the case of Gibraltar, its status depends upon
interpretation of a valid treaty, the wording of which in no
way addresses the issue of self-determination. Moreover, it

---

438   Generally on the legal status of Gibraltar, see A. Rigo
      Sureda, The Evolution of the Right to Self-
      Determination (1973), p. 185; T. Franck/P. Hoffmann,
      The Right of Self-Determination in Very Small Places,
      New York University Journal of International Law and
      Politics, Vol. 8 (1976), p. 331, 374.

may be argued that the rights enjoyed by Spain have a
colonial character. A third difference between the two cases
is that the arrival of the current population of Gibraltar on
the island did not have its roots in an unlawful use of
force, in contrast to the situation on the Falkland Islands
(Malvinas). In its entirety, the difference in context
between the situation in Gibraltar and that on the Falklands
(Malvinas) is so considerable that it would hardly be
appropriate to extend any conclusions drawn from the relevant
resolutions of the United Nations General Assembly concerning
Gibraltar to the situation existing on the Falkland Islands
(Malvinas).

In view of the historical setting, the situation in Ifni
lends itself more easily to comparison with the Falkland
Islands (Malvinas)[439]. Morocco asserts that Spain acquired
Ifni in violation of Moroccan rights. The issue of self-
determination arose in relation to Ifni after 1945 inasmuch
as nomadic people have for a long time travelled through this
territory and they may be considered as holders of the right
to self-determination. The United Nations General Assembly,
in resolution 2229 (XXI), called upon Spain to transfer Ifni
to Morocco. Spain took the position that the nomadic people
concerned were not yet in a position to effectively exercise
the right to self-determination. Again, in the light of the
uncertainty as to the holder of the right to self-
determination, no direct comparison with the situation on the
Falkland Islands (Malvinas) is appropriate. The above-
mentioned resolution of the General Assembly pointed out that
the transfer of sovereignty shall take place with due regard
to the aspiration of the local population. If this formula
indicates that the General Assembly took for granted the
existence of a potential holder of the right to self-
determination, the treatment of Ifni may well be considered
as a precedent establishing the priority of the right to

---

439   For details see Schwed (note 430), p. 464 with further
      references.

territorial integrity under circumstances similar to those on the Falkland Islands (Malvinas).

The third territory of interest in this context is Belize. The status of this territory was the subject of dispute between Britain and Spain for more than three centuries in the colonial period, and subsequently between Britain and Guatemala[440]. This dispute notwithstanding, the United Nations General Assembly recognised in resolution 3432 (XXX), adopted in 1975, "the inalienable right of the people of Belize to self-determination and independence". However, the treatment of Belize is also not easily subject to generalisations. British settlers already lived in Belize in the period during which Guatemala became independent. Moreover, Guatemala recognised[441] the British title to Belize in the so-called Wyke-Aycinema Convention (1859), even though Guatemala subsequently argued that this convention was null and void. Finally, it remains doubtful whether Britain really did violate Spanish rights to Belize in the 17th century. Certainly, in the context of Belize, no expulsion of an existing population by the use of force and no subsequent establishment of a new population has occurred. In view of the general relationship between the right to self-determination and the prohibition of the use of force, these peculiarities of the case will not be overlooked. It would appear, therefore, that the treatment of Belize in the United Nations General Assembly does not shed any light upon the legal status of the Falkland Islands (Malvinas).

On the basis of the above considerations it is now

---

440   As to the historical development, see J. Kunz, Guatemala v. Great Britain; In re Belize, AJIL, Vol. 40 (1946), p. 383; concerning the discussions in the United Nations see, for instance, J. Maguire, The Decolonization of Belize: Self-Determination v. Territorial Integrity, Virginia Journal of International Law, Vol. 22 (1982), p. 849 with further references.

441   BFSP Vol. 49 (1858/59), p. 7.

possible to reach a preliminary conclusion. The practice of
the United Nations is not opposed to the formulation of a
general principle according to which the right to self-
determination of an ethnically independent population cannot
be realised by secession from an existing territorial entity
if the area in question was unlawfully detached by the use of
force, if the existing population was removed from the
territory by the use of force, and if the new ethnic
population was subsequently established in the area with the
assistance of the colonial power.

The discussion so far has addressed the abstract
formulation and definition of the problem under
consideration. As indicated above, however, the practice of
the United Nations in this area will have to be considered
with specific reference to the setting of each individual
case. As the organs of the United Nations have several times
addressed the situation on the Falklands (Malvinas) and the
separate views of Argentina and the United Kingdom, it is
appropriate at this point to turn to the position of the
United Nations with regard to the territorial title and the
right of self-determination of the population currently on
the Islands.

The United Nations General Assembly has addressed the
legal situation, including the right to self-determination,
in two resolutions. Both resolution 2065 (XX) of December 16,
1965, and resolution 3160 (XXVIII) were adopted under the
heading "Question of the Falkland Islands (Malvinas)"[442]. The
starting point for the analysis of these two resolutions will
be resolution 2065. The subsequent resolution is more broadly
based and, in addition, specifically confirms resolution
2065. Resolution 2065 may be divided into three parts. The
preamble supplies a general evaluation of the dispute by the
General Assembly; the operative text contains an invitation

---

442   The two resolutions are reprinted infra in annex 35, p.
       296, and annex 36, p. 297, respectively.

addressed to Argentina and the United Kingdom to proceed with
negotiations; and third, the text also sets forth the
framework within which these negotiations are to take place.

The preamble of resolution 2065 (XX) takes note of the
existence of the dispute between the two states concerning
sovereignty over the Islands. Remarkably, the starting point
for the General Assembly consists in the recognition of the
existence of the territorial dispute and not the problem of
the right to self-determination. It will be recalled that the
issue of territorial title is terminologically and in
substance distinct from the existence or non-existence of the
right to self-determination, and that the wording of the
preamble of the resolution has to be assessed against this
background. The General Assembly invited the two parties to
initiate negotiations with a view to finding a peaceful
solution. From a legal perspective, special interest will
attach to the framework of these negotiations as set forth in
the resolution; reference is made to the provisions and
objectives of the United Nations Charter and of General
Assembly resolution 1514 (XV) and to "the interests of the
population of the Falkland Islands (Malvinas)".

The general reference to the objectives of the United
Nations Charter and to resolution 1514 (XV) hardly supplies
any basis for drawing specific conclusions concerning the
manner in which territorial rights, on the one hand, and the
right to self-determination, on the other hand, may be
reconciled in the case of the Falklands (Malvinas). It will
be noted, however, that what were referred to as "the
interests of the population of the Falkland Islands
(Malvinas)" will have to be taken into account in
negotiations. At first sight, this wording might be supposed
to indicate that the political wishes of the population must
be the major point of orientation in the negotiations.
However, such an assumption appears dubious if the wording of
resolution 2065 is compared with the terminology employed in
the United Nations Charter in the area of the norms

regulating the right to self-determination. Comparison shows that resolution 2065 speaks of the population of the Falkland Islands (Malvinas), but not of a "people". As determined in the practice of the United Nations, only a "people" may be a subject of the right to self-determination. Moreover, resolution 2065 addresses the "interests" of the population, but not their "wishes". The terminology used here is conspicuous inasmuch as Article 73 of the United Nations Charter speaks, in the case of the applicability of the right to self-determination, of the "wishes" of the people.

There is no reason to believe that the wording of resolution 2065 (XX) was chosen in ignorance or in defiance of the established terminological consensus in the context of the right to self-determination. Accordingly, the United Nations General Assembly must be deemed to consider the dispute between Argentina and the United Kingdom essentially not as a problem of self-determination. The emphasis upon the territorial dispute, indirectly referred to in the preamble, is emphasised in the operative part of the resolution. The fact that the "interests of the population" have to be considered as one element of the negotiations is not opposed to such an assessment. The inclusion of the word "interests" seems to point to an objective evaluation of the situation of the population which, on the one hand, does not amount to an exclusive criterion for the negotiations; on the other hand, the language chosen is consistent with an understanding of the principle of self-determination according to which each segment of the population has the right to oppose total integration inasmuch as its ethnic, cultural and linguistic identity is at stake.

In the context of this understanding of the substance and the wording of resolution 2065 (XX), the document appears to amount to an invitation to the parties to solve the territorial dispute without recognising a right to self-determination to be exercised at this point by the current population, while nevertheless indicating that negotiations will have to take into account the separate interests of the population which every ethnic group enjoys under current international law within the state of which it forms part.

Resolution 2065 (XX) also refers to the recommendation of the Special Committee on the Situation with regard to the Implementation of the Declaration on the Granting of Independence to Colonial Countries and Peoples. This recommendation assumes that the existing situation is of a colonial character; otherwise, it would not be comprehensible that reference is made to resolution 1514 (XV). The recommendation also refers to the existing territorial dispute and to the interests of the population of the Islands. Moreover, the recommendation calls upon the parties to take into account the opinions expressed in the general debate. Considering that these opinions were not homogeneous, the reference must be considered as an element of compromise beyond a strictly legal perspective. Resolution 2065 (XX) does not otherwise make any reference to these opinions when delineating the framework for the negotiations.

On the whole, it may not be assumed that the reference to the debates in the Special Committee should be attributed a weight which would decisively influence the substance of resolution 2065. The wording of the resolution's preamble, its substantive meaning and the wording of the operative part all point to the assumption of a territorially-based dispute between Argentina and the United Kingdom in which the right to self-determination of the current population is not recognised.

A question may be posed as to the legal basis upon which the United Nations General Assembly is competent to address a territorial dispute. In the light of Articles 11, 12, and 33 of the United Nations Charter, this question raises no complex issues. An invitation to reach a peaceful solution to a dispute may without doubt be made on the basis of the competences spelled out for the General Assembly in the provisions mentioned. It is also clear that the General Assembly has no power to decide bilateral territorial disputes; the competences of the Assembly are limited to the expression of recommendations. The particular competences of the General Assembly in the context of the existence of a right to self-determination in general and the devolution of colonial regimes within the framework of Article 73 *et seq.* of the Charter need not be discussed here. It is clear that the competences of the General Assembly are narrower in the case of strictly territorial disputes. Given this scheme of competences, and the substantive conclusions reached by the General Assembly with regard to the territorial nature of the dispute between Argentina and the United Kingdom, it was entirely appropriate for the Assembly to limit itself to a simple recommendation phrased in terms of negotiations and not to avail itself of the special powers included within the framework of Article 73 of the Charter.

What additional perspectives may be gained in this context from the substance of resolution 3160 (XXVIII), adopted in 1973? In comparison to resolution 2065 (XX), no fundamentally new orientation is apparent. Reference was also made to "the interests of the population of the Falkland Islands (Malvinas)". The fact that an additional reference was made to the "well-being of the population" cannot be said to have introduced a new element in the general legal assessment. Operative paragraph 2 of resolution 3160 (XXVIII) again demonstrates that the General Assembly essentially views the dispute as a territorial dispute. The negotiations shall take place "... in order to arrive at a peaceful solution of the conflict of sovereignty between them concerning the Falklands Islands (Malvinas)".

Here again, the measures recommended are consistent with an assumption of a bilateral territorial dimension of the legal dispute, and no independent assessment was made by the

General Assembly regarding the substance of the territorial issue. From the point of view of international law, the existence of the right to self-determination does not depend upon the will of individual states, and it is therefore, in principle, not subject to confirmation or negotiation in bilateral negotiations. From this perspective as well, resolution 3160 (XXVIII) provides indirect confirmation that the United Nations considers that the territorial dimension is the dominant one in the dispute over the Islands. The fact that the United Nations has addressed the issues of decolonisation and of self-determination in the context of the Falklands (Malvinas) is not opposed to this view. The treatment of the problem seems to indicate that, in the view of the United Nations, the colonial origin of the dispute justifies its inclusion on the agenda, as a matter of competence, while nevertheless the territorial aspect of the dispute is decisive from the perspective of the United Nations; substantive treatment of the issue within the framework of the United Nations and in relation to self-determination might be justified only in the event that, as an outcome of bilateral negotiations, the Islands would be appropriated to the colonial power.

In view of this conclusion, the discussion can now return to the direct question of the territorial status of the Falkland Islands (Malvinas). The starting point for the review of the right to self-determination was that a change in the territorial attribution of the Islands to Argentina might occur if the current population were a subject of the right to self-determination including a right to secession from Argentina. It is necessary to recall this starting point. The affirmation of the right to self-determination for the Falklands (Malvinas) might operate in the sense of a limitation of Argentine territorial sovereignty in favour of an incorporation into the territory of the United Kingdom. Absent the existence of the right to self-determination, the Argentine claim will not be affected. As was shown above, the United Nations has so far not recognised a right to self-

determination in favour of the current population, nor in
favour of Argentina, the primary dispute being of a
territorial nature. In conclusion, therefore, the practice of
the United Nations has no influence upon the territorial
rights of Argentina established above.

It may finally be questioned whether such an analysis can
be complete in one essential respect, inasmuch as no
independent inquiry into the existence of a right to self-
determination in favour of the current population on the
Islands has been made, regardless of the substance of the
pertinent resolutions of the United Nations. Would it be
possible for the United Kingdom to argue that the right to
self-determination has an objective character and that the
assumption by the United Nations of a competence to define
the right would be inconsistent with the legal nature of the
right? Two separate levels of argument have to be
differentiated in this context. On the one hand, such a case
might be based on the general view that each state has the
right to put forward its own legal position as long as this
position is not contradicted by a binding decision of an
internationally competent organ. At the outset, it was
indicated that such an argument stands up as far as it goes,
but that the objective nature of the rules of international
law is not thereby eliminated. The argument would be relevant
in the context of an objective assessment only to the extent
that the United Kingdom would assert that a definition of the
right to self-determination in an individual case does not
fall within the competence of the United Nations but has to
be deduced from general criteria not necessarily determined
by the practice of the United Nations. Certainly, one may
doubt whether the right to self-determination can only come
into existence once the United Nations has addressed the
relevant issue and has decided affirmatively. The problem is
different, however, if the question has been on the agenda of
the United Nations for years, as is the case for the
Falklands (Malvinas), and if the United Nations has clearly

indicated that a right to self-determination does not exist
in this case. Even then, it may be doubted whether the point
of view of the United Nations may be considered to be
arbitrary or whether abstract criteria affirming a right to
self-determination can be set aside by the existence of an
arbitrary practice on the part of the United Nations.

A closer inquiry will show that considerations of this
kind are too vague to influence the legal assessment of the
status of the Falklands (Malvinas). Essentially, the United
Nations has in this context not been concerned with the
application of abstract criteria for the existence of the
right to self-determination in an individual case, but has
addressed the fundamental issue of the relationship between a
territorial claim and the existence of the right to self-
determination in a factual existing situation having its
origins in the use of force, in other words with the
preconditions necessary for the existence of the right to
self-determination. As pointed out previously, the right to
self-determination developed after 1945 as a legal principle,
mainly on the basis of resolutions and decisions adopted
within the framework of the United Nations. Against this
background, the two major pillars of international customary
law, state practice and legal conviction, may be brought into
account with regard to the right to self-determination in an
appropriate manner in the contemporary state of development
of international law only upon the basis of decisions and
convictions expressed in the statements of competent organs
of the United Nations. It was shown above that in the
practice of the United Nations the illegal genesis of a
factual situation in the use of force cannot be rectified on
the basis of the right to self-determination.
Correspondingly, this practice may be considered as informing
and limiting the right to self-determination. Outside of the
framework of the United Nations, no developments are apparent
in the context of an illegal acquisition of *de facto*
sovereignty and a subsequent development of a right to self-
determination which would justify or support the

consolidation and legitimation of the situation created by
the use of force on the basis of the right to self-
determination.

In the light of this conclusion it may be asked how much
weight should be attributed to a legal opinion concerning the
right to self-determination which deviates from the practice
of the United Nations with regard to the Falklands
(Malvinas). It is apparent that such a deviation would
require a justification which cannot be shown to exist within
the framework of the currently recognised sources of
international law. If a state adopts a legal position which
is inconsistent with the generally accepted view of the
sources of international law, this position will not alter
existing law, even though it may turn out with hindsight to
have influenced the subsequent development of international
law. Moreover, in the context of a dispute over a structural
element of international law, the argument would be untenable
that opposition on the part of one state to a generally
accepted rule of law in a particular case would exclude the
applicability of the same norm in relation to the state
concerned. In other words, the objective assessment of the
contemporary legal situation in the present context must be
considered to be determined by the practice of the United
Nations; a divergent view of the law would have no influence
upon this legal situation. The claim that the population of
the Falklands (Malvinas) enjoys a right to self-determination
cannot be said to objectively have an effect different from
any other incorrect legal contention put forward by a state
which asserts its national interests and in doing so finds
itself acting contrary to the rules of international law.
Therefore, it must be concluded that the right to self-
determination as applied to the particular legal and factual
circumstances which prevail in relation to the Falkland
Islands (Malvinas) does not operate to set aside the rights
of Argentina as the legitimate territorial sovereign.

INDEX

Bibliography

D. Acevedo, The US Measures against Argentina resulting from the Malvinas Conflict, AJIL 78 (1984), pp. 323-344.

M. Akehurst, in: House of Commons, Foreign Affairs Committee, Session 1982-83, Falkland Islands, Appendices to the Minutes of Evidence, p. 440.

C. Alvarez, Las Islas Falkland o Malvinas su historia, la controversia Argentino-Británica y le guerra consiguente, Santiago de Chile (1987).

I. Arce, Las Islas Malvinas (1950).

I. Areco, Titulos de la República Argentina a la Soberania y Possessión de las Islas Malvinas (1885).

A. Asseff, Chile, Magallanes y Las Malvinas, Ceinar 8, (1982), pp. 29-49.

J. A. Barberis, La prescripción adquisitiva y la costumbre en el derecho internacional, Revue de droit international, de sciences diplomatiques et politiques, Vol. 45 (1967), p. 233.

R. P. Barston/P. W. Birnie, The Falkland Islands/Islands Malvinas Conflict: A Question of Zones, Marine Policy, Vol. 7 (1983), p. 14.

J. Basdevant, La Revolution Française et le Droit de la Guerre continentale (1901).

P. Beck, The Anglo-Argentine Dispute over Title to the Falkland-Islands: Changing British Perceptions on Sovereignty since 1910, in: Millennium, Journal of International Studies, Vol. 12 (1983), p. 6.

P. Beck, Argentina's Philatelic Annexation of the Falklands, History Today, Vol. 33 (1983), p. 39.

P. Beck, Britain's Falklands Future, The Round Table 1984, p. 139.

P. Beck, Cooperative Confrontation in the Falkland Islands Dispute: The Anglo-Argentine Search for a Way Forward: 1968-1981, Journal of Interamerican Studies and World Affairs, Vol. 24 (1982), p. 37.

P. Beck, The Falkland Islands as an International Problem, London (1988).

P. Beck, The Future of the Falkland Islands: a Solution made in Hongkong? International Affairs, Vol. 61 (1985), p.

643.

Zoraquin Becu, Inglaterra Prometto Abandonar Las Malvinas
    (1983).

F. Berber, Lehrbuch des Völkerrechts, Vol. 1 (1960).

U. Beyerlin, Humanitarian Intervention, in: EPIL, Instalment
    3 (1982), p. 211.

F. Bleiber, Die Entdeckung als Rechtstitel für den
    Gebietserwerb (1933).

Y. Blum, Historic Titles in International Law (1965).

D. Blumenwitz, Falkland oder Malvinas? Der britisch-
    argentinische Streit über die Inselgruppe im Südatlantik
    aus der Sicht des Völkerrechts, Zeitschrift für Politik,
    Vol. 29 (1982), p. 318.

C. Bluntschli, Das moderne Völkerrecht der civilisierten
    Staaten (1872).

C. Bluth, The British Resort to Force in the
    Falkland/Malvinas Conflict 1982, J. of Peace Research 24
    (1987), p. 5-20.

A. B. Bologna, Los derechos argentinos sobre las islas
    Malvinas, Revista de Estudions Internacionales, Vol. 3
    (1982), p. 799.

A. B. Bologna, Los derechos de Inglaterra sobre las islas
    Malvinas, Revista de Estudios Internacionales, Vol. 4
    (1983), p. 775.

J. Boltersdorf, Krisen und Krisenkontrolle in den
    internationalen Beziehungen am Beispiel des Falkland-
    Konflikts von 1982, Berlin (1985).

M. Bothe, Occupation, Belligerent, in: EPIL, Instalment 4
    (1982), p. 64.

D. Bowett, Self-Defense in International Law (1958).

V. Boysen, The Falkland Islands (1924).

I. Brownlie, International Law and the Use of Force by States
    (1963).

I. Brownlie, Principles of Public International Law (4th ed.
    1982), p. 135.

R. Caillet-Bois, La controversia del Nootka Sound y el Rio de
    la Plata, Humanidades, Vol. 20 (1929), p. 341.

R. Caillet-Bois, Las Islas Malvinas, Una Tierra Argentina

(2nd ed. 1948).

C. Calvo, Le droit international théorique et pratique, Vol. 1 (1887).

V. Caracciolo, La Falkland-Malvine alle Nazioni Unite (1960-1983), Riv. di Stud. Polit. Internaz. 51 (1984), p. 263-291.

L. Cavaré, Droit international public positif, Vo. 1 (2nd ed. 1961).

M. Charlton, The Little Platoon: Diplomacy and the Falklands Dispute, Oxford (1989).

I. Charpentier, La reconnaissance internationale et l'évolution du droit des gens (1956).

G. Cohen Jonathan, Les Iles Falkland (Malouines), AFDI Vol. 18 (1972), p. 235.

A. Coll (ed.), The Falkland War: lessons for strategy, diplomacy and international law (1985).

G. Connell-Smith, Latin America and the Falklands Conflict, Yb. of World Aff. (1984), p. 73-88.

E. David, Les sanctions économiques prises contre l'Argentine dans l'affaire des Malouines, Rev.Belge de Droit Internat. 18, (1984-85), p. 150-165.

Charles De Visscher, Les effectivités du droit international public (1967).

J. Dewost, La Communauté, le Dix et les "sanctions" contre l'Argentine-De la crise iranienne à la crise des Malouines, AFDI 28, (1982), p. 215-232.

C. Dias Cisneros, La Soberania de la República Argentina en las Malvinas ante del Derecho Internacional, Annuales de la Faculdad de Sciencias Jurídicas y Sociales, La Plata (1951), p. 7.

D. C. Dicke, Der Streit um die Falklandinseln oder Malvinen, Recht und Staat ..., Festschrift Scupin (1983), p. 429.

K. Doehring, Effectiveness, in: EPIL, Instalment 7 (1984), p. 70.

W. Down, The Occupation of the Falkland Islands and the Question of Sovereignty (1927).

D. Dunnett, Self-Determination and the Falklands, International Affairs, Vol. 59 (1983), p. 415.

R. Dupuy, L'impossible agression: les Malouines entre l'O.N.U. et l'O.E.A., AFDI 28 (1982), p. 337-353.

G. Edwards, Europe and the Falkland Islands Crisis 1982,
Journal of Common Market Studies, Vol. 22 (1984), p. 295.

I. Edwards, The Law Officers of the Crown (1964).

T. Elias, The Doctrine of Intertemporal Law, AJIL Vol. 74
(1980), p. 285.

Falkland Islands Review, Report of a Committee of Privy
Counsellors (Cmnd. 8787) January 1983.

J. E. S. Fawcett, Legal Aspects, in: The Falkland Islands
Dispute, Chatham House Special (April 1982), p. 6.

J. E. S. Fawcett, The Falklands and the Law, The World Today,
Vol. 38 (1982), p. 203.

J. Fawcett, in: House of Commons, Foreign Affairs Committee,
Session 1982-83, Falkland Islands, Minutes of Evidence,
Monday 17 January 1983, p. 139.

W. J. Fenrick, Legal Aspects of the Falklands Naval Conflict,
Rev. de Droit Penal Mil. et de Droit de la Guerre 24,
(1985), p. 241-268.

H. Ferns, Britain and Argentina in the Nineteenth Century
(1960).

E. Ferrer Vieyra, An Annotated Legal Chronology of the
Malvinas (Falkland) Islands Controversy (1985).

E. Ferrer Vieyra, Las Islas Malvinas y el Derecho
Internacional (1984).

J. Fisch, The Falkland Islands in the European Treaty System
1493-1833, German Yearbook of International Law, Vol. 26
(1983), p. 105.

L. Forlati (ed.), Crisi Falkland-Malvinas e organizzazione
internazionale, Padoue (1985).

H. Fox, Legal Issues in the Falkland Islands Confrontation
1982, International Relations, Vol. 7 (1983), p. 2454.

T. M. Franck, Dulce et Decorum Est: The Strategic Role of
Legal Principles in the Falklands War, AJIL Vo. 77
(1983), p. 109.

T. Franck/P. Hoffmann, The Right of Self-Determination in
Very Small Places, New York University Journal of
International Law ond Politics, Vol. 8 (1976), p. 331.

L. Freedman, Signals of war: the Falklands Conflict of 1982,
London (1990).

J. A. Frowein, Das de facto-Regime im Völkerrecht, Eine
Untersuchung zur Rechtsstellung "nichtanerkannter

Staaten" und ähnlicher Gebilde (Beiträge zum
ausländischen öffentlichen Recht und Völkerrecht, Vol.
46) (1968).

W. Fuglsang, Der Streit um die Insel Palmas (1931), p. 83.

V. Gamba, The Falklands/Malvinas War: a model for north-south
crisis prevention (1987).

J. Goebel, The Struggle for the Falkland Islands (1927).

Gomez Langenheim, Elementos para la historia de nuestras
islas Malvinas, Vol. 2 (1939).

J. F. Gravelle, The Falkland (Malvinas) Islands: An
International Law Analysis of the Dispute between
Argentina and Great Britain, Military Law Review, Vol.
107 (1985), p. 5.

L. C. Green, The Falklands, the Law and the War, Yearbook of
World Affairs 1984, p. 89.

L. Green, The Rule of Law and the Use of Force-The Falklands
and Grenada, Archiv des Völkerrechts 24 (1986), p.173-
195.

D. Greig, Sovereignty and the Falkland Islands Crisis,
Australian Yearbook of International Law, Vol. 8 (1983),
p. 20.

W. Grewe, Peaceful Change, in: EPIL, Instalment 7 (1984), p.
378.

H. Gros Espiell, El Caso de las Malvinas y el derecho a la
libre determinación de los pueblos, Anuario Hispano-Luso-
Americano de Derecho Internacional, Vol. 7 (1984), p. 27.

H. Gros Espiell, El conflicto bélico de las Malvinas, las
armas nucleares y el tratado de Tlatelolco, Riv. di Studi
Politici Internaz. 52, (1985), p. 63-80.

H. Grotius, De Jure Belli ac Pacis, Buch 3 (1625), hier
verwendet in der deutschen Übersetzung, hrsg. von W.
Schätzel (1950).

P. Groussac, Les îles Malouines (1910).

E. de la Guardia, La cuestión de las Islas Malvinas en las
Naciones Unidas, Anuario Juridico Interamericano (1986),
p. 97-140.

Hansard, Debates (3rd series), CXI, p. 1321, 1400 (1850).

F. Hassan, The Sovereignty Dispute over the Falkland Islands,
Virginia Journal of International Law, Vol. 23 (1982), p.
53.

M. Hastings, The battle for the Falklands, London (1986).

A. Heffter, Das Europäische Völkerrecht der Gegenwart (1848).

K. Heimburger, Der Erwerb der Gebietshoheit (1888).

A. von der Heydte, Discovery, Symbolic Annexation and Virtual
   Effectiveness in International Law, AJIL Vol. 29 (1935),
   p. 449.

A. von der Heydte, Völkerrecht, Vol. 1 (1958).

M. Hidalgo Nieto, La cuestión de las Malvinas, Contribución
   al estudio de las relaciones hispano inglesas en el siglo
   XVIII (1947).

B. Hillekamps, Der Streit um die Falklandinseln (1978).

A. Hindmarsh, Force in Peace (1933), p. 59.

F. Hoffmann, Sovereignty in dispute: the Falklands/Malvinas
   1493-1982, (1984).

F. von Holtzendorff, Eroberungen und Eroberungsrecht (1872),
   p. 19.

A. Hope, Sovereignty and Decolonization of the Malvinas
   (Falkland) Islands, Boston College International and
   Comparative Law Review, Vol. 6 (1983), p. 391, 408.

C. Hyde, International Law, Chiefly as Interpreted and
   Applied by the United States, Vol. 1 (2nd ed. 1947).

C. Jane, The Question of Tacna-Arica, Transactions of the
   Grotius Society, Vol. 15 (1930), p. 93.

R. Jennings, The Acquisition of Territory in International
   Law (1963).

G. W. Jewkes, Falkland Islands: Declaration on the
   Conservation of Fish Stocks and on Maritime Jurisdiction
   around the Falkland Islands, Internat. J. of Estuarine
   and Coastal L. 2, (1987), p.97-100.

E. Jiménez de Aréchaga, Boundaries in Latin America: uti
   possidetis Doctrine, in: EPIL, Instalment 6 (1983), p.
   45.

D. H. N. Johnson, Acquisitive Prescription in International
   Law, BYIL, Vol. 27 (1950), p. 332.

C. Joyner, Anglo-Argentine Rivalry after the
   Falklands/Malvinas War: Laws, Geopolitics and the
   Antarctic Connection, Lawyer of the Americas 15 (1984),
   p. 467-502.

A. Keller, O. Lissitzyn, F. J. Mann, Creation of Rights of

Sovereignty through Symbolic Acts 1400-1800 (1938).

D. Kinnay, National interest, national honor: the diplomacy of the Falkland crisis, N.Y. (1989).

J.-L. Klüber, Droits des Gens Moderne de l'Europe, Vol. 1 (1819).

M. Kohen, Alternativas para la solución del conflicto por las Islas Malvinas, Rev. de Estud. Internac. 7 (1986), p. 1145-1163.

M. Kohen, La alternativa jurisdiccional en la disputa sobre las Islas Malvinas, Rivista di Studi Politici Internaz. 55 (1988), p.395-424.

M. Kohen, La declaración britanica de una zona de pesca alrededor de Malvinas, Revista Juridica Argentina La Ley (1987), p. 940-948.

D. Koyitek, L'annexion de la Bosnie et de l'Herzegovine et le droit international public (1910).

J. Kunz, Guatemala v. Great Britain: In re Belize, AJIL, Vol. 40 (1946), p. 383.

G. Lang, Boliviens Streben nach freiem Zugang zum Meer (1966).

La Pradelle/Politis, Recueil des arbitrages internationaux, Vol. 2 (1923).

H. Lauterpacht, Recognition in International Law (1948).

M. Lindley, The Acquisition and Government of Backward Territory in International Law (1926).

J. M. Lindsey, Conquest: A Legal and Historical Analysis of the Root of United Kingdom Title in the Falkland Islands, Texas International Law Journal, Vol. 18 (1983), p. 11.

G. Lowell, The Sovereignty Dispute over the Falkland (Malvinas) Islands (1988).

I. MacGibbon, Customary Law and Acquiescence, BYIL Vol. 33 (1958), p. 115.

I. MacGibbon, Some Observations on the Part of Protest in International Law, BYIL Vol. 30 (1954), p. 293.

J. Maguire, The Decolonization of Belize: Self-Determination v. Territorial Integrity, Virginia Journal of International Law, Vol. 22 (1982), p. 849.

Malvinas, Georgias y Sandwich del Sur, ed. by Consejo Argentino para las Relaciones Internacionales (1983).

W. Manning, The Nootka Sound Controversy, Report of the
American Historical Association (1904), p. 279.

G. F. de Martens, Précis du Droit des Gens Moderne, Vol. 2
(1831).

M. McMahon, Conquest and Modern International Law (1940).

J. Meister, Der Krieg um die Falkland-Inseln 1982.
Geschichtliche Hintergründe, Strategie und Taktik der
Kriegsführung, politisch-wirtschaftliche Perspektive,
Osnabrück (1984).

W. Meng, The Caroline, in: EPIL, Instalment 3 (1982), p. 81.

W. Meng, Stimson Doctrine, in: EPIL, Instalment 4 (1982), p.
230.

G. Moncayo, Aspects juridiques de la controverse sur les Iles
Malouines (1959).

C. Moneta, The Malvinas Conflict: Some Elements for an
Analysis of the Argentinian Military Regime's Decision-
making Process (1976-1983), Verf. und Recht in Übersee
17, (1984), p. 457-473.

J. Moreno, Nuestras Malvinas (1938), 7th ed. (1956).

J. Moore, A Digest of International Law, Vol. 1 (1906).

J. Moore, International Adjudications, Vol. 6 (1933).

R. Moro, The history of the South Atlantic conflict: the war
for the Malvinas, N.Y. (1989).

L. Muñoz Azpiri, Historia Completa de las Malvinas, Vol. 1-3
(1966).

B. M. Mueller, The Falkland Islands: Will the Real Owner
Please Stand Up, Notre Dame Law Review, Vol. 58 (1983),
p. 616.

O. Gil Munilla, Malvinas, El Conflicto Anglo-Español de 1770,
Anuario de Estudios Americanos, Vol. 4 (1948).

F. S. Northedge, The Falkland Islands: Origins of the British
Involvement, International Relations, Vol. 7 (1982), p.
2167.

M. Panebianco, Regolamenti comunitari di cooperazione
politica per il mantenimento della pace e della sicurezza
internazionale ne conflitto Falkland-Malvinas, Riv. di
Diritto Eur. 23, (1983), p. 289-324.

A. Parsons, The Falklands Crisis in the United Nations, 31
March-14 June 1982, International Affairs, Vol. 59
(1983), p. 169.

A. Parsons, The Future of the Falklands: A View from Britain, International Relations 9 (1987), p. 131-139.

K. Partsch, Self-Defence, in: EPIL, Instalment 4 (1982), p. 212.

J. Pearce, The Falkland Islands Dispute, The World Today, Vol. 38 (1982), p. 161.

J. Pearce, The Falkland Islands Negotiations, 1965-1982, in: The Falkland Islands Disputes: International Dimensions, Chatham House Special, p. 1.

R. Perl, The Falkland Islands Dispute in International Law and Politics (1983).

N. Petersen, Background of the Falkland Islands Crisis, Department of State Bulletin, Vol. 82 (1983), p. 88.

C. Philippson, Termination of War and Treaties of Peace (1916).

R. Phillimore, International Law, Vol. 3 (1885), p. 41.

M. Pinto, Argentina's Rights to the Falkland/Malvinas Islands, Texas International Law Journal, Vol. 18 (1983), p. 1.

R. Pinto, La prescription en droit international public, RdC Vol. 87 I (1955), p. 387.

K. Pölitz, Die Staatswissenschaften im Lichte unserer Zeit, 5. Teil (2nd ed. 1828).

M. Pondal, Derechos de la Argentinia a las islas Malvinas pasados en autores inglesas, vol. 3 (1966), p. 257.

C. Pop, L'affaire des îles Falkland (1952).

V. Popov, The United States and the Falklands Crisis, International Affairs (Moscow) (1988), p. 121-130.

A. Pradier-Fodéré, Traité de Droit International Public, Vol. 2 (1885).

E. Premoli, Las Malvinas y el Correo argentino, p. 382.

S. Pufendorf, De Jure Naturae et Gentium, Libro Octo, Vol. II (1688).

A. Randelzhofer, Der Falkland-Konflikt und seine Bewertung nach geltendem Völkerrecht, Europa Archiv, Jg. 38 (1983), p. 685.

A. Randelzhofer, Use of Force, in: EPIL, Instalment 4 (1982), p. 265.

G. Rayneval, Institutions du Droit de la Nature et des Gens (1832).

W. Reisman, The Struggle for the Falklands, Yale Law Journal, Vol. 93 (1983), p. 287.

P. Reuter, Droit International Public (3rd ed. 1968).

A. Rigo Sureda, The Evolution of the Right to Self-Determination (1973).

G. Robson, The Falklands Election-Absentee ownership issue heats up politics, The Parliamentarian 71 (1990), p. 112-113.

N. Ronzitti (ed.), La Questione delle Falkland-Malvinas nel Diritto Internazionale (1984).

C. Rousseau, Argentine et Grande-Bretagne, Revue Générale de Droit International Public, Vol. 86 (1982), p. 724.

S. J. Rubin, The Falklands (Malvinas), International Law, and the OAS, AJIL Vol. 76 (1982), p. 594.

F. Saalfeld, Grundriß eines Systems des europäischen Völkerrechts (1809).

F. Sánchez/A. Pablo, La crisis de las Malvinas ante las Naciones Unidas, Rev. de Estud. Internac. 5 (1984), p. 923-953.

M. A. Sánchez, Self-Determination and the Falkland Islands Dispute, Columbia Journal of Transnational Law, Vol. 21 (1983), p. 557.

D. Sanders, Government Popularity and the Falklands War: A Reassessment, British J. of Political Science 17 (1987), p. 281-313.

A. Schacht, Reacción de la América latina y el tercer mundo en relación con el problema de las Islas Malvinas Decisiones de los gobiernos y los organismos latinoamericanos, Anuario Argentino de Derecho Internac. 2 (1984-1986), p. 35-52.

W. Schätzel, Die Annexion im Völkerrecht (1920).

W. Schätzel, Massaua, Wörterbuch des Völkerrechts und der Diplomatie, ed. by K. Strupp, Vol. 2 (1925).

D. Schenk, Kontiguität als Erwerbstitel im Völkerrecht (1978).

U. Scheuner, Naturrechtliche Strömungen im heutigen Völkerrecht, ZaöRV Vol. 13 (1950/51), p. 556.

U. Scheuner, Schriften zum Völkerrecht, ed. by C. Tomuschat

(1984).

T. Schmalz, Das europäische Völkerrecht in 18 Büchern (1817).

M. Schröder, Der Kampf um die Falkland-Inseln - Völkerrechtliche und europarechtliche Aspekte, German Yearbook of
International Law, Vol. 27 (1984), p. 334.

G. Schwarzenberger, The Fundamental Principles of
International Law, RdC Vol. 87 I (1955), p. 258.

G. Schwarzenberger, International Law (3rd ed. 1957).

G. Schwarzenberger, Title of Territory: Response to a
Challenge, AJIL Vol. 51 (1957), p. 308.

A. Schwed, Territorial Claims as a Limitation to the Right of
Self-Determination in the Context of the Falkland Islands
Dispute, Fordham Journal of International Law, Vol. 6
(1983), p. 443.

A. Sørensen, La prescription en droit international, Acta
Scandinavia Iuris Gentium, Nordisk Tidsskrift for
International Ret, Vol. 3 (1932), p. 145.

M. Sørensen, Principes de droit international public, RdC
Vol. 101 III (1960), p. 147.

G. Sperduti, Prescrizione, consuetudine e acquiescenza in
diritto internazionale, Rivista di diritto
internazionale, Vol. 44 (1961), p. 10.

A. Stuyt, Survey of International Arbitrations 1794-1970 (2nd
ed. 1972).

E. Suy, Les actes juridiques unilatéraux en droit
international public (1962), p. 47.

C. Symmons, The Maritime Zones Around the Falkland Islands,
ICLQ 37, (1988), p. 283-324.

H. Taylor, A Treatise on International Public Law (1902).

D. Thürer, Self-Determination, in: EPIL, Instalment 8 (1985),
p. 470.

J. Torre Revello, La Promesa secreta y el Convenio Anglo-
Español sobre las Malvinas de 1771 (1952).

J. Torre Revello, Las Islas Malvinas bajo la Soberania
española, Vol 3, p. 471.

A. Truyol y Serra, The Discovery of the New World and
International Law, Toledo Law Review 1971, p. 305.

E. de Vattel, The Law of Nations or the Principles of Natural

Law, hier zitiert nach der englischen Übersetzung von Charles Fenwick (1916).

A. Verdross, Völkerrecht (5th ed. 1964).

A. Verdross/B. Simma/R. Geiger, Territoriale Souveränität und Gebietshoheit (1980).

S. Verosta, History of the Law of Nations, 1648 to 1815, in: EPIL, Instalment 7 (1984).

Verykios, La prescription en droit international public (1934).

J. H. W. Verzijl, International Law in Historical Perspective: Part III (1970).

F. Vieyra, Las Islas Malvinas y el Derecho Internacional (1984).

R. Vinuesa, El Conflicto por las Islas Malvinas y el Derecho Internacional (1985).

W. Wagner, Der Konflikt um die Falkland-Inseln - Ein Streit um die hergebrachte Weltordnung, Europa Archiv, Jg. 37 (1982), p. 509.

C. H. M. Waldock, Disputed Sovereignty in the Falkland Islands Dependencies, British Yearbook of International Law, Vol. 25 (1949), p. 311.

William Walter, Voyage around the World, Vol. 1 (1784) (Ausgabe 1753).

R. Ware, The Case of Antonio Rivero and Sovereignty over the Falkland Islands, The Historical Journal, Vol. 27 (1984), p. 961.

N. J. Watkins, Disputed Sovereignty in the Falkland Islands: The Argentina-Great Britain Conflict of 1982, Florida State University Law Review, Vol. 11 (1983), p. 649.

H. Weber, "Falkland Islands" oder "Malvinas"? (1977).

H. Weber, Der Streit um die Falklandinseln (Malwinen) als Völkerrechtsproblem, Vereinte Nationen, Vol. 30 (1982), p. 77.

S. H. Wehberg, L'interdiction du recours à la force, RdC Vol. 78 (1951 I), p. 1.

H. Wehberg, Krieg und Eroberung im Wandel des Völkerrechts (1953).

W. Wengler, Völkerrecht, Vol. 2 (1964).

N. Wurmbrand, Die rechtliche Stellung Bosniens und der Herzegowina (1915).

G. Zimmer, Gewaltsame territoriale Veränderungen und ihre Völkerrechtliche Legitimation (1971).

A. Zuppi, El fracaso de la negociación internacional ante la renuncia al uso de la fuerza. Reflexiones en relacion al conflicto anglo-argentino, Derecho 12 (1987), p. 845-852.

Annexes

Annex 1: Geographical Fact Sheet on the Falkland Islands, South Georgia
Island and the South Sandwich Islands, prepared by the office of
the Geographer, U.S. Department of State (without date).
Source: R. Perl, The Falkland Islands Dispute in International Law
and Politics (1983), p. 537.

Falkland Islands

Number of Islands:

Two large islands and approximately 200 smaller islands and islets; East Falkland is 145 km (90 mi.) long and 89 km (55 mi.) wide. West Falkland is 129 km (80
mi.) long and 72 km (45 mi.) wide.

Area:

East Falkland	6604 sq. km. (2550 sq. statute mi.)
adjacent small islands	155 sq. km. (60 sq. statute mi.)
West Falkland	4532 sq. km. (1750 sq. statute mi.)
adjacent small islands	881 sq. km. (340 sq. statute mi.)
Total Area	12173 sq. km. (4700 sq. statute mi.)

In total area the Falklands are a little smaller than the state of Connecticut (5009
sq. miles).

Highest Elevations:

East Falkland (Mt. Usborne)	705 m	(2312 ft.)
West Falkland (Mt. Adam)	700 m	(2297 ft.)

Terrain:

The two main islands, East and West Falkland, are separated by Falkland
Sound, which ranges from 3 to 40 kilometers wide. The coastlines of the islands
are extremely irregular with numerous intricate inlets, many of which form
magnificent potential harbors.

East Falkland is almost cut in half by a pair of deep inlets. The northern portion
of the island is dominated by a rugged east-west range of hills dominated by Mt.
Usborne – the highest peak in the islands. The southern portion, known as
Lafonia, is a low, undulating plain with elevations rarely exceeding 30 meters
above sea level. West Falkland is more hilly than its neighbor. A range of hills
occupies the northern part of the island and another parallels Falkland Sound.
The hills and mountains are covered with thin layers of soil broken by rocky
outcrops, and many of the valleys are characterized by stone "runs" – accumula-
tions of closely packed boulders that look like rivers of stone flowing to the sea.
The lowlands on both islands are boggy in many places.

Climate:

The only long-term climate records available for the Falklands are the records of
observations made in Stanley. There is little precise information on how weather
and climate vary through the archipelago as a whole.

At Stanley the air temperature has never been known to exceed 26.1 °C (79 °F) or to fall below −11.1 °C (12 °F). There is little air pollution. Fog is rare except on the hills and dense fog does not occur. Rainfall at Stanley averages 63.5 cm (25 inches) per year and is spread fairly evenly throughout the year with an average of 16–21 days per month on which precipitation occurs. No month is entirely frost free. Snow falls on about 50 days during the year and has been recorded in every month. Snowfalls however are light and the snow soon melts. The prevailing winds are westerly with three quarters of the winds during the year coming from the southwest, west, and northwest. The average wind speed is approximately 17 mph. Although storms are recorded several times each month, gales with winds in excess of 55–63 mph (a whole gale) are almost unknown. Calm conditions are more frequent than storms.

Climatic Averages for Stanley:

Mean annual windspeed	17 mph
Mean annual rainfall	63.5 cm (25 inches)
Average number of days per year with precipitation	250
Mean annual temperature	5.5 °C (42 °F)

Average Daily Temperatures:

January Max	13 °C (55 °F)	January Min	6 °C (43 °F)
April Max	10 °C (50 °F)	April Min	3 °C (37 °F)
July Max	4 °C (39 °F)	July Min	−1 °C (30 °F)

Average Monthly Rainfall

January	71 mm	(2.8 in.)
April	62 mm	(2.4 in.)
July	57 mm	(2.2 in.)

Flora:

The plant community is similar to the moorland vegetation of upland Britain: grasses, heath, small shrubs, virtualy no trees. Low grade peat is available in abundance.

Fauna:

There are no known indigenous land mammals. Nice, rats, rabbits, hares, cats and, on some islands, a species of patagonian fox and guanaco occur, all were probably introduced by man. There are also sea lions, several species of seals and a number of marine mammals.

Penguins are the most striking feature of the bird life in the Falklands. There are three main species of penguin the rockhopper penguin, the Magellan penguin and the Gentoo penguin. Two other species, the macaroni penguin and the king penguin are found but both are rare. In addition to the penguins, some 60 species of bird are known to breed in the Falklands. Along the shore there are a wide variety of sea birds, including the Black-Browed albatross. Inland, around the freshwater ponds, there are two species of goose, several varieties of duck and a number of other species including several starlings, finches, Cassin's Falcon and the red-backed buzzard.

In addition to the wild life, there are an estimated 630,000 to 650,000 sheep which form the mainstay of the economy. There are also a limited number of cattle and other domestic animals.

Population:

Approximately 1,825 (of which 1,075 live in Stanley – the rest live in 30 or more settlements scattered throughout the islands). This has been a decline from the peak population of 2,400 in 1931. The labor force is about 1,100 of which over 95% are involved with agriculture, primarily sheep.

Telecommunications:

Stanley has a telephone system to which most East Falkland farms are connected, and there is a similar service on West Falkland, centered on Fox Bay. Traffic between the main islands and contact with farms on the smaller islands is by radio telephone.

Broadcasting and the Press:

The Government runs a broadcasting station at Stanley. In 1977 there were 591 ham radio operators in the territory. There is also a government-operated cable broadcasting service in Stanley, which had 274 subscribers in 1977. Periodicals published in the colony, other than the official gazette, are *The Falkland Islands Times* (published monthly) and the *Falkland Islands Journal* (published annually).

Economy:

The islands themselves are of little economic importance. The main industry on the islands is sheep raising and the entire economic organization of the islands is geared to the production of wool. The Falklands produce about two and one half million kilograms of wool each year at a value of about US $ 5 million. (By way of comparison, Argentina produces 155 million kilograms of wool per year and exports 90 million kilograms.) Other economic endeavors – meat and kelp processing, canning, mink ranching – quickly met with failure.

Transportation:

There are no railroads. There are 510 km (317 miles) of road, of which 30 km, in and around Stanley, are paved, 80 km are gravel, and 400 km are unimproved. An all-weather road running from Stanley to Darwin, at the head of Choiseul Sound, is under construction. Although many of the intricate inlets around the coast form magnificent natural potential harbors, Stanley is the only developed port for oceangoing vessels. In addition to Stanley there are four minor ports and many of the small settlements have jetties or landing places. Inter-island boat traffic is important, all heavy and/or bulky goods being shipped by boat. There is one permanent-surface airfield with a runway 1250 meters long, located approximately 8 km from Stanley. There are approximately 35 small unsurfaced landing strips which are utilized by the inter-island air service, which also utilizes float planes. In 1969, 3,867 passengers plus a large volume of cargo were carried by air and the inter-island air service made over 2,000 landings outside of Stanley.

Public Utilities:

A government-owned diesel power station with a capacity of 1,280 kW generating at 3.3 kV, 50 Hertz, supplying power to Stanley, was inaugurated in 1973. Elsewhere most of the settlements and farms have their own private generating plants. A water purification and filtration plant near Stanley provides a sufficient supply of clean water for the town.

Commerce:

All consumer goods, construction materials, vehicles, spare parts – literally everything in the Islands – come to Stanley from England by charter vessel four times a year. The same vessel picks up the wool bales from Stanley warehouses for sale in England. When the ships arrive, Stanley general stores abound with such luxuries as ice cream, butter, frozen chickens, fresh cookies, etc. which are generally sold out within the first few weeks.

Except for the general stores, Stanley has no other commercial establishments: no taxi service, laundries or dry cleaners, dressmakers, barbershops, shoe stores, or whatever.

Beef is relatively cheap but not always available. Since homes rarely have refrigerators and fresh meat is kept outside in a slat-sided cold storage box, butchering is usually postponed during warm months to avoid spoilage. Mutton is available year round and is free except for the delivery charge.

Annex 2: Falkland Islands-Memorandum by the Foreign and Commonwealth Office (127/82-83/FM), December 17, 1982 (Excerpt).

Source: House of Commons, Foreign Affairs Committee, Session 1982-83, Falkland Islands, Minutes of Evidence, Monday 17 January 1983.

Question 1

Why has the British claim to "first discovery" (which was the basis of our claim throughout the nineteenth century) apparently been abandoned?

The UK has not abandoned its claim to "first discovery" of the Falkland Islands, but we accept that there are conflicting claims and that the historical evidence available at present is obscure and uncertain. Our claim to first discovery has never of itself formed the basis for our claim to sovereignty over the Islands.

Question 2

What status does the recorded landing of Captain Strong in 1690 have in international law?

Captain Strong did not take formal possession of the Islands in the name of the Crown. But his recorded landing in 1690 is evidence of British interest in the Islands at that time.

Question 3

Is the British claim to sovereignty by virtue of early settlement (January 1766– May 1774) comparable with that of Spain (1767–1811)?

1. The British claim to sovereignty over the Falkland Islands by virtue of early settlement is based on formal possession of West Falkland and "all the neighbouring islands", claimed by Commodore John Byron in the name of HMG in January 1765. An expedition led by Captain McBride established a settlement at Port Egmont on 8 January 1766. Apart from a period between June 1770, when the British were expelled by the Spanish, and January 1771, when Britain and Spain exchanged Declarations to resolve the problem and restore the *status quo,* British occupation continued until 1774. When Britain withdrew from the Falkland Islands in 1774 for reasons of economy, a lead plaque was left behind declaring the Islands to be the "sole right and property" of George III. There is no record of any written agreement or of any formal commitment by Britain to renounce sovereignty on withdrawal from Port Egmont.

2. Spain's claim to sovereignty (as set out in the Argentine protest of 1833) is based on the formal French occupation of the Falkland Islands in April 1764. The French rights were surrendered to the Spanish Government, in exchange for a financial indemnity, in April 1767. Spanish occupation from 1774 to 1811 was undisturbed by any other power.

3. Britain never accepted the Spanish claim to sovereignty, on the basis of purchase from France, over the Falkland Islands. In particular, the fact that Spain occupied the Islands alone from 1774 to 1811 is not an indication that Britain accepted Spanish sovereignty over them. The Spanish garrison and

settlement on the Islands were withdrawn in 1811, after which the Islands remained uninhabited until the early 1820s, apart from fleeting visits by sealers and whalers of various nationalities.

Question 4

Please provide details of the alleged unofficial British assault on Buenos Aires in 1806–07.

1. In 1806 Commodore Sir Home Popham, a naval officer with ambitions to invade Spain's American dominions and acquire wealth, set sail from Cape Town for Buenos Aires with a force of about 1,640 soldiers, including the Highland 71st Regiment under Brigadier General William Carr Beresford. Popham had taken part in the capture of Cape Town from the Dutch, and having no immediate work to do, had decided on his own responsibility, without any government authority, to take an expedition to South America.

2. One 27 June 1806 Beresford's troops occupied Buenos Aires. The Spanish authorities, despite being warned that a British Force was approaching, were taken by surprise, although there was some skirmishing on the outskirts of Buenos Aires, and the Viceroy, the Marqués de Sobremonte, fled to the interior. Beresford proclaimed British sovereignty, named himself Governor, required an oath of allegiance to King George III from all officials, and shipped nearly $ 1. 1 m of prize money back to England. Beresford also issued a proclamation offering the people of Rio de la Plata the right to administer justice for themselves, the right of private property, freedom to practice Catholicism, and freedom of commerce. The port was opened to ships of all friendly nations, and customs duties were largely reduced, with a preferential tariff for British goods. Beresford also abolished State monopolies of some basic commodities.

3. Popham wrote to Cape Town asking for reinforcements, and the British Government, now heavily committed by Popham's unauthorised action, sent them out to Buenos Aires under Sir Samuel Archmuty, but meanwhile, the people of Buenos Aires, (a population of 40–50,000) helped by Santiago Liniers (a Frenchman serving in the Spanish service) rose against the British invaders and on 12 August forced them to surrender. 300 British soldiers were killed in the fighting. Most of the British prisoners were sent to the interior of Argentina. This Argentine success is known as the Reconquest in Argentina.

4. Following news of the defeat, the British Government sent out further reinforcements, and Lt General John Whitelocke was appointed to command all the troops in the Rio de la Plata area. Sir Samuel Archmuty had occupied Montevideo on 3 February 1807, and Whitelocke, on arrival there in May, assembled more than 10,000 men to retake Buenos Aires. Whitelocke entered Buenos Aires on 5 July 1807, but suffered appalling casualties in bitter fighting (over 400 killed, 650 wounded and 1,925 taken prisoner) at the hands of the well-prepared Buenos Aires militia and citizens. Whitelocke negotiated a truce on 7 July and signed an agreement whereby the entire British expedition would evacuate the River Plate. The Argentinians refer to this event as the Defence.

5. Both Popham and Whitelocke were court-martialled. Popham was severely reprimanded and Whitelocke was dismissed from the service.

Question 5

Did the Argentine formal possession of the islands in November 1820 (not 1829) occasion any British protest?

There was no British protest about Colonel Daniel Jewett's action in taking formal possession of the Falkland Islands in November 1820. There was no British diplomatic representation in Buenos Aires at the time and there is no reason to suppose that HMG knew of Jewett's action when it took place. It should, moreover, be noted that the act of possession was made in the name of a government which was not recognised either by Britain or any other foreign power at the time. No act of occupation followed the ceremony of claiming possession. The Islands remained without any effective government and Jewett quickly returned to Buenos Aires, his ship subsequently being condemned in the United States as a pirate.

Question 6

Is it the case that the United Provinces (Argentina) established a settlement in 1824 and re-established it from 1826–1833? Would this amount to "effective occupation"?

1. The United Provinces did not establish a settlement in 1824. However, in 1826 Louis Vernet, a naturalised citizen of Buenos Aires, untertook a purely private venture to establish a small settlement at Puerto de la Soledad. It was not until January 1828 that the Argentine Government issued a decree giving Vernet three years to establish a colony on East Falkland. On 10 June 1829 the same Government issued a decree setting forth its claimed rights to the Falkland Islands, based on what it regarded as inherited rights from the Spanish Viceroyalty of La Plata. At the same time the Government issued a second decree appointing Vernet as Political and Military Governor of the Falkland Islands. He himself later admitted that the foundation of the colony was entirely his own work, that he received no assistance at any time from his Government and that the Islands paid no taxation.

2. In August 1831, Vernet seized three American sealing ships in an attempt to control fishing in Falkland Islands waters. The US Consul in Buenos Aires promptly denied the Argentine right to regulate seal fishing and in December 1831, Captain Duncan of the USS Lexington landed an armed party at Puerto de la Soledad, destroyed the fort, dispersed the colonists and declared the Islands "free of all government". By the time of the arrival of the British in 1833 the Colony was in a sorry state: deserted apart from a small garrison and a few settlers of various nationalities.

3. HMG do not consider that Vernet's actions in the name of the Argentine Government amounted to effective occupation of the Islands sufficient to confer a valid title on Argentina.

Question 7

On what other occasions besides November 1829 did the British protest Argentine actions?

The British Government protested again on 28 September 1832. This British protest repeated the terms of the previous protest sent in November 1829, stating that the Argentine action assumed an authority "incompatible with His Britannic Majesty's Rights of Sovereignty of the Falkland Islands".

Question 8

Does the disbandment by force of the Argentine settlement by Captain Duncan of USS Lexington in December 1831 establish *terra nullius* status?

Captain Duncan's action is described in the answer to Question 6. In and of itself, this action would not have been sufficient to establish *terra nullius* status.

Question 9

Were the Islands taken by force in January 1833 against Argentine protests?

1. The Falkland Islands were not taken by force in 1833. The facts are as follows. In December 1832 the British Admiralty's instructions to go to the Falklands to exercise Britain's rights of sovereignty reached Captain Onslow of the warship HMS Clio. Captain Onslow occupied Port Egmont on West Falkland, which was uninhabited. He put up a signal post dated 23 December 1832, stating that the Islands belonged to Great Britain. Captain Onslow arrived at Puerto de la Soledad on 2 January 1833. He informed the settlement that he had come to take possession of the Islands in the name of His Britannic Majesty, and persuaded the Buenos Airean Commander, Pinedo, and the remaining members of his garrison, to leave peacefully. On arrival at Buenos Aires Pinedo was severely admonished for offering no resistance. The settlement at the time of Onslow's arrival was a small one comprising a number of settlers of various nationalities, several ex-convicts from the penal reserve, and a few farmhands ('gauchos').

2. Captain Onslow's own account of taking possession of the Falklands was sent in a despatch to the British Chargé d'Affaires in Buenos Aires on 19 December 1833.

"I have the honour to report H.M. Ship under my command visited Port Egmont, West Falkland, 20th December, 1832, and found on Saunders Island the ruins of our Establishment. I left, on what appeared to me to have been Fort George. a signal staff, with the following inscription:–

'Visited by H.B.M.S. Clio for the purpose of exercising the Rights of Sovereignty, 23rd December, 1832.'

"Not finding any inhabitants, or the foreign settlement alluded to in the Commander-in-Chief's instructions, at West Falkland, I sailed to Berkeley Sound, East Falkland, where I arrived on the 2nd January, 1833, and found the Settlement with 25 soldiers, under the Buenos Ayrean Flag; also a Schooner of War (the Sarandi) under the same colours. I waited upon the Commander of the Schooner, and learnt from him that he commanded both by sea and land. He informed me a mutiny had taken place, whilst he was at sea, amongst the soldiers, they had killed their Commander, and were in a state of great insubordination; so much so, that the settlers were afraid to pursue their avocations, and all appeared anarchy and confusion. I had great trouble to persuade twelve of the 'Gauchos' to remain on the Settlement; otherwise cattle could not have been caught, and the advantages of refreshments to the shipping must have ceased. I acquainted the Buenos Ayrean Commander, *civilly,* with the object of my Mission to these Islands, and requested him to haul down the Flag on shore, and to embark his Force 'he being in a possession belonging to the Crown of Great Britain; that I came to these Islands, to exercise the Right of Sovereignty over them.' At first, he consented to do so, provided I would state to him in writing, my Mission. I did so, but only observed, what I had before verbally communicated to him, and declined any further correspondence on the subject. He visited me at 5 a.m. the following morning, to request me to allow the Buenos Ayrean Flag to fly on shore, till the 5th instant; when he would sail, and take with him the force, and such of the settlers as were desirous to leave the Island. I told him his request, as far as it related to the Flag, was inadmissible, he then consented to embark the soldiers, and left me for that purpose; but I observed he still kept the Flag flying on shore. I landed immediately, hoisted the British Flag, and sent an Officer to haul down the Foreign Flag, and to deliver it on board the schooner. He sailed the evening 4th instant, taking with him part of the soldiers, with several of the inhabitants, who wished to return to Buenos Ayres. The mutineers he had placed in irons, on board the British schooner Rapid, by the consent of her Master, previous to my arrival, and had freighted for accordingly to take them to Buenos Ayres. She sailed on the 5th instant."

Question 10

Is it or has it ever been part of the British claim that by 1833 the Islands were *terra nullius?*

The British case has not been put in these terms. However, as indicated in the reply to Question 6, we do not consider that the sporadic acts of occupation and administration by Argentina in the period prior to 1833 were sufficient to confer a valid title on Argentina.

Question 11

On how many occasions between 1833 and 1968 did Argentina protest at Britain's occupation?

The Argentine Government formally protested about the British occupation of the Falkland Islands in 1833, 1834, 1841, 1842, 1849, 1884 and 1888. During this century Argentina has, in official correspondence with HMG and in many other fora, repeatedly placed on record her claim to the Falklands. It is not possible to provide a more precise figure.

Question 12

Is it the case that doubts existed within the Foreign Office over the legality of British actions in this period? (ie 1833–1968)

With a subject as complicated as the history of the Falkland Islands, it is inevitable that individual officials will have differing and in some cases conflicting views. This is natural, but it is also irrelevant. Successive British Governments have made it clear that they have no doubts about our sovereignty over the Falkland Islands.

Question 13

When the HMG suggested putting the issue of the Dependencies before the International Court of Justice in 1948, why was the Falkland Islands excluded?

The Dependencies are legally distinct from the Falkland Islands and the proposals we made to refer the issue of the Dependencies as then constituted to the International Court of Justice were made in the context of encroachment by Argentina and Chile on some of those territories. The question of the Falkland Islands being excluded from these proposals did not therefore arise.

...

Question 15

When was the argument of prescription first advanced?

Prescription is a well-recognised concept in international law, deriving initially from principles of Roman law. There has been no occasion, comparable to that of the making of the unilateral Application to the ICJ concerning the Dependencies, when this or other detailed legal arguments have been formally advanced by HMG in relation to the Falkland Islands.

Question 16

What distinction in international law is there between prescription and acquisitive prescription?

"Prescription" in international law is a means of acquiring title to territory, other than territory which is *terra nullius*, by means of long continued possession. Writers on international law tend to draw a distinction between "acquisitive prescription" and "extinctive prescription". Title by "acquisitive prescription" arises out of long-continued possession where no original source of title can be shown to exist or where possession in the first instance is in the face of an adverse title and the legitimate proprietor has taken no measures to assert his right or has been unable to do so. "Extinctive prescription" has really little to do with title; it is a concept analogous to that of limitation in domestic law and connotes essentially that failure to present a claim within a reasonable time may result in the loss of competence to enforce it. . .

Annex 3:   Malvinas Islands, Statement by the Representative of Argentina, Dr. I. Ruda, Before the UN Sub-committee III of the Special Committee on the Situation with Regard to the Implementation of the Declaration on the Granting of Independence to Colonial Countries and Peoples, September 9, 1964; UN Doc. A/AC 109/106, November 13, 1964 (Excerpt).

Mr. President:

... The Malvinas are a part of the Territory of Argentina, illegally occupied by Great Britain since 1833, following upon an act of force which deprived our country of the possession of the Archipelago. Thereupon, Great Britain then imposed a colonial regime on the area.

Since that time, since 1833, the Argentine Republic has required redress for this outrage suffered, from Great Britain. In the course of these 131 years, we have never consented – and will never consent – to have part of our national territory wrested from us by an illegal and untenable act.

We come to this Sub-Committee to restate our rights to the Malvinas to the International Community, strengthened as we are by the will and the unanimous feelings of the Argentine people, and by a sound and unbroken position of protest at the outrage maintained by all Argentine Governments that have succeeded one another since 1833.

Our intention is to persuade the International Community that the islands in question are an integral part of Argentine territory and that Great Britain's moral and legal duty is to restore them to their true owner, thereby setting the principle of the sovereignty and territorial integrity of states on a sure footing of peaceful international relations. This will fulfil the generous purposes implicit in Resolution 1514 (XV), and thus a long-awaited act of justice will have been rendered.

England is today the possessor of the Malvinas Islands, solely thanks to an arbitrary and unilateral acts of force. The Argentine authorities settled in the Island were expelled by the British Fleet. Legally speaking, this act of force cannot generate nor create any right, and, politically speaking, the events of 1833 were only another aspect of the imperialist policies that the European powers developed for America, Africa and Asia during the XIXth Century. The Malvinas may, perhaps, be considered one of the most outstanding symbols of this fortunately outmoded policy. Under the threats of its guns, the British fleet evicted a peaceful and active Argentine population that was exercising the legitimate rights that the Argentine Republic possessed as the Heir of Spain.

Prior to 1833, the English had never effectively possessed *the totality of the Malvinas Archipelago*. In 1766, they merely founded a fort of Port Egmont on one islet called Saunders Isle. In 1774, they voluntarily abandoned it and only 59 years later they appeared, in order to oust violently the Argentine population and thus set up their sole claim.

But the history of the Malvinas does not begin in 1833 – nor even in 1765. Quite the contrary, these islands were the concern of the Chancelleries of Europe many years earlier, and a number of diplomatic incidents had taken place in the XVIIIth Century that touched upon them.

In order to gauge the illegality of the British act of 1833, the previous events have to be examined – events that are not recounted in document A/AC.109/L.98/Add. 2, which this Sub-Committee had before it, but which surely prove the wantonness of the act committed in 1833.

We shall not go into a study of the question of the discoverer of the Malvinas Islands. Documentation published at the time shows conclusively that the Islands were discovered by Spanish navigators. In Spanish maps and charts of the beginning of the XVIth Century, the Islands already appeared. The first map is that of Pedro Reinel (1522–23) which shows an archipelago situated on the parallel 53°55' latitude South. Then there is the work of Diego Rivero, Principal Cartographer to Charles V who inserted the islands in the Castiglione (1526–27), Salviati (1526–27) and Rivero (1527) maps and also in two charts of 1529. Then come the Maps of Yslario de Santa Cruz of 1541, the Planisphere of Sebastian Gaboto of 1544, the Map of Diego Gutierrez of 1561 and that of Bartolome Olives of 1562 among others. It is to Esteban Gomez, of the Expedition of Magallanes in 1520, that the discovery of the archipelago must be attributed. The area was also sailed by Simon de Alcazaba in 1534 and Alonso de Camargo in 1540. All these were pilots of Spanish ships, sailing towards the Straits of Magellan, also discovered by Spain and one of the bases for its claims over the islands as being adjacent to the said straits. Sarmiento de Gambon, in 1580, took symbolic possession of the Straits in keeping with the usage of the times, and in 1584, founded a settlement.

The Dutch navigator, Sebald de Weert, in his log book for 24 January 1600, stated that he had sighted the Islands. The British contend that in 1592 John Davis, and in 1594 Richard Hawkins had discovered the Archipelago, but the truth of the matter is that the English cartography of the period does not show the islands, nor does there exist any proof that will substantiate the hypothetical discoveries.

Basically, until the middle of the XVIIIth Century, knowledge of the existence of the Islands was not certain in London, and at times they were confused with some imaginary Islands called The Pepys, which shows the degree of ignorance of the period. It was then, in 1748, that on the suggestion of Admiral Anson, England decided to send an expedition to "discover" and settle the Malvinas and Pepys Islands. Great Britain consulted Spain and in view of the latter's objections, desisted from the plan. I should like to quote here the instructions received by the British Representative regarding the communication to be made to the Spanish Court in Madrid: "Since there is no intention of making settlement in any of the afore-mentioned islands and since His Majesty's corvettes wish neither to make nor touch any part of the Spanish coast, His Majesty fails to understand how this project can in any way cause objections from Madrid." The first matter that was aired in this original diplomatic skirmish over the islands was whether the British had any right to enter the regions.

The acts of consultation of 1749, addressed to the Spanish Court, are a clear proof of England's recognition of the rights of Spain over the islands and the coasts of South America, in areas where British ships could neither sail nor trade, much less give themselves to occupation.

We shall not mention the rights granted to Spain by virtue of the Papal Bulls *Inter Coetera* and *Dudum si Quidem* or of their validity erga omnes, nor of the Treaty of Tordesillas between Spain and Portugal, in our defence of the position that we have stated, but we shall speak of the treaties between England and Spain.

The Peace Treaty of 1604 between Spain and England, returned matters and rights to the *Status quo ante bellum*, nullyfying anything that might have been obtained prior to the signature, including the so-called English discovery. Later, in the Treaty of Madrid of 1670, it was agreed that Great Britain would retain all the lands, islands, colonies and dominions she possessed in America; but this recognition of British sovereignty in North America was accompanied by a counter-recognition, whereby in another clause it was stated that "the subjects of Great Britain would not direct their trade to, nor sail in, ports or places which His Catholic Majesty possesses in the above-mentioned Indies, nor will they trade with them". Furthermore, the Treaty of Madrid of 1713 established that "His Britannic Majesty has agreed to issue the most stringent prohibitions and threatened with the most strict penalties, so that no subject or ship of the English Nation shall dare to sail to the Southern Sea nor traffic in any other part of the Spanish Indies". This provision which prohibited sailing and trading by Great Britain in areas not open to traffic at the end of the XVIIth Century was again ratified in 1713 in the Treaty of Utrecht.

Therefore, in 1749, when Great Britain tried to send the first expedition, she could not have considered the Malvinas Islands *res nullius,* and therefore open to appropriation.

In February 1764 there occurred the first essay at colonisation and then it was by a French sailor, Louis Antoine de Bougainville, who founded Port Louis in the Eastern Malvina in the name of the King of France.

Spain considered this settlement an encroachment of her rights and started negotiations with Paris to obtain handing-over of the French settlement. England then dispatched a clandestine expedition which in 1766 founded Port Egmont on Saunders Island, which is near Western Malvina, close to a place that Bougainville had christened Port de la Croisade.

In the meantime, Spain formally protested to the French Government and her rights of dominion were recognized. King Louis XV ordered Bougainville to hand over Port Louis on the compensatory payment of all expenses incurred in. The transfer was solemnly performed in a ceremony held on 1 April 1767 in Port Louis itself, thus recognizing the legal rights of the Spanish Crown to these Islands. Previously, the Government had issued a Royal Bill dated 4 October 1766 which declared the Islands to be dependencies of the Captaincy General of Buenos Aires, and Don Felipe Ruiz Puente was designated Governor. The Spanish were thus left in possession of the Port, whose name was changed to Port Soledad with Spanish settlers about and a military establishment located.

On Saunders Isle, however, there was still the small British garrison of Port Egmont which had been set up in 1766. At the time of the transfer of Port Louis by France to Spain, the British had been silent and made no reservations regarding their presumed sovereignty. Once her difficulties with France were solved, Spain turned her attention to Port Egmont, and the British garrison was evicted from Saunders Isle by the Spanish forces of the Rio de la Plata Fleet under the command of the Governor of Buenos Aires, Buccarelli, on 10 June 1770. Spain had thus reacted clearly and categorically in the face of both intruders and ensured respect for her sovereign rights, since the French had withdrawn after diplomatic pressure and the British after force had been exercised. Britain, however, felt that her honour had been impugned by the use of force against Port Egmont and presented a claim at the Court of Madrid.

The diplomatic negotiations – in which France also participated, were long and involved and a solution was finally arrived at on 22 January 1771. Spain's ambassador to London, Prince de Masserano, declared that his Sovereign "disapproves the aforementioned violent enterprise and binds himself to reestablish matters as they were prior to the episode", adding that "the restoration to His Britannic Majesty of the Port and Fort called Egmont, cannot and must not in any way affect the question of prior sovereign rights over the Malvinas Islands". This declaration was accepted by the Government of His Britannic Majesty on the same day, and under Lord Rochfort's signature, it was stated that His Britannic Majesty would consider the declaration of the Prince of Masserano, with the entire fulfilment of the agreement by His Catholic Majesty as adequate redress for the affront done to the Crown of Great Britain. From this diplomatic act, there stands out, first and outmost, the *acceptance* of the Spanish declaration, an acceptance which does not contain any rejection of the express reservation on the part of Spain, regarding sovereignty over the Islands. Great Britain's silence in the light of such an express, and written, reservation, can only be interpreted in its true form, namely, as an acceptance which, furthermore, is borne out by the original title of the British document, which is not called a "Counter-Declaration", as Lord Palmerston called it in 1834, but "Acceptance", according to the Official Edition of the State Papers of 1771.

We must also point out that in all the documentation covering these diplomatic negotiations, and in all the final papers, mention is only made of the restoration of Port Egmont to the *status quo ante,* but not of the Malvinas Islands in general, which latter area, however, was clearly included in the express declaration regarding Spanish sovereignty. Furthermore, while the negotiations were taking place, and uninterruptedly after it was restored by France, Port Soledad was occupied by the Spanish without Great Britain's making the slightest move nor reservation. What is more, as can be seen in the papers covering the restoration of Port Egmont, it is specified that the United Kingdom receives it from hands of the "Commissioner General of His Catholic Majesty in Port Soledad". Both owners found themselves face to face and respected one another for three years, but those whose rights were more legitimate had to prevail.

On 22 May 1774, the English voluntarily abandoned Saunders Isle, which at the time the British called Falkland Island (in the singular). The English, on leaving the Island, left behind a metal plate reading:– "BE IT KNOWN TO ALL NATIONS THAT FALKLAND'S ISLAND WITH THIS PORT . . .". And we must point out that Falkland's Island is mentioned in the possessive singular, which, linked to the British acceptance of the fact of the Spanish possession of Puerto Soledad, proves that the English claims were limited – during their stay in Port Egmont – exclusively to this settlement and no to entire archipelago.

Fifty-nine years were to elapse before the English returned to the Malvinas and the only title they were able to show in 1833 was this metal plate which had been removed by the Spanish and taken to Buenos Aires. Great Britain's astounding claim in 1833 was based on a presumed possession in the form of a metal plate, which was contrary to international law of the period which required, as proof and condition of dominion, effective possession.

We do not wish to go into the discussion that has lured so many scholars, namely the existence of a secret pact between the British and Spanish Crowns regarding the honourable redress in the form of the restoration of Port Egmont, and its subsequent abandonment by the British, but the English silence on the Spanish reservation regarding the Malvinas Islands is significant, as is also the fact that the British quitted these Islands almost immediately on the Spanish transfer. The truth of the matter Mr. Chairman, what we can be sure of, is that the British only stayed in the island for three years after the return of Port Egmont and that they did not go back until 1833. Fifty-nine years elapsed, during which, with no protest whatever from Great Britain, the islands remained in the possession of Spain first, and then of Argentina, which Governments exercised all prerogatives not only in Port Soledad, but in the entire Archipelago and the neighbouring seas, with the consent of the British Crown.

Spain exercised all sorts of acts of dominion over the Malvinas Islands until the Revolution of May 1810, which was the beginning of Argentine independence.

In 1776 she created the Vice-Royalty of the Rio de la Plata, including the above-mentioned islands which belonged to the Governorship of Buenos Aires – and England said nothing.

In 1777, all buildings and installations of Port Egmont were razed in order to avoid awakening the cupidity of ships flying other flags – and England still said nothing.

The Spanish Government named numerous and successive Governors of the Islands between 1774 and 1811 who exercised uninterrupted authority over them and their neighbouring seas – and still England said nothing.

England's silence over the Malvinas between 1774 and 1829 confirms her recognition of Spanish rights and her desire not to return to the Archipelago.

Not only did Spain exercise effective possession between 1774 and 1811, but Great Britain did not bring to bear any rights over Port Egmont in the different instruments dated around the end of the XVIIIth Century and dealing with territorial questions, although she had complete and public knowledge of the sovereign occupation of the Archipelago by Spain. Thus, in the 1783 Peace Treaty of Versailles, at the end of the North American War of Independence, there was a ratification of the previous stipulations of 1670, 1713 and others that prohibited the English from sailing in the Southern Seas. Even further, the conflict that was motivated by England's trying to found a settlement on Nootka Sound, on the West Coast of Canada, led to the signing of the Saint Lawrence Convention of 1790. This agreement granted freedom of navigation to the British in the Pacific on three conditions: The First, that this navigation would not be a pretext for illegal trading with Spanish dominions, it being prohibited within "ten maritime leagues from any coasts already occupied by Spain"; the second, that there be free trade between the settlements founded in the North Pacific since 1789 and those subsequently to be set up, and finally, article 7 of the convention established that "It has also been agreed, regarding both the Eastern and Western coasts of South America, and its adjacent Islands, that the respective subjects shall in the future make no settlements in those parts of the coasts situated South of the said coasts and of the adjacent islands already occupied by Spain".

This agreement did away with the contention that there were closed seas on the East or West coasts of America. But the British right to establish colonies was only recognized regarding the coasts of North America; with regard to other areas, the Spanish Crown only acknowledged mere fishing rights, and the parties bound themselves not to establish new colonies in the South Atlantic or Pacific, and what existed would remain in status quo. This was precisely the interpretation given by Great Britain to the Nootka Sound Convention signed after the incident on the Canadian frontier in 1826 between Great Britain and the United States.

When, in the 1790 Convention, Great Britain recognized the status quo existing in the South of America, she was thereby giving the definitive legal proof of her lack of grounds upon which to base her claims to set up settlements of any permanence in the Malvinas. It is, by the same token, one of the grounds for the Argentine claims over the Islands of the South. The English had no right to people the South of the coasts or Islands already occupied by Spain, that is to say, including the South of the Malvinas and of Puerto Deseado in the Patagonia. Regarding the Malvinas themselves, there had been a renunciation of any rights England might have contended, for the commitment was not to settle any place already occupied by Spain, aside from not sailing within 10 leagues of the coast.

In one word, gentlemen, after Great Britain's voluntary abandonment of Port Egmont in 1774, Spain was left as unchallenged and unchallengeable Mistress of the Malvinas Islands, and as such, she exercised absolute sovereignty over them, she occupied them, she designated authorities for them, without the slightest protest on the part of Great Britain. International instruments of the nature of those I have just cited were signed, which even reaffirmed Spain's rights, and these were the rights that the Argentine Republic inherited in 1810.

The process of Argentine independence was a long and painful one. Its armies travelled over half of America, helping in the independence of the sister countries; and this struggle was carried on without outside help and at the cost of great sacrifices. Yet, in 1820, the Government of the Argentine Republic sent the frigate "Heroina" to the Malvinas. Don David Jewett, commanding the ship, notified vessels in Malvinas waters of the Argentine laws regulating sealing and fishing in the area and informed them that trespassers would be sent to Buenos Aires to stand trial. Furthermore, in a solemn ceremony, he took formal possession of the islands that belonged to Argentina as the Heir of Spain. There was no opposition to the statement of Argentine rights over the archipelago, nor was any claim raised against it, despite the fact that the communication was published in newspapers in the United States and elsewhere.

In 1823 the Government of Buenos Aires designated Don Pablo Areguati Governor of the Malvinas Islands.

That same year, the government granted lands and also the rights of exploitation of wild cattle on the islands and of fishing on the Western Malvina, to Don Jorge Pacheco and Don Luis Vernet. An expedition took out the supplies needed for the new settlement, but it only prospered partially, due to climatic conditions which were unfavourable. In January 1826, the concessionaries again sent groups of families and these managed to remain.

The colonizing enterprise in the archipelago gained ground in the course of subsequent expeditions which took men, supplies and animals to Port Soledad.

In 1828, a decree was signed granting Vernet concessions in Eastern Malvinas and, in its desires to encourage the economic development of the archipelago, the Government of Buenos Aires declared the settlement exempt from all taxes excepting those required to ensure the upkeep of the local authorities.

At no time did England object to the Argentine settlement of the Malvinas, despite the fact that extremely important legal acts had taken place between the two countries, such as the signing of the Treaty of Friendship, Trade and Navigation of February 1825. This instrument does not contain any British reservation whatever on Malvinas Islands, and despite the action of the Commander of the "Heroina" in 1820 and other acts that the Government had carried out and authorized touching the Islands.

The settlement established under the protection of laws of the Government of

Buenos Aires had prospered and was in good condition in 1829.

This being the case, in 10 June of that same year, 1829, the Government of Buenos Aires created the Political and Military Commandancy of the Malvinas Islands, located in Port Soledad, and whose competence included all the islands adjacent to Cape Horn on the Atlantic side. The same Mr. Luis Vernet was named Commandant.

It was then, in the heyday of the expansionist eagerness of Great Britain, that the English interest in the Archipelago was awakened, an interest that was nothing but the renewal of its old aspirations of possessing lands in the South Atlantic. That had been the intention that had led Great Britain to invade Buenos Aires in both 1806 and 1807, being violently repulsed by the population both times. She had also occupied the Cape of Good Hope on the southernmost tip of Africa in 1806 and which served as a spearhead for later expansion. In 1815 she took Saint Helena and in 1816 the Isle of Tristan da Cunha.

The expansionist ambitions in the South Atlantic were again resumed by the British Admiralty, which hungered for a naval station on the strategic route, via Cape Horn, to Australia and the South Pacific, where Britain's aspirations had to compete with another European power.
Commercial interests linked with the fishing wealth also moved her and these were all tied in with her strategic desires to own a base in the South Atlantic.

Impelled by these interests, Great Britain decided to protest against the establishment of the Political and Military Command. On 10 November 1829 she made her claim, stating that the Argentine Government had assumed "an authority that is incompatible with the Sovereign Rights of His Britannic Majesty over the Islands".

Here, a brief parenthesis should be made in order to recall some of the salient facts. In 1766, England had clandestinely founded a fort and a port of Egmont on the Isle of Sounders. In 1770, the English were forced out by the Spanish fleet. In 1771 they again occupied Port Egmont, following upon reparation offered by Spain, with the corresponding reservation of sovereignty. In 1774, three years after the transfer, the British voluntarily abandoned Port Egmont and from then on, from 1772 until 1829, for over half a century, they made neither protest nor claims on the Spanish and later Argentine occupations. The truth of the matter is that during all that time, Great Britain was not interested in the Malvinas, and she only became so and turned her eyes to them when they played a part in her plans of imperial expansion. The archipelago assumed great importance for colonial navigation.

There are, in point of fact, two situations, that are independent of one another, namely a) The XVIIIth Century incident that ended for Great Britain with her withdrawal from the Islands, and b) a totally new situation, in 1829, determined by strategic factors connected with her access to her possessions in the Pacific which were threatened at the time and her fishing and sealing interests.

But it was not only the British ambitions and interests that came into play. The United States also showed an interest in protecting the sealing activities of her nationals, off the Malvinas coasts. When Vernet endeavoured to implement Argentine legislation relating to fishing, and held up three North American vessels, another powerful country came into the picture.

On May 31, 1831 the North American Corvette Lexington appeared before Port Soledad – she flew the French flag and carried signals asking for pilots and headed for the wharf. Thus the American sailors managed to land, destroyed the settlement and committed other acts of violence. The reason for this act was the rejection by the Argentine Government of a claim by the North American Consul wereby he sought the immediate return of one of the still detained fishing vessels. He also wanted the Politico-Military Commandant of the Malvinas to stop any intervention in the activities of the United States citizens in the area. The Lexington incident provoked a diplomatic clash between Argentina and the United States, which wound up with a virtual breaking off of diplomatic relations between the two countries.

During his stay in Buenos Aires, the representative of the United States established close relationship with the Chargé d'Affaires of Great Britain and their talks, which are documented in the correspondence published by their respective countries, shows that at a given moment, the interests of these two powerful states united in order to oust a young and weak country from the Malvinas Islands.

In 1832, for the third time, Argentina returned to settle in Puerto Soledad, and a new Civil and Military Governor was designated.

But the British die was cast: the British Admiralty instructed Captain Onslow to set sail for the Malvinas, and on January 3, 1833, the corvette Clio appeared off Puerto Soledad. A small Argentine vessel, the Sarandi was riding at anchor. The English captain insisted that the Argentine detachment withdraw. The difference in numbers allowed of no possible fight and added to that was the element of surprise.

The Argentine leader replied to the order by saying that "he held Great Britain responsible for the outrage and the violation of the respect due to the Republic, and its rights that were being assaulted by force – as blind as it was irresponsible" and added that "he was withdrawing, but that he refused to lower his flag".

The British thereupon lowered the Argentine flag and by force, occupied Port Soledad. Thus, by plunder, another chapter of colonial history was written. Almost all the Argentine inhabitants of the islands were then evicted.

On January 3, 1833, almost 60 years after the voluntary withdrawal of 1774, the British committed the act of force in Port Soledad in the Island of Eastern Malvina. In a place where they had never been. And by the next year, they had occupied the entire archipelago.

What I have just described is an act that is simple and easy to understand. In 1833, Great Britain, having no right on her side, could only resort to force in order to occupy the Islands. And the situation has not changed since that time: Force is still the cornerstone of Britain's presence in the Archipelago.

At the beginning of this statement we said that this act of force, this arbitrary and unilateral act was never and shall never be consented to by the Argentine Republic; and we added that it cannot generate nor create any rights for Great Britain.

But the Argentine reaction was not long in coming. The population of Buenos Aires gave vent to its indignation at the incident and in the Islands themselves, the rest of the settlers who resisted the invaders, were taken and sent to London for trial under different pretexts and never returned. On January 15, the Government protested to the British Chargé d'Affaires in Buenos Aires, who replied that he lacked instructions. On the 22nd January the protest was reiterated and the English Minister renewed his passive stand. In the meantime, the Minister Manuel V. Maza notified the American Foreign Offices of the events in a circular. The reply of Brazil is worthy of mention, for that country instructed its Minister in Great Britain to offer to his Argentine colleague in London "the most frank and diligent cooperation to ensure success to his endeavours". Bolivia also replied that she would be among the first countries "to seek reparations for such a dire *outrage*".

On 24 April 1833, the Argentine representative in London, Don Manuel Moreno, on instructions from Buenos Aires, presented a note of protest to His Britannic Majesty's Government, which he reiterated on June 17, in a lengthy and documented protest memorandum. Viscount Palmerston replied on 8 January 1834 contending that the rights of Great Britain "were based on the original discovery and subsequent occupation of the said Islands", arguments which Moreno rejected on 29 December 1834.

Since then, whenever possible, the Argentine Republic has repeated its protests at the act of force and illegal occupation.

Gentlemen: The Argentine Republic was a recently independent country, lacking in the material means of the great powers of the period yet it reacted with determination at the outrage suffered. Protests were raised a few days after the plunder of Port Soledad. Taking into account the distances and the difficulties through which the country was going, more speed could not have been expected. The outrage caused a wave of indignation all over the country and that feeling of protest still imbues the Argentines today.

Mr. Chairman, in the course of the last 131 years, we have never ceased to clamour to the deaf ears of Great Britain for the restoration of the Islands which are ours. Today, a new hope is offered the Argentine Republic, a hope that we may find the understanding and the support of the United Nations, one of whose noblest purposes is to end the colonial era all over the world.

The colonialist policies of that period have an outstanding example in the case of the Malvinas Islands.

At that time, advantage was taken of a country that was in the throes of organization and struggling, as are many new countries in Africa and Asia today, to achieve political and economic progress.

We defended ourselves on the strength of our dignity and of law, but we had no means to offer resistance. Our friends, the new nations of Latin America, also in the midst of their own formation, could only tender us their moral support for they shared our material weakness. Now was there, then, an international forum to which we might carry our complaint and the European Concert was apportioning the world and its spheres of influence according to its own interests. It was not the age of justice – it was the age when the Great Powers used force and Great Britain acted in the Malvinas in keeping with the habits of the day.

According to Lord Palmerston's note, Great Britain contended in 1834 that "the discovery and subsequent occupation" constituted the source of her rights, and added that these rights were given an additional sanction by the fact that Spain had restored the Port of Egmont to Great Britain in 1771.

As far as the discovery is concerned, we have seen that if anyone first sighted the Malvinas, it was the Spanish navigators. Apart from the historical facts, the legal problem must be examined in the light of the moment when the problem was born and we must bear in mind the fact that since the end of the XVIth Century, international law provided that for the acquisition of *res nullius* territories, occupation was necessary, and it prevailed over discovery which only offers preliminary and precarious rights and titles. This title – called inchoate title – had to be affirmed by means of effective occupation; in the XVIIIth Century neither discovery nor fictitious or symbolic occupation sufficed.

Regarding occupation, it can in no way be termed, firstly, "subsequent" to discovery since the first English sailor who is supposed to have sighted the Islands, according to the British themselves was Davis in 1592, and it was only 174 years later, that is, in 1766 that the English settled in Port Egmont. The presence of the English, challenged by the Spanish, was only in a location called Port Egmont, and lasted between 1766 and 1774, with the protests of Spain and the resulting events and voluntary abandonment. The first effective occupation was that of France in 1764, which recognized the rights of Spain, restoring the settlement to her, whereby the effective Spanish occupation antedates the British presence. The latter continued during the eight years when the English were in Port Egmont and afterwards. It has been correctly stated that the English occupation only showed negative facets: it was illegal – since it violated existing treaties; it was clandestine, that is, it was kept secret until the Spanish found out about it; it was belated, because it took place after the effective occupation of the French who handed it over to Spain; it was challenged, because Spain resisted it and made an express reservation in its regard; it was partial, because it only applied to Port Egmont whilst Spain possessed Port Soledad and the entire Archipelago; it was fleeting, for it only lasted eight years; it was precarious, for after 1774 it was no more. On the other hand, while the Spanish occupation preceded the English, it coexisted with it without disturbance and outlasted the abandonment by England. The 1833 British arguments only serve to cloak a clear fact: the use of arms against a new nation that possessed the Islands by virtue of its rights as the Heir to Spain, rights which were unchallengeable.

Gentlemen, In one hundred and thirty three years, we have been unable to evict Great Britain from the position into which she entrenched herself by force. But times have changed and today we are witnessing the twilight of colonialism, which is why British presence in the islands is an anachronism and must be eliminated. The days are gone forever when a young nation lacks voice and decision in international affairs. In the course of its entire history, my country has opposed this way of handling international relations, and we have constantly given proof of our sense of responsibility and our willingness to settle our international disputes peacefully. Almost the entire length of the Argentine frontiers were established by arbitration, without our even having resorted to violence to settle territorial problems.

Furthermore, in 1933, in the VIIth American International Conference in Montevideo, the American States set forth a fundamental doctrine of American law when they stated that "The Contracting States set forth as a definitive norm of conduct their specific obligation not to recognize territorial acquisitions or special advantages obtained by force, whether this be by the use of arms, by threatening diplomatic representations or by any other coercive measures. The territory of States is inviolable and cannot be the object of military occupation or of other measures of force imposed by another State, whether it be directly or indirectly, for any reason or even of a temporary nature."

Convinced of this, we signed the Charter of the United Nations in 1945 not only as a peace-keeping machinery and to ensure international peace and security, but also as a system whereby to find just solutions to international problems, and especially those that emanated from the colonial system. Even at the San Francisco Conference, the Argentine made an express reservation regarding our country's rights over the Malvinas Islands.

From the inception of this Organization, Argentina was well aware of the importance of Art. 73 e of the Charter. As soon as ever Great Britain began to supply information on the Malvinas, the Argentine Republic informed the United Nations – as it had so often in the past – of its rights of sovereignty over the territory. And thus, through the General Assembly, Argentina yearly reminded the organization of its rights, and stated that the information supplied by the United Kingdom on the Malvinas Islands, the Georgias and the South Sandwich in no way affected Argentine sovereignty over these territories, that the occupation by Britain was due to an act of force, never accepted by the Argentine Government and that it reaffirms its imprescriptible and inalienable rights. At the same time, in the Organization of American States, my country has advocated an end to colonial situations in America.

The Xth Inter-American Conference of Caracas in 1954 adopted Resolution 96 on Colonies and Territories occupied in America, and declared "that it is the will of the peoples of America that an end be put to colonialism maintained against the will of the peoples and also the occupation of territories". It proclaimed also "the solidarity of the American Republics with the just claims of the Peoples of America regarding territories occupied by extra-continental countries", and, finally, it repudiated "the use of force in the perpetuation of colonial systems and the occupation of territories in America".

After 1955, the United Nations was renewed by the admission of new Members, especially of those that emerged from the process of de-colonization imposed on the European powers by the new political structure of the world. Thus, a new perspective was created in our over one-hundred-year-old claim for the Islands.

When in 1960, with our support, there was adopted the now historic Resolution 1514 (XV), "Declaration on the Granting of Independence to Colonial Countries and Peoples", the process of decolonization all over the world took on a new impetus.

Clearly, calmly and constructively, our country supported and will support this process of decolonization which is taking place today with the help of the United Nations. We ourselves being a product of a similar process of independence – which we achieved by our own means – we are consistent with our historical tradition and determined supporters of the elimination of the colonial system. Thus, we wholeheartedly voted in favour of the additional resolutions to 1514 (XV), that is, Resolutions 1654 (XVI), 1810 (XVII) and 1956 (XVIII).

Today, this Sub-Committee III of the Committee of 24 is to take up the question of the Malvinas Islands.

The Malvinas Islands are in a different situation from that of the classical colonial case. De facto and de jure, they belonged to the Argentine Republic in 1833 and were governed by Argentine authorities and occupied by Argentine settlers. These authorities and these settlers were evicted by violence and not allowed to remain in the territory. On the contrary, they were replaced, during those 131 years of usurpation, by a colonial administration and a population of British origin. Today the population amounts to 2172 souls, and it is periodically renewed to a large extent by means of a constant turn-over: thus in 1962, 411 persons left and 268 arrived; in 1961, 326 left and 244 arrived; in 1960, it was 292 that left and 224 who arrived. This shows that it is basically a temporary population that occupies the land and one that cannot be used by the colonial power in order to claim the right to apply the principle of self-determination.

Our Government holds, and has thus stated it to successive General Assemblies, that this principle of self-determination of peoples, as set forth in Article 1, paragraph 2 of the Charter, must, in these exceptional cases, be taken in the light of the circumstances which condition its exercise.

Therefore, we consider that the principle of self-determination would be ill-applied in cases where part of the territory of an independent state has been wrested – against the will of its inhabitants – by an act of force, by a third State, as is the case in the Malvinas Islands, without there being any subsequent international agreement to validate the *de facto* situation and where, on the contrary, the aggrieved state has constantly protested the situation. These facts are specifically aggravated when the existing population has been ousted by this act of force and fluctuating groups of nationals of the occupying power supplanted them.

Furthermore, the indiscriminate application of the principle of self-determination to a territory so sparsely populated by nationals of the colonial power, would place the fate of this territory in the hands of the power that has settled there by force, thus violating the most elementary rules of international law and morality.

The basic principle of self-determination should not be used in order to transform an illegal possession into full sovereignty under the mantle of protection which would be given by the United Nations.

This strict interpretation of the principle of self-determination is specifically based upon Resolution 1514 (XV), whose main aim should not be forgotten, namely: to end colonialism in all its forms.

After recognizing the principle of self-determination, the Preamble of that Resolution states that the peoples of the world "ardently desire the end of colonialism in all its manifestations". It also adds that "all peoples have an inalienable right to complete freedom, the exercise of their sovereignty and the integrity of their national territory".

Article 2 of the Declaration reaffirms the principle whereby "All peoples have the right to self-determination; by virtue of that right they freely determine their political status and freely pursue their economic, social and cultural development".

But this article is conditioned by article 6, for it clearly states that "Any attempt aimed at the partial or total disruption of the national unity and the territorial integrity of a country is incompatible with the purposes and principles of the Charter of the United Nations". In its article 7, while reaffirming the above, it goes on to state that "All States shall observe faithfully and strictly the provisions of the Charter of the United Nations, the Universal Declaration of Human Rights and the present Declaration on the basis of equality, non-interference in the internal affairs of all States, and respect for the sovereign rights of all peoples and their territorial integrity".

The purposes of the Resolution – as its wording makes manifest – is quite in keeping with the true interpretation of the principle of self-determination insofar as the Malvinas Islands are concerned. Colonialism in all its manifestations must be brought to an end; national unity and territorial integrity must be respected in the implementation of the Declaration. It shall not be used to justify the outrages perpetrated in the past against newly independent countries.

Resolution 1654 (XVI), pursuant to which this Special Committee was established, stresses this fact when in its Preamble it states the deep concern on the part of the Assembly that "contrary to the provisions of paragraph 6 of the Declaration, acts aimed at the partial or total disruption of national unity and territorial integrity are still being carried out in certain countries in the process of decolonization".

The American Regional Organization adopted a resolution at its Xth Foreign Ministers' Conference setting forth "the need for extra-continental countries having colonies in the territories of America, speedily to conclude the measures defined according to the terms of the Charter of the United Nations in order to allow the respective peoples fully to exercise their right to self-determination, in order once and for all to eliminate colonialism from America". But bearing particularly in mind the situation of states whose territorial unity and integrity are affected by foreign occupation, this same resolution went on to state that it "does not refer to territories under litigation or the subject of claims between extra-continental countries and some countries of the hemisphere". This resolution was also transmitted to the United Nations.

The future of these islands, separated from the Argentine Republic, would be both illogical and unreal. Geographically they are close to our Patagonian coasts, they enjoy the same climate and have a similar economy to our own south-lands. They are part of our own continental shelf, which, by International Law and since the Geneva Conventions of 1958, belongs in all rights to the coastal State.

Their economic development on stable basis is linked to that of the Argentine Republic with which they at present have neither communication nor direct maritime trade because of the prevailing situation.

Furthermore, if we carefully analyze the same document submitted by the Secretariat of the United Nations on the strength exclusively of the information supplied by the British, we note how the colonial system manifests itself in the economic side of the life of the Islands. Ownership of the land is virtually in the hands of the Falkland Islands Company Limited, among whose Board of Directors – located in London – figure members of the British Parliament. This Company – which we have no compunction in labelling monopolistic – owns 1,230,000 acres of the best land, in outright freehold, and on them three hundred thousand sheep graze. The next largest land-owner is the British Crown with 56,500 acres. The company, and its subsidiaries, control all the export and import trade. It also holds the wool monopoly which is the main source of wealth of the Islands.

British domination of the Malvinas Islands is not only contrary to the Charter of the United Nations, but it also creates a sterile situation in a territory which could enjoy a greater economic boom if linked to its natural and legal owners. Proof positive of this is the fact that the statistics for 1912 show that there were 2295 inhabitants in the Malvinas Islands and that since that time the population has remained stagnant. According to a census taken on 18 March 1962, 2172 souls live in the Islands. It is the only human family in America that instead of increasing, shrinks.

Gentlemen: the United Kingdom has no right to continue in the Islands, nor does the spirit of our day allow of it.

Annex 4: G. Anson (Walter, ed.), A Voyage round the
world in the years 1740-44 (1748), p. 85 ff.
(Report on an English expedition in the year
1744).

As therefore it appears that our future expeditions to the South-Seas must run a considerable risque of proving abortive whilst we are under the necessity of touching at Brazil in our passage thither, an expedient that might relieve us from this difficulty would surely be a subject worthy of the attention of the Public; and this seems capable of being effected by the discovery of some place more to the southward where ships might refresh and supply themselves with the necessary sea-stock for their voyage round Cape Horn. And we have in realty the imperfect knowledge of two places, which might perhaps on examination prove extremely convenient for this purpose; the first of them is Pepys's Island, in the latitude of 47° South, and laid down by Dr. Halley, about eighty leagues to the eastward of Cape Blanco, on the coast of Patagonia; the second is Falkland's Isles, in the latitude of 51°½ nearly South of Pepys's Island. The first of these was discovered by Captain Cowley, in his voyage round the World in the year 1686; who represents it as a commodious place for ships to wood and water at, and says it is provided with a very good and capacious harbour, where a thousand sail of ships might ride at anchor in great safety, that it abounds with fowls, and as the shore is either rocks or sands, it seems to promise great plenty of fish. The second place, or Falkland's Isles have been seen by many ships, both French and English, being the land laid down by Frezier in his chart of the extremity of South America, under the title of the New Islands. Woods Rogers, who ran along the N. E. coast of these Isles in the year 1708 tells us that they extended about two degrees in length, and appeared with gentle descents from hill to hill and seemed to be good ground with woods and harbours. Either of these places as they are Islands at a considerable distance from the coast, may be supposed from their latitude to lie in a climate sufficiently temperate. It is true they are too little known to be at present recommended for proper places of refreshment for ships bound to the southward: But if the Admiralty should think it adviseable to order them to be surveyed, which might be done at a very small expence by a vessel fitted out on purpose; and if on this examination one or both of these places should appear proper for the purpose intended, it is scarcely to be perceived of what prodigious import a convenient station might prove, situated so far to the southward, and so near Cape Horn.

The Duke and Duchess of Bristol [Woods Roger's ships] "were but thirty-five days from their losing sight of Falkland's Isles to their arrival at Juan Fernandes, in the South-Seas. And as the returning back is much facilitated by the western winds, I doubt not but a voyage might be made from Falkland's Isles to Juan Fernandes, and back again in little more than two months. This even in time of peace might be of great consequence to this nation, and in time of war would make us masters of those seas.

* MOUSE MAT.
* MAYBE RAM ?! FOR LAPTOP.
* 2 MORE KEN. LOCKS. TEST BEFORE !!
* FOOD !!

Annex 5: Letter written by the Duke of Bedford, then in England Secretary of State for the Southern Department, addressed to the English Ambassador to Spain, of April 24, 1750.
Source: J. Bedford, Correspondence, Vol. II (1843), p. 48.

Whitehall, April 24, 1750

Sir,

The Board of Admiralty having proposed to his Majesty some time ago the sending out two frigates in order to make discoveries in the American seas, which might tend to the improvement of commerce and navigation in general, the King, always willing to promote the good and walfare of this subjects was graciously pleased to approve in their intention, and accordingly the sloops designed for this service are now actually fitted out in the river Thames, in order to proceed upon the intented discovery at the proper time of year for arriving in those seas during the good weather. But, as this scheme has been represented by Major General Wall, his Catholic's Minister at this court, liable to many representation at the court where you reside, and which might possibly tend towards creating an uneasiness and suspicion between his Majesty and the Catholic King, I am commanded to enclose you for your information a copy of the Earl of Sandwich's letter to me, explaining the design of the Board of Admiralty in the equipment now intented. Upon the perusal of it you will find that the full discovery of Pepys and Falkland Islands, lying to the eastward of Cape Blanco, was the first object of his undertaking, which, when completed, the ship were to return to Brazil to refit, to proceed afterwards into the South Sea in order to make further discoveries there. As these latter part of the scheme cannot be carried into execution without wooding and watering at the island of Juan Fernandez, and possibly coming some times within sight of the Spanish coasts of Chile and Peru, it is apprehended here that an attempt of this nature may alarm the court of Madrid, and give them suspicions, than his Majesty, though at present in peace with that crown, is preparing to be ready to attack upon them upon a future rupture, in a part where they are undoubtedly weak, and of which they must consequently be more than ordinarily jealous. This having been represented to the King in the light I have now stated to you, He has been pleased to direct the Admiralty to proceed no further in the projected discoveries, than what is contained in the first part of the plan laid down, and to direct the sloops to return here, after they have searched sufficiently the seas about Pepys and Falkland Islands.

As there is no intention of making any settlement in either of these islands, and as his Majesty's sloos will neither touch upon or even make any port of the Spanish coast, the King can in no shape apprehend that this design can give any umbrage at Madrid, but as it is his intention not only to adhere strictly to all that is stipulated in the last definitive treaty, but also to show all possible means of his desire to cement more and more the union and harmony so happily established between his crown and that of Spain, I am commanded to give you this full and circumstancial account of this affairs.

Annex 6: French inscription on the Islands (February 1764).
Source: R. Perl, op. cit., p. 321.

Etablissement des Iles Malouines, situées au 51 deg. 30 min. de lat. aust., et 60 deg. 50 min. de long, occid. merid. de Paris, par la Frégate l'Aigle, Capitaine P. Duclos Guyot, Capitaine de Brulot, et la Corvette Le Sphinx, Capitaine F. Chénard de la Girandais, Lieut. de Frégate, armées par Louis Antoine de Bougainville, Colonel d'Infanterie, Capitaine de Vaisseau, Chef de l'Expédition, G. de Nerville, Capitaine d'Infanterie, et P. D'Arboulin, Administrateur Général des Postes de France.

Construction d'un Obélisque décoré d'un Medaillon de Sa Majesté Louis XIV., sur les plans d' A. l'Huillier, Eng. Géogr. des Camps et Armées, servant dans l'Expédition; sous le Ministère d' E. de Choiseul, Duc de Stainville, *en Février, 1764.*

Avec ces mots pour exergue: *Conamur tennes grandia.*

Annex 7: Declaration on the occassion of the taking
of possession of the Islands, made by
Bougainville, April 5, 1764.
Source: L. Muñoz Azpiri, Historia Completa
de las Islas Malvinas, Vol. 2 (1966), p. 10.

Fuerte Saint Louis, 5 de abril de 1764.

Nous etats majors et officiers mariniers de la fregate du Roy des L'Aigle et le Spinx [sic], certifions que faisant notre route pour chercher les terres à l'Est de l'Amérique Meridionale, le mardy trente un Janvier a six heures du matin nous avons eu connoissance d'une terre dans l'est de nous distante de six lieues, par la latitude des cinquante degrez cinquante huit minutes, et par la longitude, Meridien de Paris, soixante trois degrez trente minutes; que depuis ce moment, nous avons couru ladite terre, jusqu'au Vendredy troisième fevrier, que le midy nous eumes connoissance d'une baye dans laquelle nous entrames, et mouillames le même jour a trois heures de l'apres midy; qu'après avoir reconnu la dite terre et qu'elle etoit une isle sans aucune trace d'habitants, nous en avons pris possession au nom de Sa Majesté tres Chretienne, et nous avons arboré le Pavillon du Roy sur un fort construit dans la même Baye ou nous avons ancré le Vendredy trois fevrier, nous avons en même temps pris possession de quelques autres isles adjacentes à l'isle Principale qui nous a paru avoir deux cens lieues de tour, et nous avons compris ces isles sous le nom des isles Malouines; fait au fort San Louis le 5e avril mil sept cent soixante quatre.

Annex 8: Ratification of the possession of the
         Islands by the King of France, September
         12, 1964.
         Source: L. Muñoz Azpiri, Historia Completa
                 de las Islas Malvinas, Vol. 2 (1966),
                 p. 11.

Versailles, 12 de setiembre de 1764.

Vu l'acte cy dessus et de l'autre part contenant la prise de possession des Isles Malouïnes faite en nôtre nom par les Etats Majors, Officiers et mariniers de nos Fregates L'Aigle et le Sphinx, situées à l'Est de l'Amerique Meridionale...

Nous ayant pour agréable la conduite tenuë par nos susdits sujets en cette occasion, avons par ces presentes signées de notre main, et de notre pleine puissance et autorité Royales, approuvé et approuvons, confirmé et confirmons en tant que besoin est les dites occupations et prise de possession faites en notre nom dans les dites terres et Isles, ainsi que tout le contenu au susdit acte; declarons vouloir nous maintenir et conserver dans la possession des dites terres et Isles, voulant qu'elles soient dorésnavant regardées comme faisant partie et etant de la dependance du Royaume de France et régies par les memes lois, status et ordonnances que les autres lieux, terres et pays soumis â notre obeissance.

Annex 9: Declaration made by Bougainville, issued
on the occassion of the transfer of the
Islands to Spain, October 4, 1766.
Source: R. Perl, op. cit., p. 322.

(Traduction.)

Acte signé par Monsieur Louis de Bougainville pour la remise des Malvines.

Moi, Louis de Bougainville, Colonel des armées de Sa Majesté très Chrétienne, ai reçu *six cent dixhuit mille cent huit livres, treize sols et onze deniers,* montant de l'estimation que j'ai donnée des dépenses faites par la Compagnie de St. Malo, pour équipements et fondation de ses établissements illegitimes dans les Iles Malvines, appartenant à Sa Majesté Catholique, savoir:

Quarante mille livres, payées, en à compte, à Paris, par Son Excellence le Comte de Fuentes, Ambassadeur de Sa Majesté Catholique, pour les quelles j'ai donné quittance.

Deux cent mille livres, qui doivent m'être comptées à la même Cour de Paris, suivant des traites souscrites en ma faveur par le Marquis Zambrano, Trésorier Général de Sa Majesté Catholique, sur Don Francisco Ventura Llorena, Trésorier Extraordinaire de Sa Majesté.

Et soixante-cinq mille six cent soixante et quinze gourdes trois quart, équivalant aux trois cent soixante dixhuit mille cent huit livres trois sous, onze deniers dus, au taux de cinq livres par dollars que j'ai à recevoir *à Buenos Ayres,* en à compte de lettres de change qui m'ont été delivrées, tirées par Son Excellence le Baylio Fray Don Julian Arriaga, Secrétaire d'Etat du départment général des Indes et de la Marine de Sa Majesté Catholique.

En considération de ces payemens, aussi bien que par soumission aux ordres de Sa Majesté très Chrétienne, je m'oblige à remettre, en due forme à la Cour d'Espagne ces établissemens, ainsi que les familles, maisons, travaux, bois de construction, vaisseaux en chantier ou employés à l'expédition; et, enfin, tout ce qui, sur les lieux appartient à la Compagnie de St. Malo, tel que porté sur l'inventaire, ainsi que ce qui appartient à Sa Majesté très Chrétienne, *qui en fait la cession volontaire* rennonçant pour toujours à tous droits que la Compagnie, ou tout autre intéressé, ait pu ou pourrait produire sur la Trésorerie de Sa Majesté Catholique, sans qu'ils puissent à l'avenir faire aucune demande d'argent, ou compensation quelconque. En foi de quoi, je signe le présent acte et le garantis, comme étant un des principaux intéressés, aussi bien qu'autorisé à recevoir le montant de toute la somme, conformément au Registre minute du département de l'état. A S' Ildefonse, le 4 Octobre, 1766.

(Signé) *Louis de Bougainville.*

Annex 10: Letter written by Captain Hunt (then British
Commander of Port Egmont), addressed on
December 10, 1769, to F. Ruiz Puente (then
Spanish Governor on the Islands) (concerning
British title to the Islands).
Source: Hidalgo Nieto, La cuestión de las
Malvinas (1947), p. 588.

Sir:

Y have received your letters by the Officer acquainting me that the Islands and
Coast there of belong to the King of Spain your Master: In return I am to
acquaint you that the said Islands belong to his Britannick Mayesty my Master by
right of discovery, as well as Selilement; and that the Subjects of no other Power
whatever can have any right to be settled in the said Islands, without leave from
his Britannick Majesty; or taking the Oaths of allegiance, and submiting themselves to his Government; as subjects of the Crown of Great Britain.

I do therefore in his Majestys Name and by his Orders, warn you to leave the said
Islands, and in order that you may be the better enabled to remove your effects;
you may remain six months from the date here of, at the expiration of wich you
are expected to depart accordingly.

I am, Sir, your most obedient humble Servant   *Antony Hunt.*

Annex 11: Spanish Declaration and British Counter-
Declaration, January 22, 1771 (concerning
consequences of the forceful eviction of
English settlers on the islands by Spanish
forces on June 10, 1770).
Source: British and Foreign State Papers, Vol.
22, (1833-34), p. 1387.

– Spanish Declaration –   *London, 22nd January, 1771.*

Sa Majesté Britannique s'étant plainte de la violence qui avoit été commise le 10
Juin de l'année 1770, à l'Ile communément appelée la Grande Maloüine, et par
les Anglais dite Falkland, en obligeant par la force le Commandant, et les Sujets
de Sa Majesté Britannique, à évacuer le Port par eux appelé Egmont, demarche
offensante à l'honneur de sa Couronne, le Prince de Masseran, Ambassadeur
Extraordinaire de Sa Majesté Catholique, a reçu ordre de déclarer, et déclare,
que Sa Majesté Catholique, considérant l'amour dont elle est animée pour la
paix, et pour le maintien de la bonne harmonie avec Sa Majesté Britannique, et
réfléchissant que cet évènement pourroit l'interrompre, a vu avec déplaisir cette
expédition capable de la troubler; et dans la persuasion où elle est de la récipro-
cité de ses sentiments, et de son éloignement pour autoriser tout ce qui pourroit
troubler la bonne intelligence entre les 2 Cours, Sa Majesté Catholique désavoue
la susdite entreprise violente; et, en conséquence, le Prince de Masseran déclare,
que Sa Majesté Catholique s'engage à donner des ordres immédiats pour qu'on
remette les choses dans la Grande Maloüine, au Port dit Egmont, précisément
dans l'état où elles étoient avant le 10 Juin, 1770, auquel effet Sa Majesté
Catholique donnera ordre à un de ses Officiers, de remettre à l'Officier autorisé
par Sa Majesté Britannique, le Fort et Port Egmont, avec toute l'artillerie, les
munitions, et effets de Sa Majesté Britannique et de ses Sujets, qui s'y sont
trouvés le jour ci-dessus nommé, conformément à l'Inventaire qui en a été
dressé.

Le Prince de Masseran déclare en même tems, au nom du Roi son Maitre, que
l'engagement de Sa dite Majesté Catholique, de restituer à Sa Majesté Britannique la Possession du Port et Fort dit Egmont, ne peut ni ne doit nullement
affecter *la question du Droit antérieur de Souveraineté* des Iles Maloüines,
autrement dites Falkland.

En foi de quoi, moi, le susdit Ambassadeur Extraordinaire, ai signé la présente
Déclaration de ma Signature ordinaire, et à icelle fait apposer la Cachet de mes
Armes. A Londres, le 22 Janvier, 1771.

(L.S.)   *Le Prince de Masseran.*

– British Counter-Declaration –   *London, 22nd January, 1771.*

«Sa Majesté Catholique ayant autorisé son Excellence le Prince de Masserano,
son Ambassadeur Extraordinaire, à offrir, en son Nom Royal, au Roi de la
Grande Bretagne, une satisfaction pour l'injure faite à Sa Majesté Britannique,
en la dépossédant du Port et Fort du Port Egmont; et le dit Ambassadeur ayant
aujourd'hui signé une Déclaration, qu'il vient de remettre, y exprimant, que Sa
Majesté Catholique, ayant le désir de rétablir la bonne harmonie et amitié qui
subsistoient ci-devant entre les 2 Couronnes, désavoue l'expédition contre le

Port Egmont, dans laquelle la force a été employé, *contre les Possessions, Commandants, et Sujets* de Sa Majesté Britannique, et s'engage aussi que toutes choses seront immédiatement remises dans la situation précise dans laquelle elles étoient avant le 10 Juin, 1770; et que Sa Majesté Catholique donnera des ordres en conséquence à un de ses Officiers de remettre à l'Officier, autorisé par Sa Majesté Britannique, le Port et Fort du Port Egmont, comme aussi toute l'artillerie, les munitions, et effets de Sa Majesté Britannique, et des ses Sujets, selon l'Inventaire qui en a été dressé; et le dit Ambassadeur s'étant de plus engagé, au nom de Sa Majesté Catholique, que le contenu de la dite Déclaration sera effectué par Sa Majesté Catholique, et que des duplicatas des Ordres de Sa dite Majesté Catholique à ses Officiers seront remis entre les mains d'un des Principaux Secrétaires d'Etat de Sa Majesté Britannique, dans l'espace de 6 semaines; Sa dite Majesté Britannique, afin de faire voir les mêmes dispositions amicales de Sa part, m'a autorisé à déclarer, qu'elle regardera la dite Déclaration du Prince de Masserano, avec l'accomplissement entier du dit Engagement de la part de Sa Majesté Catholique, comme une satisfaction de l'injure faite à la Couronne de la Grande Bretagne. En foi de quoi, moi, Soussigné, un des Principaux Secrétaires d'Etat de Sa Majesté Britannique, ai signé la présente de ma Signature ordinaire, et à icelle fait apposer le Cachet de mes Armes. A Londres, ce 22 Janvier, 1771.

(L.S.)   *Rochford.*

Annex 12: Inscription on the Islands by Britain in 1774, on the occassion of the departure of British forces.
Source: J. Goebel, The Struggle for the Falkland Islands (1927), p. 410.

Be it known to all Nations That Falkland's Island with this Fort, the Storehouses Wharfs Harbours Bays and Crecks thereunto belonging are the sole right and property of His most Sacred Majesty George the Third King of Great Britain, France and Ireland, Defender of the Faith, In witness whereof this Plate is set up, and His Brittanic Majesty's colours left flying as a mark of possession by S. W. Clayton, Commanding officer at Falkland's Island A.D. 1774.

Annex 13: Nootka Sound Convention (1790).
Source: British and Foreign State Papers,
Vol. 1, p. 663

Convention between Great Britain and Spain, signed at the Escurial, 28 October 1790

DAVENPORT, *European Treaties bearing on the History of the United States*, vol. IV, p. 169, takes from the Spanish ratification in the Public Record Office, London (F.O. 94/284(1)), dated 21 November 1790, the French text of this Convention relative to America, which was renewed by the Additional Articles of 28 August 1814. This text appears also in Martens, *Recueil des Principaux Traités* (1st ed.) vol. III, p. 184, (2nd ed.) vol. IV, p. 492; Ancell, *A Collection of Treaties between Great Britain and Foreign Powers, 1743–1803*, vol. II, No. 54; *British and Foreign State Papers*, vol. I, p. 663; *Hertslet's Commercial Treaties*, vol. II, p. 257; Del Cantillo, *Tratados, Convenios y Declaraciones de Paz y de Comercio*, p. 623; Calvo, *Recueil complet des Traités etc. de l'Amérique Latine*, vol. III, p. 356; Handbook of Commercial Treaties (1st ed., 1908), p. 868; Martens et de Cussy, *Recueil Manuel et Pratique des Traités*, vol. II, p. 33; and D'Hauterive et de Cussy, *Recueil des Traités de Commerce etc.*, Part II, vol. II, p. 500.

(11.)—*CONVENTION between Great Britain and Spain, relative to America.—Signed at the Escurial, the 28th of October,* 1790.

(Translation.)

LEURS Majestés Britannique et Catholique, étant disposées à terminer, par un accord prompt et solide, les différends qui se sont élevés en dernier lieu entre les 2 Couronnes, elles ont trouvé que le meilleur moyen de parvenir à ce but salutaire seroit celui d'une transaction à l'amiable, laquelle, en laissant de côté toute discussion rétrospective des droits et des prétentions des 2 Parties, réglât leur position respective à l'avenir sur des bases qui seroient conformes à leurs vrais intérêts, ainsi qu'au désir mutuel dont Leurs dites Majestés sont animées, d'établir entre elles, en tout et en tous lieux, la plus parfaite amitié, harmonie et bonne correspondance.

Dans cette vûe, elles ont nommé et constitué pour leurs Plénipotentiaires ; savoir, de la part de Sa Majesté Britannique, le Sieur Alleyne Fitz-Herbert, du Conseil Privé de Sa dite Majesté dans la Grande Bretagne et en Irlande, et son Ambassadeur Extraordinaire et Plénipotentiaire près Sa Majesté Catholique ; et de la part de Sa Majesté Catholique, Don Joseph Monino, Comte de Florida-blanca, Chevalier Grand Croix du Royal Ordre Espagnol de Charles III, Conseiller d'Etat de Sa dite Majesté, et son Premier Secrétaire d'Etat et del Despacho ; lesquels, après s'être communiqués leurs Pleins-pouvoirs respectifs, sont convenus des Articles suivans :

ART. I. Il est convenu que les Bâtimens et les Districts de Terrein, situés sur la Côte du Nord-ouest du Continent de l'Amé-

THEIR Britannic and Catholic Majesties, being desirous of terminating, by a speedy and solid agreement, the differences which have lately arisen between the 2 Crowns, have judged that the best way of attaining this salutary object would be that of an amicable arrangement, which, setting aside all retrospective discussion of the rights and pretensions of the 2 Parties, should fix their respective situation for the future on a basis conformable to their true interests, as well as to the mutual desire with which Their said Majesties are animated, of establishing with each other, in everything and in all places, the most perfect friendship, harmony, and good correspondence.

In this view, they have named and constituted for their Plenipotentiaries ; to wit, on the part of His Britannic Majesty, Alleyne Fitz-Herbert, Esq., one of His said Majesty's Privy Council, in Great Britain and Ireland, and his Ambassador Extraordinary and Plenipotentiary to His Catholic Majesty ; and on the part of His Catholic Majesty, Don Joseph Monino, Count of Floridablanca, Knight Grand Cross of the Royal Spanish Order of Charles III, Councillor of State to His said Majesty, and his Principal Secretary of State, and of the Despatches ; who, after having communicated to each other their respective Full Powers, have agreed upon the following Articles :

ART. I. It is agreed that the Buildings and Tracts of Land, situated on the North-west Coast of the Continent of North Ame-

rique Septentrionale, ou bien sur des Iles adjacentes à ce Continent, desquels les Sujets de Sa Majesté Britannique ont été dépossédés, vers le mois d'Avril, 1789, par un Officier Espagnol, seront restitués aux dits Sujets Britanniques.

II. De plus, une juste réparation sera faite, selon la nature du cas, pour toute acte de violence ou d'hostilité qui aura pû avoir été commis, depuis le dit mois d'Avril, 1789, par les Sujets de l'une des 2 Parties Contractantes contre les Sujets de l'autre; et au cas que depuis la dite époque, quelques uns des Sujets respectifs aient été forcément dépossédés de leurs Terrains, Bâtimens, Vaisseaux, marchandises, ou autres objets de propriété quelconques, sur le dit Continent, ou sur les Mers ou Iles adjacentes, ils en seront remis en possession, ou une juste compensation leur sera faite pour les pertes qu'ils auront essuyées.

III. Et, afin de resserrer les liens de l'amitié, et de conserver à l'avenir une parfaite harmonie et bonne intelligence entre les 2 Parties Contractantes, il est convenu que les Sujets respectifs ne seront point troublés ni molestés, soit en naviguant ou en exerçant leur Pêche dans l'Océan Pacifique, ou dans les Mers du Sud, soit en débarquant sur les Côtes qui bordent ces Mers, dans des endroits non déjà occupés, afin d'y exercer leur commerce avec les Naturels du Pays, ou pour y former des Etablissemens. Le tout sujet néanmoins aux restrictions et aux provisions qui seront spécifiées dans les 3 Articles suivans.

rica, or on Islands adjacent to that Continent, of which the Subjects of His Britannic Majesty were dispossessed, about the month of April, 1789, by a Spanish Officer, shall be restored to the said British Subjects.

II. And further, that a just reparation shall be made, according to the nature of the case, for all acts of violence or hostility which may have been committed, subsequent to the month of April, 1789, by the Subjects of either of the Contracting Parties against the Subjects of the other; and that, in case any of the said respective Subjects shall, since the same period, have been forcibly dispossessed of their Lands, Buildings, Vessels, merchandise, or other property whatever, on the said Continent, or on the Seas or Islands adjacent, they shall be re-established in the possession thereof, or a just compensation shall be made to them for the losses which they shall have sustained.

III. And in order to strengthen the bonds of friendship, and to preserve in future a perfect harmony and good understanding between the 2 Contracting Parties, it is agreed that their respective Subjects shall not be disturbed or molested either in navigating or carrying on their Fisheries in the Pacific Ocean, or in the South Seas, or in landing on the Coasts of those Seas, in places not already occupied, for the purpose of carrying on their commerce with the Natives of the Country, or of making Settlements there; the whole subject, nevertheless, to the restrictions and provisions specified in the 3 following Articles.

IV. Sa Majesté Britannique s'engage d'employer les mesures les plus efficaces pour que la Navigation et la Pêche de ses Sujets dans l'Océan Pacifique, ou dans les Mers du Sud, ne deviennent point le prétexte d'un commerce illicite avec les Etablissemens Espagnols; et, dans cette vûe, il est en outre expressément stipulé, que les Sujets Britanniques ne navigueront point, et n'exerceront pas leur Pêche dans les dites Mers, à la distance de 10 lieues maritimes d'aucune partie des Côtes déjà occupées par l'Espagne.

V. Il est convenu, que tant dans les endroits qui seront restitués aux Sujets Britanniques, en vertu de l'Article I, que dans toutes les autres parties de la Côte du Nord-ouest de l'Amérique Septentrionale, ou des Iles adjacentes, situées au Nord des parties de la dite Côte déjà occupées par l'Espagne, partout où les Sujets de l'une' des 2 Puissances auront formé des Etablissemens, depuis le mois d'Avril, 1789, ou en formeront par la suite, les Sujets de l'autre auront un accès libre, et exerceront leur commerce, sans trouble ni molestation.

VI. Il est encore convenu, par rapport aux Côtes tant Orientales qu'Occidentales de l'Amérique Méridionale, et aux Iles adjacentes, que les Sujets respectifs ne formeront à l'avenir aucun Etablissement sur les parties de ces Côtes situées au Sud des parties de ces mêmes Côtes, et des Iles adjacentes, déjà occupées par l'Espagne; bien entendu que les

IV. His Britannic Majesty engages to take the most effectual measures to prevent the Navigation and Fishery of his Subjects in the Pacific Ocean, or in the South Seas, from being made a pretext for illicit trade with the Spanish Settlements; and, with this view, it is moreover expressly stipulated, that British Subjects shall not navigate, or carry on their Fishery in the said Seas, within the space of 10 sea leagues from any part of the Coasts already occupied by Spain.

V. It is agreed, that as well in the places which are to be restored to the British Subjects, by virtue of the 1st Article, as in all other parts of the North-western Coasts of North America, or of the Islands adjacent, situated to the North of the parts of the said Coast already occupied by Spain, wherever the Subjects of either of the 2 Powers shall have made Settlements since the month of April, 1789, or shall hereafter make any, the Subjects of the other shall have free access, and shall carry on their trade, without any disturbance or molestation.

VI. It is further agreed, with respect to the Eastern and Western Coasts of South America, and to the Islands adjacent, that no Settlement shall be formed hereafter, by the respective Subjects, in such parts of those Coasts as are situated to the South of those parts of the same Coasts, and of the Islands adjacent, which are already occupied by Spain; pro-

dits Sujets respectifs conserveront la faculté de débarquer sur les Côtes et Iles ainsi situées, pour les objets de leur Pêche, et d'y bâtir des cabanes, et autres ouvrages temporaires, servant seulement à ces objets.

VII. Dans tous les cas de plainte, ou d'infraction des Articles de la présente Convention, les Officiers de part et d'autre, sans se permettre au préalable aucune violence ou voie de fait, seront tenus de faire un rapport exact de l'affaire, et de ses circonstances, à leurs Cours respectives, qui termineront à l'amiable ces différends.

VIII. La présente Convention sera ratifiée et confirmée dans l'espace de 6 semaines, à compter du jour de sa signature, ou plutôt si faire se peut.

En foi de quoi, nous Soussignés Plénipotentiaires de Leurs Majestés Britannique et Catholique, avons signées, en leurs noms, et en vertu de nos Pleinspouvoirs respectifs, la présente Convention, et y avons apposé les Cachets de nos Armes.

Fait à San Lorenzo el Real, le 28 Octobre, 1790.

(L.S.) ALLEYNE FITZ-HERBERT.

(L.S.) EL CONDE DE FLORIDABLANCA.

---

vided that the said respective Subjects shall retain the liberty of landing on the Coasts and Islands so situated, for the purposes of their Fishery, and of erecting thereon huts, and other temporary buildings, serving only for those purposes.

VII. In all cases of complaint or infraction of the Articles of the present Convention, the Officers of either Party, without permitting themselves previously to commit any violence or act of force, shall be bound to make an exact report of the affair and of its circumstances, to their respective Courts, who will terminate such differences in an amicable manner.

VIII. The present Convention shall be ratified and confirmed in the space of 6 weeks, to be computed from the day of its signature, or sooner if it can be done.

In witness whereof, we, the Undersigned Plenipotentiaries of Their Britannic and Catholic Majesties, have, in their names, and in virtue of our respective Full Powers, signed the present Convention, and set thereto the Seals of our. Arms.

Done at the Palace of St. Lawrence, the 28th of October, 1790.

(L.S.) ALLEYNE FITZ-HERBERT.

(L.S.) EL CONDE DE FLORIDABLANCA.

Article Secret.

Comme par l'article six de la presente convention il a été stipulé par rapport aux côtes tant orientales qu'occidentales de l'Amerique Meridionale, et aux isles adjacentes, que les sujets respectifs ne formeront à l'avenir aucun établissement sur les parties de ces côtes situées au sud des parties de ces mêmes côtes deja occupées par l'Espagne, il est convenu et arreté par le present article que cette stipulation ne restera en force qu'aussi longtems qu'aucun établissement ne sera formé dans les endroits en question par les sujets de quelqu'autre puissance. Le present article secret aura la meme force que s'il etoit inseré dans la convention.

En foi de quoi nous sous-signés plenipotentiaires de leurs Majestés Catholique et Britannique avons signé le present article secret, et y avons apposé les cachets de nos armes.

Fait à San Lorenzo el Real le vingt huit Octobre mille septcent quatre vingt dix.

El Conde de FLORIDABLANCA.   ALLEYNE FITZ-HERBERT.

Annex 14: Declarations by Argentina on the occassion
of the taking of possession of the Islands,
November 9, 1820.
Source: British and Foreign State Papers, Vol.
20 (1832-33), p. 422.

III. His Britannic Majesty being anxious that the troubles and disturbances which unfortunately prevail in the Dominions of His Catholic Majesty in America should entirely cease, and the subjects of those provinces should return to their obedience to their lawful Sovereign, engages to take the most effectual measures for preventing His subjects from furnishing arms, ammunition, or any other warlike article to the revolted in America.

The present Additional Articles shall form an integral part of the Treaty of Friendship and Alliance signed on the 5th day of July, and shall have the same force and validity as if they were inserted word for word, and shall be ratified within forty days, or sooner if possible.

Done at Madrid, this 28th day of August, 1814.

Signed   *H. Wellesley*, (L.S.)
                          M. el Duque de San Carlos, (L.S.)

National Frigate Heroina, at Port Soledad, 9th November, 1820.

Sir,

I have the honour to inform you of my arrival at the port, to take possession of these islands in the name of the Supreme Government of the United Provinces of South America. The ceremony was publicly performed on the 6th day of November, and the national standart hoisted at the fort, under a salute from this frigate, in the presence of several citizens of the United States and Great Britain. It is my desire to act towards all friendly flags with the most distinguished justice and hospitality, and it will give me the pleasure to aid and assist such as many require them, to obtain refreshment with as little trouble and expenses as possible. I have to beg of you to communicate this intelligence to any other vessel of your nation whom it may concern.

I am, Sir, etc.

D. Jewett
Colonel of the Marine of the United Provinces of
South America, Commander of the frigate Heroina.

(see the Salem Gazzette, June 12, 1821; and the Times of London, August 3, 1821; also B & FSP, XX, 422).

Annex 15: Decree issued by Argentina on August 18, 1823
(concerning certain rights on the Islands, held
by J. Pacheco).
Source: J. Muñoz Azpiri, op.cit., Vol. 2
(1966), p. 53.

Decreto:

Buenos Aires, 28 de agosto de 1823.

No estando en las facultades del gobierno el conceder privilegio exclusivo, o
derecho alguno de propiedad a los terrenos que se expresan, pero deseando sin
embargo conciliar el interés del suplicante con los límites que la autoridad tiene
en su ejercicio, le concede el permiso que solicita para transportarse a la isla de la
Soledad, una de las de Malvinas, y usufructuar en ella en ... términos que
también propone, mas en la inteligencia que semejante concesión jamás podrá
privar al Estado del derecho que tiene a disponer de aquel territorio del modo
que crea más conveniente a los intereses generales de la provincia, y lo cuàl se
verificará tan luego que sus recursos le proporcionen el poder de establecer en él
de un modo efectico y permanente. Devuélvase al interesado este escrito original cuyo decreto le servirá de suficiente garantía.

(Hay una rúbrica de Martín Rodríguez).

Rivadavia

Annex 16: Treaty of Amity, Commerce and Navigation,
entered into by Britain and Spain on
February 2 (1825) (Excerpt).
Source: British and Foreign State Papers,
Vol. 12 (1824-25), p. 29.

EXTENSIVE Commercial Intercourse having been established for a series of years between the Dominions of His Britannick Majesty, and the Territories of the United Provinces of Rio de la Plata, it seems good for the security as well as encouragement of such Commercial Intercourse, and for the maintenance of good understanding between His said Britannick Majesty and the said United Provinces, that the Relations now subsisting between them should be regularly acknowledged and confirmed by the signature of a Treaty of Amity, Commerce, and Navigation.

For this purpose they have named their respective Plenipotentiaries, that is to say; –

His Majesty The King of the United Kingdom of Great Britain and Ireland, Woodbine Parish, Esquire, His said Majesty's Consul-General in the Province of Buenos Ayres and its Dependencies; – and The United Provinces of Rio de la Plata, Señor Don Manuel José Garcia, Minister Secretary for the Departments of Government, Finance, and Foreign Affairs, of the National Executive Power of the said Provinces;

Who, after having communicated to each other their respective Full Powers, found to be in due and proper form, have agreed upon and concluded the following Articles: –

I. There shall be perpetual Amity between the Dominions and Subjects of His Majesty The King of the United Kingdom of Great Britain and Ireland, and The United Provinces of Rio de la Plata, and their Inhabitants.

II. There shall be between all the Territories of His Britannick Majesty in Europe, and the Territories of the United Provinces of Rio de la Plata, a reciprocal freedom of Commerce: The Inhabitants of the two Countries, respectively, shall have liberty freely and securely to come, with their Ships and Cargoes, to all such Places, Ports, and Rivers, in the Territories aforesaid, to which other Foreigners are or may be permitted to come; to enter into the same, and to remain and reside in any part of the said Territories respectively; also to hire and occupy houses and warehouses for the purposes of their Commerce; and, generally, the Merchants and Traders of each Nation, respectively, shall enjoy the most complete protection and security for their Commerce; subject always to the Laws and Statutes of the two Countries respectively...

XI. For the better security of Commerce between the Subjects of His Britannick Majesty, and the Inhabitants of the United Provinces of Rio de la Plata, it is agreed, that if at any time any interruption of friendly Commercial intercourse, or any rupture should unfortunately take place between the Two Contracting Parties, the Subjects or Citizens of either of the Two Contracting Parties, residing in the Dominions of the other, shall have the privilege of remaining and continuing their trade therein, without any manner of interruption, so long as they behave peaceably, and commit no offence against the laws; and their effects and property, whether entrusted to Individuals or to the State, shall not be liable to seizure or sequestration, or to any other demands than those which may be made upon the like effects or property belonging to the Native Inhabitants of the State in which such Subjects or Citizens may reside.

Annex 17: Decree issued by Argentina on January 5, 1828 (concerning the granting of certain rights and privileges to be held on the Islands).
Source: British and Foreign State Papers, Vol. 20 (1832-33), p. 420.

Decree.

Buenos Ayres, 5th January, 1828.　　(Translation.)

The Government, – taking into consideration the great benefit the Country will derive by populating the Island, the ownership of which is solicited, and that, besides the increase of commerce, which naturally must result, with other Nations, new channels will be opened to national prosperity by encouraging the important branch of Fishery, the benefit of which would flow to the Inhabitants of the Republic, which hitherto have fallen into the hands of Foreigners; – that, in the present War with the Emperor of the Brazils, and in any other in which the Republic may some future day see itself engaged, nothing can be more convenient than to find among those Islands a point of support for maritime operations, which will furnish to the Privateers safe Harbours to convey their prizes to; – that towards the settling and extension of Territory on the Southern Coasts the settlement on these Islands is a great step; – and lastly, that the great expenses required to put into execution a scheme of this nature, can by no means be compensated, but by the ownership of lands, which, if not granted, an opportunity of doing a great national good would be lost, and even the right of Sovereignty over them; – doth, in conformity to the spirit of the Law of 22nd October, 1821, cede to Mr. Lewis Vernet, Resident and Merchant of this place, the Island of Statenland, and all the lands of the Island of Soledad, excepting those that were ceded to Dr. Jorge Pacheco, by a Decree dated 13th December 1823, and which has been ratified by a Decree of this day; and excepting moreover an extent of 10 square leagues in the Bay of San Carlos, which the Government reserves for itself; with the object, and under the express condition, that, within 3 years of the date hereof, a Colony shall be established, and that at the end of that time the Government shall be informed of its state, in order to determine what it may consider convenient for the interior or exterior administration of the same.

And further, the Government, wishing to contribute as much as possible to the encouragement and prosperity of the Colony, has further determined:

First, That the Colony shall be free from every description of contribution, excepting what may be necessary for the maintainance of the local Authorities that may be established, from excise, tolls, and export duties, as also free from import duties on such merchandize as shall be introduced for the use of the Colony, which privileges are granted for 20 years, exclusive of the 3 years fixed for the establishment of the Colony.

Secondly, That, for the same term of 20 years, the Colony shall be at liberty to carry on the Fishery, free of duties at the 2 Islands whose property is ceded, in all the Islands of Malvinas, and on the Coast of the Continent south of Rio Negro of Patagonia.

Thirdly, That, in case of the population extending to the other Islands, within the period of the 3 years allowed for the establishment of the Colony, the Director of the same shall be under the obligation of informing the Government of such further Population, in order to determine what may be convenient.

The Notary of Government is hereby authorized fo furnish the Petitioner with as many Gopies hereof as he may require.

Balcarce, (Minister.)

Annex 18:   Letter written by the Duke of Wellington,
            then Prime Minister, to Sir George Murray, on
            July 25, 1829 (evaluation of the legal status
            of the Islands).
            Source: Despatches, Correspondence and Memo-
            randa of Field Marshal the Duke of
            Wellington; ed. by his son, Vol. XI
            (1877), p. 41.

I have persued the enclosed papers respecting the Falkland Islands. It is not at all clear to me that we have ever possessed the sovereignty of all these Islands. The Convention certainly goes no further than to restore to us Port Gumont, which we abandoned nearly sixty years ago.

If our right to the Falkland Islands had been undisputed at the time, and indisputable, I confess that I should doubt the expediency of now taking possession of them. We have possession of nearly every valuable post and colony in the world, and I confess that I am anxious to avoid exciting the attention and jealousy of other powers by extending our possessions and setting the example of the gratification of a desire to seize new territories. But in this case in which our right to possess more than Port Gumont is disputed, and at least doubtful, it is very desirable to avoid such acts.

I am at the same time very sensible of the inconvenience which may be felt by this country, and of the injury which will be done to us if either the French or Americans should settle upon these Islands, the former in virture of any claim from former occupancy, the latter, or both, from any claim derived by purchase or cession from the government of Buenos Ayres.

That which I would recommend is that the Government of Buenos Ayres should be very quietly but very distinctly, informed that His Majesty has claims upon the Falkland Islands, and that His Majesty will not allow of any settlement upon, or any cession to individuals or foreign nations of these Islands by Buenos Ayres, which shall be inconsistent with the King's acknowledged right of sovereignty.

I think that this is all that can be done at present. It will have the effect of impeding any settlement or cession by Buenos Ayres, and so we may suppose that the French and Americans will hear of this communication they will not be disposed to act in contravention to it unless determined upon a quarrel with this country.

Annex 19: Decree issued by Argentina on June 10, 1829
(concerning Argentine administrative organization on the Islands).
Source: L. Muñoz Azpiri, op. cit., Vol. 2
(1966), p. 63.

Buenos Aires, junio 10 de 1829.

Cuando por la gloriosa revolución de 25 de mayo de 1810 se separaron estas provincias de la dominación de la Metrópoli, la España tenía una posesión material de las Islas Malvinas, y de todas las demás que rodean el Cabo de Hornos, inclusa la que se conoce bajo la denominación de Tierra del Fuego; hallándose justificada aquella posesión por le derecho del primer ocupante, por le consentimiento de las principales potencias de Europa y por la adyacencia de estas islas al continente que formaban el virreinato de Buenos Aires, de cuyo gobierno dependían. Por esta razón habiendo entrado el gobierno de la República en la sucesión de todos los derechos que tenía sobre estas provincias la antigua metrópoli y de que gozaban sus virreyes, ha seguido ejerciendo actos de dominio en dichas islas, sus puertos y costas, a pesar de que las circunstancias no han permitido hasta ahora dar a aquella parte del territorio de la República la atención y cuidados que su importancia exige, pero siendo necesario no demorar por más tiempo las medidas que pueden poner a cubierto los derechos de la República, haciéndole al mismo tiempo gozar de las ventajas que puedan dar los productos de aquellas islas, y asegurando la protección debida a su población; el gobierno ha acordado y decreta:

Art. 1. – Las Islas Malvinas y las adyacentes al Cabo de Hornos en el mar Atlántico, serán regidas por un comandante político y militar, nombrado inmediatamente por el gobierno de la República.

Art. 2. – La residencia del comandante político y militar será en la Isla de la Soledad, y en ella se establecerá una batería, bajo el pabellón de la República.

Art. 3. – El comandante político y militar hará observar por la población de dichas islas las leyes de la República, y cuidará en sus costas de la ejecución de los reglamentos sobre pesca de anfibios.

Art. 4. – Comuníquese y publíquese.

Salvador María del Carril
Rodríguez.

Annex 20: Memorandum by the British Colonial Office,
July 10, 1829 (concerning legal status of
the Islands).
Source: W. Down, The Occupation of the Falk-
land Islands and the Question of
Sovereignty (1926), p. 323.

Memorandum on the Falkland Islands

The expediency of resuming possession of these Islands has lately been brought under the consideration of the Colonial Department from more than one quarter. Their importance as affording a secure Naval Station for our Ships of War can scarcely be doubted, and since the increase of our Trade with South America and the Pacific their occupation has been strongly urged by the Merchants.

Lord Anson's voyage first demonstrated the advantage of a friendly Port nearer to Cape Horn than the Brazils – especially if this country should be engaged in war; and the observations which are to be found in the account of the voyage which was compiled under his Lordship's directions, sufficiently show the opinions on this point which were entertained by that great Navigator.

When at the head of the Board of Admiralty Lord Anson decided upon carrying into effect that accurate survey of these Islands which his acquaintance with their Geographical position had led him to recommend – and in the year 1743, some Ships of War were ordered to prepare for that service. This design appears, however, to have been abandoned in consequence of the representations of Spain, and it was not revived until the year 1764, when Commodore Byron was sent out by Lord Egmont to take possession of the Falkland Islands in the name of His Britannic Majesty.

Previous to this period it would appear, that although these Islands were occasionally visited by the English who were in fact the first discoverers by the Dutch and by the French, yet that the Spaniards, during the whole of this long course of years, never even touched there. They, indeed, in the discussions which took place on their aggression in 1770, maintained a priority of discovery which they were never able to substantiate but this claim was only brought forward to support the more general one of exclusive right to all the Magellanic Regions, as they are termed. A claim which has never been admitted by this country, and which forms the only ground upon which their supposed right to these Islands can be built. Should the Spanish Government of the present day think fit to revive their ancient pretensions.

To demonstrate this satisfactorily, it will only be necessary briefly to recapitulate the course of events in regard to these Islands, since the period when their occupation became a question of importance.

In the year 1764 a Frigate was equipped at St. Maloes by M. Bougainville, a French Officer in the Army, for the chief purpose, as he is said to have conceived, of indemnifying France for the loss of Canada by the discovery of a Southern Continent, or of exploring the large Islands which were known to exist in that quarter, and of forming a Settlement on one of them, which it was considered, would prove an important station for the French East India Ships to touch at on their voyage.

M. Bougainville appears to have returned to France after a very short stay in the most Eastern of these Islands and to have been soon after sent out again to cede the Settlement which he had formed there to Spain, in consequence of a formal complaint made by that Court to the French Government against the occupation of this Island – the Settlement was accordingly surrendered to a Governor sent from Buenos Aires, who changed the name of Port Louis, which had been given it by Bougainville to Port Soledad.

It is not satisfactorily made out what portion of these Islands were included in this cession, or whether the English were privy to the transaction, although it would appear from the following circumstance that neither party were acquainted with the proceedings of the other. In the Chart of the Falkland Islands belonging to the 4th Edition of Bougainville's Voyage Point A. in one of the Islands is described as "Baye Francaise lieu ou étoit l'établissement Francois, occupé aujourd'hui par les Espagnols. Les pointes B. sont ceux où on *soupconne* que les Anglais sont établis".

It has been considered as not improbable that the British Settlement would have been abandoned, had time for reflection been given, but instead of sending a formal complaint to the British Court as the Spanish Government had done in the case of France, the Commandant of Port Soledad issued orders to the new settlers to retire, and on their refusal a small vessel of War was sent to reconnoitre the Port. This was followed by the appearance before Port Egmont of the Governor of Buenos Ayres with a large Military force and after a show of resistance for the sake of form, the English surrendered the Island by Capitulation, and to prevent their conveying the first intelligence of this aggression their ships were detained for 20 days. This took place in 1770, and it was not until the year 1771 that the negotiations which ensued were brought to an amicable termination – and a convention was settled by which the Spanish Govt agreed to the restitution of Port Egmont from which the English had been forcibly driven, and by which the act of the Governor of Buenos Ayres in dispossessing them was disavowed.

The Spanish Ambassador, Prince Masserano at the time when he communicated the orders of his Court in regard to the restoration of Port Egmont to Gt. Britain, distinctly declared that "such restoration could not and ought not to affect the question of the prior right of Sovereignty of the Malouine or Falkland Islands".

The Convention was vehemently assailed in Parliament at the time, and the Government were accused of pusillanimity in allowing the question of right to remain undecided. It was observed too by the Opposition of that day that the Spaniards had only made restitution of Port Egmont and not of the Falkland Islands generally.

It was in this conjuncture that Dr. Johnson was called in to the aid of the Administration of that day. His object being to reconcile the public to the course which had been taken, he seems to have considered that one mode of doing so was by treating the subject of the dispute as one of comparative insignificance and by stigmatising it at the same time as a Possession which would only be valuable as the seat of contraband and unauthorized traffic.

In 1774 these Islands were abandoned by the British, as it would seem from the letter of the Secretary of State on ground of economy but the Claim of Sovereignty on the part of the King of England was asserted at the time of withdrawing from these possessions, and it is apprehended that the same right, although it has not since been exercised, has not, nevertheless, been abrogated by disuse.

It hat been asserted, although, it would appear, without foundation, that the relinquishment of these Islands by the British after a sufficient length of possession to satisfy the national honour, formed part of the Compact at that time entered into with Spain; but no trace is to be found of any correspondence of this description, and the Falkland Islands are not mentioned in any subsequent Treaty between this country and the Spanish Government.

The Right of this Country to these Islands has always been maintained in our discussions with the Spanish Govt as well on the ground of prior discovery, as of prior settlement, and it is clear that Spain has acquired no additional right to them since the period when her supposed claims were successfully resisted by Great Britain. The exact time when the Spaniards returned to these Islands has not been ascertained, but according to a Report recently sent home by Mr. Parish His Majesty's Chargé d'affaires at Buenos Ayres, it would appear that until the breaking out of the South American Revolution, they were in the habit of maintaining a Guard on one of the Islands for the superintendence of Convicts who were sent there for punishment, and also a small Vessel of War, which, as well as the Guard was annually relieved from Buenos Ayres.

By the last Accounts from the same quarter it would seem that the Government of Buenos Ayres assumed the power of disposing of these Islands. They are reported to have at various times granted to individuals the privilege of catching Seals, and the wild *Cattle* which are to be found there, and according to the statement of Mr. Parish "they have now some thoughts of reoccupying them in the same manner and for the same purpose as the Spaniards did".

There is great reason to believe that the Accounts sent home by Capt. Mc.Bride, the successor of Commodore Byron, while employed on that Station, of the barrenness of the Falkland Islands and of the inhospitable nature of the Climate are not to be depended upon; the abundance of wild animals which have bred there would disprove the one statement, and the luxuriant herbage which is found there would lead to a belief that the temperature of the Atmosphere is not so destructive to vegetation as has been represented.

The Falkland Islands are three or more in number, but two only have, as yet, been selected for settlement, of which that to the Westward was the seat of the English Establishment at Port Egmont. All accounts agree in the deficiency of timber, but turf for fuel is found in abundance – the Port is represented to be safe and capacious...

Should it be the determination of Government to resume possession of this important post, it is presumed that it may be done at little expence, by sending out a small Ship of War, with a Party of Marines who might proceed to occupy the original Settlement at Port Egmont. The houses then erected might probably be repaired at a trifling expence, and if it be thought expedient gradually to abandon the Australian Provinces as the Penal Settlement for Male Convicts (as the advanced state of these Colonies, and the change in popular feeling in regard to the dread of transportation to that quarter would seem to point out) a large Detachment of that Class might be sent out with advantage to the Falkland Islands for the purpose of completing the Public Works which will necessarily be required there.

The expence of transporting them to this new Quarter will be less than to New South Wales, as the voyage to the Falkland Islands may be estimated upon an average at 12 Weeks whilst 17 are considered a fair Passage to Botany Bay.

Annex 21: British protest of November 19, 1829, against
Argentina decree of June 10, 1828.
Source: British and Foreign State Papers,
Vol. 20 (1832-33), p. 346.

The Undersigned has the honor to inform His Excellency, the Minister of Foreign Affairs, that he has communicated to his Court the Official Document published by the Government of Buenos Ayres on the 10th of June last, containing certain provisions for the Government of the Falkland Islands.

The Undersigned has received the order of his Court to represent to His Excellency, that the Argentine Republic, in issuing this Decree, have assumed and authority incompatible with His Britannic Majesty's rights of Sovereignty over the Falkland Islands.

These rights, founded upon the original discovery and subsequent occupation of the said Islands, acquired an additional sanction from the restoration, by His Catholic Majesty, of the British Settlement, in the year 1771, which, in the preceding year, had been attacked and occupied by a Spanish Force, and which act of violence had led to much angry discussion between the Governments of the 2 Countries.

The withdrawal of His Majesty's Forces from these Islands, in the year 1774, cannot be considered as invalidating His Majesty's just rights. That measure took place in pursuance of a system of retrenchment, adopted at that time by His Britannic Majesty's Government; but the marks and signals of possession and property were left upon the Islands: when the Governor took his departure, the British Flag remained flying, and all those formalities were observed which indicated the rights of ownership, as well as an intention to resume the occupation of the Territory, at a more convenient season.

The Undersigned, therefore, in execution of the Instructions of his Court, formally protests, in the name of His Britannic Majesty, against the pretensions set up by the Government of Buenos Ayres, in their Decree of the 10th of June, and against all acts which have been, or may hereafter be, done, to the prejudice of the just rights of sovereignty which have heretofore been exercised by the Crown of Great Britain."

The Undersigned, &c.   *Woodbine Parish.*

Annex 22: Memorandum by the King's Advocate in
London, July 23, 1829 (concerning status
of the Islands).
Source: W. Down, op. cit., p. 181.

In obedience to your Lordship's commands I have the honour to report that the right which this country acquired by the original discovery and subsequent occupation of the Falkland Islands cannot be considered as in any manner affected by the transactions which occurred previously to the year 1774. So far from these rights having been abandoned, they have been always strenouosly asserted and mantained, particularly in the memorable discussions with Spain referred to in your Lordship's letter, which terminated in the restoration of the English Settlement and Fort which have been taken by the Spanish forces. The claim, therefore, to these islands now advanced by Buenos Ayres cannot be admitted upon any supposed acknowledgment or recognition of the right of Spain by this country; if it is capable of being mantained upon any ground, it must be upon the supposition that the withdrawing of the British troops in 1774, and the non occupation of these Islands since that time, ammounted to a virtual abandonment of the right originally acquired, and that being unoccupied, the Islands in question reverted to their original state, and liable of become the property of the first person who might take possession of them. But I apprehended that no such effect is to be attributed to either or both of these circunstances. The symbols of property and possession which were left upon the Islands, sufficiently denote the intention of the British Government to retain those rights which they had previously acquired over them, and to reassume the occupation of them whenever convenient opportunity should occur.

Upon this ground, I am humbly of the opinion that the rights acquired by this country to the Falkland Islands, are not invalidated by any thing which has occurred previous or subsequent to the year 1774.

Annex 23: Circular Letter, written by the Argentine
representative on the Islands, addressed to the
captains of the ships stationed on the Islands,
October 16, 1830.
Source: L. Muñoz Azpiri, op. cit., Vol. 2
(1966), p. 327.

Port Luis (Falkland Islands).
To Captain...

Sir:

The undersigned, governor of the Falkland Islands, Tierra del Fuego and ady-
acencies, doth hereby, in compliance whith his duty and expressed in a decree
passed by the government of Buenos Aires, on the 10th. June 1829, to watch
over the execution of the laws respecting the fisheries of which decree the
annexed is a translation, inform you that the transgression of those laws will not,
as heretofore, remain unnoticed.

The undersigned flatters himself that this timely notice which he gives to all
masters of vessels in the fishcries on any part of the coast under his jurisdiction
will induce them to desist since a repetition will expose them to become a lawful
prize to any vessel of war belonging to the Republic or to any vessel which the
undersigned may think proper to arm in use of his authority for executing the
laws of the Republic.

The undersigned further warns persons against the practice of shooting cattle on
the East Falkland Islands the same being private property and however innocent
the act may be in those that are not aware of this circunstance, it becomes, of
course, highly criminal in those who willfully persist in such acts and renders
them liable to the rigor of the laws in similar cases.

On the other hands those who are in want of provisions or refreshments can
receive them on moderate terms by applying at the new colony at the head of
Berkeley Sound where no ports charges are to be paid, desertion of men
discouraged and any assistance rendered to those that may stand in need of it by
the undersigned,

Luis Vernet

Annex 24: Instructions by British authorities to
Commander Onslow, despatching ship to the
Islands in order to exercise sovereign rights,
November 28, 1832.
Source: G. Whitington, The Falkland Islands
Compiled from Ten Years Investigation
on the Subject (1840), p. 12.

The Right Honorable the Lords Commissioners of the Admiralty, having, in
persuance of his Majesty's pleasure, signified to me their directions to despatch a
ship of the squadrom under my orders to Port Egmont, in the Falkland Islands
for the purpose of exercising the rights of sovereignty there, and of acting at the
said Islands as in a possession belonging to the crown of Great Britain, you are
hereby required and directed to put to sea to-morrow morning in his Majesty's
sloop Clio, under your command, and to proceed with all expedition to Port
Egmont, for the purpose of exercising the rights of sovereignty over the said
Islands, and of acting thereat as in a possession belonging to the crown of Great
Britain accordingly. On your arrival at Port Egmont you will immediately
restore the symbols of his Majesty's sovereignty over the Falkland Islands,
consisting of the block-house, the flag-staff, and flag, formerly erected there by
England; if you find that such symbols have dissappeared or fallen into decay,
you will, with that view, hoist the British union flag on shore, and to proceed to
repair Fort George if any part of it remains, or to construct a new small fort or
blockhouse on its ancient site, of adequately dimensions, on which, when it is
completed, you will erect a permanent flag-staff and keep the British union flag
constantly hoisted.

Should you find at Port Egmont any persons professing to be British subjects,
you are to call them publicly, before you, and register names, ages and occupations, together with the time they may have residing in the Falkland Islands; and
in the event of there being also at that port any foreign persons, occupied in
peaceful pursuits, you will explain to them the relation in which they are to
continue to hold themselves to the crown of Great Britain, whilst they remain in
the British settlement of the Falkland Islands; you will endevour to ascertain, as
near as possible, the numbers and nations of any such foreigners, but you are not
to disturb them in their agricultural or other inoffensive employments. So soon
as you have accomplished this service at Port Egmont, you will charge the most
respectable British subject in the place, if there be one, to preserve the British
flag, and to keep it duly hoisted; and should nothing unforeseen have arisen
during your stay, to require your further presence there, you are to set out on
your return, to give an account of your proceedings to the Commander-in-Chief,
for the information of the Lords Commissioners of the Admiralty and his
Majesty's Government.

Such will be your routine, if you meet with no impediment; but should you find,
on your arrival at Fort Egmont, any foreign persons in military force, who,
affecting to be in possession of that fort, may have hoisted a foreign flag, or shall
attempt to resist your landing or operations, in obedience to these instructions,
you are, in first place, to acquaint the chief person commanding such force with
the object of your mission; request to be informed of the reason of the force

under his command being there in a British settlement; and, in terms of civility, require that the flag, if any be hoisted, be immediately struck, and that the force may be quickly withdrawn. Your will then wait his reply and, should he promptly comply with your request, you will, under due caution, afford every facility in your power for the embarkation and orderly departure of the foreign force in question, with any property to wich such force may have a just claim; but if, on the contrary, your request for that flag be struck, or for such foreign military force being withdrawn, should be refused, and objections of any sort be raised against compliance, you are, providing you deem the force of the sloop under your command adquate to the duty of forcible expulsion, to command, in the name of his Majesty, the said foreign person exercising chief authority, and all foreign military persons whomsoever to lay down their arms and quit forthwith at their peril, the British possession. And if, after this command, any further hesitation or resistance be attempted, you are to compel them to depart; observing that, in the event of your being obligated to have recourse to his painful measure, which you are only to adopt in the last extremity; you are to execute it with all possible moderation, consistent with its effectual accomplishment. And you to admit of no compromise or evasive delay under any pretence whatever, if there be vessels present to convey such military persons away; it being his Majesty's purpose to keep up mantain his sovereign rights over these Islands. If however, there should be no means of conveyance from the island for such foreign military persons, they are to be disarmed, and left there until further measures can be taken for their removal. Should you on the other hand, be of opinion that any such foreign forces which you may find at Port Egmont, or in any other port or place in the said Islands, are decided superior to the force of the Clio, which is scarcely to be expected; and it might therefore be imprudent to attempt to expel them by arms, you must the, should your request for their quiet departure be rejected, most solemny protest in writing, in the name of the King, against such forcible resistance and hostility in the British territory, and warm such chief person in command, and all persons whomsoever, of the lamentable consequence which must inevitable and suddenly follow so gros violation of the law of nations, and specially of the dignity and sacred rights of Great Britain. Excepting this protest, you are to enter into no written correspondence whatever with any such military persons holding forcible possession of his majesty's dominions; not to recognise them by any of your proceeding in any other view than as illegal intruders. And if, after your final protest, the person exercising chief command of such foreign force, should still refuse to resign possession of the place, you are to proceed with all possible despatch to join the Commander-in-Chief for further orders. But as it is desirable than his Majesty's minister at Buenos Aires should be made acquainted as early as possible with the results, whatever it may be, of your visit to the Falkland Islands, you will call in on your return at Monte Video, whence you will forward to that gentleman a concise report of your proceedings; and should you not find the Commander-in-Chief in the River Plate, you will hear intelligence of his position, and resume your exertions to rejoin him without a moment's delay.

Given on board of Warspite, Rio de Janeiro, this 28th Nov. 1832. T. Baker, Rear Admiral and Commander-in-Chief, to John James Onslow, Esq. Commander of his Majesty's sloop Clio. By command of the Commander-in-Chief, Alexander Kant, Secretary.

Annex 25: Request by Commander Onslow to the representative of Argentina, to withdraw from Islands, January 2, 1833.
Source: British and Foreign State Papers, Vol. 20 (1832-33), p. 1197.

The British to the Buenos Ayres Commander.
His Majesty's Sloop, Clio,

Berkeley Sound, 2nd January, 1833.

Sir,

I have to acquaint you that I have received directions from His Excellency the Commander-in-Chief of His Britannic Majesty's Ships and Vessels of War, on the South American Station, to exercise the rights of Sovereignty over these Islands, in the name of His Britannic Majesty.

It ist my intention to hoist, to-morrow morning, the National Flag of Great Britain on shore; when I request you will be pleased to haul down your Flag, and to withdraw your Forces, taking with you all the stores, &c., belonging to your Government.

I am, & c.   *J. J. Onslow,* Commander.

Annex 26: Protest by Argentina against forceful taking
of possession by Britain, January 22, 1833.
Source: British and Foreign State Papers,
Vol. 20 (1832-33), p. 1198.

The Undersigned, Minister of Grace and Justice, charged provisionally with the Department of Foreign Relations of the Argentine Republic, is directed by his Government to address the Chargé d'Affaires, *ad interim,* of His Britannic Majesty in this City, and to inform him, than, on the 2nd instant. His Britannic Majesty's Sloop of War *Clio,* anchored in the Port of San Luis, in the Island of La Soledad, one of the Malvinas, for the purpose of taking possession of them as belonging to His Britannic Majesty; – Captain Onslow of the said Vessel stating that he had positive orders to hoist the British Flag on shore, within 24 hours. He had already done so in other Ports of the Islands, and finally did the same in that of La Soledad, in defiance of the Protest of the Commander of the Schooner-of-War *Sarandi;* who was there in fulfilment of the Orders of his Government, but which, through a fatality of unforeseen circunstances, he could not strictly perform, by forcibly resisting the occupation of the Islands.

The Undersigned abstains, for the present, from expatriating on the inconsistency of such a violent and rude proceeding in a time of profound Peace, when the close and friendly relations between the 2 Governments on the one hand, and on the other the moderation, cordiality and purity of intentions, of which England has made ostentation, gave no reason to expect that the confidence in which the Argentine Republic reposed would be so unceremoniously violated. Nevertheless, in fulfilment of the Orders of his Government, and in its name, and in consideration of what we owe to our own dignity, to posterity, and to the deposit which the United Provinces have entrusted to the Government of Buenos Ayres, and in short, to the whole World, whose eyes are fixed upon us, – the Undersigned protest, in the most formal manner, against the pretensions of the Government of Great Britain to the Malvina Islands, and its occupation of them; as likewise against the insult offered to the Flag of the Republic, and against the damages which the latter has received and may receive in consequence of the aforesaid proceedings, and whatever may hereafter take place on the part of the British Government in this respect.

The Chargé d'Affaires, whom the Undersigned addresses, will be pleased to transmit this Protest to his Government, and manifest the decided resolution of this Republic to sustain its rights; at the same time that it desires to maintain inviolate the friendly relations which it has hitherto cultivated with Great Britain, and that Peace may prosper and be perpetual between the Two States.

God preserve the Chargé d'Affaires many years.

Manuel Vicente de Maza.

Annex 27: Protest by Argentina, June 17, 1833
(Excerpt).
Source: British and Foreign State Papers,
Vol. 20 (1833-34), p. 1366.

Protest

The Undersigned Minister Plenipotentiary of the United Provinces of Rio de la Plata, has the honor of addressing to His Excellency Viscount Palmerston, Principal Secretary of State for Foreign Affairs, the present Memoir and Protest upon the proceedings of His Britannic Majesty's Government, in assuming the sovereignty and possession of the Malvinas, otherwise called the Falkland Islands, and in forcibly stripping the said United Provinces of a part of their territory and dominion.

But previously to resorting to this mode of upholding the sovereign rights of his government, the undersigned had, on the 24th of April last, the honor of requesting that His Majesty's Government would be pleased to inform him if they had really given orders to eject Buenos-Ayrean garrison from the Malvinas, as pretended, by Captain Onslow of His Majesty's corvette, Clio; and also whether they did authorize and would recognize the declaration, also alleged to have been made, respecting the right of dominion to those islands, because on the arrival here of the correspondence from Buenos Ayres, dated the 14th of January, it was made known, from private intelligence which found its way into the London newspapers, that the Buenos-Ayrean garrison and colony in the Malvinas, together with a ship of war, the Sarandi, stationed in that part of the Argentine republic, had been forcibly constrained to withdraw upon an intimation from the said Captain Onslow, who declared that he was going to take, and did take, possession of the islands in the name of His Britannic Majesty, notwithstanding a pending discussion thereupon.

An explanation of this sort was the more called for from the circumstance of the Argentine Government not having, up to that period, received any notification of the fact, excepting what was incidentally afforded to them by the arrival at Buenos Ayres, on the fifteenth of the same month of January, of their garrison and colonists who had been expelled in a manner so surprizing; nor had their legation at this court any other notion of His Majesty's Government's intentions than what fell verbally from a chief person in the department for foreign affairs, signifying to the undersigned that instructions, relative to the discussion, were about to be given to the newly-appointed Minister to Buenos Ayres, Mr. Hamilton, but who has not yet quitted Paris.

His Excellency Lord Palmerston replied on the 27th of the same month of April "that the proceedings of the Commander of the Clio took place in consequence of instructions given by His Majesty's government to Admiral Baker, the late Commander-in-Chief of the South American station; that this admiral had orders to send a ship of war to the Malvina Islands, there to exercise the ancient and undoubted rights of sovereignty which," according to His Exellency, "are vested in His Majesty, and to act in that quarter as in a possession belonging to the crown of Great Britain, and, of course, in case of meeting in those islands, any foreign persons or military force, not acknowledging the sovereignty of His Majesty, the commander of the ship-of-war was to request such persons and such military force to withdraw, and he was to assist them with the means of doing so."

The note of His Excellency Lord Palmerston, concludes with stating that "the said instructions were made known by Admiral Baker to His Majesty's Legation at Buenos Ayres."

If, however, this information, so transmitted to His Majesty's Legation, was truly intended to come to the knowledge of the Argentine government, in order that they might not be taken by surprize at the meditated deprivation, as may be supposed from the existing amity between the two countries and the courtesies usually observed between governments, it is very painful to remark that the British Legation did not comprehend it in this manner, since they gave no information, nay more, they absolutely forgot, or denied, that they had any thing to communicate on the subject. By the correspondence received in the month of May last, it appears that on the 16th of January, two days after the return of the garrison to the roadsted of the capital the Minister for Foreign Affairs of the Republic officially communicated to His Majesty's chargé d'affaires "that he had just learned that the commander of the corvette of war Clio had occupied the site of La Soledad in the Malvinas, and hoisted the English flag, where that of the Argentine Republic was before flying; that this unexpected event had deeply affected the feelings of the Buenos-Ayrean government, and although nothing colorable could be found to warrant it, yet considering that the chargé d'affaires, to whom he addressed himself, must be possessed of information in a procedure that compromized the rights of the Republic, he requested from him the necessary explanations."

The answer of His Majesty's chargé d'affaires was expressly, in his note of the 17th of January 1833, that "he had not received instructions from his court to make any communication to the government of Buenos Ayres upon that subject."

In the absence of all explanation, anterior or subsequent to the act of deprivation, the Buenos-Ayrean government proceeded to verify the fact by the depositions of their expelled officers from whose testimony it appeared that, on the 4th of January 1833, there anchored in Port Luis de la Soledad de Malvinas, His Majesty's corvette Clio, J. J. Onslow, Commander, who, at three in the afternoon of that day, went on board the ship of war Sarandi, and intimated to her commander that he came to take possession of the Malvinas as belonging to His Majesty's crown; that he had positive orders to hoist there the English flag, within twenty-four hours, as he had already done in other ports of the islands, and peremptorily demanded that, on the following day, the flag of the Republic should be lowered also on shore; that the commander of the Sarandi refused to comply with that demand, protesting against the insult and the violation of the rights of the Republic; that, determined not to yield, excepting to superior force, he forbade the inhabitants ashore from striking the Argentine flag there; that at nine in the morning, however, of the following day, three armed boats with marines and seamen landed from the Clio in Port Luis, and, fixing a staff on the dwelling of an Englishman at some distance from the house of the Commandancy, hoisted the English flag, and then proceeded to lower, with their own hands, the flag of the Republic which was then flying.

It is essential to a right view of the question, thus untowardly renewed, as to the sovereignty of the Malvinas, to divide their history into three distinct parts.

1st. The discovery originally, or simultaneously, made by different European nations.

2nd. The formal occupation of them, from 1764 to 1774; and the consequent dispute between Spain and England.

3rd. Their state from the ending of that dispute; and under what uncontroverted sovereignty they have existed down to the present day, that is, for the last sixty years.

This naturally leads to the question of – whether the sovereignty of the Malvinas has been, and is still vested, in the crown of Great Britain? – or – whether it has been, and is still, vested in the United Provinces of the Rio de la Plata?

The history of the Malvinas is one of the simplest and best authenticated upon record; and yet, – either because it relates to times when there existed a mania for discovering remote and unpeopled lands; or because new dominions were acquired on very lax principles, and in a manner very indefinite when the law of nations was still imperfect; or because the lively, though ephemeral, interest, taken in an ancient dispute, may have given rise to some erroneous traditions or national prejudices, – the matter has sometimes been confounded in a very extraordinary manner, wholly contrary to what might have been expected from the evidence of public documents of sufficient solemnity, and of easy access. Even geographical errors have arisen: *Puerto de la Cruzada, or Port Egmont,* has been spoken of as comprehending *Port Luis, or Port de la Soledad,* &c.; and, by another error, a part, and not the greatest part, of the Malvinas has been strangely mistaken for the whole of them.

It has been sometimes pretended that the first glimpse, whether accidental or otherwise, of an until then unknown country, by a *civilized and christian people,* gave a title of seignory over the newly-seen land in favor of that nation to which the navigators, or persons figuratively styling themselves discoverers belonged.

This mode of appropriation of a territory, in virtue of a casual view thereof, was so vague; so far from reasonable; so liable to interminable disputes; and it was almost always so nearly impossible to decide upon the jarring pretensions of different European nations, that it has very properly ceased to be accounted a good title to dominion; and although attempts have been made to remove uncertainties, by the obervance of certain forms on taking possession, such as the military ceremonial of landing under salutes – hoisting the national colors – erecting crosses – or leaving other memorials, – the same inconveniences and uncertainties continued until, at length, by an understanding, which may be called universal, and more conformable to the principles of reason and philosophy, it was agreed or admitted that – to establish a right to dominion, the fortuitous act of discovery, or a momentary possession, is not sufficient: – it must be a formal and tranquil settlement, which includes habitation and culture.

With reference to this principle, a modern Publicist says "the simple fact of having been the first to discover, or to visit, an island, &c., abandoning it afterwards, appears to be an insufficient title when no permanent vestige of possession, and will, remains; and it is not without reason that frequent disputes have arisen between nations, as among philosophers, as to whether crosses, flagstaffs, inscriptions, &c. be sufficient to give, or preserve, the exclusive dominion to a country not in culture." (De Martens Précis du droit des gens modernes de l'Europe).

It is not therefore, of much importance, in the present day, to ascertain which was the nation that first caught sight of the Malvinas, as they are called by the French und Spaniards – Falkland Isles, by the English – Sabal, and Gibbel de Wert, by the Dutch – and Pepys by others, – because neither the discovery alone, nor the name, can be taken as deciding, or proving, any thing touching the sovereignty and possession of those islands.

But if this point were in any way interesting, and if there be some data to clear it from obscurity, all the probabilities concur in awarding to Spaniards the claim of being the earliest discoverers.

It is undeniable that Fernando Magallanes, in the service of Spain, – who gave his name to the Straits which terminate the southern continent, and divide it from Tierra del Fuego – was the first navigator who visited those regions, which he did in October 1520, long before the Rio de la Plata was discovered, and when scarcely twenty-seven years had elapsed since the grand discovery of the New World by Columbus. Magallanes must have seen the Malvinas, and would hardly neglect the proper forms according to the usages of his time, and so generally practised by his cotemporaries in enterprizes of this nature to caracterize them as fruits of their own exertions in honor of their sovereign. Eight years afterwards the Straits were passed by the Spaniard Loiza, who was followed by navigators of the same nation – Alcozaba in 1535 – Villalobos in 1549, and others. For more than a century the navigation to the Pacific was by way of Magellan's Straits, and this navigation, which was entirely in the power of Spain, then exclusive mistress of Chili and Peru, must have given frequent opportunities to her mariners for exploring the islands referred to, and which were situated on their route.

Sir Francis Drake, in the service of England, entered the Straits in 1578. To him has been ascribed the discovery of Cape Horn, and he might also have seen the Malvinas. His observations, however, left all in so much uncertainty that, 196 years afterwards, the celebrated Captain Cook on his second voyage of discovery, in the year 1774, was still without any accurate idea of the configuration of the Cape, nor did he know whether it formed a part of Tierra del Fuego. The general opinion has pronounced that Jacob le Maire, in the service of the Dutch republic, was the first discoverer of Cape Horn: his voyage took place in 1616.

If English writers have wished to fix upon Davis, the companion of Cavendish, the fortuitous discovery of the Malvinas in 1592, in the reign of Queen Elizabeth, and remark that two years afterwards they were visited by Sir Richard Hawkins, who gave them the name of Maidenland in honor of his sovereign, still it cannot be denied that this was an act so transient that in 1598 the States of Holland believed that they had discovered them anew, and denominated them the Isles of Sabal de Wert, in compliment to the admiral of that expedition.

France has also contended for the honor of the first discovery by means of vessels sent expressly from St. Malo, between 1700 ans 1708. These voyages acquired for the islands the name of Malouines, or Malvinas, which has been generally preserved to them on all charts that are not English; and no doubt exists that it was the French who first took formal possession of them; who established the first settlement in them; and who first inhabited them.

Respecting the original discovery, there remains to be noticed two opinions not devoid of force: the first is that of Monsieur de Bougainville, chief of the French colony in the Malvinas, who, in the printed account of his second voyage to them, observes "I believe that the first discovery can be attributed solely to the famous navigator Amerigo Vespucci who, in the third voyage that he made for the discovery of America, explored the northern coast of them in 1502. He certainly did not know whether they formed part of an island, or of the continent, but from the route that he followed; from the latitude to which he attained; and even the description which he gives of the island, there is no difficulty in deciding that it was that of the Malvinas."

The other opinion is that broached by the British Naval Chronicle, of 1809, which states that "although the discovery of the Malvinas has been attributed to Davis, they were very probably seen by Magellan, and others who followed him."

To finish, here, the controversy, namely, if no nation whatever could produce other titles to the Malvinas than – first discovery, unsupported by actual possession – it is clear that Spain, during the period now under consideration, is the only who could justify any species of right to what may be deemed accessory, points, or outworks of the continent, and immediately conducive to its security; and it was more reasonable for Spain to keep the points adjacent to her American coasts, than to forego her claims, in favor of another power separated by there thousand leagues of ocean. At least the Malvinas, until then, might be looked upon as being without an owner, *res nullius*.

It may be further inferred, from the foregoing, that there exists no positive, or satisfactory, proof that English navigators were the first who discovered those islands.

Having settled the first point of this enquiry, – namely, *the primitive discovery of the Malvinas, unfollowed by occupation,* – we now come to the second, that is to say, their formal occupation from 1764 to 1774, and the consequent dispute between Spain and England. From a doubtful and questionable title, that of – *the first discovery* – we pass on to a real title, firm and mainfest, that of – *first possession;* – and here occurs, in an authentic manner, the proof that *the people by whom the first European settlement was made, and possession first taken, were the French.*

Monsieur de Bougainville, Colonel of Infantry and Captain in the French navy, was the first founder of a colony, in those islands, with the leave and under the sanction of Louis XV. He sailed from St. Malo on the 15th of September 1763 and arrived at this islands on the 3rd of February 1764, when he found them totally destitute of inhabitants and without any traces of ever having been cultivated. Having caused houses to be built for his colonists, together with a warehouse and a small fort on the easternmost island, which was afterwards called *Port Louis,* or the *Port de la Soledad de Malvinas,* he, on the 17th of March, erected an obelisk, under which was deposited a medallion of his Sovereign, bearing an inscription commemorative of the event. He returned to France in quest of further aids for the enterprise thus begun: and early in 1765 revisited that colony which thrived unmolested, but at length he had orders from his court to deliver it to Spain, which orders he complied with on his third voyage to the Malvinas in 1767. The details of all these circumstances are extant in the work of that officer, entitled "*Voyage autour du Monde, par la Frégate du Roi, la Boudeuse, et la Flûte l'Etoile en* 1766, 1767, 1768, et 1769. – Paris 1771."

Spain who had complained of the establishment in the Malvinas, and who regarded it as intrusive, did nevertheless respect the possession, and the title of first occupant *(favor possessionis)* vested in the French government, nor was the cession of the colony negotiated without stipulating for a considerable sum, as an indemnification, the payment of which is certified in a receipt signed by Monsieur de Bougainville on the 4th of October 1766...

By this instrument Monsieur de Bougainville acknowledged to have received from Spain six hundred and eighteen thousand one hundred and eight livres, thirteen sous, and eleven deniers, to re-imburse the St. Malo company their expences in forming their settlements in the Malvinas, and it is worthy of passing remark that more than half that sum, or 62,625 dollars, was received in bills paid by the treasury of Buenos-Ayres.

Meanwhile in England where, it would appear, nothing was known of that French colony, Commodore *Byron* was sent, in 1765, a year after the settlement of Port Louis, to take the islands in the name of His Britannic Majesty, but this officer did no more than enact some pretensive ceremonies in *Port Egmont.* In 1766 he was succeeded by Captain *Macbride* who, with a military force, landed at that place, and built a fort. Now it is quite clear that the arrival of this expedition, under Captain *Macbride* at one of the Malvinas, is the epoch at which British occupancy began, and that this was subsequent to the occupancy of the French. In other words, the French had anticipated, by two years, the English settlement, – not with flags and salutes but, – with inhabitants, habitations, and actual culture. The fact, then, – supported by historical evidence, of the most authentic character, and even by English authorities, – is that the first occupancy belongs indisputably to the French.

In what manner the concurrent parties (the English and the French) behaved towards each other is apparent from the testimony of Monsieur de Bougainville in his before-cited work, chap. 3, pag. 52 to 53 where he says, "Yet, as we have just observed, Commodore *Byron* had come, in the month of January 1765, to reconnoitre the Malvinas islands. He had touched at the west of our settlement in a harbour which we had already denominated *Puerto de la Cruzada,* and had taken possession of those islands for the crown of England, without leaving, there, any inhabitant. It was not until 1766 that the English sent a colony to settle in the Puerto de la Cruzada, which they had named *Port Egmont;* and Captain *Macbride* commandant of the frigate, *Jason,* came to our settlement in the beginning of December of the same year. His pretension was that these lands belonged to the King of Great Britain; he threatened to make a forcible landing if continued resistance was opposed to him; paid a visit to the commandant; and, on the same day, put to sea."

"Such was," he adds, "the state of the Malvina Islands when we delivered them up to the Spaniards, *whose original right was thus corroborated by that which we incontestably derived from the fact of our being the first occupants.*"

The court of Spain appointed Don *Felipe Ruiz Puente* to receive the Malvinas from the French authorities, in virtue of the before-named convention, and in virtue of orders to the same effect from His Most Christian Majesty. Puente announced his arrival, to the Governor of Buenos-Ayres, Don *Francisco Buccarelli,* in a despatch of the 25th of April 1767, stating that on the 27th of March, the forms of the cession had been fulfilled.

After the Spaniards had been installed in the dominion, and possession, of this heretofore French colony, with the sanction of its founders, and by the payment of a price, which gave to this transaction all the character of a perfect contract, – they were nevertheless disquieted by an intimation, brought in a ship from the English colony of *Port Egmont,* that these islands belonged to the crown of Great Britain. This intimation was answered, by the Spaniards, with an expression of their surprise at a proceeding which disallowed their rights; and said, that they were within the dominions of their own sovereign, therefore, it was for the English to go away. This answer appears to have been natural, since the Spaniards had long been accustomed to observe that England did not deny their prior claim, to those islands. An English author (Miller, History of the Reign of George III.) says, – that in 1744 the English projected an establishment in the Malvinas, on the recommendation of Lord *Anson,* after his voyage round the globe, as the best place for establishing a port of refreshment before doubling Cape Horn. Preparations were made, about ten years afterwards, – when the same Admiral *Anson* was placed at the head of the Admiralty, – for carrying his plan into effect, but it was *opposed by the King of Spain, as the islands belonged to him.* The Spanish ministry declared that if the object of the voyage were to form an establishment in the islands, it would be an act of hostility towards Spain, the mistress of them; but that if it was merely curiosity he would give whatever information was desired without the necessity of incurring the expense of expeditions for its gratification. On perceiving this, (adds the author) the English desisted from that enterprize.

Nor did the Spaniards confine themselves to answering in the terms observable above, for they made remonstrance directly with the settlement at *Port Egmont,* giving instructions to their cruizers to protest, to the English officers, that it was contrary to the faith of treaties for them to come into those dominions without the express consent of His Catholic Majesty. This is apparent from the official correspondence of Don *Felipe Ruiz Puente* in the archives of Buenos-Ayres.

At length this alteration acquired a new interest from the expedition sent from Buenos Ayres in the beginning of 1770 by the governor *Buccarelli,* under the commandant of the Royal Marine, Don *Juan Ignacio Madariaga,* to expel the colony from Port Egmont; and on the 10th of June in that year was signed a capitulation by which the British forces and subjects were to retire from the island within a specified period, and which they did, it being allowed that, until their departure, the English flag should remain hoisted at their barracks on shore; but that the artillery and other warlike stores should be left behind.

In order to establish the circumstances and details of this incident, the most extraordinary that occurs in the history of the Malvinas, and to obviate repetitions, the Undersigned may be permitted to refer to the *State Papers,* published in the *Annual Register* of 1771, (Vol. XIV, seventh edition, London, 1817.) in which occurs the correspondence of the commandant *Madariaga;* the capitulation of the British forces in *Port Egmont;* the dispute that subsequently arose out of it, between England and Spain; and the adjustment thereof, on the 22nd of January 1771, by the Prince of *Masserano,* ambassador from Spain to London, and accepted by the Earl of *Rochford,* secretary of state for foreign affairs to His Britannic Majesty.

...

-Thus terminated the dispute between England and Spain respecting the Malvinas, or rather respecting Port Egmont. Henceforward, that is to say from 1771, there occurs no complaint, or quarrel; no compulsion, or violence; and if Great Britain, reinstated in possession of the disputed point, abandons it three years afterwards, (in May 1774) it must have been because she was either impelled to do it of her own free-will, or, as we shall soon see, at the dictation of her own honour, and by her engagement contracted in the convention of the 22nd of January.

By this treaty we see the English re-possessed of Port Egmont, and satisfied. We see the Spaniards also continuing in possession of Port Luis, in the same group of islands, and in immediate vicinage. Both possessors are in front of each other; they observe each other near at hand; and they respect each other. The islands are very small, to be an appendage of two crowns. One of the two possessors must preponderate as the more ancient, and, therefore, the more true.

The first glance at the convention of the 22nd of January 1771, suggests peculiar reflections. The Spanish government protest, in this solemn instrument, that the restitution of Port Egmont is not to operate to their prejudice, and *reserve to themselves their rights to the sovereignty of the islands.* His Britannic Majesty's government, in the precise act of answering this instrument and of accepting it, do not advert to that clause. Is not this admitting the reservation with which Spain invested herself? At least this silence was not the way to resist or invalidate her claim; and it really appears that the opportunity, or perhaps the necessity, of answering it by a counter-reservation, could not be more natural, or more obvious, considering all the circumstances of the case. This gives birth to a very strong suspicion that, below the surface of this transaction, there was something mysterious, but withal of so much importance, that it affected, and decided, the nature of the convention. Hence it was that it had scarcely seen the light, when it excited the astonishment of a no less wary, and accomplished, statesman than the illustrious Earl of Chatham, when, on the 6th of February in that year, he made a motion for laying before the twelve judges, the following questions: –

"1st. Whether, in consideration of law, the Imperial Crown of this realm can hold any territories or possessions thereunto belonging, otherwise than in sovereignty?"

"2dly. Whether the declaration or instrument, for the restitution of the port and fort called Egmont, to be made by the Catholic King to His Majesty, under a reservation of disputed right of sovereignty, expressed in the declaration or instrument stipulating such restitution, can be accepted or carried into execution, without derogating from the maxim of law, before referred to, touching the inherent and essential dignity of the Crown of Great Britain?"

On the other hand, could it have been credible that a convention which apparently left two rival jurisdictions on the same spot, was formed, or was ever intended to be permanent?

Whence could have originated the persuasion common to English historians, geographers, and other writers of the time, who agree uniformly, and with express reference to the convention of the 22nd of January 1771, *that Great Britain ceded the Malvinas Islands to Spain?* Can they all be in error? Is it possible that national historians treating, *ex professo,* of the restitution of Port Egmont to Great Britain, would call it neither more nor less *a cession of all the Falkland Islands to Spain on the part of England,* if such had not been really the case?

The Undersigned might, here, make numerous citations from those authorities which afford evidence of the cession; but he will confine himself to the mention of one production of that period, also English, which pointedly clears up the mystery attending the convention of the 22nd of January. "Anecdotes of the Right Honorable William Pitt, Earl of Chatham, Vol. III., chap. 39." states: –

"While Lord Rochford was negociating with Prince Masserano, Mr. Stuart M'Kenzie was negociating with Monsieur François, Secretary to the Embassy of France at the court of London. At length, – about an hour before the meeting of parliamant on the 22nd January 1771, – a declaration was signed by the Spanish ambassador, under French orders, and a French indemnification, for the restitution of Falkland's Islands to his Britannic Majesty, *but the important condition upon which the declaration was obtained, was not mentioned in the declaration. This condition was that the British forces should evacuate Falkland's Islands as soon as convenient after they were put in possession of Port and Fort Egmont.* And the British ministry engaged, as a pledge of their sincerity to keep that promise, that they would be the first to disarm.

"Two days after the Spanish ambassador had signed the declaration, he received orders of recall; but his fate was like that of Mr. Harris; in a short time afterwards he received orders to remain.

"In the month of February 1771, the Spanish minister at Madrid hinted to Mr. Harris, the intention of the Spanish court, to require, of the British ministry, *a perfection of engagements as they were understood.* Mr. Harris's dispatch, containing this hint, was received by the minister on the 4th of March. Three days afterwards, the Spanish messenger arrived, with orders to Prince Masserano to make a positive demand of the cession of Falkland Islands, to the King of Spain. The Spanish ambassador first communicated his information of these orders to the French ambassador, with a view of knowing if he could concur with him in making the demand. On the 14th they held a conference with Lord Rochford on the subject. His Lordship's answer was consonant to the spirit he had uniformly shewn. The reply from France was civil, but mentioned the family compact. The answer from Spain did not reach London until the 20th of April. In the mean time, the ministers held several conferences with Mr. Stuart Mackenzie. The result of the whole was, the English set the example to disarm; and *Falkland's Islands were totally evacuated and abandoned in a short time afterwards, and have ever since been in the possession of the Spaniards.*"

This disclosure which, – by the rules of impartial criticism, – cannot but be allowed to have considerable weight, is confirmed, – with respect to the cession or relinquishment of the Malvinas on the part of England, – by two dispatches from the Spanish Minister Arriaga, who signed the order of the 7th February 1771, for the restitution of Port Egmont, and who, on the 9th of April 1774, told the viceroy of Buenos-Ayres, and the governor of the Malvinas, that *the Court of London had* offered *to abandon the establishment in the great Malvina,* which was the same with Port Egmont. Authentic copies of these dispatches, taken from the archives of Buenos Ayres, where the originals exist, are in the possession of the Undersigned, who believes them to be of sufficient importance to require that he should cite them literally:

"By the annexed copy of a dispatch, you will be acquainted with the information this day given to the Governor of the Malvinas, relative to *the* offer *of the Court of London to abandon the establishment which they made in the great Malvina,* of which, by order of the King, I apprise you that you may, on your part, make dispositions for its fulfilment. God preserve you many years.

Aranjuez, 9th of April 1774."

(Signed)   *Don Julian de Arriaga.*

Sr. Don Juan José Vertiz.

"Offers *being made, as they are, by the Court of London, to relinquish* the settlement made by them in the great Malvina, withdrawing thence the few troops and inhabitants who were there, the King desires that you be made acquainted with this matter, in order that you may consequently observe, with due prudence and caution, whether the English do, in fact, abandon the said settlement, without undertaking to form any other in the immediate vicinity; and that, having ascertained that they have done that in the terms set forth, you will, from time to time, renew your exertions to make sure that they do not return to that quarter, informing me most precisely of whatever may occur at present, or at any future time: which instruction I communicate to you by His Majesty's order, to be exactly complied with, until, on a future opportunity, a more complete idea be given of all that pertains to this subject. God preserve you many years.

Aranjuez, 9th April 1774."

(Signed)   *Don Julian de Arriaga.*

"P. S. Until farther advices, which I shall address to you, you are not to deviate from the letter of the instructions I now give you: nor allow any one to proceed to the said relinquished settlement, except those whom you send for the purpose on which they are ordered.

To the Governor of the Malvinas."

In fact, on the 22nd of May 1774, three years after the restitution, we see England peacefully withdrawing her settlement from Port Egmont without any one having compelled her to this step, and without the occurrence of any new altercation, or violence. The former dispute was terminated; and it would be an anachronism to confound this voluntary egress, with the ejection in 1770 by the expedition of Buccarelli. The fact, then, of this pacific abandonment comes singularly in support of the reality of the *cession,* or, as some English writers explain it, the fulfilment of the contract by each party, for *"the Spaniards fulfilled their engagement by restoring Port Egmont, and the English fulfilled theirs by abandoning it after such surrender."*

Lieutenant Clayton who commanded in Port Egmont in the name of His Britannic Majesty, left an inscription, on a leaden plate, bearing date the 22nd of May 1774, in which he declared that the *Falkland Islands,* as well as the fort of Port Egmont, and its warehouses, stores, &c. belonged, of right, solely to His Majesty George III.; in further proof of which he also left hoisted the British flag.

But, in the first place, if an inscription were sufficient to preserve a dominion, that of Lieutenant Clayton's was long subsequent to the French inscription of 1764, and, for that reason, is of no validity. In the second place, it is over-done, for it seeks to invalidate the Spanish dominion of *Port Luis,* acknowledged in the convention of the 22nd of January 1771. Lastly, it was illegal if, as there is reason to believe, the relinquishment of Port Egmont was in consequence of an agreement on the part of the government to which he belonged; an agreement not the less binding because it was secret.

It has been said that this inscription, and this flag, thus left behind, were intimative of an intention of returning to occupy the territory at a more convenient opportunity; which, by the way, does not appear to have occurred until after the lapse of sixty years.

Notwithstanding, it is requisite to observe that if this *intention* was effective, it cannot be reconciled with the faith that was pledged; and the question would resolve itself into, – whether Great Britain had offered to withdraw from those islands. Then, to prove that intention, it was requisite to leave other more permanent vestiges of possession and will. It is clear, that if neither exterior signs of that nature, nor even the priority of discovery sufficed for a title of dominion, conformably to established opinions, as little could they suffice for its preservation, and transmission.

Property merely intentional must yield to formal and physical property. It may also be observed, as singularly strange, that the very act of the evacuation which puts an end to the possession, should have the effect of extending the *ideal* dominion, to points which England never obtained, to *all the Malvina Islands,* and specially to *Port Luis,* or *Puerto de la Soledad,* called, by the English,

Berkeley Sound. It might be asked whether Lieutenant Clayton, on completely abandoning Port Egmont, could impose a *veto* to all nations of the globe, that they should never inhabit the islands which he left desert, nor make use of them for cultivation, as of an abode which the *hand, and the will, of the Creator* had destined for man. In especial manner it may be remarked that, this interdict could not be extended to Spain, whom England had admitted, and treated with, as sovereign of the isle, to the eastward, in which is situated Port Luis.

From what has been stated, it results that the claims of Spain to the Malvinas, were – her *formal occupation* of them; the purchase of them from France, at a price agreed on; and the cession, or relinquishment, of them by England *(derivative occupation.)* This closes the period of the ten years, just passed in review, or the dispute between the two crowns from 1764 to 1774.

"Property is acquired *de jure* by an occupation without defect; it is preserved by a *continued possession.*" (Günther's Völkerrecht.)

This Spanish occupation then continued without disturbance on the part of any other power; and it is worthy of remark, in the public treaties that subsequently took place between England and Spain, no allusion, or reference, is made to those islands, the inference being, that the ancient question was considered as definitively settled. Here might be given a list of Spanish Governors who held command in the islands, and resided constantly in Port Luis, in immediate dependance on, and at the expense of the vice-regal government of Buenos Ayres.

It is well known to all the World that, by the Revolution which took place on the 25th of May 1810, and the solemn Declaration of Independence on the 9th of July 1816, a political Community was constituted, in the jurisdiction of Buenos Ayres, under the name, style, and title of "The United Provinces of the Rio de la Plata," – which has been recognized by Great Britain, and other principal nations. This political Community could not exist without territory, as where there is no independence of territory there can be no sovereign state, and thus as the community acquired the right of treaties, and that of competency to negociate with foreign powers, it also acquired the right of state property *(jus in patrimonium republicae.)* The United Provinces, consequently succeeded Spain in the rights which that nation, from whom they separated, had possessed in that jurisdiction. The Malvinas had always been a part of that country, or of that district, and, as such, they formed part of the dominion, or public property, of the new state, *(patrimonium reipublicoe publicum;)* and were claimed, inhabited, and garrisoned by its subjects. The sovereignty of the islands which ceased, in the Spanish government, on the Independence of America, could not pass in succession to England, nor revive a question, and claims that were extinct.

Supported by so great, and so solid, a basis; – strong in the justice of their cause, and in the consciousness of their rights, – The Government of the Republic protested, on the 22nd of January 1833, to the British Legation in Buenos Ayres, against the expulsion of their garrison and settlement from the Malvinas, and against the assumption of sovereignty which has been made in them, in the name of Great Britain, &c., giving orders to the Undersigned to reiterate this Protest to the Government of His Britannic Majesty.

Therefore, the Undersigned, – in fulfilment of his orders and instructions, – protests formally in the name of the United Provinces of the Rio de la Plata, against the sovereignty lately assumed in the Malvina Islands by the crown of Great Britain, and against the espoliation and ejection, of the Republic's settlement in Port Luis, otherwise called *Puerto de la Soledad,* by His Britannic Majesty's corvette Clio, with demand for reparation claimable in such cases for *lexion* inflicted, as well as for every act consequent on that proceeding.

The United Provinces make this just demand to the honour of His Britannic Majesty's Government, and to the opinion of an impartial World.

London, June 17th 1833, Year the twenty-fourth of the liberty, and eighteenth of the Independence of the United Provinces of the Rio de la Plata.

(Signed)   *Manuel Moreno.*
                    His Excellency,
                    The Right Honorable Viscount Palmerston, G.C.B.

Annex 28:   Response by Britain, January 8, 1834,
to the protest by Argentina of June 17,
1833 (Excerpt).
Source: British and Foreign State Papers,
Vol. 22 (1833-34), p.1384.

The Undersigned, &c. has the honour to acknowledge the receipt of the Note of M. Moreno, &c., dated the 17th of June last, in which he formerly protests, in the name of his Government, "against the Sovereignty lately assumed in the Malvina (or Falkland) Islands, by the Crown of Great Britain."

Before the Undersigned proceeds to reply to the allegations advanced in M. Moreno's Note, upon which his Protest against this act on the part of His Majesty is founded, the Undersigned deems it proper to draw M. Moreno's attention to the contents of the Protest which Mr. Parish, the British Chargé d'Affaires at Buenos-Ayres, addressed, in the name of his Court, to the Minister for Foreign Affairs of the Republic, on the 19th of November, 1829, in consequence of the British Government having been informed that the President of The United Provinces of the Rio de la Plata had issued Decrees, and had made Grants of Land, in the nature of Acts of Sovereignty over the Islands in question.

That Protest made known to the Government of The United Provinces of the Rio de la Plata: –

1st. That the Authority which that Government had thus assumed, was considered by the British Government as incompatible with the Sovereign Rights of Great Britain over the Falkland Islands.

2dly. That those Sovereign Rights, which were founded upon the original Discovery and subsequent Occupation of those Islands, had acquired an additional sanction from the fact, that His Catholic Majesty had restored the British Settlement, which had been forcibly taken possession of by a Spanish Force, in the year 1771.

3rdly. That the withdrawal of His Majesty's Forces from the Falkland Islands, in 1774, could not invalidate the just rights of Great Britain, because that withdrawal took place only in pursuance of the system of retrenchment adopted at that time by His Majesty's Government.

4thly. That the Marks and Signals of Possession, and of Property, left upon the Islands, the British Flag still flying, and all the other formalities observed upon the occasion of the departure of the Governor, were calculated not only to assert the rights of Ownership, but to indicate the intention of resuming the Occupation of the Territory at some future period.

Upon these grounds, Mr. Parish protested against the pretensions set up on the part of the Argentine Republic, and against all acts done to the prejudice of the just rights of Sovereignty theretofore exercised by the Crown of Great Britain.

The Minister for Foreign Affairs of the Republic acknowledged the receipt of the British Protest, and acquainted Mr. Parish that his Government would give it their particular consideration, and that he would communicate to him their decision upon the subject, so soon as he should receive directions to that effect.

No Answer was, however, at any time returned, nor was any objection raised, on the part of the Government of The United Provinces of the Rio de la Plata, to the rights of Great Britain, as asserted in that Protest; but the Buenos-Ayrean Government persisted, notwithstanding the receipt of that Protest, in exercising those acts of Sovereignty against which the Protest was specially directed.

The Government of The United Provinces of the Rio de la Plata could not have expected, after the explicit Declaration which had been so formally made of the right of the Crown of Great Britain to the Islands in question, that His Majesty would silently submit to such a course of proceeding; nor could that Government have been surprised at the step which His Majesty thought proper to take, in order to the resumption of rights which had never been abandoned, and which had only been permitted to lie dormant, under circumstances which had been explained to the Buenos-Ayrean Government.

The Claim of Great Britain to the Sovereignty of the Falkland Islands having been unequivocally asserted and maintained, during the Discussions with Spain, in 1770 and 1771, which had nearly led to a War between the 2 Countries, and Spain having deemed it proper to put an end to those Discussions, by restoring to His Majesty the Places from which British Subjects had been expelled; the Government of the United Provinces could not reasonably have anticipated that the British Government would permit any other State to exercise a right, as derived from Spain, which Great Britain had denied to Spain herself; and this consideration alone would fully justify His Majesty's Government in declining to enter into any further explanation upon a question which, upwards of half a century ago, was so notoriously and decisively adjusted with another Government more immediately concerned.

But M. Moreno, in the Note which he has addressed to the Undersigned, has endeavoured to shew that, at the termination of the memorable Discussions referred to between Great Britain and Spain, a Secret Understanding existed between the 2 Courts, in virtue of which Great Britain was pledged to restore the Islands to Spain at a subsequent period, and that the evacuation of them, in 1774, by His Majesty, was the fulfilment of that pledge.

The existence of such a Secret Understanding is alleged to be proved; 1st. By the reservation, as to the former right of Sovereignty over the Islands, which was contained in the Spanish Declaration, delivered at the time of the restoration of Port Egmont and its Dependencies to His Majesty; and, 2ndly. By the concurrent description of the Transaction, as it took place between the Parties, given in certain Documents and Historical Works.

Although the reservation referred to, cannot be deemed to possess any substantial weight, inasmuch as no notice whatever is taken of it in the British Counter-Declaration, which was exchanged against it; and although the evidence adduced from unauthentic Historical Publications cannot be regarded as entitled to any weight whatever, with a view to a just decision upon a point of International Rights; yet, as the Allegations above-mentioned involve an imputation against the good faith of Great Britain, to which His Majesty's Government cannot but feel sensibly alive, the Undersigned has been honoured with the King's Commands to cause the Official Correspondence with the Court of Madrid, at the period alluded to, to be carefully inspected, in order that the circumstances which really took place upon the occasion might be accurately ascertained.

That inspection has accordingly been made; and the Undersigned has the honour to communicate to M. Moreno the following Extracts, which contain all the material information that can be gathered from that Correspondence relative to the Transaction in question.

...

M. Moreno will perceive that the above authentic Papers, which have been faithfully extracted from the Volumes of Correspondence with Spain, deposited in the State Paper Office, contain no allusion whatever to any Secret Understanding between the 2 Governments, at the period of the restoration of Port Egmont and its Dependencies to Great Britain, in 1771; nor to the evacuation of Falkland Islands, in 1774, as having taken place for the purpose of fulfilling any such Understanding. On the contrary, it will be evident to M. Moreno, that their contents afford conclusive inference that no such Secret Understanding could have existed.

The Undersigned need scarcely assure M. Moreno, that the Correspondence which has been referred to, does not contain the least particle of evidence in support of the contrary supposition, entertained by the Government of the United Provinces of the Rio de la Plata, nor any confirmation of the several particulars related in M. Moreno's Note.

The Undersigned trusts, that a perusal of these details will satisfy M. Moreno, that the Protest which he has been directed to deliver to the Undersigned, against the re-assumption of the Sovereignty of the Falkland Islands by His Majesty, has been drawn up under an erroneous impression, as well of the understanding under which the Declaration and Counter-Declaration relative to the restoration of Port Egmont and its Dependencies were signed and exchanged between the 2 Courts, as of the motives which led to the temporary relinquishment of those Islands by the British Government; and the Undersigned cannot entertain a doubt but that, when the true circumstances of the case shall have been communicated to the knowledge of the Government of The United Provinces of the Rio de la Plata, that Government will no longer call in question the right of Sovereignty which has been exercised by His Majesty, as undoubtedly belonging to the Crown of Great Britain.

The Undersigned requests, &c.

M. Moreno.

Palmerston.

Annex 29: Response by Argentina, December 29, 1834,
to the Note by Britain of January 8, 1834
(Excerpt).
Source: W. Down, op. cit., p. 240.

The U.S. Minister Plenipotentiary of the United Provinces of the River Plata, having sent to his Government the communication of H. E. Visct. Palmerston of the 8th of January 1834, by which he was pleased to reply to the protest of the 17th of June 1833 against the violent occupation and assumption of the Sovereignty of the Falkland Islands by H.M. Government, has received special orders to reply to that communication with the arguments which he has the honour of exhibiting in the present note.

To this end, he cannot avoid observing that H.E.'s answer leaves still undecided the question of right, the only one which is essential relatively to this subject, turning on the fact as to who has been, and never has ceased to be, the Sovereign and legitimate possessor of those Islands.

The point of right must necessarily be determined not by the antiquity of the pretensions of the parties, but by the impartial and just estimation of the Titles which they have supposed, and still suppose to possess concerning the subject of the present dispute. These titles being those of Sovereignty, it is clear that they cannot exist simultaneously in two independent nations or Governments, and that whether they be compared with each other, or examined separately and directly, we shal be able to arrive at the knowledge of their whole legal validity.

The United Provinces have proved by unexceptionable documents that their Titles to the Falkland Islands or to the Isle of Soledad or Port Louis (separated from Port Egmont by a straight or channel of the Sea) are: *lawful purchase from France, priority of occupation and formal cultivation and inhabitation;* and, finally, notorious and tranquil *possession* for more than half a century, up to the moment when they were dislodged by force on the 5th of January 1833. These Titles are founded on the principle that the priority of occupation confers real and exclusive dominion over the unappropriated object, a principle laid down in the codes of nations as derived from eternal justice, which principle is the basis on which rests the inviolability of every private and public property, and which Blackstone calls it's true ground and foundation. "Occupancy", he says, "is the true ground and foundation of all property." (Book II Ch. 15) A nation cannot produce any better right to the spot it has on the surface of the globe, than that it was the first to possess itself of that spot; that it has created the wealth distributed in its district, and that it has recommended that spot by its labour to the subsistence and fortunes of its posterity. It would be difficult to meet with a title more ancient than this, more venerable and more universally admitted.

On the part of Gt. Britain the reply of H.E. only mentions the *priority of discovery;* but the discovery alone, without the occupation of the thing, has never been held in any jurisprudence a preferable title to that of real occupation; on the contrary, it has always been questioned whether the said priority can establish a valid title; and it is remarkable that England herself has maintained in other disputes with Spain that the mere discovery of a country does not confer property and Sovereignity when discovery has not been followed by occupation.

If it be supposed that English Navigators were the first to discover or *see* the Falkland Islands, a supposition, however, which is contrary to the best evidence of history, it is a fact abundantly established, that they did not occupy or form any colony in them. It is an undisputed fact that the English establishment in West Island or Port Egmont by Capt. M'Bride (the only one of the Falkland Isles ever possessed by England) was not made till two years after East Island or Soledad was already formally inhabited and occupied by another nation.

On the other hand, the priority of discovery, for which there are no other documents than the historical evidence of the voyages authorised by various Governments to that part of the world, is of necessity limited to proceedings which are equivocal and of so little moment that that alone must suffice for repudiating it in the present case as a title of property...

It would therefore seem that the error of one of the parties in the present dispute proceeds from the starting point. England deduces her right to the Islands from the priority of her discovery, which it has been shown above of what description it was. The United Provinces derive theirs from the priority of occupation.

The U.S. has confined himself here to stating this pre-eminent right of *prior occupation*, which incontestably belongs to the United Provinces; but there is besides another right which if not supereminent is at least as respectable as the other, that of *possession*, which must not be confounded with the former, – that tranquil and bona fide possession which the United Provinces had of the disputed territory 'till they were expelled without previous intimation by the mere exercise of force. It ought not to be forgotten that it is a principle of universal jurisprudence, and especially of the laws of England that the simple possession of an object which may belong to another protects the possessor, insomuch that they even require the owner or claimant to proceed only by legal investigation, arbitration or amicable adjustment to recover it, and by no other means, which principle as one of mutual security and respect is likewise adopted by the international laws.

It seems that the reply of H.E. considered the protest of Mr Parish, H.M. Chargé d'affaires (on the 19th of November 1829) as a sufficient notice preparatory to force and despoliation. But the protest of Mr Parish on occasion of the decree of the Government of Buenos Ayres of the 10th of June of that year, relative to the establishment of "Soledad" has been the only act of the British Government tending to couple the present question with its pretensions of 1770. According to all legal forms, the protest only renewed a discussion which had rested and was perhaps relinquished and forgotten for more than half a century. The Minister for Foreign Affairs of the Republic surprised at such a claim which he had no idea could be entertained by H.M. Government, contented himself for the moment with acknowledging the receipt of the Protest, and promising a formal answer, which would contain an investigation of all that bore on the subject, but if such an answer, which required some time, was not returned, neither is it known that it had been demanded and pressed for by the diplomatic Agent of H.M. ...

... Great Britain acknowledged that Spain had made the *primitive discovery,* but it contended that the discovery not having been accompanied or followed by *occupation* and *cultivation,* she could found no title of exclusive property in favor of the discoverer. Such was the doctrine supported before Parliament by Mr Pitt, the Minister, in the discussion of the message relative to that dispute (vide Debates) and such is the reason for which it has been said before, that England professed that the mere discovery of a territory confers no property and

Sovereignty, when discovery has not been followed by occupation. It is therefore inferred that the French and Spaniards *having been the first who occupied and cultivated* the Falkland Islands, it is they who must be considered as the masters and proprietors of those Islands according to the principles of H.M. Government itself.

It cannot be alleged against the United Provinces that they wish to revive a question which had been set at rest for more than half a century: on the contrary, the invasion of the Schooner Clio on the 5th January 1833 is what has altered and disturbed the state of things as left by the Convention of the 22nd January 1771.

If the expedition of the Clio had limited itself to West Island (Port Egmont) it might be said that the Government of H.B.M. had re-instated itself in the *status quo* which the ancient Convention left. But the expedition of the Clio went to East Island (Port Soledad) which never was English, requiring the instant evacuation of the garrison and citizens of another state, and possessed itself of properties and objects of value not belonging to subjects of H.M. This procedure overturns directly the principles recognised in 1771, – it transfers to the British flag a territory never before trod by an English foot, with buildings stock and cultivation, which were the products of the industry of another nation; – a nation of the American continent which under the favor of Providence that rules the destinies of mankind has succeeded to the territorial rights of Spain in that jurisdiction, and to which are infallibly due the considerations of justice claimed by every independent people...

Accordingly the Government of the United Provinces, having reconsidered the subject in all it's bearings, finds itself under the necessity of declaring that it cannot acquiesce in the conclusion which the reply of H.E. Viscount Palmerston of the 8th of January 1834 draws from it. It repeats and confirms its protest of the 17th June 1833 against the Sovereignty assumed over the Falkland Islands by the Crown of Great Britain, and begs that the Republic may have restored to it East Island and it's Establishment in Port Soledad in the same state that they were previous to the invasion of H.M. Schooner Clio on the 5th of January 1833.

The present reclamation is founded on such evident rights that the Government of the United Provinces doubts not but that it will be admitted immediately by the Government of H. Brit. My. in conformity with the principles of justice which characterize it.

In conclusion, it remains only for the U.S. to request H.E. the Duke of Wellington etc.

Manuel Moreno

Annex 30: Protest by Argentina, December 18, 1841
(Excerpt).
Source: British and Foreign State Papers,
Vol. 31 (1842-43), p. 1003.

The Undersigned, Minister Plenipotentiary of the United Provinces of Rio de la Plata, has the honour to address his Excellency the Earl of Aberdeen, Her Majesty's Principal Secretary of State for Foreign Affairs, with the view of calling his attention to the discussion pending between the Government of the United Provinces, and that of Her Britannic Majesty, touching the sovereignty of the Malvina Islands, called by the English, Falkland Islands, especially respecting the Eastern Island, or Soledad, and Port Luis, of which the British Government took possession on the 5th of January, 1833, thereby despoiling the United Provinces of that ancient territory and legitimate possession of the Republic.

The Undersigned, in the performance of his duty, and in obedience to orders received from his Government to proceed with the discussion of this subject, and to press it upon the attentive consideration of Her Majesty's Government, feels persuaded that, in the present state of the question, he is relieved from any other duty than that of referring to the proofs contained in the papers produced in the course of this discussion, namely, the protest in the name of the United Provinces, of the 17th of June, 1833; the answer of Viscount Palmerston, then Minister to His Majesty, dated the 8th of January, 1834, and the reply of the Undersigned, of the 29th of December of the same year, in which are set forth with due care, and at full length, the principles and bases of the rights involved in this case.

But it may be permitted to the Undersigned to state summarily that the spoliation of which the United Provinces complain, refers: 1st. To the sovereignty and dominion of the Malvina Islands, particularly the Eastern Island. or Soledad, and Port Luis; 2ndly. To the legal, *bona fide,* and peaceable possession enjoyed by them for more than half a centuary of the said Eastern Island, or Soledad, and Port Luis; 2 points which it is of consequence to avoid confounding, as the complete possession, evidently protected by the best titles and most just right (that is, the purchase from France by a public and well-known contract, the subsequent colonization and cultivation, and, finally, the creation and collection on the spot of property, buildings, and cattle) must give to the United Provinces an incontrovertible right to an immediate and equitable compensation.

The Undersigned may be also permitted to say, that while the note of Viscount Palmerston, the Minister who directed the spoliation complained against, presents nothing but vague and erroneous ideas and assertions in regard to the question of the Malvinas, his Excellency mistaking the geography of the islands, and appearing to assume that the Eastern Island, or Soledad, at all times in possession of the Spaniards, which is 130 miles long and 80 miles broad, is, or has been, a dependency of the Western Island, or Port Egmont, which is only 100 miles long, and about 50 broad; the Government of the United Provinces confirming, on every occasion, the indisputable titles which it produced in its protests of the 17th of June, 1833, and the 29th of December, 1834, has never desisted from declaring, in its annual messages to the Legislature of the State, its great regret that it has not hitherto obtained that satisfaction to which it believes itself entitled, and which it claimed in vain from the preceding Administration.

The Undersigned having thus fulfilled the orders which he has received from his Government, deems it his duty to close this note in the words of his last communication: "This claim is founded on rights so evident, that the Government of the United Provinces does not doubt that it will be attended to without dealy, by His Britannic Majesty's Government, acting in conformity with the principles of justice by which it is characterized."

The Undersigned, & c. Manuel Moreno

The Earl of Aberdeen, K.T.

Annex   31: Protest by Argentina, July 31, 1849.
        Source: L. Muñoz Azpiri, op. cit., Vol. 2
        (1966), p. 195.

Al señor Ministro de Relaciones Exteriores:

El infrascrito tiene el honor de dirigirse al señor Ministro para poner en conocimiento del Excmo. Gobierno la notable incidencia ocurrida en la sesión de la Cámara de Comunes del 27 de julio próximo pasado, con ocasión de haber preguntado Mr. Baillie al Ministerio si era cierto que el gobierno de Buenos Aires reclamaba las islas Malvinas, y, en este caso, qué es lo que se ha hecho en la materia, y estado en que se halla el asunto.

Notando alguna discrepancia en el relato que hacen los diarios, como más o menos se puede en la imperfección del arte taquigráfico de personas *verbatum* y estricamente la conversación, ha consultado el infrascrito varios de ellos, tomando del relato del "Times", que es siempre considerado más correcto, la respuesta que dio S. E. el vizconde Palmerston, como sigue:

«Lord Palmerston dijo que se había hecho reclamación hace muchos años de parte de Buenos Aires a las islas Malvinas (‹Falkland Islands›), y se había resistido por el gobierno británico que la Gran Bretaña siempre había disputado y negado el derecho de España a las Malvinas; y así, no estaba dispuesto a ceder a Buenos Aires lo que había negado a España: Diez o doce años ha, habiendo estado desocupadas por algún tiempo dichas islas, la Gran Bretaña tomó posesión de ellas, y ha mantenido allí desde entonces un establecimiento; y *creía muy desacertado querer revivir una correspondencia que había cesado por la aquiescencia de una de las partes y la perseverancia de la otra*» (artículo del "Times", acompañado).

De esta declaración del vizconde le pareció al infrascrito ser su deber el protestar inmediatamente; y lo ha hecho por la nota que va aquí acompañada, en copia, distinta y señaladamente contra el concepto o aserción ambigua y errónea de retiro de la reclamación de la República y consentimiento en la usurpación de las islas Malvinas por el gobierno británico, reservándome el señalar después otras actitudes bien graves que se observan en la respuesta sobre la historia y estado de la discusión que no era oportuno comprender en dicha representación.

Dios guarde a V. S. muchos años.

Manuel Moreno

Annex 32: Response by Britain, August 8, 1849, to
Protest by Argentina of July 31, 1849.
Source: L. Muñóz Azpiri, op. cit., Vol. 2
(1966), p. 197.

Sir,

I have the honour to acknowledge the receipt of your note of the 31th. July stating that the reply wich *(sic)* I was reported by some of the London Newspapers to have made to a question put to me by Mr. Baillie in the House of Commons en *(sic)* the 27th. of July, did not correctly describe the State of the question between the British Government and Buenos Aires respecting the Falkland Islands; and I have the honour to acquaint you that whatever the Newspapers may have represented me as having said on the occasion above referred to, I have always understood the matter in question to stand exactly in the way described by you in your letter.

I have the honour to be, with the highest consideration, Sir, your most obedient humble servant.

Palmerston

Annex 33: Note by Argentina to Britain, January 2,
1885.
Source: L. Munoz Azpiri, op. cit., Vol. 2
(1966), p. 213.

Nota y Memorándum del Canciller Ortiz al Ministro Monson

Ministerio de
Relaciones Exteriores

Buenos Aires, enero 2 de 1885.

El secretario de Estado y ministro de Relaciones Exteriores que suscribe ha
tenido el honor de recibir una nota de S. E. el E. E. y ministro plenipotenciario
de Su Majestad Británica en la que, en virtud de instrucciones de su gobierno,
tiene ocasión de hacer la representación que enuncia fundada en circunstancias
que han dado ya tema para las comunicaciones confidenciales que han mediado
entre ambos.

Agrega S. E. el señor ministro de Su Majestad Británica que por ley del 18 de
setiembre último el Congreso nacional autorizó el pago al Instituto Geográfico
Argentino de la suma de 25.000 pesos nacionales para cubrir los gastos de la
publicación del mapa de la República que actualmente prepara; que el día 8 del
corriente mes publicó «El Nacional» la afirmación de que el mencionado mapa
incluiría las islas Falkland o Malvinas como territorio argentino y que este aserto
ha sido aceptado como auténtico por otros dos diarios de la capital sin que tal
afirmación se haya contradicho ni oficial ni periodísticamente.

De estos precedentes deriva Su Excelencia que un mapa para el cual ha votado el
Congreso una suma de dinero, no puede ser ni será considerado por el gobierno
de Su Majestad Británica y por el resto de las naciones de otra manera que por un
mapa oficial; y no obstante las razones que verbal y confidencialmente el
infrascrito ha expuesto a S. E. sobre la prematura consulta que le ha dirigido
respecto del mapa que se halla en preparación, y de cuya exactitud no sería
posible formar juicio ni adelantar opinión oficial en ningún sentido desde que tal
obra se realiza bajo exclusiva responsabilidad de un instituto particular, S. E.
manifiesta que en vista de instrucciones terminantes que ha recibido, no puede
dejar duda alguna en cuanto al alcance que su gobierno atribuiría a la inclusión
como territorio argentino en un mapa levantado con la sanción directa y por
cuenta del Congreso nacional de un grupo de islas que forman parte de los
dominios de la Corona británica y que por tales razones no tiene otra alternativa
que la de hacer constar la formal protesta que hace en su elevado carácter contra
tal inclusión, manifestando, con ese motivo, que al mismo tiempo que el gobierno de S. M. Británica lamenta que sucedan actos como el que nos ocupa, adhiere
sinceramente a los sentimientos que atribuye con toda seguridad al gobierno
argentino y que tienen como norma el deseo y la intención de mantener las
relaciones entre la Gran Bretaña y la República Argentina en la misma base de
amistad y de armonía en que han descansado felizmente durante tantos años.

Ha sido bajo los expresados conceptos que el infrascrito ha dado cuenta a S. E. el
Sr. Presidente de la República de su enunciada nota y Protesta, que le ha sido
dirigida el 27 del pasado por el E. E. y ministro plenipotenciario de Su Majestad

Británica, y no obstante la anticipación con que S. E. el Sr. Presidente de la República ha encargado al infrascrito de contestarle expresándole al mismo tiempo los deseos que abriga por que una solución amistosa ponga término a la solución pendiente sobre la soberanía de las Malvinas.

Tomada en su doble aspecto de forma y de fondo, la protesta es inconsecuente con la historia, con el derecho y con los hechos.

Bajo el punto de vista puramente geográfico carece de fundamento desde que no se refiere a hechos producidos, como sería la publicación evidente del mapa, y el gobierno argentino no podría en ningún caso tomarla en consideración desde que se trata de meras conjeturas y afirmaciones noticiosas de los diarios cuyos juicios no es de práctica rectificar oficialmente, porque el gobierno se reserva la facultad de autorizar o no las publicaciones de ese carácter aunque sean costeadas, como al presente, por el tesoro nacional.

Por otra parte, y aun suponiendo que el mapa de que se trata se hubiera ya publicado y contuviera las indicadas islas como parte integrante de la República Argentina, el gobierno de Su Majestad Británica no debería hallar en eso un motivo fundado de protesta desde que esa inclusión no modificaría en nada el estado en que se han considerado siempre las Malvinas, cuya cuestión, como S. E. ha tenido la deferencia de manifestármelo, se halla pendiente y sujeta a la solución de los gobiernos. Esto en lo que se refiere al fin ostensible de la protesta con respecto a la publicación del mapa. Ahora, en cuanto al fondo de la nota que es la afirmación incondicional, de que el grupo de las Malvinas forma parte de los dominos de Su Majestad Británica, cumple el infrascrito recordar a S. E. que la ocupación actual de ese Archipiélago no está asegurada por título indiscutible de dominio; que la soberanía de esas islas ha sido objeto de largas discusiones en el pasado y en el presente siglo, habiendo quedado definitivamente asegurados los derechos de España desde 1774, en que se levantó el establecimiento inglés de Puerto Egmont, hasta 1810; y desde esa fecha en poder de la República Argentina emancipada.

La actual ocupación por Inglaterra data de 1833 en que fue violentamente tomada la Gran Malvina o isla de la Soledad, donde *existía* una guarnición y una colonia argentina.

Esa ocupación agraviante de un territorio donde jamás había *existido* ningún establecimiento de la Corona británica fue enérgicamente protestada por la legación argentina en Londres, y después de una ilustrada discusión con el gabinete de Su Majestad Británica, la protesta, fundada en títulos que por la emancipación habían retrovertido a la República Argentina, quedó pendiente, lo mismo que la negociación de que había sido objeto.

Tal es el estado de la cuestión Malvinas. El infrascrito se complace en que S. E. el señor ministro de Su Majestad Británica le haya prestado ocasión para demostrarle los fundamentos en que el gobierno argentino se apoya para sostener los derechos de soberanía de la República en las citadas islas, como lo hace en el memorándum que tiene el honor de adjuntarle, y espera de la habitual cortesanía del ministro de Su Majestad que quiera elevarlo a conocimiento de su gobierno, confiando en la seguridad que tiene el gobierno argentino de la rectitud de Su Majestad Británica que la discusión aplazada será nuevamente abierta por la contestación que el abajo firmado espera a sus observaciones, y resuelta por los medios amistosos y de derecho que hoy adoptan las naciones civilizadas para arreglar cuestiones de este género.

Esperando que la solución definitiva del dominio histórico y legal de las Malvinas ha de ser un motivo más para estrechar las constantes y reales relaciones existentes entre los dos países, el ministro que suscribe aprovecha esta nueva oportunidad para reiterar a S. E. el enviado extraordinario y ministro plenipotenciario de Su Majestad Británica, las seguridades de su alta consideración.

Francisco J. Ortiz

Annex 34: Response by Britain, November 14, 1887,
to Argentine note of January 2, 1885.
Source: L. Muñoz Azpiri, op. cit., Vol. 2
(1966), p. 352.

Señor Ministro: Tengo el honor de acusar recibo de vuestra nota de 3 del corriente, en la que llamáis la atención a un memorándum fecha 2 de enero de 1885, referente a las islas Falkland, que fue comunicado al ministro de S. M. en Buenos Aires por el ministro argentino de Relaciones Exteriores.

Permitidme observar que en agosto de 1886, el representante de S. M., sir Pakenham, por instrucciones del secretario de Estado de S. M., recordó al doctor Ortiz, ministro argentino de Relaciones Exteriores, las notas dirigidas sobre el asunto de las islas Falkland a don M. Moreno el 8 de enero de 1834 y el de 15 de febrero de 1842, y la nota del conde de Aberdeen de 5 de marzo de 1844, en las cuales don M. Moreno fue informado de que, en cuanto concernía al gobierno británico, la discusión estaba cerrada, y manifestó a S. E. que estando los consejeros de S. M. en aquel tiempo enteramente conformes con las vistas expresadas en las notas de 8 de enero de 1834 y 15 de febrero de 1842, no podía consentir en reabrir el asanto.

Sin embargo, en consecuencia de haberse manifestado en la memoria publicada por el departamento argentino de Relaciones Exteriores que no se había dado respuesta al gobierno argentino respecto al asunto de las islas Falkland, se mandó orden al ministro de S. M. en Buenos Aires con fecha 5 de setiembre último para informar al ministro de Relaciones Exteriores argentino, por escrito, de la comunicación verbal hecha al doctor Ortiz en agosto de 1886.

Tengo el honor de ser con la más alta consideración, señor ministro, vuestro más obediente y humilde servidor.

(Firmado) Por el marqués de Salisbury.

Th. V. Lister

Annex 35: Note by Argentina to Britain, June 12, 1888
(concerning proposal for arbitral settlement
of dispute)
Source: Muñoz Azpiri, op. cit., vol. 2 (1966),
p. 360

Señor Encargado de Negocios:

He tenido el honor de recibir la comunicación de S. S., fecha 13 de abril último, en que S. S. manifiesta, por encargo de S. E. el ministro de Estado de S. M. B., qué el gobierno de S. M. se niega a entrar a discutir sus derechos a las islas Falkland (Malvinas) porque en sentir del mismo ese derecho no ofrece duda ni dificultad de especie alguna.

He llevado al conocimiento de S. E. el Sr. Presidente de la República una respuesta que tan poco armoniza con los antecentes de la cuestión y extrañando S. E. el desío que se nota en sus términos, respecto del punto principal que se ventilaba en las notas cambiadas con el señor Pakenham que era dejar establecido el estado de la discusión relativa a la protesta argentina por la toma de las islas Malvinas en 1833, me ha encargado a su vez el Sr. Presidente exprese a S. S. para que se sirva trasmitirlo al secretario de Estado de S. M. B., que no obstante la resolución que tiene a bien comunicarle, de negarse a discutir los derechos que pudiera tener a la soberanía de dichas islas, el gobierno de la República no cree comprometidos los suyos por esa declaración ni menos por el silencio que el gobierno inglés guarda ante las indicaciones de someter el asunto a arbitraje hechas por el gobierno argentino, quien mantiene y mantendrá siempre sus derechos a la soberanía de las islas Malvinas de que fue violentamente privado en plena paz.

Aprovecho la oportunidad para reiterar a S. S. las seguridades de mi consideración más distinguida.

N. Quirno Costa

Annex 36: UN Resolution 2065 (XX) - Question of the
Falkland Islands (Malvinas), December 16,
1965

2065 (XX). Question of the Falkland Islands (Malvinas).

The General Assembly,

Having examined the question of the Falkland Islands (Malvinas),

Taking into account the chapters of the reports of the Special Committee on the Situation with regard to the Implementation of the Declaration on the Granting of Independence to Colonial Countries and Peoples relating to the Falkland Islands (Malvinas), and in particular the conclusions and recommendations adopted by the Committee with reference to that Territory,

Considering that its resolution 1514 (XV) of 14 December 1960 was prompted by the cherished aim of bringing to an end everywhere colonialism in all its forms, one of which covers the case of the Falkland Islands (Malvinas),

Noting the existence of a dispute between the Governments of Argentina and the United Kingdom of Great Britain and Northern Ireland concerning sovereignty over the said Islands,

1. *Invites* the Governments of Argentina and the United Kingdom of Great Britain and Northern Ireland to proceed without delay with the negotiations recommended by the Special Committee on the Situation with regard to the Implementation of the Declaration on the Granting of Independence to Colonial Countries and Peoples with a view to finding a peaceful solution to the problem, bearing in mind the provisions and objectives of the Charter of the United Nations and of General Assembly resolution 1514 (XV) and the interests of the population of the Falkland Islands (Malvinas);

2. *Requests* the two Governments to report to the Special Committee and to the General Assembly at its twenty-first session on the results of the negotiations.

Annex 37: UN Resolution 3160 (XXVIII) - Question of
the Falkland Islands (Malvinas), December
14, 1973

3160 (XXVIII). Question of the Falkland Islands (Malvinas)

The General Assembly,

Having considered the question of the Falkland Islands (Malvinas),

Recalling its resolution 1514 (XV) of 14 December 1960 containing the Declaration on the Granting of Independence to Colonial Countries and Peoples,

Recalling also its resolution 2065 (XX) of 16 December 1965, in which it invited the Governments of Argentina and the United Kingdom of Great Britain and Northern Ireland to proceed without delay with the negotiations recommended by the Special Committee on the Situation with regard to the Implementation of the Declaration on the Granting of Independence to Colonial Countries and Peoples with a view to finding a peaceful solution to the problem of the Falkland Islands (Malvinas), bearing in mind the provisions and objectives of the Charter of the United Nations and of resolution 1514 (XV) an the interests of the population of the Falkland Islands (Malvinas),

Gravely concerned at the fact that eight years have elapsed since the adoption of resolution 2065 (XX) without any substantial progress having been made in the negotiations,

Mindful that resolution 2065 (XX) indicates that the way to put an end to this colonial situation is the peaceful solution of the conflict of sovereignty between the Governments of Argentina and the United Kingdom with regard to the aforementioned islands,

Expressing its gratitude for the continuous efforts made by the Government of Argentina, in accordance with the relevant decisions of the General Assembly, to facilitate the process of decolonization and to promote the well-being of the population of the islands,

1. *Approves* the chapters of the report of the Special Committee on the Situation with regard to the Implementation of the Declaration on the Granting of Independence to Colonial Countries and Peoples relating to the Falkland Islands (Malvinas) and, in particular, the resolution adopted by the Special Committee on 21 August 1973 concerning the Territory,

2. *Declares* the need to accelerate the negotiations between the Governments of Argentina and the United Kingdom of Great Britain and Northern Ireland called for in General Assembly resolution 2065 (XX) in order to arrive at a peaceful solution of the conflict of sovereignty between them concerning the Falkland Islands (Malvinas);

3. *Urges* the Governments of Argentina and the United Kingdom, therefore, to proceed without delay with the negotiations, in accordance with the provisions of the relevant resolutions of the General Assembly, in order to put an end to the colonial situation;

4. *Requests* both Governments to report to the Secretary-General and to the General Assembly as soon as possible, and not later than at its twenty-ninth session, on the results of the recommended negotiations.

2202nd plenary meeting
14 December 1973

Annex 38:   Census for Falklands (Malvinas), (1851-1980)
Source: Doc. A/37/582, p. 10.

Table

The population in the Census years 1851-1980

Year	Population
1851	287
1861	541
1871	811
1881	1,510
1891	1,789
1901	2,043
1911	2,272
1921	2,094
1931	2,392
1946	2,239
1953	2,230
1962	2,172
1972	1,957
1980	1,813

Annex 39:   Falkland Islands (Malvinas), Working Paper
            prepared by Secretariat of Special Committee on the
            Situation with Regard to the Implementation of the
            Declaration on the Granting of Independence to
            Colonial Countries and Peoples, August 5, 1981
            (concerning developments up to 1981)
            Source: UN Doc. A/AC 109/670

UNITED NATIONS
GENERAL
ASSEMBLY

Distr.
GENERAL

A/AC.109/670
5 August 1981

ORIGINAL: ENGLISH

SPECIAL COMMITTEE ON THE SITUATION WITH
REGARD TO THE IMPLEMENTATION OF THE
DECLARATION ON THE GRANTING OF
INDEPENDENCE TO COLONIAL COUNTRIES
AND PEOPLES

FALKLAND ISLANDS (MALVINAS)

Working paper prepared by the Secretariat

CONTENTS

FALKLAND ISLANDS (MALVINAS) 1/

1. GENERAL

1.   The Falkland Islands (Malvinas) lie in the South Atlantic, some 772 kilometres
north-east of Cape Horn. They comprise 200 islands and cover a total area of
11,961 square kilometres. There are two large islands, East Falkland and West
Falkland. Apart from a number of small islands, the Dependencies consist of
South Georgia, 1,287 kilometres east-south-east of the Falkland Islands (Malvinas)
and the uninhabited South Sandwich Islands, some 756 kilometres south-east of
South Georgia.

2.   At the last census, held in 1972, the population of the Territory, excluding
the Dependencies, numbered 1,957, almost all of whom were of European descent,
mainly of British origin. Of this total, 1,079 lived in Stanley, the capital.
The preliminary results of the December 1980 census showed a total of 1,812
resident civilians in the Territory.

2. CONSTITUTIONAL AND POLITICAL DEVELOPMENTS

A. Constitution

3.   The constitutional arrangements for the Territory, introduced in 1949 and
amended in 1955, 1964 and 1977, are outlined in earlier reports of the Special
Committee. 2/ Briefly, the governmental structure consists of: (a) the Governor
appointed by the Queen (currently Mr. Rex Masterman Hunt); (b) an Executive
Council consisting of two ex officio members (the Chief Secretary and the
Financial Secretary), two unofficial members appointed by the Governor and two
elected members of the Legislative Council, elected by the members of that Council;
(c) a Legislative Council consisting of the Governor who presides, two ex officio
members (the Chief Secretary and the Financial Secretary) and six members elected
on the basis of universal adult suffrage: and (d) a Court of Appeals set up in
July 1965 to hear and determine appeals from the courts of the Territory.

4.   Elections under the amended constitutional arrangements were held in
October 1977, and the newly elected Legislative Council was sworn in on
21 November 1977. There remains one nominated member of the Legislative Council
owing to the fact that one of the elected seats was not contested.

5.   It will be recalled 3/ that, in a speech to the newly elected Legislative
Council in June 1978, the Governor suggested that the Council might consider from
time to time how the newly instituted constitutional and legislative arrangements
were working. He said that readjustments might be possible in one or two respects,
and invited the members to submit their views on the matter. At a meeting of the
Legislative Council in June 1980, Mr. W. H. Goss, one of the members, stated
that with the prospect of elections in 1981, the Council should consider revising
the Constitution. In his opinion, the community was too small to have two
Councils, which had led to considerable duplication of work and documentation. He
felt that there should be only four elected members of the Legislative Council, all
of whom would serve on the Executive Council.

B. Public service

6.   According to information provided to the United Kingdom House of Commons, 4/
the territorial Government employs 315 persons, including those employed on a
contract basis. The policy of the Government is to give all members of the public
service every opportunity to enhance their capabilities through further training,
thereby reducing the need to recruit officers from abroad. In a speech in June 1978,
the Governor stated that proposals would be submitted to the Legislative Council
for expanding the training scheme for nurses and introducing in-service
secretarial and clerical training in the public service for school leavers. Efforts
were also being made to encourage training overseas, not only in academic
institutions but through individually arranged working attachments.

2/ Official Records of the General Assembly, Twenty-fifth Session, Supplement
No. 23 (A/8023/Rev.1), vol. IV, chap. XIX, annex, paras. 4-7; and ibid.,
Thirty-third Session, Supplement No. 23 (A/33/23/Rev.1), vol. IV, chap. XXVIII.
annex I, paras. 4-7.

3/ Ibid., Thirty-fourth Session, Supplement No. 23 (A/34/23/Rev.1), vol. IV,
chap. XXVIII. annex, para. 5.

4/ Parliamentary Debates, House of Commons, 17 December 1980, col. 313.

7.   A review of the salary structure of the public service was expected to be
made in December 1980 by Mr. H. P. Ritchie, a Salaries Commissioner from the
United Kingdom. The Falkland Islands Civil Service Association, in a circular
dated 9 September 1980, urged the full participation of all its members in the
review, stating that one of the most important problems facing the Association was
the reduction of "the immense emoluments gap" between locally recruited officers
and those recruited abroad. The Association also felt that the review should
cover the loss of free medical and dental treatment and the need for periodic
adjustments to the cost-of-living bonus.

C. Relations between the Governments of
Argentina and the United Kingdom

8.   Detailed information concerning relations between the Governments of Argentina
and the United Kingdom on the question of the Falkland Islands (Malvinas) prior
to 1980 is contained in earlier reports of the Special Committee. 5/

9.   On 28 and 29 April 1980, a ministerial meeting was held at New York on the
question of the Falkland Islands (Malvinas) and related issues in the South
Atlantic. The delegations were led by Commodore Carlos Cavándoli, Under-Secretary
for External Relations and Worship of Argentina, and Mr. Nicholas Ridley, Minister
of State at the United Kingdom Foreign and Commonwealth Office. Mr. Adrian Monk,
a member of the Falkland Islands Legislative Council, was part of the United
Kingdom delegation.

10.   Reporting to the United Kingdom House of Commons on the meeting, Mr. Ridley
stated that "the exchanges were conducted in a cordial and positive spirit. Each
side was able to reach a better understanding of the other's position. No decisions
were taken, though it was agreed that contacts on day-to-day matters between the
islands and Argentina should be expanded ...". 6/ Subsequently, in response to
questions in Parliament, Mr. Ridley said that arrangements had been set in hand
to institutionalize contacts between the islanders and the Argentines in Government
and the private sector with whom there was co-operation on economic and supply
matters. 7/

11.   On 25 September 1980, during the thirty-fifth session of the General Assembly,
Brigadier Carlos W. Pastor, Minister for External Relations and Worship of
Argentina, and Lord Carrington, United Kingdom Secretary of State for Foreign and
Commonwealth Affairs, held a meeting at New York.

12.   On 11 November, by its decision 35/412, the General Assembly, on the
recommendation of the Fourth Committee, decided to defer consideration of the
question of the Falkland Islands (Malvinas) until its thirty-sixth session and
requested the Special Committee to keep the situation in the Territory under
review.

13.   In November 1980, Mr. Ridley paid his second visit to the Territory, and on
2 December, reported to Parliament about it as follows:

"We have no doubt about our sovereignty over the islands. The Argentines,
however, continue to press their claim. This dispute is causing continuing
uncertainty, emigration and economic stagnation in the islands. Following
my exploratory talks with the Argentines in April, the Government has been
considering possible ways of achieving a solution which would be acceptable
to all the parties. In this, the essential is that we should be guided by
the wishes of the islanders themselves.

_____

5/ For the most recent, see Official Records of the General Assembly, Thirty-
fourth Session, Supplement No. 23 (A/34/23/Rev.1), vol. IV, chap. XXVIII, annex,
paras. 7-17; and A/AC.109/615, paras. 6-14.

6/ Parliamentary Debates, House of Commons, 8 May 1980, col. 224.

7/ Ibid., 14 May 1980, col. 1473.

"I therefore visited the islands between 22 and 29 November in order
to consult island councillors and subsequently, at their express request, all
islanders, on how we should proceed. Various possible bases for seeking a
negotiated settlement were discussed. These included both a way of freezing
the dispute for a period or exchanging the title of sovereignty against a
long lease of the islands back to Her Majesty's Government.

"The essential elements of any solution would be that it should preserve
British administration, law and way of life for the islanders, while releasing
the potential of the islands' economy and of their maritime resources, at
present blighted by the dispute. It is for the islanders to advise on which,
if any, option should be explored in negotiations with the Argentines. I have
asked them to let me have their views in due course. Any eventual settlement
would have to be endorsed by the islanders, and by this House." 8/

In response to a question on the wisdom of placing the lease-back proposal on the
negotiating table, Mr. Ridley stressed that none of the options had been put to
the Argentine Government for negotiation. They were for discussion among the
islanders, who would decide whether they wished any of them to be pursued.

14. According to The Times (London) of 27 November, the options put to the
islanders, in addition to those mentioned by Mr. Ridley, included: (a) the outright
transfer of sovereignty to Argentina; (b) the institution of a condominium
arrangement similar to that which existed in the New Hebrides under France and the
United Kingdom; and (c) the breaking off of negotiations.

15. On 28 November, The Times reported that during a meeting of the Sheepowners'
Association in the Territory, Mr. Ridley had stated that under the lease-back
proposal "your life style would not be changed, and there would be new financial
benefits from fishing, tourism, and oil, which would commence as soon as possible
after the change".

16. According to the January 1981 issue of The Falkland Island Times (a local
newspaper), Mr. Monk and another member of the Legislative Council visited their
constituents in order to ascertain their views on the options open to them.
Mr. Monk also addressed the entire community in radio broadcasts on 1 and
2 January 1981. He urged the islanders not to cede their sovereignty and to
maintain the position that they were British and wished to remain so.

17. On 7 January, the Legislative Council of the Territory, by a vote of 7 to 1,
adopted a motion asking the United Kingdom Government to continue discussions with
the Argentine Government with a view to reaching an agreement which would freeze
the dispute over sovereignty for a determined period of time. Mr. Monk, who cast
the vote against the motion, expressed the view that there should be no further
discussion of the question between Argentina and the United Kingdom.

18. On 23 and 24 February, a further round of talks was held at New York. The
Argentine delegation was headed by Commodore Cavándoli and included the Argentine
Ambassador to the United Kingdom. The United Kingdom delegation, led by
Mr. Ridley, included the United Kingdom Ambassador to Argentina as well as Mr. Monk
and Stuart B. Wallace, both members of the territorial Legislative Council.

19. According to press reports, although the Argentine delegation rejected the
proposal that there be a "freeze" on the question of sovereignty, as the islanders
had requested, the talks were considered to have been cordial. No date was set
for the resumption of negotiations which, it appeared, would not take place until
after a general election was held in the Territory.

20. On their return to the Territory after the talks, Messrs. Monk and Wallace
met with the other members of the Legislative Council. Subsequently, in a press
conference, it was reported that the Argentine delegation, in a direct appeal to
the councillors, had offered to make the islands a "most pampered region" and to

---

8/ Ibid., 2 December 1980, cols. 195-196.

maintain the democratic, legal, social and educational systems of the Territory, if the inhabitants gave up United Kingdom sovereignty in favour of Argentine sovereignty.

21. Since elections are scheduled to be held in the Territory before November 1981, the present Council believes that any decision on the future of the negotiations should be left to the new Legislative Council.

3. ECONOMIC CONDITIONS

A. Shackleton report

22. It will be recalled 9/ that a report entitled Economic Survey of the Falkland Islands, 10/ prepared by Lord Shackleton, was issued by the United Kingdom Government in 1976. In the introduction to the report, it was stated that the terms of reference were very wide since it was intended to provide an over-all survey of the economic prospects of the Territory in all sectors. In order to assess fully the development potential of the Territory, account had to be taken of the social dimensions of the situation. The terms of reference excluded any political consideration, however, and the report was thus based on the premise that the political status of the Territory would remain as it had been over the past 150 years. It was none the less stated that in certain proposed areas of development, particularly those related to the exploitation of offshore resources, "co-operation with Argentina - even participation - should, if possible, be secured".

23. As reported above (see para. 13), Mr. Ridley indicated in December 1980 that, until there was a solution to the political problem, there could be no development of the Territory's economy or its maritime resources. Later that month, in response to a question in the House of Commons on the implementation of the Shackleton report, Mr. Ridley expanded on this theme, stating:

"We desperately want to develop the economy of the islands. My honourable friend mentioned improved farming and markets for farming produce. A great deal of credit is needed to open up those possibilities, and we must get commercial banks to perform their functions in the islands. There is also the question of revenue from the rich harvest of fish and the possibility - there can be no certainty - of finding oil. He wanted us to exert our undoubted rights over the fishing zones and the economic zones that surround not only the islands, but our dependencies. My honourable friend mentioned the vexed question of Magellanes Este, the oil block that straddles the median line. Nothing would give us more pleasure than to be able to say that we had agreed the median line, and that we and the Argentine respected that median line, so that oil exploration and exploitation could go ahead.

...

"We also believe that there is a need for good communications. The airport, the supply of fuel, the air and sea services, education and advanced health services are all adequate at present, but they depend on Argentina for their provision.

"The difference of interpretation between my honourable friend and myself is over how we achieve these aims. That must be made more particular by asking the effect of the long-run dispute with Argentina on these questions. At present, the relationship between Great Britain and Argentina is good and friendly. We are still negotiating in a series of talks with the Argentine Government, as we were for many years before this Government took over. In spite of that, it is still not possible to declare those 200-mile fishery

---

9/ Official Records of the General Assembly, Thirty-third Session, Supplement No. 23 (A/33/23/Rev.1), vol. IV, chap. XXVIII, annex I, paras. 17-21.

10/ London, H.M. Stationery Office, 1976.

zones, to get the licence fees from foreign fishing in those zones, to explore or exploit oil, or to legalize the position of Southern Thule. Even the commercial banks are unwilling to set up the islands, because of the political risks.

"These hazards are real. It must be recognized that solving these problems requires an over-all political settlement. The economy of the islands, even at this time of relative peace, co-operation and good relations, is still in decline. The population declined last year from about 1,800 to about 1,700. It must be apparent to my honourable friend that even with the status quo, these problems cannot be solved and they are leading to a worsening economic condition in the islands.

...

"My honourable friend seemed to believe that, in spite of these political difficulties, which I can assure him are very real, there was a solution which consisted of pumping more money into the islands. My honourable friend quoted the Shackleton report. I can tell him that a very large number of the recommendations have been implemented - 49 out of 90. Of the remainder, 14 have been rejected, 20 are in train and 7 are undecided. I concede that the bulk of the recommendations in terms of money have not been implemented because we come immediately to the question of the runway, and the vast proportion of the work that has not been done is the new runway to the airport.

"There are two reasons why it has not been done, both of which seem equally valid to me now. The first is that a runway to take large jets would require the existence of some commercial demand. With 1,700 people in the islands, it is unsurprising that that demand is very small. No commercial airline has expressed any interest in running long-haul jet services there because they frankly and rightly believe that the traffic would not be available." 11/

B. General

24. The economy of the Territory continues to be overwhelmingly dependent on sheep farming for wool production. The grasslands are generally poor, owing to difficult climatic and soil conditions, and the resulting yield per hectare is low. Research into the improvement of pastures and related aspects of sheep farming is being conducted by the Grasslands Trial Unit (GTU), established in 1975 and entirely financed by the United Kingdom Government. In July 1979, the staff of GTU was increased from 4 to 6. GTU has also been providing assistance to the territorial Government on agricultural matters pending the recruitment of an agricultural officer.

25. In 1978/79, the latest year for which figures are available, there were 659,012 sheep in the Territory, an increase of 10,646 over the record figure of the previous year. The distribution was as follows: East Falkland, 377,237; West Falkland, 213,743; and other islands, 68,032.

26. The economy is closely tied to the price of wool on the world market, which has tended to remain static in the past few years while production costs have continued to rise. None the less, in 1979, exports of wool amounted to 2,133 metric tons, bringing earnings of £2,463,615, 12/ compared to 1978 earnings of £2.0 million. Exports of hides and skins totalled 48 metric tons in 1979, with a value of £38,636 (£3,457 in 1978). It will be recalled that, in November 1977,

_____

11/ Parliamentary Debates, House of Commons, 18 December 1980, cols. 996-998.

12/ The local currency is the pound sterling.

an expert in the tanning and processing of sheepskins and hides paid a visit to the Territory to advise on the development of this activity. 13/

27. During the period under review, sheepowners in the Territory sought assistance in the preparation of wool clip for marketing. A member of the New Zealand Wool Board spent some time in the Territory demonstrating techniques of proper evaluation and classification of the wool clip and ways in which the clip could be made more attractive to buyers.

28. The Falkland Islands Company (FIC), registered in the United Kingdom in 1851, is the major contributor to the economy, and the development of the Territory is closely tied to the growth of the company. As the owner of almost half the sheep of the Territory and an equivalent proportion of the land, FIC is the largest producer of wool and controls much of the local banking, commerce and shipping.

29. Other potential areas of economic development include tourism, fisheries and the processing of kelp into alginates. At one time, Alginate Industries, Ltd., was making plans for the production of alginate in the Territory, but discontinued them in 1977. In the past years, new approaches have been made to commercial companies. The Taiyo Fishing Company of Japan and, more recently, the White Fish Authority of the United Kingdom have been carrying out research into the fishing resources of the Territory. There are stocks of king crab and of krill, a small prawn high in protein; several countries are interested in the exploitation of the latter.

30. Tourism, which is based on the abundance of marine and bird-life in the Territory, including breeding colonies of albatross, seals and geese, was the subject of a recent study in which the Government invested some £25,000. Recent reports indicate that Mr. Julian Fitter, the tourism expert who made the study, has set up an organization called Falkland Wildlife to take tourists by ship to visit the wild-life areas of the Territory.

31. The possibility that large oil deposits exist in the Territory and its off-shore areas has aroused the interest of several major oil companies. In 1978, the United Kingdom Government reported that two private companies had completed seismic surveys in the waters surrounding the islands, one of which had been made on behalf of the Argentine and United Kingdom Governments. The results of the survey, according to reports in the press, were "more encouraging than discouraging". Oil companies and consultants feel that oil exploration in the area is now an economic proposition, and according to The Times (London), several large companies have projected expenditures totalling some £130 million for exploration in the waters between Tierra del Fuego and the Territory.

32. In mid-February 1981 it was announced that the largest Argentine off-shore oil strike had been made near the Patagonian coast. The well, discovered by the Shell company, is reported to have a flow rate of approximately 2,000 barrels per day. It is located in an area adjacent to Magellanes Este, a concessionary licensing block for which tenders are now being sought and which is within 154 kilometres of the Falkland Islands (Malvinas). The block also straddles what the United Kingdom regards as the "putative" median line between Argentina and the Territory (see also para. 23 above).

33. As noted above, the Territory specializes in the production of wool for export and depends heavily on imported goods for the satisfaction of local requirements.

In 1979, imports totalled £2,502,251. The United Kingdom continues to absorb most of the Territory's exports and to provide most of its imports. Recently, attempts have been made to increase trade relations between the Territory and the Argentine mainland, and also with Chile.

13/ Official Records of the General Assembly, Thirty-third Session, Supplement No. 23 (A/33/23/Rev.1), vol. IV, chap. XXVIII, annex I, para. 23.

34. According to the approved budget estimates for 1980/81, ordinary revenue would amount to £2,213,201 (compared with the revised estimates of £2,338,530 for 1979/80), while expenditure would amount to £2,284,320, leaving a deficit of £71,119. The principal items of revenue were customs duties, internal revenue, posts and telecommunications and municipal services, which were estimated at £1,321,150. The principal items of expenditure were public health (£257,381), public works (£254,256), education (£223,640), posts and telecommunications (£191,500) and civil aviation (£302,289). Capital expenditure for 1980/81 was estimated at £891,605, of which £520,770 was to come from United Kingdom aid. The major projects to be financed by United Kingdom aid were the school hostel project (£250,000) and the roads project (£180,090). The major items of development expenditure from local funds were housing (£100,000) and roads (£45,160).

35. In 1971, the Governments of Argentina, the Falkland Islands (Malvinas) and the United Kingdom signed a Communications Agreement at Buenos Aires, designed to improve economic, social and cultural co-operation between the Falkland Islands (Malvinas) and Argentina. Air communications between Argentina and Stanley are operated on a weekly basis by Líneas Aéreas del Estado (LADE), a State-owned Argentine airline. The permanent airport at Stanley, constructed with United Kingdom aid at a cost of £6 million and by Argentine technicians, was opened to traffic on 1 May 1979. The airport was designed to take aircraft up to the size of the Hawker Siddeley HS-748 or other medium-haul aircraft.

36. Following the publication of the Shackleton report, the United Kingdom Government agreed to carry out a survey of the internal transport service (road, sea and air) in the Territory. This led to the initiation of a road development programme, the first stage of which is the construction of an all-weather road from Stanley to Darwin. The internal air service run by the territorial Government was expanded in 1979 by the addition of a twin-engine land-plane to the fleet of sea-planes which make unscheduled flights between the settlements and Stanley.

4. SOCIAL AND EDUCATIONAL CONDITIONS

37. During the period under review, the labour situation in the Territory continued to decline due to emigration. Vacancies continue to exist in the agricultural industry of the islands, mainly for skilled mechanics. The development projects currently under way are reported to have put a strain on available labour, and in some cases, their completion has been delayed. According to The Observer (London) of 18 January 1981, a proposal to counteract the decline in the population of the Territory by encouraging the immigration of people from St. Helena, another United Kingdom colony in the South Atlantic, attracted hundreds of applicants, including persons from the United Kingdom. The territorial Government, however, had intended to start with a pilot scheme of four families, in which the men would be suitably qualified tradesmen whose wives could be employed in clerical positions in the Government.

38. The Government maintains a 17-bed general hospital at Stanley, providing medical, surgical, obstetric and geriatric care. Of the original 27 beds, 10 have been converted to provide hostel accommodations. The Medical Department is responsible for public health and sanitation in the Territory and employs one senior medical officer, two medical officers and other staff. A general practitioner is available in the town, while a flying-doctor service reaches the outlying farm settlements.

39. The installation at the hospital of new X-ray equipment, acquired at a cost of £32,000 with funds from the United Kingdom, was to have been completed late in 1980. Expenditure on public health for the year 1980/81 was estimated at £257,381.

40. According to information submitted by the administering Power, there were 313 pupils attending the 11 government schools, which are staffed by 32 teachers. Education is free and attendance compulsory in Stanley for children between the ages of 5 and 15 years, and outside Stanley, for those between the ages of 7 and

15 years. Education is provided mainly at the primary level, except at the
Senior School at Stanley, which offers secondary education in a limited range of
subjects up to the ordinary level of the General Certificate of Education.
In 1978, scholarships for secondary education abroad were discontinued and in 1979,
it was announced that overseas education allowances would also be discontinued
once the current beneficiaries had completed their studies. The Argentine
Government provides an unlimited number of scholarships for secondary education
of students from the Territory, as well as two teachers of Spanish for the schools
at Stanley. Estimated expenditure on education for the year 1980/81 amounted
to £223,640.

Annex 40: Discussion in UN Security Council, April 3, 1982.
Source: UN Doc. S/PV 2350

UNITED NATIONS

SECURITY

COUNCIL

PROVISIONAL

S/PV.2350
3 April 1982

ENGLISH

PROVISIONAL VERBATIM RECORD OF THE TWO THOUSAND
THREE HUNDRED AND FIFTIETH MEETING

Held at Headquarters, New York,
on Saturday, 3 April 1982, at 11 a.m.

President:	Mr. KAMANDA wa KAMANDA	(Zaire)
Members:	China	Mr. LING Qing
	France	Mr. LOUET
	Guyana	Mr. KARRAN
	Ireland	Mr. DORR
	Japan	Mr. NISIBORI
	Jordan	Mr. NUSEIDEH
	Panama	Mr. ILLUECA
	Poland	Mr. WYZNER
	Spain	Mr. PINIES
	Togo	Mr. ADJOYI
	Uganda	Mr. OTUINU
	Union of Soviet Socialist Republics	Mr. TROYANOVSKY
	United Kingdom of Great Britain and Northern Ireland	Sir Anthony PARSONS
	United States of America	Mr. LICHENSTEIN

This record contains the original text of speeches delivered in English and interpretations of speeches in the other languages. The final text will be printed in the Official Records of the Security Council.

Corrections should be submitted to the original speeches only. They should be sent under the signature of a member of the delegation concerned, within one week, to the Chief of the Official Records Editing Section, Department of Conference Services, room A-3550, 866 United Nations Plaza, and incorporated in a copy of the record.

82-60458/A

The PRESIDENT (interpretation from French): The Security Council will now resume its consideration of the item on its agenda.

The first speaker is the Minister for Foreign Affairs of Argentina, His Excellency Mr. Nicanor Costa Mendez. I welcome him and invite him to make his statement.

Mr. COSTA MENDEZ (Argentina) (interpretation from Spanish): Perhaps the beginning of my statement may be considered repetitive, but I consider it none the less useful to state that the reason for the calling of these meetings lies in the Malvinas Islands, which is part of Argentine territory and which was illegally occupied by the United Kingdom in 1833 by an act of force which deprived our country of that archipelago.

The British fleet in 1833 displaced by force the Argentine population and the authorities which were exercising the legitimate rights that belonged to the Republic at that time as the heir to Spain.

Legally speaking, that act of force cannot give rise to any right at all, and politically the events of 1833 were one more reflection of the imperialist policy which the European States carried out in the nineteenth century at the expense of America, Africa and Asia. Hence, we can say today that this is a colonial problem in the most traditional sense of that political and economic phenomenon.

Since 1833, the Republic of Argentina has been claiming reparation from the United Kingdom for the great wrong done. The Republic of Argentina has never consented to that act of usurpation of its national territory, usurpation carried out by unacceptable and illegal means. All the successive Governments of Argentina, regardless of party or faction, have remained united and steadfast in their position during those 149 years of strongly protesting against that arbitrary occupation.

(Mr. Costa Mendez, Argentina)

No one can have the slightest doubt as to the historic role of the United Nations in the decolonization process. This is perhaps the area in which the United Nations has proved most fruitful, a task that it has carried out most effectively, one that has changed the course of international relations. Proof of this is that the original membership of 54 has increased to 157. Many of the young nations represented here in the Council have been freed from the colonial yoke, and their contribution to the organized international community is of such magnitude that I do not need to mention it - far less to emphasize it.

Of the 54 original Members 20 belong to the Latin American Group, and their decisive influence in the early days of the Organization must be recognized. That group of nations was very active in giving impetus to the decolonization process. The Latin American Group was, if we may say so, a champion of that cause, because it had suffered from the effects of colonization. We too had been colonies; we too had fought the hard struggles for national independence.

One of the last vestiges of colonialism on Latin American territory ended yesterday. The claims that my country has been making repeatedly since 1833 have enjoyed the support of the decisions of the world Organization, and of the individual assistance of these new nations just emerging from the colonial era.

Despite the Organization's efforts and my country's arduous and careful work, time passed and brought with it only continued frustration, resulting from the evasive tactics and time-wasting manoeuvres of Great Britain - and all that despite the many alternatives put forward by Argentina and despite the imagination and flexibility with which we approached negotiations.

Two days ago the Permanent Representative of my country made reference here to the willingness and readiness on our part demonstrated by the facilities offered in 1971 in terms of communications and other concessions to the inhabitants of the islands. Those 1,800 inhabitants, as the United Kingdom representative

(Mr. Costa Mendez, Argentina)

said yesterday, would fit without difficulty into this chamber. They have been and are the subject of constant concern in Argentina, which has given them attention that I venture to say, with all due respect, they have not received from their "homeland". The Government of Argentina is always careful to respect individual rights and physical integrity.

Yesterday Argentina stated that its position did not represent any kind of aggression against the present inhabitants of the islands, whose rights and way of life - and I stress this - will be respected in the same way as those of the countries freed by our liberators. Troops will be used only when absolutely necessary and they will not in any way disturb the inhabitants of the islands; quite the contrary, they will protect the institutions and inhabitants, since they are part of us. This is a most solemn commitment by the Government of Argentina to the international community.

The United Kingdom has invoked the presence of the inhabitants of the Malvinas Islands as an excuse for its colonial presence in those islands. But I ask members: What, then, is the pretext for that presence in the South Sandwich or South Georgia Islands? I here, as the Times of London said in an editorial of 29 March last, the only natives, according to the Commonwealth and Foreign Offices, were seals - and in the present state of international law seals do not enjoy the right to self-determination?

In view of the fact that my country opened up communications, the British Government did not seem too concerned over the physical and historical isolation in which the inhabitants of the islands lived.

I shall not go into details about the change in the standard of living brought about by the facilities offered by Argentina. As the President of my country has said, we are ready to guarantee all the individual rights of the inhabitants. But we cannot allow anyone to use those 1,800 persons as something enshrined in international law as a "population".

(Mr. Costa Mendez, Argentina)

In previous statements the characteristics of that group of persons have
been dealt with, but I must say again here that, to a large extent, those persons
are officials of the British Government and a large number of them are employees
of the Falkland Islands Company, a typical colonial firm - a complete anachronism:
a colonial corporation of those who had letters patent from the eighteenth century
the trade branch of colonialism and imperialism: history offers various examples
of this.

Those foreigners with interests there, with no right other than trade and
colonial ones, are those who most strongly and systematically have prevented the
British Government from taking action.

Of necessity, the recalcitrant attitude of the British Government that I have
mentioned brought about tension and difficulties. More than once peace and
security in the region were threatened by the persistent colonial presence.

We have already mentioned in another statement the Shackleton incident of
1976, an episode - and I wish to emphasize this although I am sorry to have to
cite this - that supplies a fine example of the Inter-American Committee's
resolution, which states:

"Threats to peace and security in the region, together with flagrant
violations of international rules on non-interference, are constituted
by the presence of foreign war ships in American waters, and also by the
announcements made by the British Government concerning their dispatch
of other vessels."

It would seem that this would apply equally well today.

The foregoing episode and the episode I have mentioned which was the
immediate origin of the present situation are both covered in the statement made
by the Permanent Representative of my country and the letter dated 1 April 1982
from my Government to the Security Council which has been circulated as document
S/14940

That incident was serious, but was made even more serious by the United
Kingdom because it sent warships to the region in a clear attempt at
intimidation, which constituted a real threat to my country and to the continent.
Hence the statement I have just read out about the Shackleton episode from the
Inter-American Committee is still fully valid in 1982.

The military preparations and the despatch of warships to the region by
the United Kingdom, to which I have already referred, explain and justify the
actions taken of necessity by the Government of Argentina in defence of its rights.

Some delegations here have stated that my Government acted hastily.
I leave it to the Council to judge, but I must point out that it seems difficult
to describe my country as acting hastily when, with the greatest respect for
peaceful solutions, it has borne with a situation of continued usurpation of
its territory by a colonial Power for 150 years. Argentina has wisely,
patiently and imaginatively negotiated on its long-standing claim
but the United Kingdom has not given the slightest indication of being flexible

(Mr. Costa Mendez, Argentina)

nor made a single just proposal. Furthermore, we have been accused in this chamber
of violating Article 2 (3) and (4) of the United Nations Charter. No provision
of the Charter can be taken to mean the legitimization of situations which have
their origin in wrongful acts, in acts carried out before the Charter was adopted
and which subsisted during its prevailing force. Today, in 1982, the purposes
of the Organization cannot be invoked to justify acts carried out in the last
century in flagrant violation of principles that are today embodied in international
law.

Throughout the years we have celebrated the excellent results of the
irreversible march of history typified by decolonization and at the same time,
while we were celebrating and taking part in that process, our frustration was
growing because of the conviction that the United Kingdom was not ready to
give up the territory it had usurped from Argentina. The accession of emerging
peoples to international politics and the change in international society are a
result of the historic process I mentioned at the beginning of my statement.
This is a real force, and this real force in the world order was reflected in the
establishment of the Non-Aligned Movement, which my country joined in 1973
and in which it takes part as an active member. That Movement promotes the
eradicating of historical injustices, whether they be political or economic.
Members of the Non-Aligned Movement, as our Permanent Representative has
already said, have repeatedly recognized and acknowledged the justice of the
Argentine claim and our country's sovereignty over the Malvinas Islands,
the South Georgia and Sandwich Islands, they have already stated that the
principle of self-determination does not apply in this case for special historical
reasons I have already explained.

The representative of the United Kingdom said that he had doubts about
being able to arrive at an agreement with the representative of my country
as to the historical vicissitudes. That is possible, but it would seem
difficult for us not to agree on the facts of history which are absolutely
indisputable.

The Government of Argentina has not invaded any foreign territory, as
the United Kingdom claims. As was stated very simply by the President of my
country,

"Safeguarding our national honour and without rancour or bitterness,
but with all the strength that comes from being in the right, we have recovere
a part of our national heritage".

The same cannot be said of the United Kingdom Government vis-à-vis our country.

Apart from the case which concerns us today, in 1806 and 1807 British
expeditionary forces attacked and temporarily occupied the city of Buenos Aires
and its suburbs, a historical fact that may not be well known to everybody.
On both occasions the British troops were repelled by the Argentine people.
In 1840 and in 1848 the Government of Great Britain organized naval blockades

(Mr. Costa Mendez, Argentina)

against the Republic of Argentina, and, to abide by historical facts, it is
rather strange to notice that another colonial power, France, whose representative
was so quick to rally to the colonial position yesterday, was already associated
in 1848 with these colonial ventures since it took part in the blockade that
year that I have mentioned.

All that is by way of providing the Council with the background. None
the less, I want to mention something familiar to all members of the Council.

Yesterday France made reference to the Malvinas Islands and even mentioned
them by their English name, ignoring the General Assembly decision which provides
that in referring to the islands they shall be called the Malvinas Islands and
the Falkland Islands - always using both names. The representative of France
and all representatives of the French-speaking nations in the Organization
cannot be unaware that the name Malvinas has its origin in the famous trip
made by Bougainville from Saint Malo to the Archipelago; it became "Malouines",
which was hispanized to "Malvinas".

I dare not think that there may be ideological or political subtleties
underlying this historical error of language, but I mention it because it is
surprising.

I have made reference to something of which everyone is aware: the spirit of
conciliation and the firm resolution of successive Governments of Argentina to
seek by peaceful means a solution to our dispute with Great Britain. Furthermore,
everyone is aware that on several occasions our Government has had to discourage
sectors of the Argentine community that considered that the total lack of response
from the British community made imperative the use of other means. Recent events
have affirmed our presence in the islands, and we have offered every guarantee
and safeguard so that the new state of peace may be maintained. We have again here
told the British Government that we are ready and willing to negotiate and to
hear its position. But we must make it absolutely clear in this chamber that
any change or disturbance in the peace that may come about from now on in the
area of the islands will be the sole responsibility of the United Kingdom.

There is something of which members may not be so aware. The Government
of Argentina, after very lengthy negotiations, all fruitless in view of the
reluctance of Great Britain, finally proposed a written paper to institutionalize
the meetings and to structure the talks so that we could move forward to a
peaceful, honourable and just solution. We thus handed the British Embassy a
document before a meeting that was to be held on 4 February 1982 with the express,
formal and pressing request that it should be answered on the occasion of the
meeting. The British delegation, always cordial in matters of form, agreed to
the meeting but gave no response to our presentation despite our urgent request.
We called upon the meeting to set a date for the response. No date was agreed
to. We asked that it should be before the end of March. We were told that they
would think about it, but that it was not possible to give any date at that time.

(Mr. Costa Mendez, Argentina)

I want to tell members that Argentina felt great discouragement, sadness, and frustration at hearing all that non-news. And yet, despite that recalcitrance, despite that inexplicable reluctance, the Government of Argentina offered a press release that we believed to be extremely important. I shall now read it out:

"The representatives of Argentina and the United Kingdom, at a meeting in New York in February, have considered an Argentine proposal for the establishment of a system of monthly meetings with a pre-established agenda, the venue to be established beforehand, presided over by officials from the highest echelons. Such meetings will have the purpose of speeding up to the utmost the on-going negotiations to arrive at recognition of Argentine sovereignty over the islands and of thus obtaining substantial results within a time-limit which at this stage of the talks must of necessity be short.

"Argentina has negotiated with Great Britain with patience, honesty and good faith for more than 15 years within the framework mentioned in the relevant resolutions of the United Nations to arrive at a solution to the dispute over the sovereignty of the islands. The new system is an effective measure to arrive at a prompt solution.

"However, if this does not come about, if there is no response from the British side, Argentina reserves the right to put an end to the operation of such a mechanism and freely to choose the procedure it deems most fit in accordance with its interests."

This forewarning was given to the representative of Great Britain. There was not, and there has not been as yet, any reply except the presence of HMS Endurance in the Georgias and a note from Lord Carrington the terms of which I shall refrain from mentioning for various reasons.

I now wish to make reference to the draft resolution submitted by the United Kingdom. It speaks volumes that the terms are absolutely identical to those put forward more than 22 years ago in this same chamber in the case of Goa, when Portugal was hanging on to its colonial power, which consumed it and gave rise to a new Portugal. That resolution sought to deny India its territorial rights, just as an attempt is being made here to deny my country its proper rights. That draft resolution was thrown out by the Council because it was merely a defence, an expression of continuing colonialism.

The United Kingdom is the only other party to this dispute. It is the only sponsor of the single draft resolution before the Council. This also is strange. In trying to deny us our territorial integrity and our right to it, the United Kingdom calls for the withdrawal of the Argentine troops which recovered the Malvinas for national sovereignty. If the United Kingdom took those islands through an illegitimate act of force, why has it not withdrawn in the last 149 years on the basis of the same principles that

it is today invoking in order to avoid this conflict, which now seems
to be of such deep concern to it?

Obviously I am at variance with the draft resolution submitted by
the United Kingdom, but I wish to say that I am in agreement on one point.
The Republic of Argentina is threatening nobody, the Republic of Argentina
is not carrying out acts of aggression or hostility against anyone. It is
of no interest to us to have any armed confrontation with anybody at all.
We are ready to negotiate through diplomatic channels. I would say that
again: we are willing to negotiate through diplomatic channels any
differences we have with the United Kingdom except our sovereignty, which
is not open to negotiation.

We have a clear conscience about our rights, and we shall maintain them
with firmness and prudence until we arrive at a proper and peaceful settlement.
It is useless to whip up emotions when there is clear justice, as in our case.
Our policy, the policy of Argentina has, at all time been lofty, conciliatory
and prudent - and there is no evidence to the contrary. I am sure that it
will lose none of those attributes here.

The PRESIDENT (interpretation from French): The representative of
the United Kingdom has asked to speak in exercise of the right of reply and I
call on him.

Sir Anthony PARSONS (United Kingdom): I have no intention of speaking
polemically vis-à-vis the representative of Argentina any more than he did so
in his own statement, and any more than my Government has any intention or
desire of disturbing the peace in the South Atlantic. I should simply like to
make a number of points at this stage in the discussion.

First, I should like to go back to the reason why I called for an
immediate meeting of the Council two days ago. This was not - I repeat: not -
in any sense to discuss the rights or wrongs of the very-long-standing issue between
Britain and the Republic of Argentina over the islands in the South Atlantic.
This was not in any sense my intention. I was summoned two or three days ago
by the Secretary-General, acting on his own initiative and on press reports that
had come to his notice, and he extended to me a call for my Government to exercise
restraint in what appeared to him to be an incipiently serious situation.
Shortly after my conversation with the Secretary-General I received information
from my Government that an armed attack by Argentina on the Falkland Islands was
imminent. I therefore took the step - exceptional for the British Government -
of asking the President of the Security Council for an immediate meeting. My
only intention in calling for a meeting of the Council was that the Council should
act in such a way as to pre-empt, to deter, any threat of armed force and to

(Sir Anthony Parsons, United Kingdom)

conduct itself in its finest role: defusing a growingly dangerous situation.
That was my only objective in calling for a meeting of the Council.

As has been said many times round this table, you, Mr. President, issued an
appeal on behalf of the same Council the same evening, unanimously, calling
on both sides to exercise restraint and to refrain from the threat or use of force.

The following morning my delegation learnt, to its very great distress,
that that appeal had not been heeded by one party and that Argentine armed
forces had invaded the Falkland Islands.

My object in calling for a second meeting of the Council again had nothing
whatsoever to do with the rights or wrongs of the long-standing issue between my
country and the Republic of Argentina. It was not in any sense concerned with the
merits; it was entirely in response to this armed invasion. That is why I called
for a second meeting of the Council.

I should like to go on to make one or two observations on certain points
which the Foreign Minister of Argentina raised in his statement.

I think I am right in saying that he suggested that the immediate origin of
the present crisis was the incident which had taken place in South Georgia some
days, or even two or three weeks, previously.

I find that contention impossible to accept. This was an incident of relative
triviality. It was a question of the resolution of what we, the United Kingdom
Government, considered to be the illegal presence of 10 scrap-metal dealers on
the island of South Georgia. We had no intention of resolving that incident by
the use of force. It would have been bizarre, ludicrous, for the Government of
the United Kingdom to bring an incident of that dimension to the Security Council.
We had no doubt that we would be able to resolve it peacefully with the Government
of the Republic of Argentina. And I cannot see how this very small dispute could
conceivably justify the armed invasion of a group of inhabited islands located
800 miles away from the point at which the 10 scrap-metal dealers were located.

The Foreign Minister of Argentina also stated that his Government had not
acted hastily in using force to assert its claim over the Falkland Islands and he
referred to the state of negotiations between his Government and mine. Earlier in
his statement he referred to our manoeuvres, our evasive tactics, our procrastination
over the years. Of course, I cannot accept these charges.

At the risk of wearying the Council, I wish to give our side of the state of
negotiations as they were before this very grave crisis exploded.

There was a meeting in New York, at ministerial level, between the British
and Argentine Governments in late February this year, at which were present also
elected representatives of the people of the Falkland Islands. At the end of that
meeting a joint communiqué was agreed between the two Ministers who were conducting
the negotiations. The communiqué read as follows:

"The British and Argentine Governments held a meeting at ministerial
level in New York on 26 and 27 February 1982 to discuss the Falkland

(Sir Anthony Parsons, United Kingdom)

Islands question within the negotiating framework referred to in the
relevant resolutions of the United Nations General Assembly.
The British and Argentine delegations were led respectively by
Mr. Richard Luce, Member of Parliament, Minister of State at the Foreign
and Commonwealth Office in London, and Ambassador Enrique Ross,
Under-Secretary of State at the Ministry of Foreign Affairs and Worship
in Buenos Aires. The meeting took place in a cordial and positive spirit.
The two sides reaffirmed their resolve to find a solution to the
sovereignty dispute and considered in detail an Argentine proposal for
procedures to make better progress in this sense. They agreed to inform
their Governments accordingly."

The next thing that happened was that the Government of the Republic of
Argentina unilaterally published the statement to which the Foreign Minister
referred and which, indeed, he quoted in extenso in his statement.

That statement by the Government of Argentina differed from the joint
communiqué which we thought had been agreed at ministerial level in New York.
It contained a final sentence quoted by the Foreign Minister of Argentina,
which read as follows:

"However, should this not occur" - that is, the early solution of the dispute
"Argentina reserves the right to terminate the working of this negotiating
mechanism and to choose freely the procedure which best accords
with her interests."

The fact that the Government of Argentina unilaterally published its
own statement when we believed that there would be a joint publication of an
agreed communiqué, and the presence in the statement of that final sentence,
caused great alarm to the people of the Falkland Islands and, indeed, it
caused a certain controversy within the British Parliament and apprehension in
the British Government.

We have since been trying to reconcile this issue and to get back to an
agreed statement which would enable a negotiating process to begin. Unfortunately,
we now find ourselves in the situation which we are today debating.

I would like to refer to another proposition which, if the interpretation
was correct, I understood the Foreign Minister of Argentina to include in his
statement. I understood him to say that the principles in the Charter
relating to the settlement of international disputes by peaceful means - I refer
of course to Article 2, paragraphs 3 and 4 - were not necessarily applicable
to situations which arose before the Charter was adopted.

If my understanding of the Foreign Minister's meaning is correct, I submit
to the members of the Council that this is an extremely dangerous doctrine. The
world is distressingly full of crisis situations, which have from time to time
exploded into hostility in every continent on the globe. A large number of
those situations have their origins years, decades, centuries before the United

(Sir Anthony Parsons, United Kingdom)

Nations Charter was adopted in 1945. If the proposition were to be accepted that the use of force was valid for situations which originated before the Charter was adopted, by heaven I believe the world would be an infinitely more dangerous and flammable place than it already is.

I said at the outset of my statement that I had not come here to enter into the rights and wrongs of the problem of sovereignty between the Republic of Argentina and my own country. It has been very widely aired by other speakers this morning, and I would just like to say one or two words which relate to it.

The Foreign Minister of Argentina argued that the people of the Falkland Islands are not a population in international law. Those 1,800 or 1,900 people are not recent arrivals in the Islands. The vast majority of them were born there to families which had been settled there for four, five, six generations since the first half of the nineteenth century. In the judgement of my Government, whether they are 1,800 or 10,000 or 18 million, they are still entitled to the protection of international law and they are entitled to have their freely expressed wishes respected.

These have been the only objectives of my Government in that area for a very long time. I cannot believe that the international community takes the view that Britain in the 1980s has a "colonialist" or "imperialist" ambition in the South Atlantic. The proposition is self-evidently ludicrous. We threaten nobody; we have simply concerned ourselves with the protection of the interests and respect for the wishes of the small population of the Islands.

Finally, it has also been argued that this was not an invasion because the Islands belong to Argentina, a proposition which of course my Government contests. But the fact is that the United Kingdom has been accepted by the United Nations - by the General Assembly, by the Committee of 24 - as the Administering Authority. It therefore flies in the face of the facts and in the face of reason to suggest that this was not an armed invasion.

Annex 41: Statement by United States, May 22, 1982, in the
UN Security Council
Source: Press Release by United States, USUN 37 (82),
May 22, 1982

UNITED STATES MISSION TO THE UNITED NATIONS

PRESS RELEASE

'99 UNITED NATIONS PLAZA
NEW YORK, N Y 10017

FOR RELEASE ON DELIVERY
CHECK TEXT AGAINST DELIVERY

Press Release USUN 37(82)
May 22, 1982

STATEMENT BY

AMBASSADOR JEANE J. KIRKPATRICK

UNITED STATES REPRESENTATIVE TO THE UNITED NATIONS

IN THE SECURITY COUNCIL

ON THE QUESTION CONCERNING THE SITUATION IN THE
REGION OF THE FALKLAND ISLANDS (ISLAS MALVINAS)

MAY 22, 1982

Mr. President, I should like to begin by expressing
the appreciation of my government for your judicious and
skillful leadership of the affairs of this Council in this
deeply troubled time, as we seek a solution to the tragic
conflict underway in the South Atlantic.

We desire to express in this public arena our gratitude
to the Secretary General for his tireless and determined

efforts to find a peaceful resolution to the conflict between
the United Kingdom and Argentina. The Secretary General
knows, as we should like the world as well to know, that he
enjoyed the active support and cooperation of the United
States in his search for a peaceful resolution of the conflict.

This conflict poses a particularly acute problem for
persons and nations who love peace and also for this
international body whose very raison d'etre is to promote
and ensure the peaceful settlement of disputes.

The United States stands behind the principle that
the use of force to settle disputes should not be allowed
anywhere, and especially in this hemisphere where a significant
number of territorial disputes remain to be solved
diplomatically. For the United States, the Falkland crisis
has been and still is a particularly agonizing, tragic event.
As the whole world knows, we have a longstanding alliance
and, beyond that, the closest relations of friendship with
Great Britain, the country from which our political
institutions, law and language derive. But we have not
forgotten for a moment our close geographical, economic and
political relations with our Latin neighbors. We do not only
care about this hemisphere, we are part of this hemisphere,
and we share many of the aspirations, goals and dreams of all
nations of the Americas. Our own culture and society are
deeply influenced by a growing Hispanic population. We can
never turn our backs on, or be insensitive to, hemispheric
goals and aspirations that we ourselves have promoted and
defended.

That is why the United States tried so hard to avoid
the conflict on the Falklands, why we are hoping so intensely
to reduce and isolate it, and why we are eager and ready
to back any realistic diplomatic initiative which will put
a just end to it. And we especially mean to stay in close
touch with our Latin neighbors while efforts are made to solve

this tragic conflict, in order to restore peace with honor
so, that once again we can concentrate our efforts on the
resolution of our problems. The quicker we put this tragic
conflict behind us, the quicker we can begin building our
future. And there, as always, Latin America will find how
deeply the U.S. is committed to the cause of peace and
prosperity in our hemisphere.

Mr. President, as the fighting intensifies and
the cost in lives mounts in the South Atlantic, I think we
all share a sense of anguish that it has not yet been
possible to prevent this tragic conflict.

We have all come to appreciate how deep the roots
of the conflict are. Britain, in peaceful possession of the
Falkland Islands for 150 years, has been passionately devoted
to the proposition that the rights of the inhabitants should
be respected in any future disposition of the Islands. No
one can say that this attitude, coming from a country that
has granted independence to more than 40 countries in a generation and a half, is a simple reflex to retain possession.

Yet we know too how deep is the Argentine commitment
to recover islands they believe were taken from them by
illegal force. This is not some sudden passion, but a long-
sustained national concern that also stretches back 150
years, heightened by the sense of frustration at what Argentina
feels were nearly 20 years of fruitless negotiation.

From the start it has been widely recognized that the
conflict engages basic principles without which a peaceful
international order cannot stand. Unless the principle is
respected that force must not be used to settle disputes, the
entire international community will be exposed to chaos
and suffering. And unless the right of self-defense is
granted, only those countries that use force first will
have the protection of law.

The Security Council was profoundly right to reassert those principles in Resolution 502, which forms the indispensable framework in which a peaceful solution has been sought and will ultimately be found. It is of fundamental importance that both Argentina and Britain have accepted Resolution 502 in its entirety.

For the United States, the conflict has a special poignancy. We do not take -- have never taken -- any position on the underlying claims. Britain is a country to which we are bound by unique ties of friendship, values, and alliance. And Argentina is also an old friend, a country of immigrants and settlers like our own, a country with which we share the enormous human and national potential of the New World experience.

That a conflict of such dimensions should take place, and that it should occur here, in the Western Hemisphere -- whose countries havelong shared a particular commitment to each other, to their mutual welfare and to peace -- causes us the deepest concern. This conflict, however urgent, cannot be permitted to obscure the common engagement of all American states to the rule of law and to the well-being of this hemisphere.

So it was natural that the United States should make a particular effort to help Argentina and Britain find a solution.

That effort began before April 2nd, when we offered to the two sides our good offices to help find a solution to the South Georgia incident.

After April 2nd, both President Galtieri and Prime Minister Thatcher asked the United States to see whether it could be of assistance. At President Reagan's direction, Secretary of State Haig undertook two rounds of intense discussions in both capitals. Finally, on April 27th, as prospects for more intense hostilities arose, we put forward

a proposal. It represented our best estimate of what the
two parties could reasonably be expected to accept. It was
founded squarely on Resolution 502 by providing for a cessation
of hostilities, withdrawal of forces, and a political
settlement of the dispute.

The British government indicated that it would seriously
consider our proposal, although it presented certain real
difficulties for it. However, the proposal was not acceptable
to Argentina.

Immediately afterward, President Belaunde of Peru,
after consultation with Secretary Haig, took the initiative
to put forward a much simplified peace plan, also drawing on
the fundamental elements of Resolution 502.

On May 5th a draft text was forwarded by Peru to
Buenos Aires; we forwarded the same text to London.

Britain made clear that it could seriously consider
the proposal. Argentina chose not to consider it, asking
instead that the Secretary General use his good offices as,
of course, it was its full privilege to do.

Mr. President, the tragic conflict before us also
has special poignancy for the United Nations. It is precisely
the kind of problem this organization was created to resolve.
The Charter commits us "... to bring about by peaceful means,
and in conformity with the principles of justice and international
law, adjustment or settlement of international disputes or
situations which might lead to a breach of the peace." "To
develop friendly relations among nations based on respect
for the principle of equal rights and self-determination of
peoples, and to take other appropriate measures to strengthen
universal peace;
"To achieve international cooperation in solving international
problems...

"To be a centre for harmonizing the actions of nations in
the attainment of these common ends."

The United Nations record in dealing with this conflict
is commendable. The Security Council responded rapidly to the
Argentine seizure of the Islands. The fact that both parties
accepted Resolution 502 proves that it was a constructive
response.

The Secretary General's determined and imaginative
efforts were, of course, fervently welcomed by all of us.
Again the elements of settlement seemed to be present or nearly
present. Again peace eluded us. I believe the institutions
of the United Nations have functioned in this crisis in the
manner foreseen by its founders and its Charter. We can be
proud of it; proud, especially, of the Secretary General.

We have already heard his account of his search for a
formula that could resolve the conflict. I think all of us
have been deeply impressed by the skill and sensitivity, by
the judgment and fairness that the Secretary General brought
to this task. That his effort has not so far succeeded does
not mean that it has not realized important gains, notably
in the establishment of a mutually acceptable concept of
negotiations. The United States will wholeheartedly support
any initiative that can help Argentina and Britain make
peace with honor.

· Despite all our efforts, the problem is not solved.
Young men die in icy waters, on freezing beaches.

The dispute that appeared to many to be simple has
nonetheless proved extraordinarily difficult to resolve. But
we must not abandon the effort. Resolution 502, with its
concept of linked and simultaneous cessation of hostilities,
withdrawal of forces, and negotiations, must remain the
framework of the search for peace. The problem is too
important -- for the rule of law, for the future of the

Americas, for many of us friends of Britain and Argentina --
not to make an all-out effort to settle this tragic conflict,
so costly in every way.

Annex 42: Statement, US Assistant Secretary of State, August 5,
1982 (concerning attitude of United States)
Source: R. Perl, op. cit., p. 569

PREPARED STATEMENT OF
THOMAS O. ENDERS
ASSISTANT SECRETARY OF STATE
FOR INTER-AMERICAN AFFAIRS
BEFORE THE
SUBCOMMITTEE ON INTER-AMERICAN AFFAIRS
U.S. HOUSE OF REPRESENTATIVES
WASHINGTON, D.C.
August 5, 1982

1.

Mr. Chairman: I was delighted to receive your invitation to review with this Committee the impact of the Falklands/
Malvinas Islands conflict on the Inter-American System
and specifically on U.S. relations with Latin America.

The clash between Argentina and the United Kingdom
erupted suddenly, then as quickly disappeared from the
headlines. It left in its wake some haunting questions
-- about how to prevent war in the hemisphere, about the
future of Inter-American cooperation, even about regional
stability and progress.

This is not the first time that these islands have
vividly illustrated the risk of massive repercussions from
modest origins. These "few spots of earth which, in the
desert of the ocean, had almost escaped notice" once brought
"the whole system of European empire" to the point of convul-
sion. The remark is from Thoughts on the Late Transactions
Respecting Falkland's Islands, written by Samuel Johnson
in 1771.

This prepared statement addresses the disturbing consequences of the 1982 Falklands/Malvinas crisis beginning
in Part 6. Parts 2-5 record something of the origins and
course of the conflict itself.

2.

The territory immediately at issue consists of 2 main
islands and some 200 smaller ones located in the South
Atlantic 480 miles north-east of Cape Horn. The islands
cover a total area of 4,700 square miles. Their terrain
is alternately boggy and hilly, the environment wind-swept
and virtually treeless. Samuel Johnson described it as
"a bleak and barren spot in the Magellanick Ocean of which
no use could be made". But Johnson never went there to
see for himself. A U.S. Foreign Service Officer who did

so more than two centuries later in the course of her consular duties reported that "work is hard but life is simple
and not uncomfortable." According to the 1980 census,
the population was 1,813 -- down from the 1931 peak of
2,392. The predominant economic activity is the production
of fine wool.

It is their relationship to the outside world rather
than their marginal profitability that has made these islands
a source of seemingly endless contention. Even their name
reflects disagreement: though in English they are known
as the Falklands, in the Spanish-speaking world they are
invariably known as the Malvinas. There is even controversy
over which European first sighted the islands in the 16th
century.

But the central dispute has always been over sovereignty.
In 1770, England, France, and Spain almost went to war
over small outposts embodying competing claims to exclusive
dominion on the islands. That crisis was resolved pragmati-
cally when Spain restored to England the settlement of
Port Egmont on Saunders Island off West Falkland, founded
orginally by English settlers in 1766, then seized by Spain.
In turn, Spain kept Port Louis, which had originally been
founded by France in 1764 on East Falkland. Both Spain
and England maintained their broader sovereignty claims.

In 1774, apparently for reasons of economy, England
withdrew from Port Egmont, leaving behind a leaden plaque
declaring that "Falkland's Island" was the "sole right
and property" of King George III. From 1774 to 1811 the
islands were administered without challenge by a succession
of Spanish governors under the authority of the Viceroyalty
of La Plata in Buenos Aires.

In 1820, Argentina formally claimed sovereignty over
the then uninhabited islands as the successor to Spain.
In one of the many ironies of this history, the Frigate
Heroina sent to enforce Argentina's control was commanded
by David Jewett, one of the many British subjects who fought
in the Wars of Liberation in the service of the Argentine
Republic. In 1826, Argentina established a new capital
at the protected harbor of Stanley on East Falkland. In
1833, after a series of incidents over fishing rights,
one of which had led to action by the USS _Lexington_ against
Argentine authorities, the corvette HMS _Clio_ reasserted
Britain's claim.

For nearly a century and a half -- until an Argentine
naval force invaded Port Stanley last April 2 -- Britain
administered the islands, first as a Crown Colony, then
as a self-governing dependency. The royally chartered
Falklands Islands Company undertook the first large-scale

settlement of the islands, and provided ships that made
four or five round trips a year to Britain exchanging the
islands' wool and hides for everything from chocolates
to building materials.

3.

Argentina's commitment to recover territories Argentines
believe were illegally wrested from them by force is documented in countless pamphlets, articles, and books, some
of them distributed widely in Latin America. For the past
40 years or so, the claim to the "Malvinas" has been an
important component of Argentine nationalism, endorsed
by prominent civilian and military leaders across the political spectrum.

Immediately after World War II, Argentina moved its
claims beyond the bilateral exchanges that had marked its
efforts to recover the islands in the nineteenth and early
twentieth century. At inter-American conferences in Rio
in 1947, Bogota in 1948, Washington in 1953, and Caracas
in 1954, Argentine delegations introduced resolutions pressing Argentina's claims within a general framework of decolonization. In the arctic summer of 1947-48, an Argentine
task force of two cruisers and six destroyers conducted
maneuvers off the islands, but left when Britain dispatched
warships in response.

Argentine diplomacy registered a significant gain
in 1964. Since 1946, the United Nations had treated the
U.K. as the Administering Authority under Chapter XI of
the U.N. Charter. United Nations General Assembly resolution
2065(XX) called upon Argentina and the United Kingdom to
initiate talks with a view to resolving their conflicting
sovereignty claims peacefully. Confidential bilateral
talks began in 1966. With numerous ups and downs and occasional interruptions, Argentine-U.K. negotiations continued
for sixteen years. Agreements were reached providing for
Argentine facilitation of air travel and communications,
postal and medical services, education and oil supply.
The two sides remained far apart, however, on the basic
issue of sovereignty and such related issues as land ownership and residence by Argentines. The last pre-crisis
round of talks took place in New York in February 1982,
ending barely six weeks before Argentina attempted to settle
the matter by force.

It has been said that Britain's approach reflected
a stubborn colonialist reflex. The fact that over the
last generation no fewer than nine members of the Organization of American States have received their independence
in peace and good will from Great Britain suggests that

the situation was rather more complex. The resident islanders, hardy individuals predominantly of Scottish and Welsh
extraction, proved to be satisfied with British rule and
adamantly united in opposing Argentine claims. Throughout
the negotiations, Britain stood by the proposition that
the rights and views of the inhabitants must be respected
in any future disposition of the islands.

The standoff became rooted in principle as well as
nationality: Britain arguing for self-determination, Argentina
for territorial integrity.

4.

The United States has at no time taken a legal position
on the merits of the competing sovereignty claims. In
the nineteenth century, U.S. officials made clear that
-- because the British claims antedated 1823 -- the United
States did not consider the reassertion of British control
a violation of the Monroe Doctrine. The U.S., however,
refused to become embroiled in the sovereignty issue, and
took no position on Argentine and British sovereignty claims.

Thirty-five years ago, at the signing of the Final
Act of the 1947 Rio Conference which created the Rio Treaty,
the United States delegation, headed by Secretary of State
George C. Marshall, made clear our view that the Rio Treaty
is without effect upon outstanding territorial disputes
between American and European states -- and explicitly
refused to endorse Argentina's claim.

U.S. neutrality on the question of sovereignty has
been confirmed repeatedly since then -- at the Organization
of American States and the United Nations as well as during
the recent fighting. I reassert it again today, before
this body: The United States takes no position on the
merits of the competing claims to sovereignty, nor on the
legal theories on which the parties rely.

For the record, I would like to add that although
we of course have an interest in peace there as elsewhere,
the United States has no direct interest in the islands.
Because some comments abroad have suggested otherwise,
I state explicitly that the United States has never had,
and does not now have, any interest in establishing a military base of any kind on these islands. The only occasion
on which any U.S. military presence has ever been contem-
plated was in April-May 1982 as a contribution to a peaceful
resolution had one been agreed to between Argentina and
the United Kingdom.

5.

Argentina's surprise military occupation of the islands beginning April 2 provoked dismay and apprehension throughout the international community. The next day, April 3, the United Nations Security Council adopted Resolution 502, demanding immediate cessation of hostilities and withdrawal of Argentine troops, and calling on Argentina and the U.K. to resolve their differences diplomatically. Invoking the right of self-defense under Article 51 of the UN Charter, the U.K. dispatched a war fleet toward the islands.

The looming military confrontation put the inter-American system under great stress. Some said that because war would pit an American republic against an outside power, the Rio Treaty required that all its members come to the assistance of the American republic.

Others said that the inter-American system -- which protects regional order based on law and the peaceful settlement of disputes -- could in no way be interpreted to support the resort to force to settle a dispute.

The United States' position was that because the unlawful resort to force did not come from outside the hemisphere, this was not a case of extra-continental aggression against which we were -- and are -- all committed to rally.

These different responses to a conflict for which the Inter-American system was not designed led to heated exchanges among Foreign Ministers at the meeting of the Rio Treaty Organ of Consultation that began April 26. Two days later, the Organ adopted by a vote of 17-0-4 (the United States abstaining) a resolution that urged an immediate truce, recognition of the "rights of sovereignty of the Republic of Argentina over the Malvinas (Falkland) Islands and the interests of the islanders," and called for "negotiation aimed at a peaceful settlement of the conflict."

Negotiation of a peaceful settlement of the conflict had in fact been the central objective of the United States' response to the crisis.

U.S. efforts to encourage a negotiated settlement began even before the initial use of force. In late March, we offered to the two sides our good offices to help find a peaceful solution to an incident on South Georgia Island on March 19 when an Argentine salvage team was threatened with expulsion for operating without British permission. On April 1, learning that Argentine military action appeared imminent, President Reagan called President Galtieri to urge that Argentina desist from the use of force.

After Argentina forcibly occupied the islands, both
President Galtieri and Prime Minister Thatcher encouraged
the United States to see whether it could be of assistance
in finding a solution. At President Reagan's direction
Secretary Haig undertook two rounds of intense discussions
in each capital.

On April 27, as prospects for more intense hostilities
increased, the United States put forward a proposal of
its own. It represented our best estimate of what the
two parties could reasonably be expected to accept. It
was founded squarely on U.N. Security Council Resolution
502, which both sides asserted they accepted.

The U.S. proposal called for negotiations to remove
the islands from the list of Non-Self-Governing Territories
under Chapter XI of the U.N. Charter. It specified that
the definitive status of the islands must be mutually agreed,
with due regard for the rights of the inhabitants and for
the principle of territorial integrity. And it referred
both to the purposes and principles of the U.N. Charter,
and to the relevant resolutions of the U.N. General Assembly.

Those negotiations were to be completed by the end
of the year. Pending their conclusion, an interim authority
composed of Argentina, Britain, and the United States was
to oversee the traditional local administration, to be
sure that no decision was taken contrary to the agreement.
Argentine residents of the islands were to participate
in local councils for this purpose. During the interim
period travel, transportation and movement of persons between
the islands and the mainland were to be promoted and facilitated without prejudice to the rights and guarantees of
the inhabitants.

The proposed interim authority of three countries
was to make proposals to facilitate the negotiations, including recommendations on how to take into account the wishes
and interests of the inhabitants, and on what the role
of the Falkland Islands Company should be.

Should the negotiations not have been completed by
year's end, the United States was to be asked to engage
in a formal mediation/conciliation effort in order to resolve
the dispute within six months.

The British government indicated that our proposal
presented certain real difficulties but that it would seriously consider it. However, the proposal was not acceptable
to the Argentine Government, which continued to insist
that any solution must have a predetermined outcome.

On April 30, in light of Argentina's continued unwill-
ingness to compromise, we took concrete measures to underscore that the United States could not and would not condone
the unlawful use of force to resolve disputes. The President
ordered limited economic and military measures affecting
Argentina, and directed that we would respond positively
to requests for materiel support for British forces, but
without any direct U.S. military involvement. Secretary
Haig's statement announcing these measures emphasized our
belief that no strictly military outcome could endure,
that a negotiated settlement would be necessary in the
end, and that the United States remained ready to assist
the parties in finding that settlement.

On May 5, President Belaunde of Peru took the initiative
to put forward a new peace plan, drawing also on the fundamental elements of Resolution 502. We worked closely with
him. The simplified text forwarded by Peru to Buenos Aires
and London called for: an immediate cease-fire; concurrent
withdrawal and non-reintroduction of forces; administration
of the islands by a contact group pending definitive settlement, in consultation with the elected representatives
of the islanders; acknowledgement of conflicting claims;
acknowledgement in the final settlement of the aspirations
and interests of the islanders; and an undertaking by the
contact group to ensure that the two parties reached a
definitive agreement by April 30, 1983.

Britain made clear that it could seriously consider
the proposal. Argentina asked instead for the U.N. Secretary
General to use his good offices as, of course, it was its
full privilege to do.

By this time, however, the military tempo was rapidly
overtaking the negotiators. On May 2, two torpedoes from
a British submarine sank the General Belgrano, Argentina's
only cruiser. On May 4, a sea-skimming missile from an
Argentine jet devastated the HMS Sheffield, a modern British
destroyer. Despite intense new efforts by the U.N. Secretary-
General, the war we had worked so hard to avoid had come
in earnest.

By June 14, when the Union Jack was again raised over
Port Stanley, what Horace Walpole had in 1770 called "a
morsel of rock that lies somewhere at the very bottom of
America" had become the improbable scenario of bitter fighting. More than a thousand men and women were dead. Billions
of dollars had been expended. Emotions had surfaced in
both countries that promise to make this issue and others
even harder to resolve in the future.

6.

I said at the outset that the South Atlantic war faces us with several haunting questions.

Perhaps the most fundamental is how better to prevent war in the future in this hemisphere.

Many of us feared as soon as Argentina acted April 2 that the fighting would escalate. Argentina, it is true, did not cause casualties in its takeover. But that did little to diminish the shock. Any use of force invites further use of force. The shock in this case was increased because the two countries were both linked in friendship to us and to each other. It grew when brave men on both sides began to risk and lose their lives. But perhaps the deepest shock came because war between states had been virtually unknown in the Americas in our time.

In the world as a whole, some four million persons have lost their lives in armed action between states since the Second World War. Including the toll in the South Atlantic, fewer than four thousand of them have died in the Western Hemisphere. The countries of Latin America spend less of their national resources for arms than any other area in the world. Their military expenditures come to only 1.4 percent of GNP -- a quarter of the average in the Third World as a whole.

The South Atlantic war -- the fact of major fighting and the clear advantages demonstrated by modern weapons -- means that military institutions, throughout the hemisphere but especially in South America, have powerful new claims to resources. Because Latin America's military institutions and arsenals are relatively modest in size, demands for advanced weapons systems and for the expertise to maintain and employ them are likely to increase. Governments will also look for self-sufficiency in defense industries, for bigger stocks of weapons.

Budgetary limitations will of course constrain purchases, but we would be mistaken to expect arms modernization to be deferred as a result of the South Atlantic conflict. On the contrary. The duration and intensity of the fighting called into question the assumption that the Inter-American System guarantees that interstate conflicts in this hemisphere would be limited to a few days of actual fighting.

A new emphasis on military preparedness in a region long plagued by territorial disputes and military involvement in politics would undeniably challenge every member of the Inter-American System.

The hemisphere is laced with territorial questionmarks. The prevalence of territorial tensions (e.g., among Argentina-Chile-Peru-Bolivia-Ecuador, Colombia-Venezuela-Guyana, Nicaragua-Colombia, Guatemala-Belize) puts a premium on the peaceful settlement of disputes. To take just one example, tensions between Guatemala and Belize (the only place in the hemisphere other than the Falklands where the U.K. stations combat troops) will continue to fester if unresolved.

The challenge to regional peacekeeping is far from hopeless, however. The U.S. response to the crisis may serve to deter others from resorting to force. Moreover, the Inter-American System equips the New World with the means to prevent or control the conflicts that have kept other continents from realizing their potential.

Machinery exists to anticipate disputes and permit their peaceful and definitive settlement: various Inter-American arbitration and conciliation agreements, OAS peace-keeping mechanisms, the International Court of Justice, even the Treaty of Tlatelolco, which established the world's first nuclear free zone in a populated area. What appears lacking is the will to use this machinery to prevent and resolve contentious problems. The U.S. and other countries of the area have at one time or another been involved in calming or negotiating most of them. But this is a branch of hemispheric diplomacy that deserves fresh attention.

The interest of American states is clearly to avoid arms races. Even where competitive procurement cannot be avoided altogether, they will want to see that existing disputes are not needlessly exacerbated. U.S. arms sales as a proportion of South American purchases fell from 75 percent in 1960 to 25 percent in 1970, and 7 percent in 1980. The reduction in training and in-depth contacts between the U.S. and most South American militaries has been equally precipitous.

These patterns raise a question worth pondering in the wake of the Falklands/Malvinas episode. Can the United States maintain a degree of military access and communication with the states of South America so as to help maintain the regional balance of power with such limited personnel, doctrinal, and materiel relationships?

A related challenge is to prevent regional conflicts from having strategic consequences, changing the East-West balance. This is a real problem, for history shows the Soviet Union and its proxies are ready and eager to take advantage of instability. Should Moscow be willing to provide arms at bargain prices as it did to Peru in the

1970's, economic constraints on Latin American purchases
of military equipment from traditional Western sources
could give the Soviets a unique opportunity to forge closer
links with established governments in South America. Cuba
(and Nicaragua) rushed forward to exploit the Falklands
crisis. In Argentina some talked of playing the Cuban
card. We do not believe Argentina will turn to the country
that harbors in its capital the extremely violent Argentine
terrorist organization -- the Montoneros. But Cuba will
be working hard to use the crisis to lessen its current
isolation within the hemisphere.

7.

A second legacy of the conflict is the need to overcome
resentments of the United States that were triggered by
the crisis.

Although the immediate emotional strains of the crisis
are already receding, the perception of the U.S. as a reliable ally to Latin American nations in times of crisis
will take time to restore.

The commitment of the United States to the hemisphere
and its institutions has been called into question. I
have already noted the importance we attach to the OAS,
that we have taken no position on the question of sovereignty,
and that in our view no Rio Treaty action could apply to
this particular contingency. Nonetheless, U.S. support
for what on May 29 the second meeting of the Rio Treaty
Organ of Consultation condemned as an "unjustified and
disproportionate" U.K. military response was taken by some
to mean that the U.S. commitment to the Inter-American
System was superficial at best.

The fact that the conflict remained localized and
ended relatively rapidly helped mitigate damage to U.S.
interests. Nonetheless, our bilateral relationships with
certain countries have unquestionably been affected adversely.
The most severe impact is obviously on relations with Argentina
But Venezuela, Panama, and Peru were also highly critical
of our support for the United Kingdom's military response,
and will be watching closely the future evolution of the
sovereignty issue. In contrast, U.S. relations with most
other South American countries, Mexico and the Caribbean
Basin appear less affected.

The lasting effects of this mood, which varies from
country to country, will depend on how the post-crisis
situation evolves and what posture we adopt. Reactions
may change as the position taken by the United States is
better understood. But the widespread view that the United

States does not take Latin America seriously could increase
North-South and non-aligned rhetoric and inhibit cooperation
in support of U.S. interests. The argument that the United
States and United Kingdom acted as industrialized powers
cooperating to keep a developing country "in its place"
makes us once again a target for anti-colonialist and anti-
imperialist emotions that will make it harder for us to
accomplish our objectives.

     It would be wrong to conclude from such reactions
that the U.S. should not have acted as it did. There can
be no position for the United States other than to oppose
the unlawful use of force to settle disputes.

     The first lesson for U.S. policy is that that this
is a time for steadiness of purpose rather than for grandiose
gestures, statements, or proposals. During the coming
months, it will be especially important that we meet our
commitments, protect our interests and respond to those
of our neighbors in a meaningful and resourceful manner.

     The Caribbean Basin Initiative is vitally important
in this regard. Many Basin countries now wonder whether
our contribution to the CBI will ever materialize. If
Congress were not to act, the concerns these countries
now express about their future and our commitment to them
would deepen, widening opportunities for Soviet and Cuban
adventurism. It is now up to the United States to deliver.

     We must maintain our commitment in Central America,
where democratic processes are vulnerable, and where fragile
government institutions face a major challenge from Cuban
supported guerrilla movements. Our political, economic
and security assistance is essential to help them meet
this challenge and make progress toward democracy, economic
development, and the effective protection of human rights.

     While we must continue to seek innovative solutions
to the problems of our immediate neighborhood, we must
understand what is happening in South America is also important to us. This was evident in the midst of the Falklands
conflict -- for example, in the visit of President Figueiredo
to Washington. The conflict between Argentina and the
United Kingdom was a major topic of discussion. The exchange
made clear that the positions of the U.S. and Brazil differed, but that our basic interests and objectives were
similar. For several years now, we have simply not given
South America the attention its place in the world and
our interests warrant.

                         8.

     This brings me to a third challenge, the conundrum
of our relations with Argentina. Despite our many similarities, U.S.-Argentine relations have seldom been close.

The President's vision of region-wide cooperation
had led us to make efforts to improve ties to South America,
including Argentina. In the case of Argentina, however,
those efforts had not yet borne fruit by the time of the
crisis. We must continue to seek a dialogue that can develop
the bilateral and multilateral framework for more fully
cooperative relations.

During the South Atlantic crisis, our ties with Argentina
proved too weak to promote effective cooperation in support
of common interests. Repeated efforts were made by us
and by others -- before the Argentine landing on the islands,
again when the British fleet was approaching, and again
when the U.S. and Peruvian and UN peace plans were advanced
in turn -- to explain to Argentine leaders what would happen
if they did what they proposed to do. Although our predic-
tions consistently proved accurate, they were not believed.
Communication failed utterly.

Our objectives with Argentina today include encouraging
economic recovery, peaceful resolution of the dispute between
the U.K. and Argentina, and, of course, political comity.
Yet our ties to the government in Buenos Aires are now
more limited than previously. How long this will last
depends on several factors. But the fundamental point
is that we all share a compelling interest in an Argentina
that is true to hemispheric traditions and free of foreign
communist influence. We do not want the Soviets to be
their only alternative. Neither do they. We all should
be prepared to help Argentina maintain conditions in which
its people can realize their free world vocation.

So we must begin, in orderly fashion, to build the
solid, realistic relationship so evidently lacking until
now.

9.

Finally, the South Atlantic crisis has highlighted
economic problems in South America and throughout the hemisphere.

Even before the crisis, many of the region's countries were feeling the effects of the world recession on
their development. The problems vary. Virtually all depend
heavily on international trade and on access to international
financial markets. Some have contracted substantial debt.
The South Atlantic crisis could crystallize doubts about
stability and creditworthiness on a region-wide level,
particularly if arms procurement were to divert resources
from development priorities.

The major lesson here is the need for cooperation
in economic management -- not merely with Argentina, but
with Brazil, Venezuela and Mexico.

Many of the problems now associated with the South
Atlantic crisis have been developing for some time. The
growing assertiveness and needs of major developing countries
are not new. Let us hope that the crisis will strengthen
our ability to work more realistically together.

10.

Before the crisis erupted in the South Atlantic, we
had already begun to develop more sustained hemispheric
relationships.

-- We had started to achieve with Mexico a relationship that reflects its exceptional importance
   to the U.S. and its role in world affairs. Now
   comes the harshest test of that new relationship,
   as the economic slowdown in both countries threatens
   to aggravate all our joint accounts: trade, finance, immigration. We must be steadfast.

-- We had committed ourselves to help countries of
   the Caribbean Basin protect themselves against
   outside intervention, strengthen or develop democratic institutions, and overcome economic disas-
   ters. Now we must deliver.

-- We were beginning to respond to new realities
   in South America, rebuilding close bilateral relations with each country after a decade of drift,
   when the shadow of the South Atlantic crisis fell
   across our efforts. Now we must relaunch those
   efforts, joining others to maintain the network
   of constructive relationships that is essential
   to peace.

What this crisis may ultimately mean for the United
States is not that our recent decisions were wrong -- they
were right -- but that the accummulation from our past
decisions reveals a flaw in our outlook. We have pursued
an a la carte approach, ignoring our friends when it suited
us, yet demanding their help or agreement when it served
our interest. We took too much for granted, and invested
too little. When we needed close and effective dialogue
on April 2, we didn't have it.

When a fight in distant islands reverberates around
the world, the fundamental lesson is not how little we
need each other but how closely connected we are. Our
task is to make interdependence work, not against us, but
for us. This requires long term commitments that will
enhance our ability to influence events and protect our
interests.

Legal Aspects of Falklands/Malvinas Crisis Negotiations

This paper addresses three aspects of the negotiations
which occurred during April and May of 1982 to avert the war in
the South Atlantic: the United States posture on the underlying
dispute over sovereignty of the Islands; the content of the
three most intensive settlement efforts, focusing on the two in
which the United States was most closely involved; and the consideration given to use of the International Court of Justice.

U.S. Position on Claims to the Islands

Throughout the more than 200-year history of this dispute,
the United States has maintained a legal neutrality on the competing United Kingdom and Argentine claims to the Falklands/
Malvinas, urging that their dispute be resolved through peaceful
means in accordance with international law. In the post-World
War II era, the United States has abstained on United Nations or
Organization of American States resolutions that implied a
position on the merits.

United States neutrality is also reflected in the United
States position on the non-applicability of the Monroe
Doctrine. Because the dispute over the Islands predated the
Monroe Doctrine, and because the United States took no position
on the dispute over sovereignty, the State Department long ago
expressed the view that the reinsertion of a British presence on
the Islands in 1833 was not a new attempt at colonization, and
that the Doctrine is thus inapplicable.

In addition to declining to take a position on the merits,
the United States has not taken a position on the underlying
legal theories on which the parties rely. Specifically, the
United States has taken no view on the relative weight to be
given to Britain's position on self-determination for the
Islanders, and Argentina's emphasis on the principle of
territorial integrity with the mainland. The application of
the principle of self-determination to the Falklands has raised
a number of legal questions in view of the size and origin of
the population, the existence of other legal principles which
may be applicable given the history and nature of the dispute,
and, in particular, the interpretation placed by Argentina on
the principle of territorial integrity contained in United
Nations General Assembly decolonization resolutions such as
Resolution 1514 (XV).

This United States position of neutrality was maintained
throughout, and facilitated our attempts to mediate, the crisis.

While remaining neutral on the merits of the dispute, the
United States has acknowledged the fact of longstanding United
Kingdom administration of the Islands. The United States has
accordingly dealt with the United Kingdom on matters related to
the Islands and has on occasion acquiesced in United Kingdom
accession to bilateral agreements and international conventions
on behalf of them. The United States position in such instances
has been consistent with acknowledgment of the United Kingdom's

de facto responsibility for the Islands' foreign relations as the administering authority in peaceful possession. This pragmatic policy of dealing with the administrator in de facto control is also that of the United Nations, which has accepted from the United Kingdom, as the administering authority, annual reports under Chapter XI of the United Nations Charter regarding Non-Self-Governing Territories.

April-May 1982 Negotiations

There were three intensive efforts after the Argentine occupation of the Islands to avert the coming military confrontation; each resulted in textual elaborations of the positions of both sides on acceptable outcomes on the range of issues involved in a package to promote a peaceful settlement. All of these efforts addressed four common elements:

--a cease-fire, linked to a mutual withdrawal of forces within a short period, and a commitment on non-reintroduction of forces, subject to third-party verification (this element was consistent with United Nations Security Council Resolution 502, operative paragraphs 1 and 2 of which called for an immediate cessation of hostilities and withdrawal of Argentine forces from the Islands);

--interim administrative arrangements for the Islands, based on some form of third-party supervision of local government, including provision for Argentine accesss to the Islands during this period;

--the composition and definition of the functions of the third-party mechanism to assist the parties in implementation of an agreement; and

--a framework for negotiations to reach a definitive settlement, including a deadline or target date, and the role in such negotiations for third-party assistance.

Each side, of course, approached these common elements from a different perspective, which in some cases shifted as the diplomatic and military situation changed over time. The United Kingdom was willing to consider variations on the form of administration of the Islands, subject to certain basic guarantees in respect of local rights and institutions. It was prepared to accept third-party assistance in implementation of an agreement, subject to inclusion of some role for the United States. United Kingdom insistence on a cease-fire coupled with immediate withdrawal of Argentine forces from the Islands remained firm, consistent with its legal position based on Article 51 of the United Nations Charter relating to self-defense, and United Nations Security Council Resolution 502. The United Kingdom also insisted that nothing in an agreement prejudice the final outcome of the negotiations. This insistence focused in particular on the drafting of a formula on future negotiations that was neutral on the issue of sovereignty, and on provisions to control Argentine intercourse with the Islands at pre-war levels, consistent with a 1971 agreement between the two countries.

Argentina, in turn, sought either effective interim control of the Islands' administration, including freedom of access to the Islands, or assurance that the formula on a definitive settlement would automatically result in confirmation of Argentine sovereignty over the Islands at some fixed future time. While accepting the concept of a cease-fire linked to mutual withdrawal of forces, Argentina sought an immediate United Kingdom withdrawal of its units to home bases; the United Kingdom viewed such a formula for the withdrawal period as imbalanced (since Argentine forces would remain within close range of the Islands) and as removing a necessary deterrent to Argentine violation of the terms of an agreement. Argentina sought drafting of the negotiation mandate to emphasize decolonization and the principle of territorial integrity with the mainland, and resisted references to a right of self-determination on the part of the Islanders which were desired by the United Kingdom. Argentina, in light of the long history of prior talks with the United Kingdom, took the position that the mandate had to be placed under a firm and short deadline date.

Both sides shared an evaluation that provisions on interim arrangements and the framework for reaching a definitive settlement were interlinked elements of the negotiation, each prepared to be flexible in one area for gains in the other.

The three principal initiatives are discussed below, and the resulting texts are attached.

United States Proposal of April 27. The first effort, that of Secretary Haig, culminated in a fairly detailed set of proposals to the two parties on April 27. It was based on the three strenuous weeks of consultations he had held in London, Buenos Aires and Washington, and our best perception of what might ultimately prove acceptable to each side. Its approach, and many of its elements, reappeared in subsequent proposals to and by the two parties.

The United States draft memorandum of agreement provided for an integral cease-fire and withdrawal linkage. The formula for providing for balanced withdrawals proved troublesome in each of the three negotiations, given the vastly different geographic perspectives of each side. The United States proposal resolved the problem by a formula based on parity in reinsertion time, rather than on conventional but more difficult geographic withdrawal distances. These commitments, and that of non-reintroduction of forces into the Islands and defined surrounding areas, were to be verified by the United States.

The proposal called for immediate steps to terminate simultaneously the various economic and financial measures each party had adopted, and for the United Kingdom to request termination of similar measures taken by its allies.

Local self-government on the Islands was to be restored. The office of Governor was to remain vacant, and its powers exercised by the next-ranking official, appointed by the United Kingdom. The local Executive and Legislative Councils were to be retained, but augmented by representation of the small local Argentine resident population by means of at least one representative in each Council, and by inclusion of two Argentine Government representatives in the upper, Executive Council. A

Special Interim Authority was to be created, composed of a
representative of each side and of the United States. The
flags of each constituent country were to be flown at its
headquarters. The Authority was to have supervision over Island
administration, exercised by means of a veto power in the event
the Authority, by majority vote, deemed an act of the local
government to be inconsistent with the agreement. In all other
cases, the Authority was called upon to ratify expeditiously
all local decisions, laws and regulations.

The proposal called for decolonization of the Islands as
the negotiation objective. This was framed in terms of
removing the Islands from the list of Non-Self-Governing
Territories under Chapter XI of the United Nations Charter.
The potential means were not limited, but the conditions for
their definitive status had to be mutually agreed. The
negotiation mandate maintained neutrality on the competing
legal positions of the two sides, noting that of each by
short-hand references to due regard for the rights of the
inhabitants and the principle of territorial integrity.
Reference was made to relevant United Nations General Assembly
resolutions (which would include general decolonization
resolutions and specific resolutions on the subject of the
Falklands/Malvinas).

Foreshadowing the contact group concept utilized in later
proposals, the United States formulation provided a role for
the Special Interim Authority to catalyze the negotiations with
recommendations to the two sides, in particular on the sensi-
tive issues of how to take into account the wishes of the
Islanders and the role of the Falkland Islands Company. If the
negotiations did not prosper by the deadline date (December 31,
1982), a second phase of negotiations, under a new six-month
target date, was to occur in which the United States would, act
as a mediator/conciliator to press for an agreement.

With respect to contacts with the mainland, the draft
agreement stated a principle of promotion and facilitation of
non-discriminatory travel, commercial, communications, and
other links. The proposal provided for recommendation by the
Authority to the two Governments of specific measures on such
matters, and for securing the views of the local Councils on
the recommendations. These provisions were balanced by an
obligation to respect the traditional rights and guarantees of
the Islanders.

The United Kingdom, which had not yet landed on the
Falklands/Malvinas or suffered any serious combat losses, found
the proposal difficult, but was willing to give it "serious
consideration." This was the only time the United Kingdom
considered a proposal to cover the South Georgia and South
Sandwich Dependencies as well as the Falklands/Malvinas
(sensitivity to the implications of use of the English and
Spanish names for the Islands resulted in the United States
proposal defining the island groups by coordinates).

Despite many attractive features for the Argentines, the
Argentine Foreign Minister replied on April 29 that the
Government of Argentina could not accept the formulation since

it gave them neither effective interim control nor assurances
of obtaining sovereignty as a result of the negotiation process.

Peru-United States Proposal. At the initiative of the
President of Peru, and with our cooperation, another effort was
launched, culminating on May 5 with a more skeletal proposal,
limited in geographic scope to the Falklands/Malvinas. A
cease-fire and withdrawal of forces were inseparably linked,
but all implementing detail was to be deferred for decision by
a Contact Group composed of representatives of Brazil, Peru,
the Federal Republic of Germany and the United States.

The Contact Group was to verify the military provisions of
an agreement. It would assume administration of the government
of the Islands in consultation with the elected representatives
of the Islanders, and ensure that no actions were taken inconsistent with the agreement. All details on implementation of
administration--financial questions, applicable law, administrative, legal and appointive links to Britain, the role of the
Councils, the exercise of powers of the office of Governor--were
to be deferred for later decision by the Contact Group . The
result conceivably might have paralleled the United States proposal once elaborated, but the door was open to other variations
of third-party administration and the role to be played there-
under by the existing local institutions.

The existence of the parties' differing legal positions was
noted; the proposal also included an acknowledgment that the
"aspirations and interests" of the Islanders were to be "included" in a definitive settlement.

Finally, the Contact Group assumed a responsibility to
attempt to ensure that the two governments reached a negotiated
agreement on the future of the Islands by April 30, 1983.
Again, the detail of modalities for the negotiation, and the
role and procedures of the Contact Group in facilitating a
result, were deferred for later decision. The negotiation
formula was neutral, but included a deadline date as Argentina
desired.

The United Kingdom indicated that it was willing to give
this proposal serious consideration; Argentina, after the
initiation of talks under the auspices of the United Nations
Secretary-General, preferred to shift the focus of negotiations
to New York.

United Nations Negotiations. With continued change in the
military situation and, from the United Kingdom's perspective,
in the wake of failure to secure agreement on the basis of
substantial concessions reflected in the United States and
Peruvian proposals, the positions of both sides hardened in a
number of respects as evidenced by the texts each side publicly
released at the breakdown of these talks in late May.

Both sides accepted the concept of a United Nations
administration with generally defined authority. This formulation reflected a substantial concession by the United Kingdom
on maintenance of administrative links to Britain in favor of

local self-rule under United Nations supervision. Again,
critical details would have had to be defined in implementing
agreements or by United Nations Security Council resolution.
United Nations verification of military disengagement provisions
was also accepted by both sides in principle, as well as the
auspices of the United Nations Secretary-General to conduct the
negotiations.

The publicly-released positions permitted identification of
very limited other common ground. The United Kingdom sought to
subject a United Nations administration to local law and
practices, "in consultation with" the Islands' representative
institutions, which Argentina resisted. Argentina sought
immediate, expanded access to the Islands, which the United
Kingdom would not accept for fear that the population and
character of the Islands might be unilaterally altered during
the interim period. Argentina desired a firm deadline for
negotiation to be followed, if necessary, by reference of the
dispute to the United Nations General Assembly for decision; the
United Kingdom rejected recourse to the General Assembly, and
continued to consider a rigid timetable unrealistic. On these
and other points (e.g., extent of geographical coverage; military withdrawal details; self-determination references), the two
sides ended far apart.

The Secretary-General made last-minute proposals to the two
sides before the talks unraveled. Prime Minister Thatcher, as
events overtook these suggestions, simply noted that Argentina
could not possibly have accepted them. We are unaware of any
formal Argentine response. To our knowledge, the content of
these suggestions was not publicly released.

Subsequent Developments. The United Kingdom and Argentine
texts tabled at the conclusion of the Secretary-General's first
round of negotiations remain the final textual elaboration of
their views on settlement issues. There followed efforts in the
Security Council to negotiate a resolution that would substitute
for an agreement, notably involving a useful Brazilian draft
text. None was the subject of intensive substantive negotiation.   These efforts culminated in the Security Council's
adoption, on May 26, of Resolution 505, which asked the
Secretary-General to renew his good offices to secure a
cease-fire; and in the United Kingdom-United States veto, on
June 4, of a Spanish/Panamanian draft resolution that sought a
cease-fire and implementation of the previous Security Council
Resolutions, under verification of the Secretary-General, but
with inadequate detail on withdrawal procedures and other
elements to serve as a mutually agreeable vehicle for settlement
of the conflict.

Possible Role for the International Court of Justice

The focus of United Nations General Assembly resolutions on
the subject, the efforts of both countries over sixteen years,
and of the peace-making efforts in the spring, was on a
negotiated settlement of the dispute.

The United States Government is committed to the use of the
International Court of Justice to resolve legal disputes,
consistent with Article 36(3) of the United Nations Charter.

The submission to a Chamber of the Court of our differences with Canada over delimitation of a maritime boundary in the Gulf of Maine is a concrete example. The dispute on sovereignty over the Falklands/Malvinas is an issue which the Court could appropriately decide. United States negotiators this spring raised this matter with both sides. Neither has ever indicated a willingness to have recourse to the Court over the Falklands/Malvinas. The case does not fall within the compulsory jurisdiction of the Court, and the agreement of both parties is thus necessary to submit the case for binding decision.

The United Kingdom on two occasions since World War II sought to submit to the Court the related dispute on sovereignty over the South Georgia and South Sandwich Island Dependencies, but Argentina did not agree to do so.

The United States continues to believe that a peaceful solution to this long-standing controversy is required, consistent with the United Nations Charter obligations of both parties, and it may be that posible use of the Court will be reconsidered among the other possible settlement options, including renewed negotiations, that would be consistent with Article 33 of the Charter.

Annex 43: Resolutions passed by UN General Assembly on Falkland
Islands (Malvinas), between 1982 and 1990

37/9.   Question of the Falkland Islands (Malvinas)[19]

The General Assembly,

Having considered the question of the Falkland Islands
(Malvinas),

Aware that the maintenance of colonial situations is incompatible with the United Nations ideal of universal peace,

Recalling its resolutions 1514 (XV) of 14 December 1960,
2065 (XX) of 16 December 1965, 3160 (XXVIII) of 14
December 1973 and 31/49 of 1 December 1976,

Recalling also Security Council resolutions 502 (1982)
of 3 April 1982 and 505 (1982) of 26 May 1982,

Taking into account the existence of a *de facto* cessation
of hostilities in the South Atlantic and the expressed intention of the parties not to renew them,

Reaffirming the need for the parties to take due account
of the interests of the population of the Falkland Islands
(Malvinas) in accordance with the provisions of General
Assembly resolutions 2065 (XX) and 3160 (XXVIII),

Reaffirming also the principles of the Charter of the United
Nations on the non-use of force or the threat of force in
international relations and the peaceful settlement of international disputes,

1.   *Requests* the Governments of Argentina and the United
Kingdom of Great Britain and Northern Ireland to resume
negotiations in order to find as soon as possible a peaceful
solution to the sovereignty dispute relating to the question
of the Falkland Islands (Malvinas);

2.   *Requests* the Secretary-General, on the basis of the
present resolution, to undertake a renewed mission of good
offices in order to assist the parties in complying with the
request made in paragraph 1 above, and to take the necessary
measures to that end;

3.   *Requests* the Secretary-General to report to the General Assembly at its thirty-eighth session on the progress
made in the implementation of the present resolution;

4.   *Decides* to include in the provisional agenda of its
thirty-eighth session the item entitled "Question of the Falkland Islands (Malvinas)".

55th plenary meeting
4 November 1982

[19] See also sect. I, footnote 10, and sect. X.B.6, decision 37/404.

38/12. Question of the Falkland Islands (Malvinas) [33]

The General Assembly,

Having considered the question of the Falkland Islands (Malvinas),

Aware that the maintenance of colonial situations is incompatible with the United Nations ideal of universal peace,

Recalling its resolutions 1514 (XV) of 14 December 1960, 2065 (XX) of 16 December 1965. 3160 (XXVIII) of 14 December 1973. 31/49 of 1 December 1976 and 37/9 of 4 November 1982,

Recalling also Security Council resolutions 502 (1982) of 3 April 1982 and 505 (1982) of 26 May 1982,

Having received the report of the Secretary-General on his mission of good offices, [34]

Regretting the lack of progress in the implementation of resolution 37/9,

Aware of the interest of the international community in the resumption by the Governments of Argentina and the United Kingdom of Great Britain and Northern Ireland of their negotiations in order to find as soon as possible a peaceful and just solution to the sovereignty dispute relating to the question of the Falkland Islands (Malvinas),

Taking into account the existence of a *de facto* cessation of hostilities in the South Atlantic and the expressed intention of the parties not to renew them,

Reaffirming the need for the parties to take due account of the interests of the population of the Falkland Islands (Malvinas) in accordance with the provisions of General Assembly resolutions 2065 (XX), 3160 (XXVIII) and 37/9,

Reaffirming also the principles of the Charter of the United Nations on the non-use of force or the threat of force in international relations and the peaceful settlement of international disputes,

1. *Reiterates* its request to the Governments of Argentina and the United Kingdom of Great Britain and Northern Ireland to resume negotiations in order to find as soon as possible a peaceful solution to the sovereignty dispute relating to the question of the Falkland Islands (Malvinas);

2. *Takes note* of the report of the Secretary-General on the implementation of General Assembly resolution 37/9; [34]

3. *Requests* the Secretary-General to continue his renewed mission of good offices in order to assist the parties in complying with the request made in paragraph 1 above, and to take the necessary measures to that end;

---

[33] See also sect. I. footnote 6. and sect. X.B.5. decision 38/405.
[34] A/38/532.

4. *Requests* the Secretary-General to submit a report to the General Assembly at its thirty-ninth session on the progress made in the implementation of the present resolution;

5. *Decides* to include in the provisional agenda of its thirty-ninth session the item entitled "Question of the Falkland Islands (Malvinas)".

59th plenary meeting
16 November 1983

39/6. Question of the Falkland Islands (Malvinas)[14]

The General Assembly,

Having considered the question of the Falkland Islands (Malvinas) and having received the report of the Secretary-General,[15]

Recalling its resolutions 1514 (XV) of 14 December 1960, 2065 (XX) of 16 December 1965, 3160 (XXVIII) of 14 December 1973, 31/49 of 1 December 1976, 37/9 of 4 November 1982 and 38/12 of 16 November 1983, together with Security Council resolutions 502 (1982) of 3 April 1982 and 505 (1982) of 26 May 1982,

Reaffirming the principles of the Charter of the United Nations on the non-use of force or the threat of force in international relations and the obligation of States to settle their international disputes by peaceful means and recalling that, in this respect, the General Assembly has repeatedly requested the Governments of Argentina and the United Kingdom of Great Britain and Northern Ireland to resume negotiations in order to find as soon as possible a peaceful, just and definitive solution to the sovereignty dispute relating to the question of the Falkland Islands (Malvinas),

Observing with concern that, in spite of the time which has elapsed since the adoption of resolution 2065 (XX), the prolonged dispute has not yet been resolved,

Aware of the interest of the international community in the settlement by the Governments of Argentina and the United Kingdom of all their differences, in accordance with the United Nations ideals of peace and friendship among peoples,

Taking note of the communiqué issued by the representatives of the Government of.Switzerland and the Government of Brazil at Berne on 20 July 1984,[16]

Reaffirming the need for the parties to take due account of the interests of the population of the Falkland Islands (Malvinas) in accordance with the provisions of General Assembly resolutions 2065 (XX), 3160 (XXVIII), 37/9 and 38/12,

---

[14] See also sect. I, footnote 6, and sect. X.B.5, decision 39/404.
[15] A/39/589.

1. *Reiterates its request* to the Governments of Argen-.ina and the United Kingdom of Great Britain and Northern Ireland to resume negotiations in order to find as soon as possible a peaceful solution to the sovereignty dispute and their remaining differences relating to the question of the Falkland Islands (Malvinas);

2. *Requests* the Secretary-General to continue his renewed mission of good offices in order to assist the parties in complying with the request made in paragraph 1 above, and to take the necessary measures to that end;

3. *Requests* the Secretary-General to submit to the General Assembly at its fortieth session a report on the progress made in the implementation of the present resolution;

4. *Decides* to include in the provisional agenda of its fortieth session the item entitled "Question of the Falkland Islands (Malvinas)".

46th plenary meeting
1 November 1984

40/21. Question of the Falkland Islands (Malvinas)[34]

The General Assembly,

Having considered the question of the Falkland Islands (Malvinas) and having received the report of the Secretary-General,[35]

Aware of the interest of the international community in the peaceful and definitive settlement by the Governments of Argentina and the United Kingdom of Great Britain and Northern Ireland of all their differences, in accordance with the Charter of the United Nations,

Taking note of the interest repeatedly expressed by both parties in normalizing their relations,

Convinced that such purpose would be facilitated by a global negotiation between both Governments that will allow them to rebuild mutual confidence on a solid basis and to resolve the pending problems, including all aspects on the future of the Falkland Islands (Malvinas),

1. *Requests* the Governments of Argentina and the United Kingdom of Great Britain and Northern Ireland to initiate negotiations with a view to finding the means to resolve peacefully and definitively the pending problems between both countries, including all aspects on the future of the Falkland Islands (Malvinas), in accordance with the Charter of the United Nations;

2. *Requests* the Secretary-General to continue his renewed mission of good offices in order to assist the parties in complying with the request made in paragraph 1 above, and to take the necessary measures to that end;

3. *Requests* the Secretary-General to submit to the General Assembly at its forty-first session a report on the progress made in the implementation of the present resolution;

---

[34] See also sect. I, footnote 7, and sect. X.B.6, decision 40/410.

4.   *Decides* to include in the provisional agenda of its forty-first session the item entitled "Question of the Falkland Islands (Malvinas)".

95th plenary meeting
27 November 1985

41/40.   Question of the Falkland Islands (Malvinas)[90]

The General Assembly,

Having considered the question of the Falkland Islands (Malvinas) and having received the report of the Secretary-General,[91]

Aware of the interest of the international community in the peaceful and definitive settlement by the Governments of Argentina and the United Kingdom of Great Britain and Northern Ireland of all their differences, in accordance with the Charter of the United Nations,

Taking note of the interest repeatedly expressed by both parties in normalizing their relations,

Convinced that such purpose would be facilitated by a global negotiation between both Governments that will allow them to rebuild mutual confidence on a solid basis and to resolve the pending problems, including all aspects on the future of the Falkland Islands (Malvinas),

1.   *Reiterates its request* to the Governments of Argentina and the United Kingdom of Great Britain and Northern Ireland to initiate negotiations with a view to finding the means to resolve peacefully and definitively the problems pending between both countries, including all aspects on the future of the Falkland Islands (Malvinas), in accordance with the Charter of the United Nations;

2.   *Requests* the Secretary-General to continue his renewed mission of good offices in order to assist the parties in complying with the request made in paragraph 1 above, and to take the necessary measures to that end;

3.   *Requests* the Secretary-General to submit to the General Assembly at its forty-second session a report on the progress made in the implementation of the present resolution;

4.   *Decides* to include in the provisional agenda of its forty-second session the item entitled "Question of the Falkland Islands (Malvinas)".

84th plenary meeting
25 November 1986

---

[90] See also sect. I, footnote 6, and sect. X.B.6, decision 41/414.
[91] A/41/824.

42/19.   Question of the Falkland Islands (Malvinas)[62]

The General Assembly,

Having considered the question of the Falkland Islands (Malvinas) and having received the report of the Secretary-General,[63]

Aware of the interest of the international community in the peaceful and definitive settlement by the Governments of Argentina and the United Kingdom of Great Britain and Northern Ireland of all their differences, in accordance with the Charter of the United Nations,

Taking note of the interest repeatedly expressed by both parties in normalizing their relations,

Convinced that such purpose would be facilitated by a global negotiation between both Governments that will allow them to rebuild mutual confidence on a solid basis and to resolve the pending problems, including all aspects on the future of the Falkland Islands (Malvinas),

1.   *Reiterates its request* to the Governments of Argenntina and the United Kingdom of Great Britain and Northern Ireland to initiate negotiations with a view to finding the means to resolve peacefully and definitively the problems pending between both countries, including all aspects on the future of the Falkland Islands (Malvinas), in accordance with the Charter of the United Nations;

2.   *Requests* the Secretary-General to continue his renewed mission of good offices in order to assist the parties in complying with the request made in paragraph 1 above, and to take the necessary measures to that end;

3.   *Requests* the Secretary-General to submit to the General Assembly at its forty-third session a report on the progress made in the implementation of the present resolution;

4.   *Decides* to include in the provisional agenda of its forty-third session the item entitled "Question of the Falkland Islands (Malvinas)".

72nd plenary meeting
17 November 1987

---

[62] See also sect. I, footnote 10, and sect. X.B.6, decision 42/410.
[63] A/42/732.

43/25.   Question of the Falkland Islands (Malvinas)[57]

The General Assembly,

Having considered the question of the Falkland Islands (Malvinas) and having received the report of the Secretary-General,[58]

Aware of the interest of the international community in the peaceful and definitive settlement by the Governments of Argentina and the United Kingdom of Great Britain and Northern Ireland of all their differences, in accordance with the Charter of the United Nations,

Taking note of the interest repeatedly expressed by both parties in normalizing their relations,

Convinced that such purpose would be facilitated by a global negotiation between both Governments that will allow them to rebuild mutual confidence on a solid basis and to resolve the pending problems, including all aspects on the future of the Falkland Islands (Malvinas),

1.   *Reiterates its request* to the Governments of Argentina and the United Kingdom of Great Britain and Northern Ireland to initiate negotiations with a view to finding the means to resolve peacefully and definitively the problems pending between both countries, including all aspects on the future of the Falkland Islands (Malvinas), in accordance with the Charter of the United Nations;

2.   *Requests* the Secretary-General to continue his renewed mission of good offices in order to assist the parties in complying with the request made in paragraph 1 above, and to take the necessary measures to that end;

3.   *Also requests* the Secretary-General to submit to the General Assembly at its forty-fourth session a report on the progress made in the implementation of the present resolution;

4.   ¯ *Decides* to include in the provisional agenda of its forty-fourth session the item entitled "Question of the Falkland Islands (Malvinas)".

54th plenary meeting
17 November 1988

---

[57] See also sect. I, footnote 8, and sect. X.B.6, decision 43/409.
[58] A/43/799.

Annex 44: Statements by Argentina and United Kingdom to UN
Special Committee in 1983 (concerning issue of self-
determination)
Source: UN Doc. A/AC.109/PV.1238, p. 71 ff.

Sir John THOMSON (United Kingdom): Thank you, Mr. Chairman. It gives me
much pleasure, Sir, as this is my first opportunity to address the Committee, to
offer you my belated congratulations on your election by acclamation as the
Committee's Chairman. You will know, Mr. Chairman, that we have always attached
great importance to the work of the Committee of 24, not only because it addresses
issues of direct concern to my Government but because it lies at the heart of many
of the ideals and aspirations for which the United Nations stands. The high
reputation enjoyed by the Committee has been due in no small part to the efforts

JP/sm/ap   A/AC.109/PV.1238
                                       72
                                      (Sir John Thomson, United Kingdom)

of your predecessors. We are confident that you will continue to maintain the
exacting standards that they have set. You have the right combination of
qualifications and abilities. We in the United Kingdom, as the Administering Power
responsible for more than half the Territories that appear on the agenda of this
Committee, are happy to extend to you our fullest co-operation.

I have to speak today on an item that, regrettably, remains a serious bone of
contention between the United Kingdom and the Government of Argentina. Last year's
conflict in the South Atlantic, although it took us all by surprise, was an
unfortunate reality, and its consequences are still with us. The Argentine invasion
of the Falklands is part of history. It is true that in his speech to the General
Assembly last year the Argentine Foreign Minister managed to avoid all reference to
it, but it is no good trying to pretend that it did not take place or that it is not
important. The fact is that Argentina did invade the Falkland Islands, and,
moreover, in direct defiance of a call by the Security Council to refrain from the
use or threat of force, and in open violation of basic Charter principles about the
peaceful settlement of disputes and the right to self-determination. No meaningful
discussion of the Falkland Islands can take place except against that background. It
is most unfortunate, but we have to live with the facts as they are.

The Islanders last year suffered an act of unashamed and unprovoked aggression.
Their way of life was shattered and their pastoral economy was severely disrupted.
Now the Islanders want to be left along to reconstruct their own future, secure in

the knowledge that the United Kingdom has both the political will and the material
means to deter, but, if unfortunately necessary, to repel future attempts to take
the Islands by force. The Islanders want to remain British and to manage their own
affairs. If anyone doubts that, let him visit the Islands; let him listen to the
Islanders' elected representatives.

These are not half-truths quoted out of context, slanted to support our refusal
to negotiate the transfer of sovereignty over the Falkland Islands to Argentina.
That is all that Argentina means by negotiation. These are plain facts, to which
Councillors Cheek and Blake, whom the Council has just heard, have attested from
personal experience. Anyone who can read, anyone who was even remotely close to the
events of last year, can understand that Argentine rule is not wanted in the
Falkland Islands.

JP/sm/ap   A/AC.109/PV.1238
                                       73-75

                              (Sir John Thomson, United Kingdom)

I listened to some of the glowing things that Mr. Betts and Mr. Rozee said
about life in the Argentine. With their practical experience of living in the
Argentine, they are no doubt speaking accurately. Many Falkland Islanders know what
conditions are in the Argentine. Nevertheless, they do not want to be ruled by the
Argentine. The rule of the Argentines is simply not wanted in the Falkland Islands.
The Argentine forces were regarded as usurpers, not, as some would believe, as
liberators. It is simply a question of demonstrable and observable fact. Nor is it
surprising. When one's home is seized, it is natural that one does not like the
people who seized it. This has happened all too often around the world. All the
peoples in Africa, the Middle East, Europe, Asia and the Falklands who have been
invaded cry out to us to take a stand on principle, a stand on the Charter of the
United Nations.

The Committee of 24 has received and considered British reports on the
Falklands under Article 73 of the Charter for over 25 years. It is not necessary,
therefore, in this body to enter into any argument about that. The record is clear.
Suffice it for me to say here that we have no doubt as to our sovereignty over the
Falkland Islands, and the moral and political validity of our title is resoundingly
endorsed by the present-day facts. A settled and self-sustaining community with its
own institutions and administration and a growing measure of self-government has
seen uninterrupted development on the Falkland Islands since the 1830s. How many
independent States, let alone dependent Territories, can claim a political and
historical pedigree of such stability and quality? The Islanders have recently
celebrated 150 years' continuous settlement on the Islands. Many have families
going back six and seven generations. The Falkland Islands are their home and,
like other people, they wish to determine their own destiny.

AW/18   A/AC.109/PV.1238
                                      76
(Sir John Thomson, United Kingdom)

In the Committee of 24, it is above all appropriate to speak of obligations, particularly the obligations placed by the Charter on the United Kingdom as the administering Power for the Falkland Islands. Those are responsibilities I hope no one in this Committee would seek to question. In the Charter provisions on **self-determination**, as well as in Article 73, we find chapter and verse showing that the British Government's responsibilities towards the people of the Falkland Islands and their Charter obligations mutually support and reinforce one another. Our policies have firm Charter backing and we will continue to pursue them.

The principal concern of this Committee is the economic and political well-being of non-self-governing peoples and, in particular, their right to self-determination. I have no doubt that Committee members know Article 73, resolution 1514 (XV) and the Friendly Relations Declaration by heart, but I hope they will bear with me if I quote from them today.

The first part of Article 73 is particularly significant:

"Members of the United Nations which have or assume responsibilities for the administration of territories whose peoples have not yet attained a full measure of self-government recognize the principle that the interests of the inhabitants of those territories are paramount".

These are profound words; they are strong words. If we as the administering Power accept that the interests of the inhabitants of the Falkland Islands are paramount, how can we negotiate with another Government about transferring sovereignty when that is manifestly contrary to what the people of the Islands see as their interests? The administering Power cannot move in direct contradiction to the wishes of the people of the Territories concerned. How can we say that their interests and their wishes stand in direct opposition to one another? Administering Powers accept as a sacred trust the obligation to promote to the utmost /their/ well-being . In particular, they undertake

"to ensure, with due respect for the culture of the peoples concerned, their political, economic, social and educational advancement, their just treatment, and their protection against abuses".

AW/18   A/AC.109/PV.1238
                                      77
(Sir John Thomson, United Kingdom)

May I add, in parentheses, Sir, that an invasion by 10,000 troops is an abuse indeed.

And it is the obligation of this Committee to support us in so doing. May

I repeat - it is the obligation of this Committee to support us in carrying out our responsibilities as administering Power to ensure, with due respect for the culture of the people concerned, their political, economic, social and educational advancement, their just treatment and their protection against abuses. The abuses come from one direction only.

Some, though I would hope not members of this Committee, which has always maintained that factors such as the size of the population and geographical isolation should not militate against any people's right to self-determination in accordance with the Charter, may argue that Article 73 allows the interests of the inhabitants to be overridden. But it is surely not for one country to lay down where another people's interests lie. The inhabitants of a settled and largely self-governing Territory like the Falklands must surely be the best judge of that.

Suggestions to the contrary can only encourage interference in the internal affairs of other States and the unprincipled use of force. It is of course the classic argument used by those who wish to further their territorial ambitions. But for the United Kingdom as administering Power to accept that argument would be to acquiesce in handing over a people to alien and unwanted rule. It is not the sort of argument which the Committee of 24 by its very nature could accept. For it runs directly counter to the Declaration on the Granting of Independence to Colonial Countries and Peoples, which states that:

"The subjection of peoples to alien subjugation, domination and exploitation constitutes a denial of fundamental human rights, is contrary to the Charter of the United Nations and is an impediment to the promotion of world peace and co-operation." (resolution 1514 (XV)

That seems to me a fairly comprehensive statement which applies directly to the Falklands.

I have dwelt at some length on the responsibilities placed on us by the Charter because it leads to the heart of the matter. It is the origin of my Government's co-operation with this Committee. The Committee has repeatedly declared its belief in the inalienable right of self-determination. Inalienable' is a very strong word. It means birthright; it means you cannot get rid of it:

A/AC.109/PV.1238
                                 78-30
                                     (Sir John Thomson, United Kingdom)

it means that the Falklanders have a right of self-determination which no one can take from them. The United Kingdom shares that view. In the process of decolonization, which this year will see a further two dependent Territories, Saint Kitts-Nevis and Brunei, achieve independence, we have held fast to that principle. There is no reason if, for example, the people of Tokelau, the Cocos Islands and Pitcairn can enjoy the right to self-determination, the people

of the Falkland Islands cannot. This right is the right recognized in General
Assembly resolution 1514 (XV), the Declaration on the Granting of Independence
to Colonial Countries and Peoples, which lies at the origin of this Committee.
Forgive me, Sir, if I repeat what must already be so familiar to members of the
Committee, but the second operative paragraph of the Declaration is particularly
relevant:

> "All peoples have the right to self-determination: by virtue of that
> right they freely determine their political status and freely pursue
> their economic, social and cultural development." (ibid)

This is another very clear statement.

These words have been taken up into the International Covenants on Civil
and Political Rights and on Economic and Social Rights, both of which have been
ratified by the United Kingdom and extend to the Falkland Islands. They
admirably and succinctly summarize what we stand for in the case of the Falkland
Islanders. Moreover, the General Assembly itself has repeatedly asserted that
self-determination is an inalienable right, of equal standing to other
fundamental human rights. The General Assembly continues to assert that right on
behalf of the remaining dependent Territories and also on behalf of certain other
peoples. The right of self-determination, as propounded by the international
community, offers many small and powerless peoples a moral and legal safeguard
against being overwhelmed, assimilated or conquered by ambitious and unscrupulous
neighbours. Like other human rights, self-determination is a concept which can
be convenient to certain Governments on some occasions and inconvenient when it
runs counter to their untramelled exercise of arbitrary power. This is not,
however, a reason to set it aside, on the contrary, such situations require that
the principle be asserted with great conviction. It would not be reasonable to
believe that members of a Committee seriously concerned with the future of the
people of the remaining Non-Self-Governing Territories are willing to be
selective in their application of this inalienable right.

JVII/19   A/AC.109/PV.1238
          31

         (Sir John Thomson, United Kingdom)

I should like members of this Committee to be in no doubt of our
determination not to shirk our responsibilities under the United Nations
Charter. The right to self-determination of any people, however small, is too
precious a commodity to be sacrificed to satisfy the political whims of one
particular country. There is much to talk about with the Argentine Government,
and we should like nothing better than to normalize relations with a country
with which, prior to last year's events, we were bound with close ties of
friendship and co-operation in a variety of fields. We have never denied the
existence of serious differences between the United Kingdom and the Government

f Argentina. What we will not countenance is Argentina's insistence that
its claims be accepted in advance. We continue to hear threats, some open
some implied, of further Argentine military action. That surely is no way
for the Argentines to win friends in the Falklands, or, for that matter,
in the United Nations.

The Committee of 24 has just heard the people of the Falklands speak through
their freely elected representatives. They have also just heard two petitioners,
Mr. Rozee and Mr. Betts, speak in what I thought was in a rather interesting way.
I am sure that Mr. Betts' wish for his remarks to be heard in the Falklands will
be gratified. I have no doubt it will be reported: it is a free society
there. It is really strange for him to continue to believe that the
islanders may have a doubt about what rule they wish to live under. Perhaps
he would like to return to his family in the Falklands and find out what they
think.

Mr. Rozee asked, "Who are the islanders?" and he replied rhetorically
that "Were they not the normal day-to-day people?". Well, yes, indeed the
normal day-to-day people have voted. They have expressed their views to the
world press. They have expressed their views through their elected
representatives. It is their elected representatives who have spoken here
today, and that is surely what this Committee is all about. Its purpose is to
make sure that the administering Power does right by the people of the
Territory concerned. The people have spoken. The United Kingdom will do its
part, and I am sure the United Nations will uphold its principles.

JVM/19   A/AC.109/PV.1238
                                      82
                               (Sir John Thomson, United Kingdom)

I have just expressed in detail the United Kingdom's views about the
subject matter of this debate in the Committee of 24, namely, the advancement
of the people of the Falkland Islands and the protection of their rights.
I have to observe, however, that a text has been submitted by Venezuela in
A/AC.109/L.1486 for a draft resolution that would have the Committee deny or
ignore its own cardinal principles. It would also take the Committee outside
its proper field by seeking to have it pronounce, or purport to pronounce, on
matters which appear as a separate item on the agenda of the thirty-eighth session
of the General Assembly, as they did last year. The United Kingdom is not a
member of this Committee. We therefore have no vote on any decision or
resolution taken by the Committee of 24. Our vote and our voice will be
expressed in the General Assembly itself when the agenda item on the question
of the Falkland Islands is debated there. But it is my duty, as the representative
of the administering Power, to point out to the Committee why the Venezuelan
resolution would conflict with the Committee's own principles, and it may be of
help to members of the Committee if I now do so.

I would say that the reference in the preamble to the maintenance of colonial situations being incompatible with the United Nations ideal of universal peace is offensive. Our principal concern has always been to promote the interests of the inhabitants of the Falkland Islands, and that appears to be their view: they appear to have accepted that that is what we have been doing and are continuing to do. Our concern has also been to defend their right to live in peace and security under a Government of their own choosing. That, too, is something that the Falkland Islanders appear to accept that we are doing. The small population of the Islands pose no threat to anyone. It is evident, unfortunately, that Argentina does.

In its other preambular paragraphs the draft resolution also takes a biased and prejudicial slant which makes it unacceptable to my Government. The paragraph which refers to a solution "to the sovereignty dispute" is cast in a way which implies that the outcome of any negotiations must be the only one that only Argentina considers acceptable - that is, a transfer of sovereignty over the Falkland Islands to Argentina. Neither in that nor in any other paragraphs do we find reference to the fundamental question of the rights of the people of the Falkland Islands.

JVM/19   A/AC.109/PV.1238
                                  83

                              (Sir John Thomson, United Kingdom)

My Government is also obliged to take a sceptical attitude towards the paragraph which refers to the "expressed intention" of the parties not to renew hostilities. Since this language was incorporated in General Assembly resolution 37/9 last year, the Argentine Government has done nothing to enhance the credibility of its professions of peaceful intent. It has steadfastly refused to demonstrate convincingly that it considers that hostilities have ceased permanently or that it renounces the use of force in the further pursuit of its claim. It was, after all, the Argentine Minister of Defence, who may be expected to know about such matters, who in May stated that diplomacy was not the only option Argentina had, and noted that there had been "only" a de facto cessation of hostilities. The Argentine attitude, in other words, remains menacing; the threat of force remains; and these are not circumstances in which negotiations could be expected to produce a useful result.

The Argentines have made much of their expressed intention to safeguard the "interests" of the population of the Falkland Islands. But Argentine actions in 1982 unfortunately demonstrated how they interpreted this interest of the Falkland Islanders. They put at risk the lives of the Islanders and sought to impose on them their alien laws instead of inalienable self-determination. A sharp contrast. They also sought to impose their alien regulations, language and school curricula. The Islanders, moreover, are conscious that the Argentine legal system has failed to protect its own and foreign nationals from

the serious abuses of human rights about which my own and other Governments have
expressed their concern, and a reference solely to the interests of the
Islanders is no substitute for the right of self-determination, which we expect
this Committee to recognize.

The final preambular paragraph and subsequent paragraphs refer to the
principles of the Charter on the peaceful settlement of international disputes
and call on my Government and that of Argentina to resume negotiations. But
the draft resolution appears to neglect the facts and the consequences of events
in 1982. It simply is not realistic to pretend that there was no invasion of
the Falkland Islands, that there was no occupation by 10,000 troops. It happened
most unfortunate, but it is a fact. My Government and that of Argentina were
in that very year engaged in negotiations about matters in dispute between them.

JVM/19   A/AC.109/PV.1238
                                    84-85

                                        (Sir John Thomson, United Kingdom)

A joint communiqué - and I emphasize the word "joint" - issued at the end of the
last round of talks in March 1982 characterized those talks as "cordial and
positive". One month later, Argentine forces invaded the Falkland Islands in
flagrant violation of the fundamental principles of the Charter. Argentina has
demonstrated no regret over that action and, as I have already noted, appears to
preserve the option of a further resort to force. Argentina's sole objective
remains the transfer of sovereignty over the Islands, irrespective of the wishes
of the inhabitants of that territory. No negotiations begun against that
background could possibly have a useful outcome.

BG/20   A/AC.109/PV.1238
                                      86

                                        (Sir John Thomson, United Kingdom)

It is for the reasons I have just set out that my Government does not
propose to resume negotiations with Argentina about the Falkland Islands.
I wish to make clear in this Committee, however, that my Government has
taken and supported several initiatives aimed at reducing tension and at
developing a more normal bilateral relationship between Argentina and the
United Kingdom. It is a matter of regret that Argentina has shown no
interest in responding to those initiatives but maintains a sterile attitude
of confrontation and of menace. Serious indications by Argentina that it is
prepared to respond to those initiatives or is otherwise ready to work
towards the restoration of mutual confidence will find my Government
receptive. But the Argentine authorities must recognize the consequences
of their actions and work for a gradual restoration of confidence. This, rather

than unrealistic and hypocritical calls for negotiations, must be the path
to follow.

So much for the Venezuelan draft.

In August of last year this Committee decided to continue its
consideration of the Falkland Islands at its 1983 session, subject to any
directives which the General Assembly might give in that connection at its
thirty-seventh session; it also decided to transmit the relevant documentation
to the General Assembly in order to facilitate consideration of the item there.
It is not for the United Kingdom, as a non-member of this Committee, to say
whether the Committee ought to adopt any decision of a different kind this
year. In our view, what the Committee is duty bound to do, in whatever
form it thinks best, is to re-emphasize the inalienable right of the people
of the Falkland Islands to self-determination in accordance with the United
Nations Charter and other relevant documents, including resolution 1514 (XV).
That would undoubtedly facilitate consideration of the question of the Falkland
Islands by the General Assembly in due course. As I have already said, the
right to self-determination of any people, however small, is too precious
a commodity to be sacrificed to satisfy the political whims of one particular
country.

BG/20   A/AC.109/PV.1238
                                  87

Mr. MUÑIZ (Argentina)(interpretation from Spanish): I should like
to thank you, Mr. Chairman, and the other members of the Special Committee
for giving me this opportunity to participate in the consideration of a serious
colonial question the continuation of which violates the legitimate and
inalienable rights of my country and is a cause of serious concern to the entire
Latin American region.

Since this is the first time that my delegation has spoken in the debates
of the Special Committee during 1983, may I, first of all, tell you, Sir, how
pleased we are at your unanimous election to your office. We are certain that,
under your expert leadership, this important body will continue to be one of
the most effective instruments in the United Nations struggle against
colonialism. As the distinguished son of a continent which has suffered
more than any other from the ills of colonialism, you are in the best possible
position to understand the legitimacy and urgency of the demand of those of us
who continue to have a part of our territory under foreign domination.

We also extend our congratulations to the other officers of the Committee
whose contribution is also of great importance to the success of this body's
work.

The members of the Special Committee are sufficiently familiar with the background of the question of the Malvinas Islands. That makes it unnecessary for me to reiterate today the solid historical and legal basis of Argentina's rights over the Malvinas, South Georgias and South Sandwich islands. In this connection, I shall confine myself to reaffirming previous statements by my Government in which that basis has been broadly expressed, in particular the statement of the Minister for Foreign Affairs of my country in the plenary General Assembly at its thirty-seventh session on 2 November 1982. I should

BG/20   A/AC.109/PV.1238
                               88

like to recall that Argentine rights have been explicitly recognized by the overwhelming majority of the international community, including in particular the countries of the Latin American region of which the Malvinas, Georgias and South Sandwich Islands are an inseparable part, and the Non-Aligned Movement. In spite of the broad international consensus, the close and unassailable link between the Islands and Argentina continues to be disregarded by the United Kingdom, which since 1833 has illegally and forcibly occupied and colonized those Territories.

The existence of sufficient grounds for Argentina to demand the return of the islands in dispute has been explicitly and formally acknowledged by the General Assembly and the Special Committee in important decisions, among them, I should like to underscore, resolutions 2065 (XX), 3160 (XXVIII), 31/49 and 37/9. Those resolutions constitute an essential frame of reference for the decolonization of the Malvinas Islands. Because they stem from the organ to which all the Members of the United Nations, including Argentina and the United Kingdom, have voluntarily recognized principal competence to guide and oversee the process of decolonization, they form a body of laws which Argentina and the United Kingdom could not disregard without challenging international law. It is therefore important to recall exactly what that frame of reference established by the General Assembly for the decolonization of the Malvinas Islands is.

First of all, and as is natural, the Assembly has included the Malvinas Islands among colonial Territories subject to the process of decolonization. It is not superfluous for me to mention this point which is so obvious, because for a year now the highest authorities of Great Britain have been affirming, even in Parliament, that the Malvinas, Georgias and South Sandwich Islands are "sovereign British territory". In other words, the United Kingdom now wishes to annex a foreign territory located more than 10,000 kilometres from London which the British Government itself in 1946 included in the list of Territories to be decolonized. The British Government has gone to

the extreme of considering the description of its presence on those islands
as colonial as "offensive".

BG/20   A/AC.109/PV.1238
                                    89-90
                                              (Mr. Muñiz, Argentina)

     Secondly, the General Assembly has recognized the existence of a sovereignty
dispute between Argentina and the United Kingdom over the Malvinas Islands. This
point is of legal and political importance. It means that the British
claim of sovereignty over the colony has no international recognition. It
also makes the political future of the Territories in the dispute dependent
on prior solution of the question of sovereignty. Recognition of the existence
of a dispute of sovereignty constitutes the cornerstone of the doctrine prepared
by the General Assembly on the question of the Malvinas Islands and it explains
why certain principles the application of which has been followed in connection
with other colonial Territories have been expressly excluded from the frame of
reference to which I have just alluded.

     I should also like to recall that the inclusion of this item was decided
upon for the first time by this Special Committee in 1964 in a decision
which has served as a basis for all the subsequent resolutions of the General
Assembly on the subject and which implied clear rejection of the British
reasoning. On that occasion the Special Committee accepted the Argentine
reasoning that the question of the Malvinas Islands constituted a special
case of decolonization, with the particular characteristic of there being a
dispute of sovereignty the solution of which was an essential and inevitable
prerequisite to the determination of the Territory's political future.

RM/21/gt   A/AC.109/PV.1238
                                     91
                                              (Mr. Muñiz, Argentina)

     Thirdly, the General Assembly inspired by the general principle that
enshrines the right of States to territorial integrity and by operative
paragraph 6 of resolution 1514 (XV), affirmed in resolution 3160 (XXVIII) that
the solution of the conflict of sovereignty was the way - that is, the only way -
to put an end to the colonial situation of the Malvinas Islands. It is
evident, therefore, that any British measure aimed at determining the political
future of the colonial Territory outside that framework would lack legal effect
in the eyes of the international community.

     Fourthly, the General Assembly also established that there are only two

parties to this dispute, namely, the Argentine and British Governments. This
is logical, since in a dispute of this type the parties can only be the States
involved.

Fifthly, the Assembly has repeatedly asked both Governments to resolve the
dispute through negotiations. As is known, Argentina has always supported
that course of action, since negotiations between the parties constitute
the principal and most effective of the means enshrined in the United Nations
Charter for the solution of international controversies. The British attitude
has been otherwise. A special investigatory commission appointed last year
by the Government of the United Kingdom, the Frank Commission, and, more
recently the Foreign Relations Sub-Committee of the British House of Commons
have admitted that during the 17 years prior to the conflict in the South
Atlantic the United Kingdom had been reluctant to enter into negotiations with
Argentina over sovereignty. Nor have the members of those investigatory bodies
been unaware of the role that policy has played in creating the conditions of
the 1982 crisis. Although I shall refer to the present situation in the
South Atlantic later, I should like at this juncture to point out that at the
present time the British Government is not only maintaining that attitude, it
is even attempting to impose a military solution and is pursuing a dangerous
policy of increased provocation against Argentina.

RM/21/pt   A/AC.109/PV.1230
                                           92
                                          (Mr. Muñiz, Argentina)

Sixthly, the General Assembly has emphasized the need for the Argentine
and British Governments to take into account in their negotiations the interests
of the present inhabitants of the territories in dispute. That formulation
is also a key one. It is, furthermore, logical and intelligent.

It is a key formulation because more than any other it responds to the
particular circumstances of the territories that are in dispute between Argentina
and the United Kingdom, particularly the need to guarantee respect for the
fundamental Charter principle that enshrines the right of States to territorial
integrity. It is logical because it would be unthinkable at this stage in
the development of our civilization and of international relations for two countries
to resolve a dispute over sovereignty without taking into account the well-being,
traditions and cultural identity of the inhabitants of the Territory in question.
Lastly, the formulation is intelligent because, owing to its broad and
comprehensive nature, it strikes a balance between Argentine rights, the
responsibilities of the administering Power and the concerns of the
1,800 Islanders.

Of course no one can ignore the fact that the United Kingdom has questioned the inclusion of the word interests" in resolutions adopted with regard to the question of the Malvinas Islands. Nor can anyone be unaware of the ambiguous and self-interested attitude the United Kingdom has always maintained in connection with the right of colonial peoples to self-determination. Diego Garcia, among others, is a specific and timely point of reference.

Actually it is only natural for the General Assembly and this Special Committee to have adopted a position rejected by the United Kingdom. When the British took over the Malvinas Islands illegally and by force they expelled from the Territory not only the Argentine authorities but also the indigenous population of the Territory, a population of Argentine origin. Since then, Argentines have not been allowed either to own property or to reside permanently in the Islands.

RM/21/ap   A/AC.109/PV.1238
        93
          (Mr. Muñiz, Argentina)

The original Argentine population was then replaced by officials and employees of the British Government and of the Falkland Islands Company, which, as has been recognized within the United Kingdom itself and as can be seen in the Secretariat's working paper, has a monopoly over economic activity and land ownership in the Islands. Those British officials and employees comprise 70 per cent of the present population of the Islands.

Hence, if the present population were to be recognized as having a right to self-determination, that recognition would only favour the United Kingdom, which acts through its dependents and through the employees of the Falkland Islands (mpany.

As is obvious, this would be a grotesque distortion of the right to self-determination, which would be used not to put an end to a colonial situation but, rather, to legitimize the indefinite prolongation of that very colonial situation at the expense of the inalienable right of a State to its territorial integrity. It would be tantamount to recognizing a right to self-determination for the inhabitants of Walvis Bay or the illegal settlers in the occupied Arab territories, and it would establish a serious precedent with regard to other colonial enclaves in the territories of Member States. It would be tantamount to endorsing colonial expansion and aggression against third States. It would make possible the triumph of colonialism through a gross manoeuvre designed to make improper use of the instruments established by this Organization precisely in order to guarantee the elimination of colonialism. In any event, the real holder of the right to .lf-determination in the Malvinas Islands is the Argentine people, from whom he Territory has been taken illegally and by force.

The unjustified British attacks against the General Assembly and this Special Committee do not take into account the fact that the International Court of Justice, in its advisory opinion of 1975, handed down the clear

RM/21/pt   A/AC.109/PV.1238
                                          94-95
                                                    (Mr. Muñiz, Argentina)

interpretation that there is no single, immutable form for the decolonization of colonial Territories and recognized that each colonial entity has an individual nature and that the particular circumstances prevailing in each situation must determine the principle and right to be applied. In fact, this position was firmly upheld by the United Kingdom itself during the drafting of the United Nations Charter and during negotiations preceding the adoption of General Assembly resolution 1514 (XV), and it is now upheld by London with regard to several of the colonial Territories it still administers. The anachronistic policy of confrontation with Argentina and with international law that is being pursued by the United Kingdom with regard to the Malvinas Islands is therefore even more incomprehensible.

I have dwelt on the fundamental aspects of the resolutions of the General Assembly on the question of the Malvinas Islands because they offer the sole frame of reference for a solution to the present confrontation between Argentina and the United Kingdom that will be not only just, legal and peaceful, but also realistic, intelligent and lasting. In fact, there is no alternative to those resolutions that can, at the same time, guarantee a solution respectful of international law and the final eradication of tension in the South Atlantic. The clearest proof of this is the present situation around the Islands. The British claim that the future of the disputed Territories should be determined independent of the resolutions of the General Assembly dangerously prevents the return of peace and stability to the region.

RG/22   A/AC.109/PV.1238
                                          96
                                                    (Mr. Muñiz, Argentina)

The lack of a viable and legal alternative to the resolutions of our Organization was clearly recognized by the international community when on 4 November 1982 the General Assembly took its first decision following the conflict in the South Atlantic: resolution 37/9. The importance of that resolution is undeniable. It reaffirms all prior relevant resolutions

of the General Assembly and the standard applicable to the decolonization of
the Territory continues to be the same as that existing before the crisis,
whose military outcome in no way enhanced the non-existent British title
{ r the Malvinas, South Georgia and South Sandwich Islands.

Together with this explicit endorsement of its prior resolutions on
this issue, in its resolution 37/9 the General Assembly once again requests
the Argentine and British Governments to resume negotiations in order
peacefully and as promptly as possible to resolve the sovereignty dispute.
It also includes a request to the Secretary-General of the Organization to
resume his good offices which were begun during the South Atlantic conflict.

Since the adoption of resolution 37/9, Argentina has repeatedly
expressed in statements and communications to the Secretary-General its desire
to co-operate in the search for a negotiated solution to all - I repeat: all -
its problems with the United Kingdom, including aspects related to the
definitive disappearance of tension in the South Atlantic, in accordance with
the decisions of the Organization. The working paper prepared by the Secretariat
in connection with this issue in document A/AC.109/752 contains a list and a
summary of the many official documents in which this position of my country
has been expressed.

As I have already stated, the attitude of the British Government has been
exactly the opposite. Not only has it failed to recognize resolution 37/9
but it has at the same time implemented a policy of growing provocation against
Argentina.

Indeed, its refusal to negotiate has been accompanied by a massive
militarization of the territories usurped from Argentina. My country has already
denounced before the Secretary-General and the President of the Security Council
the seriousness of the situation which, because of its characteristics and
magnitude, clearly suggests the British intent to prolong indefinitely its
colonial presence in the Islands and, equally serious, to incorporate them in

RG/22

A/AC.109/PV.1238
98

(Mr. Muñiz, Argentina)

and serious source of harm to my country affecting the interests of the
Argentine State and fishing activities, which represent an important sector
of national production.

In summary, the British attitude is incompatible with the Charter of the
United Nations, in particular with its provisions establishing the obligation of
States to settle their international disputes peacefully, and with the
General Assembly resolutions to whose contents I have already referred.
No excuse can justify the British refusal to comply with the basic obligation which

as a Member of the United Nations it has assumed under the Charter and General
Assembly resolutions to seek a peaceful and negotiated solution to its problems
with Argentina and refrain from taking provocative measures that contribute
to increasing tension in the South Atlantic.

It can therefore come as no surprise that the British Government can find
no argument to respond to those who, such as members of my Government and of
some responsible sectors of the United Kingdom itself, have pointed out this grave
violation of international commitments and of the principles and norms regulating
international coexistence.

The violation of the Charter by the United Kingdom cannot even be founded
on the need for Argentina to comply with formalities that are not demanded under
international law. Argentina has repeatedly declared that it is not its intention
to resume hostilities. Furthermore, Argentina, together with 19 other Latin
American countries, is a sponsor, of resolution 37/9, which contains a paragraph
along those lines. The 14 and a half months that have elapsed since the cessation
of hostilities confirm the strict compliance with those statements. That long
period without armed hostilities in addition has legal effect. What explanation
can there then be for the British insistence on placing artificially at the centre
of this problem this already resolved aspect of the 1982 crisis? We can only
conclude that the sole real explanation is the afore-mentioned intention to
establish a military base on the Islands as part of a policy of strategic expansion,
especially since, as is natural, if the United Kingdom were to accept compliance
with the Charter and resolution 37/9, setting aside that aggressive plan and
leaving without effect the illegal exclusion zone, relations between the two
countries would register an immediate and significant change.

RG/22   A/AC.109/PV.1238
                                   99-100
                                          (Mr. Muñiz, Argentina)

As my Government has already pointed out, the British policy is even
less understandable if account is taken of the fact that for its implementation
it uses as additional justification a supposed desire to protect the
rights and guarantee the future of the present inhabitants. In fact, and as
has also been recognized in the United Kingdom, the policy of fortifying the
Malvinas Islands is bound to result in deep and negative changes in the
lifestyle of the islanders. Above all, that policy lacks viability, since
it guarantees a permanent state of confrontation with Argentina and
Latin America, which are called upon to play a fundamental role in the economic
progress and political future of the Territory. It is known that a peaceful
negotiated and just solution to the sovereignty dispute would make it possible
for related questions - for example, questions related to respecting and

guaranteeing the lifestyle of the Islands, their well-being, traditions and cultural identity - to be given, as is natural, special consideration and be properly met, including through international guarantees and safeguards and special statutes that could be negotiated.

JP/dkd   A/AC.109/PV.1238
                                          101

(Mr. Muñiz, Argentina)

Argentina demonstrated its concern in this connection in the course of negotiations lasting 17 years. The negotiators from Argentina repeatedly presented to their British counterparts proposals containing a system of guarantees and safeguards for the population of the islands. It was the British lack of receptiveness that made it impossible to do more thorough work on this important question, lack of receptiveness to the extent that the Islanders themselves were not made fully aware of the concern demonstrated by Argentina.

My Government is confident that the United Kingdom authorities will come to understand that a prolongation and worsening of the present confrontation with Argentina cannot be a realistic or viable option. The occupation of the Malvinas, South Georgia and South Sandwich Islands is today as illegal as it was in 1833.

On the basis of all these considerations, my Government hopes that, as is proposed in draft resolution A/AC.109/L.1483, the Special Committee will ratify the principles applicable to the decolonization of Territories under disputed sovereignty. My Government also hopes that in ratifying those principles the Special Committee will make a new appeal to both parties to resume their negotiations with a view to putting an end as soon as possible, in a peaceful, just and definitive way, to that dispute, and that it will express its support for the Secretary-General's present mission of good offices. My Government wishes to express once again its gratitude to Mr. Perez de Cuellar for his valuable efforts during the past year in connection with this issue. At the same time, we reiterate to him our intention to continue to give him all the co-operation he requires, in accordance with the mandate given him by the General Assembly.

Lastly, I should like to emphasize that a decision by the Committee along the lines that I have just mentioned would meet not only the just position of my country but also the interests of all of Latin America, which, as is well known, has made of decolonization and the return of the Malvinas Islands to Argentina a regional cause. My country cannot fail to reiterate its special gratitude to the States of Latin America, whose firm support for Argentina in this problem constitutes one of the most concrete and effective manifestations

JP/dkd/ap   A/AC.109/PV.1238
                                         102
                                              (Mr. Muñiz, Argentina)

of regional unity. We also extend our thanks to the other members of the
international community which support us and to the Non-Aligned Movement, which
explicitly and firmly reiterated at the recent Summit in New Delhi its support
for Argentina's rights.

                    The meeting rose at 6.45 p.m.

Annex 45: Statements by Argentina and United Kingdom to UN
Special Committee in 1984 (concerning developments
between 1982 and 1984)
Source: UN Doc. A/AC.109/PV.+1261, p.11 ff.

But it is not only this separation that causes my anxiety; it is also this
uncertain situation brought about by the existence of the so-called military
fortress which Great Britain has established in the archipelago and which,
according to many official statements in the United Kingdom, protects the liberty
and free will of the population. This military fortress constitutes an irritating
source of hostility not only to the Argentine Republic, but also to all that part
of South America in general.

I observe with real regret that the land of my birth, instead of developing in
at atmosphere of peace, has been turned into an enormous military camp, where the
necessities and human rights of the islanders are largely disregarded. Prospects
for improvement are scant.

While Great Britain introduces sophisticated arms to the Falklands/Malvinas,
the infrastructure which could improve the possibilities of a better life for the
islanders has diminished, or at least has not improved, and time is showing that
their outlook is apparently becoming gloomier.

It gave me great pleasure when I learned that a meeting had taken place
between Argentine and British negotiators in the middle of this year, but I also
felt a great sense of frustration when I learned that the meeting had been broken
off because of the British refusal to discuss anything concerned with sovereignty.

Not only is what I have just said saddening, but there is an obstinate policy
motivated by hidden interests that impede the achievement of a solution to the
Falklands/Malvinas question. And the old-style British colonial system still puts
off the development of the land of my birth.

In view of the foregoing, I appeal to you, Sir, and to this Committee, to do
everything possible to arrive at a negotiated solution to this sovereignty dispute,
in accordance with the decisions of the United Nations which, I understand, have
since 1965 urged an end to this controversy which affects the population of the
Falklands/Malvinas and that of the Argentine mainland.

Mrs. Coutts de Maciello withdrew.

The CHAIRMAN: I call on the representative of the United Kingdom as the
Administering Power concerned.

Mr. MARGETSON (United Kingdom): Mr. Chairman, it gives my delegation
great pleasure to see you re-elected by acclamation to the important position you

A/AC.109/PV.1261
12

(Mr. Margetson, United Kingdom)

now hold. It is both significant and appropriate that a representative of a
leading and active member of the Commonwealth, a country which became independent
through peaceful decolonization, should be honoured with the chairmanship of this
Committee.

This afternoon we have heard the testimony of two elected representatives of
the Falkland Islanders - I stress "elected representatives". They are members of
the Falkland Islands Government; there is no doubt as to their right to speak on
behalf of the inhabitants of the Falkland Islands. We heard from three other
petitioners who spoke as individuals and who represent no one but themselves. The
Committee will, of course, judge the weight to be attached to their evidence.

As you know, Mr. Chairman, my delegation has a long and honourable record of
constructive co-operation with the Committee of 24 over the Territories for which
my country is the administering Power. It is the first time I have had the
privilege of addressing this Committee, but I am happy to follow the tradition
established by my predecessors. It is a tradition which I hope will be sustained
on both sides. My delegation believes that we all, Committee members and
administering Powers alike, stand to benefit from a genuinely constructive and
informative exchange. I hope that our discussions will be guided not by external
political considerations or narrow national interests but, as the Charter
envisages, by concern for the interests and aspirations of the people of the
Territories in question, and the need to find real and practical solutions to which
all parties can willingly subscribe.

It is in this spirit that I have the privilege of addressing the Committee on
the question of the Falkland Islands, which, despite our best efforts, continues,
regrettably, to constitute an impediment to the normalization of relations between
Argentina and my country. I do not intend to speak at great length. Nor do I wish
to rake over old coals or to reopen old wounds. The arguments that have been
deployed in this Committee and in the General Assembly are familiar to all. We
have always been conscious of our responsibilities under Article 73 of the Charter
towards non-self-governing peoples and the concomitant principle of self-
determination, so often enshrined in resolutions of this Committee as an
inalienable right. In the Committee of 24, concerned as it is with dependent
peoples, my delegation has sought, and I think logically, to concentrate on the
inhabitants of the Falkland Islands, their rights and their aspirations.

A/AC.109/PV.1261
13

(Mr. Margetson, United Kingdom)

It has therefore been a matter of regret that the Argentine delegation has sought instead to turn the debate into a bilateral dispute, involving not people but land. The focus for it has indeed been exclusively on territory, which it argues is rightfully its. It has gone further and argued that the principle of territorial integrity supersedes that of self-determination, and that self-determination, conveniently, does not apply in this case. Inalienable rights are not, in the view of my country, disposed of as simply as that. Such inalienable rights are not the gift of this Committee or any other United Nations body. I therefore regret greatly that this Committee and subsequently the General Assembly have adopted resolutions that have failed even to mention the right of self-determination of the Falkland Islanders. They have also prejudged the outcome of negotiations in Argentina's favour and made only scant and indirect reference to the tragic events of 1982, for which the then military Government of Argentina was to blame.

That the Committee of 24 and the General Assembly could have taken such a position remains a major disappointment to us. But we have not been discouraged. On the contrary, we have persevered with the task of promoting the rights of the Islanders, as the Charter would have us do, and sought to improve bilateral relations when this was possible. We were naturally pleased by the Secretary-General's report of 27 October 1983 to the General Assembly on the Falkland Islands (A/38/532), in which he expressed his belief that the resumption of dialogue, coupled with the adoption of confidence-building measures, could contribute to a normalization of the situation in the South Atlantic and open the way towards a lasting solution of the problem. It was recognized that the United Kingdom and Argentina had different positions on the sovereignty issue, and it was recognized that it was clearly right and in the interests of both countries to move towards more normal relations.

The Secretary-General's report did not, of course, mark a turning point in our attitude towards talks. Rather, it provided valuable endorsement of the approach we had already taken. Ever since the end of the Falklands conflict we have consistently taken the lead in advocating realistic means of restoring more normal relations, especially in the commercial, economic and humanitarian areas. In July 1982, barely one month after the war ended, we lifted the 200-mile exclusion zone

A/AC.109/PV.1261
14

around the islands, replacing it with a 150-mile protection zone. In September of
that year we lifted the financial restrictions imposed at the time of the conflict
though this was, sadly, not reciprocated by Argentina. In subsequent months the
presidency of the European Community made no fewer than five approaches to the
Argentine authorities to suggest discussion of the normalization of economic and
commercial relations between the Community and Argentina. This had our full
support. In May last year we proposed to the Argentines that the bilateral Air
Services Agreement between Britain and Argentina, denounced by the Argentine
Government in June 1982, should be allowed to continue in force. We have also made
clear on a number of occasions that we would be prepared to accept a suitably
prepared visit by bona fide relatives of Argentine war dead to the Falklands, under
the auspices of the International Red Cross.

Following Argentina's October 1983 elections we, like many other countries,
expressed a welcome for the return of democracy to Argentina. The Prime Minister
also sent a message to President Alfonsin on the occasion of his inauguration on
10 December. Subsequently we have sent a series of messages to the Argentine
Government, through the Swiss Government, acting as our protecting Power, with the
aim of establishing a mutually acceptable basis for official talks on the
normalization of our bilateral relations. The first of these messages was sent as
early as 26 January, and a further two messages were sent in April and May,
supplemented by oral exchanges, again through the Swiss protecting Power, which
carried forward the preparatory exchanges.

We recognized that it would take time to find an agreed basis for talks. This
is why a central theme of our approach through the Swiss was to try to identify
subjects for discussion on which we considered progress was feasible and
realistic. We believed that establishing a dialogue on practical issues of concern
to both countries would give each side the chance to demonstrate that it was
capable of doing business with the other, thereby creating a new climate of
confidence between them.

A/AC.109/PV.1261
15

We also recognized that if the talks for which we were working were to have
any chance of success it would be necessary to devise a formula which met our
different positions on the sovereignty question. After much painstaking discussion
and negotiation a formula was finally agreed, on the basis of a proposal which the
Argentines themselves put forward, that if the Argentine delegation chose to raise
the question of sovereignty, the British delegation would respond that it was not

prepared to discuss it. The talks would then turn to bilateral questions of mutual
interest so that the talks would effectively proceed without prejudice to either
side's position on the sovereignty question. We were informed by the Swiss
Government that the Argentine Government had specifically agreed to this
˙rrangement.

As I explained in my letter to the Secretary-General of 2 August, distributed
as General Assembly document A/39/373, the British delegation was scrupulous in its
adherence to this agreement when talks opened in Berne last month. As had been
foreseen, the Argentine delegation did raise the issue of sovereignty. The British
delegation replied, as foreseen, that it was not prepared to discuss it and
proposed, as foreseen, that the discussion should move on to other matters of
mutual interest. Subsequently the British delegation put forward some constructive
ideas on a number of practical issues, such as the restoration of commercial and
financial relations and arrangements for the return to Argentina of the bodies of
the Argentine war dead, or, alternatively, for a visit by Argentine next-of-kin to
the graves of their relatives on the Falkland Islands. We put forward these ideas
in the conviction that this was the best way in which to build more constructive
ɤ ations between our two countries.

Unfortunately, the Argentine delegation was not willing to continue the talks
on this agreed basis. Instead it put forward a new proposition - namely, that it
was not prepared to discuss practical issues unless and until what it called a
mechanism was established for addressing the question of sovereignty over the
Falkland Islands and Dependencies. As this attempt to link consideration of
normalization of bilateral relations with discussion of sovereignty was quite
inconsistent with what had previously been agreed, the talks came to an end.

I cannot stress too strongly my Government's disappointment that so much time
and effort invested in the preparation of these talks should have come to nothing.

A/AC.109/PV.1261
16

(Mr. Margetson, United Kingdom)

Obviously an important opportunity for moving towards better bilateral relations
has been missed, an opportunity we were only too ready to seize. Why the Argentine
delegation should have chosen to set aside the agreed basis for the talks - and
agreed it most certainly was - as soon as the talks opened remains unclear to my
delegation.

As I said earlier in my statement, it is not my intention to rekindle old
animosities, nor to indulge in recrimination. But I have to say that since the
talks in Berne we have been disturbed to discover that Argentina has sought to
paint the United Kingdom as intransigent and somehow responsible for the failure of
the talks in Berne. A communiqué issued in Buenos Aires on 19 July from the

Argentine Foreign Ministry asserts that the British delegation, by stating that it was "not prepared" to discuss sovereignty, "undermined the spirit in which the invitation to the meeeting in Berne was issued". But the truth is that that statement by the British delegation and the precise language in which it was expressed formed an integral part of the prior understanding on which the invitation to the talks was based. The letter from the Chargé d'Affaires of the Argentine Mission dated 23 July talks of our attitude being

"incompatible with the declared British interest in the progressive normalization of relations between the two countries". (A/139/359, p. 2)

That is not the truth of the matter. As I have shown, we have worked hard and with genuine sincerity for talks with Argentina. We have not been inflexible nor lacking in imagination. We remain convinced that improved relations between our two countries are not only in our interests but also in those of our friends. The unfortunate outcome in Berne has not made our task any easier. We shall now need to reflect on where we should go from here. But we are not despondent. We look constructively to the future.

How then can the Committee of 24 help? In our view it can help a great deal by adopting a resolution, a constructive resolution, that should not seek to endorse one or other position of the two countries involved in this dispute, nor to bargain improved bilateral relations for sovereignty. Rather, I believe it should aim at encouraging the United Kingdom and Argentina to work to normalize relations, to establish a climate of confidence in which talks can be carried forward. Regrettably, the resolution before the Committee today once again seeks to define

A/AC.109/PV.1261
17

(Mr. Margetson, United Kingdom)

the dispute in terms of Argentina's claim to sovereignty, prejudges the outcome of negotiations in Argentina's favour and makes no reference to the Islanders' right to self-determination. I hope that Committee members will not allow themselves to be swayed by apparently innocuous language that skirts the real issues, ignores the United Kingdom's position of principle and can only encourage greater deadlock between us. I hope, too, that we can all avoid emotional statements and unnecessary reiteration of entrenched positions which can only serve to exacerbate the difficulties and differences between our two countries.

In that way the Committee could help in the difficult process of re-establishing the ties of friendship that have characterized the relationship between the United Kingdom and Argentina in the past and that we sincerely hope will characterize it again. In that way the Committee might help to lay the foundations for a solution to the problem of the Falkland Islands, consistent with the United Nations Charter and with the right to self-determination which is fundamental to the work of this Committee.

The CHAIRMAN: I thank Ambassador Margetson for his kind words addressed to me. I now call on the representative of Argentina.

Mr. MUÑIZ (Argentina) (interpretation from Spanish): Allow me to begin, Sir, by congratulating you on your unanimous election as Chairman of this important body, and on the wise, objective and effective manner in which you are carrying out your difficult task. I also thank the Committee for this further opportunity to take part in the debate on a question that directly affects the interests of my country and causes concern to the whole of Latin America.

As the Committee well knows, the question of the Malvinas Islands is a)lonial case of a special and particular nature. Allow me briefly to recall some of the factors that contributed to giving it that character.

At the time of their seizure by the United Kingdom the Malvinas Islands were not res nullius. They already belonged to Argentina, which exercised full and effective sovereignty over them through a Governor and Argentine settlers who had permanently established themselves there.

The colonial occupation was imposed by force in violation of even international law of the nineteenth century. Argentina never acquiesced in this occupation, and it will continue to claim those territories until they are

A/AC.109/PV.1261
18

(Mr. Muñiz, Argentina)

restored. Britain's lack of response to this just claim has led to a conflict over sovereignty that has been going on now for 151 years.

The 1833 aggression was not limited to the Territory alone. The original population of the islands, of Argentine origin, was expelled and completely replaced by British citizens.

Furthermore, since the middle of the nineteenth century the colonial legislation has prevented Argentines from owning land or residing permanently on the islands.

These facts will make it possible to arrive at a correct assessment of the situation of the 1,800 British citizens living on the islands and at understanding why they cannot invoke the right to self-determination.

The practice and doctrine of the United Nations system in the area of decolonization show that the right to self-determination requires a legitimate relationship of origin with a Territory and that those exercising that right should be subject to foreign domination. The present population of the Malvinas Islands does not meet those conditions.

Their relationship with the Territory is neither legitimate nor one of origin. It is based on an illegal act of force and on the expulsion of the Argentines previously settled in the Territory. It is maintained by the continuation of the colonial system and by a century and a half of discrimination against those born in my country.

Nor is the population subject to foreign domination. The islanders are full British citizens of British blood. I must once again stress that there is no indigenous population on the islands. The indigenous population was expelled from the islands by the colonial Power when it seized the Territory.

Thus, when the United Kingdom asks for recognition of the islanders' so-called right to self-determination, it is claiming that right only for itself.

In brief, in the Malvinas Islands there is a population but there is no "people" in the sense required by resolution 1514 (XV). At all events, and in accordance with the study on the right to self-determination prepared by the Special Rapporteur of the Sub-Committee on the Prevention of Discrimination and the Protection of Minorities, this distinction should be recognized in favour of the Argentines. This does not mean that the islanders do not have rights in other

A/AC.109/PV.1261
19

(Mr. Muñiz, Argentina)

contexts - for example, within the framework of the International Covenant on Civil and Political Rights.

By reason of all these facts the question of the Malvinas Islands is, I repeat, a special and particular case, not comparable to other colonial situations. Clearly, paragraph 6 of resolution 1514 (IV) and the principle of the Charter establishing and giving pride of place to the right of States to their territorial integrity is the only appropriate basis for their decolonization. Any other criterion would only give legitimacy to an unacceptable territorial plunder and perpetuate colonialism.

That is how the Committee has wisely understood the matter and its many resolutions on this case reflect these features. Indeed, all these decisions established, first, that the only way to put an end to the colonial situation with regard to the Malvinas Islands is by a peaceful and negotiated solution of the sovereignty dispute between Argentina and the United Kingdom; and secondly, that both Governments, the only parties to this dispute, should take into account the interests of those who today are living in the Territory.

The criterion of the General Assembly in its five resolutions and four consensus decisions on this subject is identical to that taken by this Committee. I should like most particularly to mention resolutions 37/9 and 38/12, which were adopted after the 1982 conflict and which therefore are of special significance.

First, resolutions 2065 (XX), 3160 (XXVIII) and 31/49 confirm that the sovereignty dispute still exists and that resolving that dispute is the only way of ʻecolonizing the Malvinas Islands and the South Georgia and South Sandwich Islands;

and secondly, they expressly reflect the interests of the international community that Argentina and the United Kingdom should resume their negotiations on sovereignty and resolve this drawn out controversy as soon as possible. As additional proof of these interests, States Members have requested the Secretary-General to continue his renewed mission of good offices by assisting the parties to carry out those resolutions.

Almost two years have elapsed since the adoption of resolution 37/9, and it is no secret that the sovereignty negotiations have not yet been resumed. The resolutions have not been complied with. The Committee will logically ask itself, why?

A/AC.109/PV.1261
20

(Mr. Muñiz, Argentina)

Who is responsible for this situation?

Let us recall what has till now been the position of the two parties up to date with regard to the resolutions. In notes to the British Government itself and to the Secretary-General and in public statements by its highest authorities, Argentina has officially committed itself to carrying out those resolutions. The United Kingdom has failed to do likewise, although it had accepted the General Assembly's competence on this question. This attitude does not benefit the process of decolonization nor does it contribute to strengthening the United Nations system, whose Charter obliges States actively to seek the settlement of their international disputes by peaceful means.

In point of fact, reluctance to implement resolutions 37/9 and 38/12 is unjustifiable.

The resolutions are based on the following: one, the Malvinas Islands is a colonial Territory that must be decolonized; two, there exists a dispute between Argentina and the United Kingdom over sovereignty of the Islands. Yet, surprisingly, in London some circles maintain that the Islands are British sovereign territory and that the dispute simply does not exist.

I do not believe that the questioning of the existence of the dispute is well founded. As everyone knows, for 17 years the United Kingdom negotiated with my country on this subject. Furthermore, it is difficult to believe that there is still anyone who maintains the right of conquest or that there exists any specific proposal to annex the Islands, situated as they are in Latin America and 13,000 kilometres from London. That is why I prefer the interpretation that these are only tactical arguments aimed exclusively at justifying the reluctance to accept the General Assembly resolutions.

I have mentioned the bases of resolutions 37/9 and 38/12. Let us now see what their objective is: the peaceful solution of the sovereignty dispute. Let us see what means they propose to achieve that end: negotiations.

As is clear, the resolutions are faithful to the Charter. Is it not an obligation incumbent upon States Members to settle their international disputes by peaceful means? Is it not recognized by all of us that negotiations between the parties constitute the most effective means of solving such disputes? And is not this the first of the means for the solution of disputes mentioned in Article 33 of

A/AC.109/PV.1261
21

(Mr. Muñiz, Argentina)

the Charter? Even without resolutions 37/9 and 38/12, are not Argentina and the United Kingdom obliged to seek a solution to their sovereignty dispute and to act, above all, in keeping with Article 33 of the Charter? The answer to all these questions is, of course, in the affirmative.

The United Kingdom Government is trying to justify its non-acceptance of resolutions 37/9 and 38/12 mainly by two arguments: on the one hand, by its commitment to respecting the desires of the Islanders. I have already fully explained the reasons for which the right to self-determination is not applicable to this case. Furthermore, it cannot be accepted than an agreement on the situation of the 1,800 Islanders is unattainable, all the less since it is the intention of my Government scrupulously to respect their interests. In point of fact, Argentina would not oppose both countries' granting special status or guarantees, even international guarantees, within the framework of the solution of this dispute. And by making this reference I should like to clarify the fact that my Government - contrary to what was stated by the representative of the United Kingdom - does not confine itself to a bilateral dispute concerning only the land and not the people.

A second British argument is that Argentina "must live with the consequences of the 1982 conflict". In reality, the consequences of that conflict are as prejudicial to Argentina as to the United Kingdom and the Islands themselves. The first to recognize this are important sectors in London which, like us - and, I am sure, the Committee - are asking themselves: Who gains from a perpetuation of the present situation? Where is this present situation leading us?

In this regard, it is useful to recall the information contained in paragraph 47 of the working document A/AC.109/788, prepared by the Secretary, referring to the visit of British parliamentarians to Buenos Aires.

I should say that the 150 years of colonial domination in the islands have also left a deep mark on my country. However, my Government is fully aware of the fact that the final solution to this dispute requires above all firm commitment to the Charter, a lofty sense of political responsibility and a rational and dispassionate exploration of the various possibilities. That is why my Government has repeatedly stated and repeats today that, without by any means abandoning the just rights of the Argentines over the Malvinas, South Georgias and South Sandwich

A/AC.109/PV.1261
22

(Mr. Muñiz, Argentina)

islands, it will strive for the restoration of those territories exclusively by
peaceful means, in accordance with the United Nations Charter and the resolutions
of the General Assembly on this matter. It is legitimate for my Government to
expect from the British Government an appropriate response to our attitude -
a response expected also by Latin America, which is firmly supporting Argentine
sovereignty over the Malvinas Islands and which with equal firmness calls for its
security interests to be respected.

As is known, the United Kingdom has installed a powerful military base in the
Malvinas Islands. There are more than 4,000 military troops in the islands. There
are nuclear submarines, as well as warships and aircraft with nuclear capacity. A
strategic airport has been constructed which can receive long-range bombers.
Furthermore, two sophisticated radar systems have been installed, and we have no
certainty that missiles have not been placed there.

At a time when Latin America is facing urgent socio-economic needs and trying
to consolidate its democratic institutions in a permanent manner, the British
Government's obstinate determination to impose colonialism on our coasts, its
refusal to negotiate and its obstinacy in militarizing the South Atlantic is quite
simply incomprehensible. I have no doubt that important sectors in Britain,
friends of the United Kingdom and the Committee itself see things as I do.

The problems that Argentina and the United Kingdom are facing are complex.
That is why the Argentine Government will continue to lend every effort to seek
imaginative and flexible ways and means of resuming negotiations on sovereignty
along with negotiations on bilateral relations. The British Government, the
protecting Powers and the Secretary-General are aware of our initiatives and the
realistic and conciliatory spirit in which we have taken them. It is with the same
spirit that my Government attended the meeting held in Berne on 18 and 19 July of
this year at the invitation of the Governments of Brazil and Switzerland.

It is important for this debate to determine whether in that first direct
contact the parties did or did not manifest a readiness to implement
resolutions 37/9 and 38/12, or whether at least they recognized the need to set in
operation some machinery that would enable them to achieve that goal. I repeat:
this is what is really important, not the procedural aspects explained by the
representative of the United Kingdom.

A/AC.109/PV.1261
23

In this regard, I shall confine myself to reading out the appropriate paragraph from the communiqué issued by the representatives of Switzerland and Brazil in Berne on 20 June:

"... the Argentine side reaffirmed that, in its view, it was necessary to discuss the establishment of machinery" - I repeat: the establishment of machinery - "that would make it possible to initiate a discussion in connection with sovereignty over the islands. The United Kingdom side reaffirmed that Her Majesty's Government was not prepared to enter into discussion of the question of sovereignty." (A/39/364, p. 3)

This is the Committee on decolonization; it is difficult for it to be interested in questions such as trade exchanges between Argentina and Great Britain. I would gladly leave aside that and other questions completely alien to the thrust of our debate. However, British insistence on giving them priority and restricting the Berne meeting merely to their consideration obliges me to make some additional comments.

In accordance with what was agreed through the protecting Powers, the Berne meeting was to be informal and with an open agenda; no subject was to be excluded in advance. In consequence, the Argentine representatives reiterated the fact that the question of sovereignty was unquestionably the central point, the very raison d'être of the problems between the two countries. That is why they added that the solution of the existing differences in the various areas of our bilateral relations would be possible in so far as appropriate machinery was set up to settle the dispute, in accordance with the relevant resolutions of the General Assembly.

Argentina's position is logical. It is evident that if the sovereignty dispute did not exist bilateral relations would be different. What kind of solidity or credibility would Argentine-British relations have if this problem were not dealt with?

The British Government has shown interest in re-establishing more normal relations with Argentina on practical and realistic bases. My Government has welcomed this interest and shares it. However, I cannot fail to point out, with frustration, that what the British Government has to date considered as "practical and realistic" is only the indefinite postponement of any discussion - and I am not even talking about negotiations - on sovereignty. In other words, this course is incompatible with that aim.

A/AC.109/PV.1261
24

As I stated in my letter of 23 July last to the Secretary-General (A/39/359), despite the regrettable lack of tangible progress in Berne, the Argentine Government remains firmly committed to the quest for a peaceful negotiated solution of the sovereignty dispute with the United Kingdom, in accordance with the relevant resolutions of the General Assembly. As a result, my Government will continue to offer all its co-operation to the renewed mission of good offices undertaken by the Secretary-General in accordance with the mandate of resolutions 37/9 and 38/12 and the actions of the Protecting Powers.

To sum up, our position is clear. Argentina will never give up the Malvinas Islands, South Georgia or the South Sandwich Islands. Our rights over those Territories are inalienable and we shall not cease to call for their restitution. To that end, we shall follow the course set out by the Charter and the General Assembly in its relevant resolutions, and we shall exhaust all diplomatic channels and fully respect the obligation to solve this controversy by peaceful means - above all, through negotiations, as I stated before.

Not only Argentina but Latin America and the whole international community as well hope that the British Government will respond appropriately to this attitude and the principles that underlie it. An appropriate manifestation of these hopes is contained in draft resolution A/AC.109/L.1525, the main paragraphs of which only reflect fundamental principles and essential obligations set out in the Charter.

The CHAIRMAN: I welcome Ambassador José Francisco Sucre Figarella to this Committee to which his delegation has contributed so much, and call on him.

Mr. SUCRE FIGARELLA (Venezuela) (interpretation from Spanish): In a constant spirit of solidarity, but also with renewed hope, the delegation of Venezuela has the great and historical satisfaction of bringing before the Special Committee on decolonization for consideration a draft resolution on the question of the Malvinas Islands, co-sponsored by the other two Latin American members of this Committee, Cuba and Chile.

Our solidarity with the Argentine cause prevails over any transitory circumstances, because it corresponds to one of the essential principles of our historical philosophy - our belief that any colonialism must be eliminated. When one looks over the background which determines Argentina's sovereignty over the Malvinas Islands, irrefutable proof emerges: the foreign presence is only the

A/AC.109/PV.1261
27

(Mr. Sucre Figarella, Venezuela)

lose. It would be an important lesson to which the democratic régime in Argentina, and all of Latin America, would be truly receptive.

It is regrettable that the recent Bern conference, held last July, when the two Governments met for the first time, produced nothing positive and that the opportunity was lost to begin negotiations. On the contrary, the conference stressed secondary matters - which could indeed be dealt with, but without losing sight of the main objective: restoration of usurped sovereignty to its legitimate holders.

I wish to conclude on a note of optimism. I trust that the Committee will warmly and widely welcome this draft resolution. It is a draft resolution aimed ot merely at rectifying a past injustice, but at opening the way to a future of understanding between two nations which traditionally were friends.

The CHAIRMAN: I shall call now on representatives who wish to speak in exercise of their right of reply.

Mr. MARGETSON (United Kingdom): The representative of Venezuela mentioned the problem of British military expenditure on the Falkland Islands. He said, if I understood him correctly, that this was without any treaty provision to justify it and was only for prestige. I am sorry if I have to labour the obvious point, but, as I think all of us in this room know, before 1982 we had on the Falkland Islands 40 marines. I can only wish that that was the case today, but, unfortunately, events of 1982, as one of the petitioners has reminded us, taught us a lesson. I do not think that there is any country represented in the United Nations which would be so foolish in those circumstances as to defend the islands with 40 marines after a massive invasion. I do not think there has to be any treaty provision to justify what is really a simple matter of common sense.

I wonder if I could also make two brief comments on the speech of the representative of Argentina. First of all, at the start of his speech he laid great emphasis on history. Indeed, it appeared to be rather fundamental to his whole position. As he has given his version of the history of the events of the ninteenth century, may I be permitted to give mine.

First, the islands were, in fact, abandoned by Spain in 1811, that is to say five years before Argentina's declaration of independence. After that, and until 1820, the islands were mostly deserted, apart from occasional visits by fishermen

A/AC.109/PV.1261
28

(Mr. Margetson, United Kingdom)

of various nationalities. In the years after 1820 there were, most certainly, various colonizing ventures from Buenos Aires which were planned. But these were essentially private in nature and were never effectively carried out. The representative of Argentina mentioned that there was a Governor. Indeed, in 1829 the Buenos Aires Government appointed a Hamburg merchant, one Herr Vernet, as Governor of the islands: a Hamburg merchant. But his authority was never recognized by other Powers.

So one comes to the question, "Was there a settled Argentine population in the islands in 1833?" In fact, the islands were practically deserted when a British naval officer, Captain Onslow, arrived in East Falkland in January 1833. Those that were there asked to be repatriated to Buenos Aires, and when the British naval vessel HMS Challenger arrived in the Falklands in January 1834 the township was deserted.

As will be clear, therefore, the British did not take the Falklands by an act of force in 1833. British occupation of the islands in 1833 and 1834 took place without a shot being fired, and Britain has administered the islands continuously since that time.

Lastly, may I just make a comment on the question of the Berne talks. The Argentine Ambassador has said how important it is that both parties should recognize the need to implement United Nations resolutions. I wonder if I could say that it is surely important that Argentina should have recognized the need to implement the agreed basis for the talks in Berne. Unfortunately, this did not happen, and I regret it greatly. But, as I said, we are not despondent. We look constructively to the future. I was very pleased to hear some of the words spoken by the representative of Argentina about the spirit in which he was, and would be, approaching this matter, and I can only reiterate that my Government will not be inflexible or lacking in imagination.

There is therefore, I think, some hope for the future in this unhappy dispute.

Mr. MUÑIZ (Argentina) (interpretation from Spanish): I can assure the Committee that it is not our intention unnecessarily to prolong this debate, much less to contribute to inflaming it. I can tell members that it has been our unvarying concern not to foster a climate incompatible with a constructive and calm

A/AC.109/PV.1261
29

analysis of the problems between Argentina and the United Kingdom; we maintain that spirit.

I referred in my statement to the course that should be taken in order to overcome the present differences between Argentina and the United Kingdom. I think it would be useful to reiterate some of those ideas, although I do not feel it necessary to dwell on considerations regarding the historical arguments, since I have made lengthy statements on other occasions in this same forum on that subject. One must simply ask: Were Argentine citizens expelled from the Malvinas Islands or not? Were their authorities expelled or not? Was the Argentine flag flying? When the United Kingdom signed the 1825 agreement with Argentina did it make any claims regarding the sovereignty of the Malvinas Islands? At that time was not Argentina effectively occupying the islands? Immediately after the occupation of 1833, did not the Argentine Government call upon the Government of the United Kingdom to restore the Malvinas Islands? And did not other Latin American countries, such as Brazil, join it in that demand? I do not think I need say anything more.

My Government is aware of the many questions that need to be resolved, and we do not minimize their importance or their urgency. Indeed, we even agree about the interest of certain points mentioned by my British colleague. In truth, the Argentine Government is interested in the solution of all the problems with the United Kingdom and is not attempting to set any order of priorities regarding the speed of and timeframe for the resolution of those problems. Our approach is practical and realistic.

But precisely because we are trying to be practical and realistic we cannot, and must not, forget the reason for these bilateral problems: The sovereignty dispute is not some intellectual abstraction; it is not a subject of mere academic interest. It is a real dispute that led to a conflict between the two countries. Thus, Argentina's stress on the resumption of a dialogue on this subject too is completely logical. As I have already pointed out, that dialogue is indispensible if we are to rebuild stable and credible relations, as we desire.

I wish expressly to reiterate to this Committee that we have the best of intentions; we have the greatest desire to find a peaceful and final solution with the United Kingdom and to establish the most cordial, close and fruitful relations with that country.

Annex 46: Developments in 1985 and 1986 (Lifting of import
ban by United Kingdom; proposal by Argentina to
negotiate; meeting between Argentine President and
Mr. Kinnock, UK Opposition Leader; UK decision to
withdraw from Special Committee on Decolonization).
Sources: UN Doc. A/40/468; A/40/478; A/40/496;
A/40/646; A/40/662; A/41/23 (Part VII).

**UNITED
NATIONS**

General Assembly

Distr.
GENERAL

A/40/468
9 July 1985

ORIGINAL: ENGLISH

Fortieth session
Item 23 of the preliminary list*

QUESTION OF THE FALKLAND ISLANDS (MALVINAS)

Letter dated 8 July 1985 from the Acting Permanent Representative
of the United Kingdom of Great Britain and Northern Ireland to
the United Nations addressed to the Secretary-General

I have the honour to enclose the text of a written statement concerning
relations between the United Kingdom and Argentina which was made in Parliament on
Monday, 8 July.

I should be grateful if you could arrange for this letter and its enclosure to
be circulated as a document of the General Assembly under item 23 of the
preliminary list.

(Signed) P. M. MAXEY
Acting Permanent Representative of
the United Kingdom of Great Britain
and Northern Ireland

* A/40/50/Rev.1.

A/40/468
English
Page 2

ANNEX

Relations between the United Kingdom and Argentina

On 8 July 1985, Mr. Timothy Renton M. P., Parliamentary Under-Secretary at the Foreign and Commonwealth Office, gave a Written Reply to the following Parliamentary Question:

"To ask the Foreign and Commonwealth Secretary if he is considering any early development in relations between the United Kingdom and Argentina."

The text of Mr. Renton's Written Reply was as follows:

"The twin objectives of our policy are: to fulfil our commitments to the Falkland Islanders: and to restore more normal relations between Britain and Argentina.

"The question of sovereignty over the Falkland Islands is not for discussion. In our view, better relations with Argentina can only realistically be achieved by seeking agreement on practical issues. Commercial and economic relations offer a natural opportunity for progress of this kind. We have on a number of occasions made it plain to the Argentine Government that we are willing to discuss this subject. They have not so far responded to any of these initiatives.

"We have accordingly decided ourselves to take a fresh step to promote improvement in this field. We are lifting, with effect from midnight tonight, the ban on imports from Argentina which has been in place since April 1982.

"The International Monetary Fund have stressed the importance of increased trade for the recovery of the Argentine economy and for the resolution of their debt problems. That is important for international financial stability and for the consolidation of Argentine democracy. We have consistently played a constructive part in the relevant negotiations in the IMF and the Paris Club. The announcement which I am making today will enable Argentina to recognise that if trade is to flourish it has to be a two-way street, and so to lift their restrictions on imports from Britain. It will also benefit British industry, by restoring access to Argentine raw materials, and employment in the United Kingdom.

"Argentina now has the opportunity to respond to our initiatives and thereby to open the way to further steps towards more normal relations between Britain and Argentina."

In the House of Lords, on 8 July, Lady Young, Minister of State at the Foreign and Commonwealth Office, issued a parallel Written Reply to a similar question.

**UNITED
NATIONS**

General Assembly

Distr.
GENERAL

A/40/478
12 July 1985
ENGLISH
ORIGINAL: SPANISH

Fortieth session
Item 23 of the preliminary list*

QUESTION OF THE FALKLAND ISLANDS (MALVINAS)

Letter dated 11 July 1985 from the Chargé d'affaires a.i. of
the Permanent Mission of Argentina to the United Nations
addressed to the Secretary-General

On instructions from my Government, I have the honour to write to you in order
to forward a press communiqué (see annex) issued on 10 July by the Ministry of
Foreign Affairs and Worship of the Argentine Republic in connection with item 23 of
the preliminary list.

I request you to arrange for this letter and the attached press communiqué to
be circulated as a document of the General Assembly and brought to the attention of
the Special Committee on decolonization.

(Signed) Luis E. CAPPAGLI
Chargé d'affaires a.i.

---

*   A/40/50/Rev.1.

85-20615 1594q (E)

/...

A/40/478
English
Page 2

ANNEX

Press communiqué dated 10 July 1985

Statement by the Minister for Foreign Affairs
and Worship of Argentina

What separates the Argentine Republic from the United Kingdom is the question of sovereignty over the Malvinas, South Georgia and South Sandwich Islands.

This is the basic problem; if it did not exist, neither would there exist difficulties with respect to trade, economic and diplomatic relations.

This is not to say that the transfer of sovereignty is essential in order to bring about the resumption of trade and diplomatic relations. It merely means that such resumption would have solid foundations once the matter which separates the two nations ceases to be ignored by one of them.

The Secretary-General of the United Nations upheld this view in his report to the General Assembly at the thirty-ninth session by stating: "Such measures could conceivably, in my view, facilitate addressing the issue that lies at the core of their current estrangement, in order to achieve a lasting solution of the problem".

The United Kingdom Government is quite correct in its observation that we must advance step by step in order to rebuild mutual trust and solve all our problems. That is a realistic and appropriate position. What is not realistic is the attempt to advance step by step in secondary matters, brushing aside all treatment of the fundamental discrepancy.

In this regard, the Argentine Government has taken note of the United Kingdom Government's decision to terminate the ban imposed on imports from Argentina in 1982. According to the official announcement, this measure reflects the United Kingdom's desire to improve relations with Argentina.

This is a positive development; it is to be appreciated at its true worth and welcomed, and it betokens the prestige achieved by the Argentine democracy in the international community.

As the United Kingdom communiqué states, it is of benefit to the parties that trade between the two nations should flourish. But there can be no doubt that for trade to flourish it is necessary to have stable political conditions and mutual trust. Firstly, a stable relationship requires that the central issue separating our two nations should not be ignored; secondly, mutual trust requires the elimination of threats to the security of the Argentine Republic of any type, such as the threat presented by the excessive and disproportionate militarization of the Islands, and the maintenance of the so-called protection zone.

Accordingly, although we are today witnessing a genuinely more flexible British policy, we have to seek prompt and realistic responses to all the other

/...

A/40/478
English
Page 3

questions that need to be considered, because otherwise we would discover that only the practical questions of interest to United Kingdom policy were being dealt with and that everything else was being ignored.

We stress that the discussion on sovereignty is a specific question par excellence, since on it the rest depends and without it, after all, those so-called practical questions would become illusions.

Hence it has been the policy of the Argentine Republic, upheld by numerous decisions of the United Nations and other multilateral forums, to maintain that the problem of sovereignty must necessarily be included in any type of negotiation undertaken with the United Kingdom.

Not only is this a legitimate demand, it is also a realistic appraisal of the situation; it certainly does not signify a specific position in the agenda of the negotiations or a predetermined date for the solution of all the issues.

The Argentine Government hopes that the United Kingdom's lifting of the ban on imports constitutes the profound expression of a negotiating spirit, and it is to confirm this that it is proposing to the United Kingdom Government some important steps forward.

Accordingly, it invites the United Kingdom Government to initiate negotiations in the course of the next 60 days, and to this end it is prepared to embark on the necessary preparations forthwith, either through the mission of good offices entrusted by the General Assembly to the Secretary-General of the United Nations or, if preferred, through friendly Powers that represent the respective interests.

The Argentine Government has not deemed it necessary to make a formal declaration of cessation of hostilities, the de facto existence of which has been recognized in various resolutions of the United Nations. However, if this matter is viewed by the United Kingdom Government as the remaining obstacle to the initiation of negotiations, the Argentine Government would be prepared to make the declaration as soon as the United Kingdom Government agrees to initiate the general negotiations repeatedly recommended by the international community.

The Argentine Government, in its desire to strengthen peace through the diplomatic channel, trusts that it will receive a prompt and favourable response to this proposal.

**UNITED
NATIONS**

A

General Assembly

Distr.
GENERAL

A/40/496
18 July 1985

ORIGINAL: ENGLISH

Fortieth session
Item 23 of the provisional agenda*

QUESTION OF THE FALKLAND ISLANDS (MALVINAS)

Letter dated 17 July 1985 from the Deputy Permanent Representative
of the United Kingdom of Great Britain and Northern Ireland to the
United Nations addressed to the Secretary-General

   I have the honour to refer to my letter of 8 July 1985, circulated as document
A/40/468, and to the letter to you dated 11 July 1985 from the Chargé
d'affaires a.i. of the Permanent Mission of Argentina, circulated as document
A/40/478.

   I enclose a statement issued by the Foreign and Commonwealth Secretary of the
United Kingdom on 12 July, which referred to the statement by the Minister for
Foreign Affairs and Worship of Argentina enclosed with the letter under reference
from the Chargé d'affaires of Argentina.

   I should be grateful if you could arrange for this letter and its enclosure to
be circulated as a document of the General Assembly under item 23 of the
provisional agenda, and for this letter to be brought to the attention of the
Special Committee on the Situation with regard to the Implementation of the
Declaration on the Granting of Independence to Colonial Countries and Peoples,
together with my letter of 8 July.

(Signed) P. M. MAXEY
Deputy Permanent Representative

---

*   A/40/150.

A/40/496
English
Page 2

ANNEX

Statement issued by Sir Geoffrey Howe, Secretary of State for Foreign and Commonwealth Affairs of the United Kingdom, 12 July 1985

..

The Statement issued on 10 July by the Argentine Foreign Ministry is a disappointing response to the initiative we took in lifting the ban on Argentine imports.

The Argentine Foreign Ministry has acknowledged that our action was a positive step. But their statement does not indicate any willingness to reciprocate directly. Instead, it calls upon Britain to enter into discussions, which must include discussion of sovereignty over the Falkland Islands, within 60 days.

Our statement of 8 July made it absolutely clear that we are not prepared to discuss sovereignty. This has been the Government's position all along, as the Argentine Government well knows. Yet the Argentine Government continues to insist that any practical steps to promote better bilateral relations with Britain, including a formal cessation of hostilities, must be dependent on a condition which it knows to be unacceptable. This is neither realistic nor constructive.

We hope that Argentina will reconsider its response and show a willingness to take practical steps, as Britain has done, to begin the long process of restoring confidence between our two countries and developing a more normal bilateral relationship.

**UNITED
NATIONS**

A

General Assembly

Distr.
GENERAL

A/40/646
17 September 1985
ENGLISH
ORIGINAL: SPANISH

Fortieth session
Item 23 of the provisional agenda*

QUESTION OF THE FALKLAND ISLANDS (MALVINAS)

Letter dated 16 September 1985 from the Permanent
Representative of Argentina to the United Nations
addressed to the Secretary-General

I have the honour to transmit to you the text of the press communiqué issued
on 12 September by the Ministry of Foreign Affairs and Worship of the Argentine
Republic, containing the statement by Mr. Dante M. Caputo, Minister for Foreign
Affairs and Worship, concerning the question of the Malvinas Islands (see annex).

I should like to request that this letter and its annex be circulated as a
document of the General Assembly under item 23 of the provisional agenda.

(Signed) Carlos Manuel MUNOZ
Ambassador
Permanent Representative

---

*   A/40/150.

A/40/646
English
Page 2

ANNEX

Press communiqué dated 12 September 1985 issued by the Ministry
of Foreign Affairs and Worship of the Argentine Republic

Statement by Mr. Dante Caputo, Minister for Foreign Affairs and Worship

Buenos Aires, 12 September:

The 60-day period following the invitation which the Argentine Government
extended, through me, to the United Kingdom Government, to resume negotiations on
the question of the Malvinas Islands within that period, ended on 11 September. In
that invitation, the Argentine Government also said that it was prepared to embark
on the necessary preparations forthwith, either through the mission of good offices
entrusted to the Secretary-General by the United Nations General Assembly or
through the friendly protecting Powers who represent the countries' respective
interests.

That invitation was couched in the broadest and most flexible terms in order
to permit a resumption of the dialogue between the two nations in accordance with
the guidelines provided by United Nations resolutions, with which my country
complies fully.

The spirit in which we extended that invitation foresaw the possibility of
coming to the fortieth session of the United Nations General Assembly with a
negotiating process already under way which would show that a peaceful attitude and
a desire to resolve the problem existed between our two nations.

Such a development would have been a positive response to the repeated calls
by the international community to achieve a just, peaceful and lasting settlement
of the dispute over the Malvinas, South Georgia and South Sandwich Islands.

In the year marking the fortieth anniversary of the United Nations, such an
event would have signified a reaffirmation of the contribution which this
organization has made to the peaceful settlement of international disputes, which
is one of the guiding principles of the Charter.

Thus far, however, the United Kingdom Government has given no positive
response to the Argentine invitation. This blatant indifference shows how little
importance the United Kingdom, a permanent member of the Security Council, attaches
to the Organization's decisions.

The United Kingdom Government has emphasized the need to restore trust between
the parties, yet it refuses to resume the dialogue, thereby ignoring the appeals of
the international community and contradicting its own statements.

What is more, the Argentine Government's repeated offers have met with utter
refusal on the part of the United Kingdom to consider the issue that lies at the
heart of the conflict between the two nations and is the source of their other
differences. These differences would no doubt be resolved gradually were the
United Kingdom to agree to resume negotiations with the Argentine Republic.

/...

A/40/646
English
Page 3

We therefore appeal to the reason and good sense of the United Kingdom authorities, which cannot continue to ignore the existence of a dispute which they have acknowledged on numerous occasions.

"The Argentine Government is still waiting for a positive response from the United Kingdom Government and, to this end, renews the invitation to embark on comprehensive negotiations on the question, without pre-conditions or predetermined dates, within a framework governed by the principle of good faith which must prevail in international relations.

The democratic Argentine Government reiterates once again its pledge that the interests of the inhabitants of the Islands must be taken care of during the negotiations, to which end it is prepared to guarantee their traditions, lifestyle and customs and grant the necessary safeguards.

There is thus no remaining justification for the United Kingdom's conduct other than the attempt to perpetuate an anachronistic and illegal colonial situation, ignoring United Nations mandates applicable to the situation.

We must none the less emphasize yet again that the passage of time will not weaken the resolve underlying Argentina's claim, nor its conviction as to the need to settle peacefully a dispute which is preventing the normalization of relations between the two nations.

**UNITED
NATIONS**

General Assembly

Distr.
GENERAL

A/40/662 /
19 September 1985
ENGLISH
ORIGINAL: SPANISH

Fortieth session
Item 23 of the provision agenda*

QUESTION OF THE FALKLAND ISLANDS (MALVINAS)

Letter dated 19 September 1985 from the Permanent Representative of
Argentina to the United Nations addressed to the Secretary-General

I have the honour to enclose herewith the text of a press release issued on
18 September 1985 by the Ministry of Foreign Affairs and Worship of the Argentine
Republic in connection with the meeting held in Paris on that same date between
His Excellency the President of Argentina, Dr. Raúl Alfonsín, and the Leader of the
Labour Party and Her Majesty's Opposition in the United Kingdom Parliament, the
Rt. Hon. Neil Kinnock, M.P.

I would ask that this note and its annex be circulated as a document of the
General Assembly, under item 23 of the provisional agenda, and brought to the
attention of the Special Committee on decolonization.

(Signed) Carlos Manuel MUÑIZ
Ambassador
Permanent Representative

---

*   A/40/150.

85-25571 2398b (E)   /...

A/40/662
English
Page 2

ANNEX

Press release issued on 18 September 1985 by the Ministry of
Foreign Affairs and Worship of the Argentine Republic

On 18 September 1985, in Paris, the President of the Argentine Republic,
Dr. Raúl R. Alfonsín, met with the Leader of the Labour Party and Her Majesty's
Opposition in the United Kingdom Parliament, the Rt. Hon. Neil Kinnock, M.P. They
were accompanied by the Argentine Minister for Foreign Affairs, Dr. Dante Caputo,
and the Labour Party Chief Spokesman on Foreign Affairs, the
Rt. Hon. Denis Healey, M.P.

President Alfonsín and Mr. Kinnock were in agreement on the importance of the
present progress of democracy in Latin America, not only for the people of the
region, but also for development, stability and justice in the world as a whole.

Mr. Kinnock expressed his appreciation of the re-establishment and advance of
democracy in Argentina and the significance of the effective measures adopted by
the Government of President Alfonsín to defend human and civil rights, including
the re-establishment of judicial authority calling to account those who had so
grievously violated them.

Both agreed that the main threat to democracy and peace in Latin America was
the continuing economic crisis. Democratic stability in the continent is obviously
closely linked to the possibility of growth in its economies. The main obstacles
to the efforts of the developing countries are the world financial system which
denies the necessary resources for development and maintains interest rates at
crippling levels, the distortion of world trade through the increase of
protectionism and the deterioration of the terms of trade for those countries.

President Alfonsín and Mr. Kinnock agreed on the need for urgent and
substantial reforms to the present world economic system. In particular, they
considered that Latin American foreign debt must be dealt with politically by the
Governments of both creditor and debtor countries with the aim of ensuring the
development of the region and, consequently, sustaining democratic systems.
President Alfonsín and Mr. Kinnock emphasized that such reforms would have mutual
advantages of stability and employment for developed and developing countries
throughout the world.

Both expressed a firm desire for rapid progress in the peace negotiations in
Central America undertaken by the Contadora Group, and Mr. Kinnock emphasized the
importance of the recent establishment of the Support Group to those negotiations,
made up of democratic Governments of the Latin American continent, including the
Government of the Argentine Republic.

President Alfonsín and Mr. Kinnock underlined the responsibility of the
democracies of Latin America and Europe to work to secure peace and economic
development in the Central American region, and also stressed the importance of a
determination on the part of all parties that attitudes and negotiations should be

/...

A/40/662
English
Page 3

constructive and directed towards ensuring self-determination, demilitarization, respect for human rights and economic development in the region.

Both agreed on the need for the re-establishment of diplomatic and commercial relations between the Argentine Republic and the United Kingdom. To that end, they expressed their desire that negotiations should be initiated to explore the means of resolving the outstanding problems between the two countries, including all aspects of the future of the Falkland Islands (Malvinas).

They also jointly stressed the importance for the inhabitants of those islands of effectively guaranteeing the preservation of their customs, their ways of life and traditions, as well as respect for forms of administration, education and social and economic organization. In that connection, Mr. Kinnock stressed the fundamental importance of taking fully into account the interests of the inhabitants of the islands, and President Alfonsín pointed to the range and the extent of the rights guaranteed by Argentina's democratic Constitution.

President Alfonsín and Mr. Kinnock expressed their appreciation to the Socialist International Secretariat for facilitating their useful meeting.

CHAPTER X*

FALKLAND ISLANDS (MALVINAS)

A. Consideration by the Special Committee

1.   At its 1294th meeting, on 18 March 1986, by adopting the suggestions relating to the organization of its work put forward by the Chairman (A/AC.109/L.1577), the Special Committee decided, inter alia, to take up the question of the Falkland Islands (Malvinas) as a separate item and to consider it at its plenary meetings.

2.   The Special Committee considered the Territory at its 1304th and 1308th meetings, on 12 and 14 August 1986, respectively.

3.   In its consideration of the item, the Special Committee took into account the provisions of the relevant General Assembly resolutions, including in particular resolution 40/57 of 2 December 1985 on the implementation of the Declaration on the Granting of Independence to Colonial Countries and Peoples. By paragraph 12 of that resolution, the Assembly requested the Committee "to continue to seek suitable means for the immediate and full implementation of General Assembly resolution 1514 (XV) in all Territories that have not yet attained independence and, in particular: ... to formulate specific proposals for the elimination of the remaining manifestations of colonialism and to report thereon to the General Assembly at its forty-first session". The Committee also took into account Assembly resolution 40/21 of 27 November 1985 concerning the Territory. Further, the Committee took into account the relevant provisions of Assembly resolution 35/118 of 11 December 1980, the annex to which contains the Plan of Action for the Full Implementation of the Declaration, as well as Assembly resolution 40/56 of 2 December 1985, relating to the twenty-fifth anniversary of the Declaration on the Granting of Independence to Colonial Countries and Peoples. The Committee also took into account the relevant provisions of the Political Declaration adopted by the Ministerial Meeting of the Co-ordinating Bureau of the Movement of Non-Aligned Countries, held at New Delhi from 16 to 19 April 1986 1/.

4.   During its consideration of the item, the Special Committee had before it a working paper prepared by the Secretariat containing information on developments concerning the Territory (A/AC.109/878).

At the 1304th meeting, on 12 August, the Chairman drew attention to a draft resolution on the item sponsored by Chile, Cuba and Venezuela (A/AC.109/L.1607).

7.   At the same meeting, the Chairman informed the Special Committee that the delegation of Argentina had expressed the wish to participate in the Committee's consideration of the item. The Committee decided to accede to the request.

8.   At the same meeting, the representative of Venezuela, in a statement to the Special Committee (see annex) introduced draft resolution A/AC.109/L.1607, referred to in paragraph 5.

9.   At-the same meeting, statements were made by the representatives of Argentina and Cuba (see annex).

10. At the same meeting, the Special Committee adopted the draft resolution (A/AC.109/L.1607) by 20 votes to none, with 4 abstentions (see para. 14). The representative of Sweden made a statement (see annex).

12. The delegation of the United Kingdom, the administering Power concerned, did iot participate in the Committee's consideration of the item. At the outset of the year, the Permanent Representative of the United Kingdom to the United Nations stated in his letter dated 30 January 1986 addressed to the Chairman that:

> "My Government have decided that the United Kingdom will henceforth not take part in the work of the Special Committee on decolonization or its sub-committees ... we shall continue strictly to fulfil our responsibilities under the United Nations Charter towards our Non-Self-Governing Territories, particularly the responsibilities set out in Article 73. We shall also inform the Secretary-General of any relevant political and constitutional developments in those Territories."

13. In a related context, the Special Committee, at its 1296th meeting, on 4 August, adopted a resolution on the question of sending visiting missions to Territories (A/AC.109/875) in which, in "expressing its regret at the decision of the Government of the United Kingdom of Great Britain and Northern Ireland not to take part in the related work of the Special Committee, and noting with serious concern the negative impact which the non-participation of the United Kingdom has had on its work during the year, depriving it of an important source of information (.1 the Territories under the administration of the United Kingdom", the Committee appealed to the Government of the United Kingdom to reconsider its decision not to participate in the work of the Special Committee, and urged it to permit the access of visiting missions to the Territories under its administration. 2/

Annex 47: Working Paper prepared by Secretariat of UN Special
Committee, August 5, 1988 (concerning developments
until 1988)
Source: UN Doc. A/AC 109/962.

SPECIAL COMMITTEE ON THE SITUATION WITH
REGARD TO THE IMPLEMENTATION OF THE
DECLARATION ON THE GRANTING OF
INDEPENDENCE TO COLONIAL COUNTRIES
AND PEOPLES

FALKLAND ISLANDS (MALVINAS)

Working paper prepared by the Secretariat

CONTENTS

88-19670   0452a (E)   /...

A/AC.109/962
English
Page 2

FALKLAND ISLANDS (MALVINAS) 1/

I. LAND AND PEOPLE

1.   The Falkland Islands (Malvinas) comprise two large islands, East and West
Falkland, and some 200 smaller ones, covering a total area of approximately
12,173 square kilometres. They are situated in the south Atlantic, some
772 kilometres north-east of Cape Horn and about 480 kilometres east of the
southern Argentine mainland. South Georgia is an island of 3,592 square kilometres
situated about 1,300 kilometres east-south-east of the Falkland Islands (Malvinas)
group and the South Sandwich Islands, covering an area of 311 square kilometres,
lie about 750 kilometres east-south-east of South Georgia. Neither of them has an
indigenous or permanent population.

2.   The population of the Falkland Islands (Malvinas), according to the
preliminary results of the census held in November 1986, is 1,916 inhabitants,
excluding military personnel and contract workers employed by offshore
contractors. Based on the same census, the population of Stanley, the capital, is
estimated at 1,231, and that of the "Camp" settlements outside Stanley at 647.
According to the previous census of 1980, of the total population of 1,813, 1,360
were born in the Islands and 302 in the United Kingdom.

3.   Since 1982, 50 residents who had departed in the wake of the conflict have
returned, while another 50 have migrated from the United Kingdom. 2/ Estimates
place the increase in population in the Falklands during the past five years at
6 per cent. 3/

II.   CONSTITUTION AND GOVERNMENT

4.   The Constitution for the Falkland Islands (Malvinas) has been in operation
since 18 April 1985. 4/ From that date South Georgia and the South Sandwich
Islands ceased to be governed as dependencies of the Falkland Islands (Malvinas)
and have their own Constitution. 5/ They continue, however, to be administered
from Stanley "purely as a matter of convenience" 6/ and the Governor of the
Falkland Islands (Malvinas) holds concurrently the office of Commissioner for the
Territories. 7/ A summary of the Constitution is set out in the 1985 working paper
prepared by the Secretariat (A/AC.109/835 and Corr.1, paras. 4-39).

5.   It was reported on 25 July 1988 8/ that Mr. William Hugh Fullerton was
appointed Governor of the Falkland Islands (Malvinas).

/...

A/AC.109/962
English
Page 3

III.   CONSIDERATION BY THE UNITED NATIONS

A.   Special Committee on the Situation with regard to the
     Implementation of the Declaration on the Granting of
     Independence to Colonial Countries and Peoples

6.   The Special Committee on the Situation with regard to the Implementation of
the Declaration on the Granting of Independence to Colonial Countries and Peoples
considered the question of the Falkland Islands (Malvinas) at its 1315th, 1324th
and 1327th meetings, on 4, 12 and 14 August 1987, respectively. Statements were
made in the course of the debate by the representatives of Argentina, Cuba and
Yugoslavia and, in explanation of vote, by the representative of Sweden
(A/AC.109/PV.1327). The delegation of the United Kingdom did not participate in
the Committee's consideration of the item (see A/41/23 (Part I), paras. 76
and 77). At its 1315th meeting, the Committee granted requests for hearings and,
at its 1327th meeting, heard statements by a representative of the Legislative
Council of the Falkland Islands and two other petitioners (A/AC.109/PV.1327).

7.   At the conclusion of the discussion, the Special Committee adopted, by
20 votes to none, with 4 abstentions, a draft resolution (A/AC.109/L.1644)
introduced by Venezuela on behalf also of Chile and Cuba (see A/AC.109/930).

8.   On 18 February 1988, the Acting Chairman of the Special Committee issued a
press statement concerning developments relating to the Territory (see annex; see
also sect. VII).

B.   General Assembly

9.   At its 3rd plenary meeting, on 18 September 1987, the General Assembly, on the
recommendation of the General Committee, decided to consider the question of the
Falkland Islands (Malvinas) directly in plenary meeting, on the understanding that
the hearings of the organizations and individuals having an interest in the
question would be held in the Fourth Committee in conjunction with the
consideration of the item in plenary meeting.

10. In their statements in the general debate at the forty-second session,
Sir Geoffrey Howe, Secretary of State for Foreign and Commonwealth Affairs of the
United Kingdom of Great Britain and Northern Ireland (A/42/PV.8), and
Mr. Dante Caputo, Minister for Foreign Affairs and Worship of Argentina
(A/42/PV.13), inter alia, outlined the positions of their respective Governments on
the question of the Falkland Islands (Malvinas). The representatives of the
following delegations also referred to the question in their statements in the
general debate: Brazil (A/42/PV.4), Uruguay and Peru (A/42/PV.5), Mexico and Cuba
(A/42/PV.7), Costa Rica (A/42/PV.8), Paraguay (A/42/PV.9), Spain (A/42/PV.13),
Colombia (A/42/PV 14), Bolivia (A/42/PV.16), Dominican Republic and Philippines
(A/42/PV.18), Panama (A/42/PV.19), Mozambique (A/42/PV.20), Ecuador (A/42/PV.21),
Honduras (A/42/PV.24), Botswana (A/42/PV.25), Saint Lucia (A/42/PV.29),
Saint Vincent and the Grenadines and Grenada (A/42/PV.33).

/...

A/AC.109/962
English
Page 4

11. The General Assembly discussed the question of the Falkland Islands (Malvinas) at its 70th and 72nd plenary meetings, on 16 and 17 November 1987. The Assembly had before it, inter alia, the report of the Secretary-General (A/42/732) submitted pursuant to resolution 41/40 of 25 November 1986, as well as the report of its Fourth Committee (A/42/731) on the hearing of two representatives of the Legislative Council of the Falkland Islands and two other petitioners, held at the Committee's 24th meeting, on 17 November (A.C.4/42/SR.24).

12. At the 70th and 72nd plenary meetings, respectively, the Minister for Foreign Affairs and Worship of Argentina and the representative of the United Kingdom made statements on the question, elucidating further the position of their respective Governments. Statements on the item were made, at the 70th plenary meeting, by the representatives of Barbados, Bolivia, Brazil, Colombia, Peru and Venezuela (A/42/PV.70) and, at the 72nd plenary meeting, by the representatives of Costa Rica, Cuba, the Dominican Republic, Mexico, Panama, the Union of Soviet Socialist Republics and Uruguay (A/42/PV.72).

13. On 17 November 1987, the General Assembly adopted, by a recorded vote of 114 to 5 (Belize, Gambia, Oman, Sri Lanka and United Kingdom), with 36 abstentions, resolution 42/19, the operative paragraphs of which read as follows:

     "The General Assembly,

          ...

          "1. Reiterates its request to the Governments of Argentina and the United Kingdom of Great Britain and Northern Ireland to initiate negotiations with a view to finding the means to resolve peacefully and definitively the problems pending between both countries, including all aspects on the future of the Falkland Islands (Malvinas), in accordance with the Charter of the United Nations;

          "2. Requests the Secretary-General to continue his renewed mission of good offices in order to assist the parties in complying with the request made in paragraph 1 above, and to take the necessary measures to that end;

          "3. Requests the Secretary-General to submit to the General Assembly at its forty-third session a report on the progress made in the implementation of the present resolution;

          "4. Decides to include in the provisional agenda of its forty-third session the item entitled "Question of the Falkland Islands (Malvinas)."

14. Statements in explanation of vote were made by the following delegations: Argentina, Botswana, France, Guatemala, Islamic Republic of Iran, Jordan, Netherlands, Sri Lanka, Sweden and United Kingdom (A/42/PV.72).

15. On 15 January 1988, the text of resolution 42/19 was transmitted to the Permanent Representatives of the United Kingdom and Argentina to the United Nations for the attention of their respective Governments.

/...

A/AC.109/962
English
Page 5

16.   The report of the Secretary-General on his renewed mission of good offices, in pursuance of paragraph 3 of resolution 42/19, will be issued in a separate document of the General Assembly at its forty-third session.

C.   Security Council

17.   At its 2800th and 2801st meetings, on 17 March 1988, the Security Council considered the letter dated 11 March 1988 addressed to the President of the Council by the Permanent Representative of Argentina to the United Nations (S/19604), in which the attention of the Security Council was drawn to "the situation created in the South Atlantic by the United Kingdom Government's decision to conduct military manoeuvres in the Malvinas Islands from 7 to 31 March 1988" (see sect. VIII).

18.   At the 2800th meeting of the Security Council, statements were made by the Minister for Foreign Affairs and Worship of Argentina, by the representatives of Brazil, the United Kingdom, and the Union of Soviet Socialist Republics and, at the Council's invitation in accordance with the relevant provisions of the Charter of the United Nations and rule 37 of the provisional rules of procedure of the Council, by the representatives of Colombia, Costa Rica, Ecuador, Mexico, Peru, Spain, Uruguay and Venezuela, as well as by the Acting Chairman of the Special Committee on the Situation with regard to the Implementation of the Declaration on the Granting of Independence to Colonial Countries and Peoples (S/PV.2800).

19.   At the 2801st meeting of the Security Council, statements were made by the representatives of Algeria, China, the Federal Republic of Germany, France, Italy, Japan, Nepal, Senegal, the United States of America, Yugoslavia and Zambia and at the Council's invitation under the Charter and the above-mentioned rule of procedure, by the representatives of Bolivia, Guatemala, Guyana, India, Nicaragua and Panama (S/PV.2801). Following further statements by the the Minister for Foreign Affairs and Worship of Argentina, the representatives of the United Kingdom and the United States of America, at the same meeting (S/PV.2801), the President of the Security Council declared that the Council had thus concluded the present stage of the discussion on the item before it.

IV.   CONSIDERATION BY OTHER INTERGOVERNMENTAL ORGANIZATIONS

A.   Organization of American States

20.   On 18 March 1988, the Permanent Council of the Organization of American States (OAS), meeting in an extraordinary session at the request of Argentina, and having heard statements of 28 delegations in the debate, adopted by 27 votes to none, with 2 abstentions (Saint Lucia and United States of America), a resolution by which the Permanent Council expressed its deep concern with the increase in tension in the south Atlantic as a consequence of the proposed military exercise (see sect. VII) and the hope that the United Kingdom would reconsider its decision with a view to creating a climate of trust for future negotiations. 9/

/...

A/AC.109/962
English
Page 6

B. Movement of Non-Aligned Countries

21. On 16 March 1988, the Co-ordinating Bureau of the Movement of Non-Aligned
Countries held a meeting in New York to hear a statement by Mr. Dante Caputo. In a
communiqué issued at the conclusion of the meeting, 10/ the Co-ordinating Bureau,
in strongly deploring the decision by the United Kingdom Government to hold
military manoeuvres in the area (see sect. VIII), declared that such a dangerous
and provocative measure was contrary to the general interest of international peace
and security. It further pointed out that the military exercises were contrary to
the pertinent United Nations resolutions which, with the express support of the
United Kingdom, declared the south Atlantic a zone of peace and co-operation.

V. POSITIONS OF THE GOVERNMENTS OF THE UNITED KINGDOM
AND ARGENTINA

22. The positions of the Governments of the United Kingdom and Argentina on the
question of the Falkland Islands (Malvinas) are set out in the statements made by
the representatives of the respective Governments to the General Assembly at its
forty-second session and to the Security Council on 17 March 1988. In brief, the
United Kingdom Government's policy is to stand by its commitments to the Falkland
islanders, while seeking to improve its bilateral relations with Argentina; it is
prepared to hold talks to that end but is not willing to have included in them the
question of sovereignty over the Falkland Islands. The Argentine Government, on
its part, accepts the relevant General Assembly resolutions and expresses its
permanent willingness for dialogue without pre-conditions and with a view to
ensuring peace in the region without altering in any manner its right of
sovereignty over the Malvinas, South Georgia and the South Sandwich Islands and the
adjacent waters.

23. In her 1987 Christmas broadcast to the Falkland islanders,
Mrs. Margaret Thatcher, the Prime Minister of the United Kingdom, repeated her
pledge not to negotiate with Argentina over the issue of sovereignty. 11/

24. In May 1988, in his opening message to the Argentinian Congress,
Mr. Raúl Alfonsin, President of the Argentine Republic, reiterated that the
Argentine Government's position on the question was based on a "negotiated solution
to disputes", on its "firm commitment to restore Argentina's inalienable rights"
and on a "prudent attitude" to avoid incidents with the United Kingdom. 12/

25. On 1 June, during the general debate at the fifteenth special session of the
General Assembly devoted to disarmament, President Alfonsín stated that his country
affirmed "the need to start a broad dialogue, with an open agenda and without
pre-conditions, with the United Kingdom of Great Britain and Northern Ireland
regarding the ongoing dispute with that State over the Territory of the Malvinas,
South Sandwich and South Georgia Islands and the surrounding seas. That dialogue
may create conditions which will facilitate the beginning of negotiations, which, I
insist, are the only method Argentina can envisage for recovering its sovereignty
over those Territories". 13/ On 2 June, Foreign Minister Dante Caputo was quoted
to have said that any kind of dialogue was possible so long as it did not involve
"raising negative precedents for our sovereignty claims". 14/

/...

A/AC.109/962
English
Page 7

26. In a press communiqué issued on 10 June 1988, 15/ the Argentine Government reaffirmed its rights over the Malvinas Islands and islands of the south Atlantic and called for the resumption of negotiations with the United Kingdom. It was reported on 3 July that Foreign Minister Caputo had reiterated the readiness of the Argentine Government to declare a formal end to hostilities with the United Kingdom in return for discussion of the sovereignty issue over the Territory. 16/

VI. UNOFFICIAL ANGLO-ARGENTINE CONTACTS

27. Contacts between Argentine and United Kingdom parliamentarians have continued within the framework of meetings of the Inter-Parliamentary Union, most recently in the Conference held at Guatemala City in April 1988.

VII. POLITICAL DEVELOPMENTS IN THE TERRITORY

28. In November 1987, 20 members of Parliament, sponsored by the United Kingdom Ministry of Defence, made a five-day visit to the Territory. 17/

29. The Secretary of State for Foreign and Commonwealth Affairs, Mr. T. Eggar, visited the Territory from 4 to 9 December 1987. During the visit he officially opened the new King Edward Memorial Hospital (see para. 72), inspected development projects and met with residents and members of the armed forces. 18/ He was reported to have told residents of Port Stanley that, although indirect contacts with Argentina had been going on for the past nine months, the United Kingdom had resolved never to give way to the question of sovereignty as long as the islanders wished to remain British.

30. In January 1988, Lord Shackleton, who was Chairman of the team that prepared the 1976 and 1982 reports on the economic conditions in the Falkland Islands (see A/AC.109/752, paras. 51-60), visited the Territory. 19/ During the visit, at which time he was presented with the "Freedom of Stanley" award, he toured the islands, visiting several development projects supported by the Falkland Islands Development Corporation. He officially opened a new lodge, tourist hotel (see para. 53) and met with independent farmers who had participated in the land redistribution programme which he had recommended in his 1982 economic report (see para. 44).

31. In January 1988, the Territory's first political party, named Desire the Right Party - Falkland Islands, was reported to have been organized with a manifesto which, inter alia, stressed the intention of the party "to ensure [that] the Islands remain British in every respect". 19/

VIII. MILITARY DEVELOPMENTS

32. On 11 February 1988, the Minister of State for the Armed Forces of the United Kingdom announced in the House of Commons 20/ that the United Kingdom intended to hold a full-scale reinforcement exercise, known as "Fire Focus", in the Territory between 7 and 31 March 1988. The exercise would involve the reinforcement of the

/...

A/AC.109/962
English
Page 8

Falkland Islands garrison's air defence and an airlift of troops to the Falklands, followed by unit exercises "to take advantage of the excellent training facilities in the Islands".

33. A press release issued on the same date by the United Kingdom Minister for Defence, 21/ stated that the exercise would involve the deployment of Royal Air Force Phantom aircraft and a significant number of troops. The communiqué further stated that the "exercise had been planned for some time and did not reflect any increase in tension in the area. The British Government's commitment to maintaining the security of the Falkland Islands is very clearly on record: exercise 'Fire Focus' is simply the means of practising its ability to discharge this commitment should the need ever arise".

34. By a letter dated 12 February 1988 addressed to the Secretary-General, 22/ the Permanent Representative of Argentina to the United Nations transmitted the text of a press communiqué issued on 11 February 1988 by the Argentine Ministry of Foreign Affairs and Worship. The communiqué, in setting out the position of the Argentine Government over the planned exercises by the United Kingdom Government, denounced the British decision as constituting a particularly serious and highly alarming development, creating new and greater tension.

35. In a letter dated 25 February 1988 addressed to the Secretary-General, 23/ the Permanent Representative of the United Kingdom, referring to the Argentine press communiqué concerning the planned exercises in the Falkland Islands in March 1988, stated: "I wish to emphasize that this is a routine reinforcement exercise. ... Our reinforcement capability has enabled us to reduce our garrison in the Falklands. This is a contribution to a lowering of tension in the region".

36. In a letter dated 23 February 1988 addressed to the Secretary-General, 24/ the Permanent Representative of Ecuador to the United Nations transmitted the text of a press release issued on the same date by the Goverment of Ecuador concerning the planned British military exercise in the Territory. On 29 February 1988, 25/ the Permanent Representative of Colombia to the United Nations transmitted to the Secretary-General the text of a statement on the subject, issued on 25 February by the Ministers for Foreign Affairs of the countries members of the Permanent Mechanism for Consultation and Concerted Political Action (Group of Eight), namely, Argentina, Brazil, Colombia, Mexico, Panama, Peru, Uruguay and Venezuela.

37. On 3 March 1988, it was reported that the Argentine Government had announced that a series of measures involving defensive alert and surveillance and warning to navigation, would be enforced as long as the British military exercises lasted. 26/

38. The British military exercises began on 16 March 1988, 27/ when 1,000 British troops were airlifted from their bases to the assembly station on Ascension Island in mid-Atlantic, from where they continued south to the Falkland Islands (Malvinas), accompanied by a Nimrod reconnaissance craft, Hercules transports and other aircraft. Advance personnel and equipment from Britain aboard a Tristan wide-bodied jet were escorted in the final approach by two of the Phantom jets permanently based at the Mount Pleasant airfield in the Territory. The exercises ended on 31 March 1988 when the British troops returned to their bases in the United Kingdom. 28/

/...

A/AC.109/962
English
Page 9

39. With the completion of the Mount Pleasant airport complex (see A/AC.109/920, para. 38), most United Kingdom troops in the Territory, estimated at about 1,800, have moved to the complex. 29/

40. The estimated cost of the United Kingdom's defence budget relating to the Territory, including campaign and garrison costs, from 1 April 1982 to the end of fiscal year 1987/88 was reported as follows: 30/

Year	Millions of pounds sterling
1982/83	780
1983/84	637
1984/85	644
1985/86	572
1986/87	402
1987/88	141

IX. ECONOMIC CONDITIONS

A. General

41. The outlook of the economy of the Falkland Islands (Malvinas), which had been almost entirely dependent on the production of wool and its export, was reported to have changed owing to the increased importance of fisheries, following the establishment in 1986 of the Falkland Islands Interim Conservation and Management Zone (see A/AC.109/920 and Corr.1, paras. 22, 28-30, 57 and 58). In a foreword to the report of the Falkland Islands Development Corporation, 31/ the Chairman of the Corporation, who is also the Governor of the Territory, stated that the Islands now had "a source of income which should provide a sizeable surplus of income over expenditure for investment in development" (see paras. 48-50). According to the administering Power, the inhabitants of the Territory continue to be principally occupied in sheep-farming.

42. The Falkland Islands Development Corporation, which became operational in 1984, advises the territorial government in matters of general economic development. The corporation is vested with the authority to approve projects up to £250,000 without reference to the United Kingdom Overseas Development Administration. The annual amounts expended by the Overseas Development Administration since 1979 were reported as follows: 32/

/...

A/AC.109/962
English
Page 10

Year	Millions of pounds sterling
1979	0.915
1980	1.015
1981	1.058
1982	4.025
1983	9.053
1984	6.016
1985	10.700
1986	10.252
1987	8.165 a/

_____

a/   Provisional estimates.

43. Following the presentation to Parliament of the Falkland Islands Economic
Survey 1982, the United Kingdom Government allocated a fund of £31 million for
development over a six-year period (1983-1988) (see A/AC.109/878 and A/AC.109/920).

B.   Agriculture, land tenure and livestock

44. The Falkland Islands Company owns approximately 43 per cent of the total
farmland. The territorial government has been acquiring the islands' huge,
absentee-owned sheep ranches and subdividing and selling them in smaller units to
local farmers, thus encouraging the evolution of a farming system based on
owner-occupation and enabling the local farmers to retain earnings at home.
According to a report, 33/ while the land purchases by the Falkland Islands
Development Corporation have helped to create 35 to 45 new farms, many islanders
believed that the programme was also destroying a traditional way of life in which
workers lived in small, self-contained settlements.

45. The Agricultural Research Centre is responsible for agricultural expansion in
the Islands and deals with specific requests for advice. Its specialists in
agronomy, sheep husbandry and animal health provide support for farmers, in
particular new landholders under the land development scheme, on technical matters,
with the supporting farm business management advice of an agricultural economist.
The Centre is reportedly developing a multidisciplinary approach based on a number
of selected contact farms. The future work programme of the Centre has been
reviewed and reorganized in anticipation of the Falkland Islands Government
assuming responsibility for it from July 1988.

46. The staff of the Agricultural Department consists of an officer-in-charge, a
veterinary officer and two other workers. The Department's budgetary provisions
for 1986/87 amounted to £65,000.

47. The total number of sheep in the Territory in 1986-1987 was 692,150, as
compared with 698,879 in 1985-1986.

/...

A/AC.109/962
English
Page 11

C. Fisheries

48.   As reported previously (see A/AC.109/920, para. 57), the United Kingdom
Government issued on 29 October 1986 a "declaration on south-west Atlantic
fisheries". As a sequel to the declaration, the Falkland Islands Interim
Conservation and Management Zone was established on 1 February 1987 to protect fish
stocks against over fishing. Vessels fishing inside the zone require a licence
from the Falkland Islands Government. Under the licensing regime, the number of
fishing vessels is limited on the basis of the fish stock. In 1987, there were 200
vessels licensed to fish in the Zone, compared with 600 in 1986, prior to the
establishment of the Zone. During the fishing season which ended in June 1988,
there were 140 vessels licensed to fish in the northern zone and 43 in the southern
zone, and 74 were licensed for fin-fish in all areas. The Falkland Islands
Government estimated that the value of the annual catch was around £450 million.

49.   Following the declaration establishing the Zone, the Falkland Islands
Government decided that, when allocating licences for fishing, preference should be
given to companies prepared to enter into a joint venture with Stanley Fisheries
Limited, a subsidiary of Falkland Islands Development Corporation. 34/ Joint
ventures controlled by Stanley Fisheries Limited with a 51 per cent share-holding
were to be funded by the fishing companies which, in addition to fishing licences,
would pay sums equivalent to the licence fee to secure the joint venture
arrangement. The amount thus paid in was to be invested in development projects,
such as the purchase and chartering of trawlers, or improvement in port and
bunkering facilities, cold stores and fish processing. Under the scheme, one such
development, commercial exploitation of crab fishing, was being undertaken by a
joint venture. A pilot salmon farm was established in 1986 by the Falkland Islands
Development Corporation.

50.   According to a statement made on 29 April 1988 in the House of Commons by the
United Kingdom Secretary of State for Foreign and Commonwealth Affairs, 35/ the
revenue to the Falkland Islands Government from fishing licences and trans-shipping
fees for the 1987/88 financial year was estimated at £18.65 million. In addition,
Stanley Fisheries Limited received joint venture premiums of £16.2 million.

51.   In a statement issued on 3 February 1988, referring to unofficial reports that
the United Kingdom Government had issued fishing licences to vessels of different
nationalities to operate in the waters of the Falkland Islands (Malvinas), the
Foreign Ministry of Argentina said 36/ that the granting of licences resulted in
increased tension in the area and conspired against the initiatives to achieve
tranquillity in the zone and prevent the depredation of resources. It said that
the Argentine Government strongly opposed the effort to internationalize the waters
around the Malvinas and rejected the establishment of such a zone by the United
Kingdom.

52.   Since February 1987 the Government has been operating a Dornier twin-engined
aircraft in the surveillance of the Interim Conservation and Management Zone. It
was reported in April 1988 37/ that the Falkland Islands Government had begun
action to curb overfishing and illegal fishing in the south Atlantic. According to
the same report, a Korean vessel was seized and a Polish trawler fined at the end

/...

A/AC.109/962
English
Page 12

of April. The Korean vessel was reportedly found illegally fishing 25 nautical
miles within the 150-mile zone; the Polish trawler, although licensed to fish, was
reportedly found illegally trans-shipping part of its catch in excess of the catch
quotas.

D. Industry

53. The Falkland Islands Development Corporation provides grants and loans for
development projects at concessionary interest rates, aimed at increasing
self-sufficiency and the export of processed and manufactured products, as well as
achieving the maximum exploitation of the country's natural resources. The
Falkland Islands Tourism, a subsidiary of the Falkland Islands Development
Corporation established in 1985, promotes the Islands as a tourist destination. It
has financed the construction of a new tourist lodge on Sea Lion Island and
assisted the establishment of tourist lodges at Port Howard and Pebble Island. The
new tourist hotel, the Lodge, was opened in January 1988.

54. With assistance from the Falkland Islands Development Corporation, a number of
small businesses have also been established, including an electrical contractor, a
garage, a retailing co-operative, and a restaurant-bar.

E. Mining

55. There is no significant mining activity in the Territory. According to the
administering Power, the area may have some oil-yielding potential, although the
enormous development costs and the unpredictable weather conditions are likely to
limit the interest of oil companies in exploiting whatever resources might exist.

F. Energy

56. The Government-owned power station has been installed at the Fox Bay East
settlement, consisting of one 40 kW and one 112 kW diesel-driven generator.
Throughout the rest of the Islands, power is generated by small-engined generators.

57. The Government is currently installing additional equipment to raise the power
station's maximum output to 4.7 megawatts. A 10 kW wind generator was installed on
Pebbles Island in 1987. Interest in solar energy is growing with small units
powering electric fences.

G. Banking

58. The only bank is the Standard Chartered Bank of the United Kingdom which
opened a branch in Stanley in 1983 and provides a full range of banking
facilities. Both British and local coinage are used, together with local currency
notes of values £20, £10, £5 and £1.

/...

A/AC.109/962
English
Page 13

H. Public finance

59. Actual ordinary revenue increased from £6.6 million in 1985/86 to
£21.6 million for the year ended 30 June 1987, resulting from the considerable
increment in fisheries revenue, which accounted for £11 million, or 55.4 per cent
of the total revenue. Other main sources of revenue were: customs and harbour
receipts, £2.1 million, (10.2 per cent); public works, £2 million (9.5 per cent);
personal and company tax, £1.2 million (5.5 per cent); post and telecommunications,
£421.125 (1.9 per cent); and aviation, £294.341 (1.4 per cent).

60. Total actual expenditure amounted to £14.2 for 1986/87, as compared with
6.6 million in 1985/86. Of that amount, £8.7 million represented ordinary
expenditure and the balance, £5.5 million, was development expenditure.

61. The Territory's main imports are food products and tobacco, manufactured
goods, machinery and transport equipment. The United Kingdom remains almost
exclusively its main trade partner. Total imports in 1986 were valued at
£5.1 million, and total exports, consisting mainly of wool, at £2 million.

62. The Territory's gross national product for 1987 was estimated at
£30.2 million, compared with £9.6 million in 1986. National income from 1983 to
1987 rose as follows:

Year	National income	Per capita income
	(Pounds sterling)	
1983	6 370 000	3 420
1984	8 010 000	4 260
1985	8 980 000	4 730
1986	9 550 000	4 980
1987	30 220 000 a/	15 000

---

a/ Includes £7.2 million for Stanley Fisheries Limited and the
joint ventures and £12 million from fishing licences.

/...

A/AC.109/962
English
Page 14

X. SOCIAL AND EDUCATIONAL CONDITIONS

A. Labour and employment

63. No unemployment is reported to exist in the Territory. As of 1 January 1988, salaries for a 40-hour work-week were as follows:

	£
Handymen	97.60 - 108.40
	(according to ability)
Labourers (aged 18 and over)	95.20
Skilled labourers	98.80 - 109.20
Tradesmen	119.20

In the Camp, minimum monthly wages for a 40-hour work-week were as follows:

	£
General labourers over 18 years of age	283.21
Foremen	303.03
Shepherds living in settlements	333.04
Shepherds living outside settlements	351.95

64. In addition, a cost-of-living adjustment, reviewed regularly and adjusted accordingly, is paid to all employees. Labourers and shepherds also receive free quarters, fuel, meat and milk.

65. Extra bonuses are paid for shearing, while labourers and shepherds add to their earnings by engaging in contract work, such as fencing and peat cutting. Employees in the Camp are given 21 days' annual holidays, including nine public holidays.

66. There were 49 overseas personnel under contract, and 125 local and other employees at end of 1987. Also, a number of St. Helenian workers were employed in short-term contracts to fill essential vacancies.

B. Housing

67. The majority of the houses in Stanley are privately owned. The Government owns a number of houses which are rented to government employees and other residents of Stanley. Housing construction continues on behalf of the Island Government and in the private sector at an overall annual growth rate of about 12 per cent.

68. In October 1987, the Government announced 38/ that various projects were being initiated to alleviate the current housing shortage. Those projects included a contract valued at £2.7 million, on a joint venture basis, to build 30 houses on the Jersey Estate with units ranging from four bedrooms to a single bedroom, including all services, roads, footpaths and streetlights, to be completed in March 1989.

/...

A/AC.109/962
English
Page 15

69. Work also began in October 1987 on a plot near Lookout Camp, where 26 houses were to be built by the Housing Corporation Ltd., a company formed by a consortium of Stanley Fisheries Limited's joint venture partners, which was awarded the contract on its bid of £2.6 million. Fourteen two-bedroom, nine three-bedroom and three large dormitory units were expected to be completed by June 1988. The complex, known locally as "fishing village", was being built primarily to house fisheries' employees.

C. Public health

70. Medical and dental treatment and drugs are free to the residents of the Falkland Islands (Malvinas). All employed persons are required to pay a medical service levy of 1 per cent of their salary and employers 1.5 per cent of the salary paid. Self-employed persons contribute 1.5 per cent of their net income.

71. There is no private system of medical care. The Medical Department employs 6 registered medical practitioners, 18 registered nurses, 6 midwives, 8 untrained nursing auxiliaries, 2 sanitary inspectors, 3 laboratory and X-ray technicians, 2 dental surgeons and 1 pharmacist.

72. A new joint civilian/military hospital, the King Edward Memorial Hospital, built at a cost of about £13 million, was formally opened on 8 December 1987. The hospital is equipped with 28 beds, including 2 for intensive care, and two for maternity units. Facilities include an operating theatre suite, a pathology laboratory, an X-ray department and a casualty resuscitation department. The hospital civilian medical service provides primary care to the population of the Territory, to some military personnel and to the crews of the fishing fleets around the islands. It also provides a flying doctor service to outlying farm settlements. Secondary care for civilian, military and fishing crews is provided by the military surgeon, the anaesthetist and the operating team at the hospital.

73. In 1986/87 estimated recurrent expenditure on all aspects of health care and public health was £470,720 and estimated special expenditure was £7,390, as compared with £355,210 and £6,040, respectively, in 1985/86. Actual expenditure on social welfare for 1986/87 amounted to £178,480, as compared with £146,420 in 1985/86. Expenditure for 1988/89 is estimated at £268,200.

D. Educational conditions

74. Education is free. Attendance is compulsory in Stanley for all children between the ages of 5 and 15 years. Outside Stanley, attendance is compulsory for all children between 5 and 15 years living within 1.6 kilometres of a settlement school and for children between 7 and 15 years living within 3.2 kilometres of a settlement school. There is virtually no illiteracy in the Territory.

75. In 1987, school enrolment totalled 384 and there were 41 teachers, of whom 35 were formally qualified. There are seven schools: two in Stanley (a senior and a junior school), one in Goose Green, one in Fox Bay East and the rest are small

/...

A/AC.109/962
English
Page 16

settlement schools. Secondary education is available only in Stanley where 130 students are enrolled. There is a government boarding hostel in Stanley with accommodation for 85 older children attending senior school and the upper classes of the junior school.

76. All instruction in the schools throughout the Islands is given in English with textbooks obtained from the United Kingdom. Spanish has lately been reintroduced in the school curriculum. Opportunities exist for students to further their education in schools in the United Kingdom, financed by the United Kingdom Government, which also makes available bursaries for tertiary training. In 1987, no students were enrolled in schools in the United Kingdom.

77. For the year 1987/88, expenditure on education was estimated at £839,540, as compared with £547,000 in 1986/87. An additional amount of £35,350 was allocated for new equipment for Stanley schools, hostel and Camp education, and £340,060 for teachers and overseas training.

E.   Human rights

78. According to the administering Power, the principles set out in the Universal Declaration of Human Rights are observed in the Territory. In addition, the administering Power has extended the International Covenant on Civil and Political Rights and the International Covenant on Economic, Social and Cultural Rights to the Territory, although they are not embodied in any one legislative instrument. The Constitution forbids the enactment of laws that are discriminatory.

F.   Status of women

79. According to the administering Power, there is no discrimination on the basis of sex in the Territory, in conformity with articles 2 and 3 of the International Covenant on Civil and Political Rights.

Notes

1/   The information contained in this paper has been derived from official United Nations documentation, from published reports and from information transmitted to the Secretary-General by the Government of the United Kingdom of Great Britain and Northern Ireland under Article 73 e of the Charter of the United Nations on 29 June 1988 for the year 1987/88.

2/   The Times (London), 17 March 1987.

3/   The Guardian (London), 16 February 1987.

4/   South Atlantic Territories; the Falkland Islands Constitution Order 1985 (Statutory Instruments, 1985/444).

/...

A/AC.109/962
English
Page 17

Notes (continued)

5/   South Atlantic Territories; the South Georgia and South Sandwich Islands
Order, 1985 (Statutory Instruments, 1985/449).

6/   Statement by the Secretary of State for Foreign and Commonwealth Affairs,
Parliamentary Debates, House of Commons, 14 March 1985, cols. 492-494.

7/   The South Georgia and South Sandwich Islands Order, op. cit., sect. 4.

8/   La Nación (Buenos Aires), 25 July 1988.

9/   United Nations Information Centre, Washington, D.C., WAP/50/3,
1 March 1988.

10/   Communiqué dated 16 March 1988.

11/   Reuters, dispatch, London, 23 December 1987.

12/   Summary of World Broadcasts, ME/0142 D/1, 4 May 1988.

13/   A/S-15/PV.2.

14/   Summary of World Broadcasts, ME/0169 iii, 4 June 1988.

15/   A/43/403, annex.

16/   Financial Times, (London), 3 July 1988.

17/   Penguin News (Stanley), 27 November 1987.

18/   Ibid., 25 December 1988.

19/   Ibid., 22 January 1988.

20/   Parliamentary Debates, House of Commons (Hansard), 11 February 1988,
532.

21/   Ministry of Defence, press release, 12 February 1988.

22/   A/43/138-S/19500.

23/   A/43/169-S/19541.

24/   A/43/164.

25/   A/43/181-S/19559.

26/   Summary of World Broadcasts, ME/0092 D/1, 5 March 1988.

/...

A/AC.109/962
English
Page 18

Notes (continued)

27/   Reuters, dispatch, Stanley, 16 March 1988.

28/   Ibid., Buenos Aires, 31 March 1988.

29/   Financial Times (London), 25 and 29 February 1988; Reuters, dispatch, Stanley, 18 March 1988.

30/   Parliamentary Debates, House of Commons, 22 October 1987, col. 873; and ibid., 28 January 1988, col. 308.

31/   British Information Services, Survey of Current Affairs, vol. 17, No. 8, August 1987, p. 256.

32/   Parliamentary Debates, House of Commons, 18 April 1988, col. 295.

33/   National Geographic, vol. 173 (March 1988), p. 396.

34/   British Information Services, loc. cit.

35/   Parliamentary Debates, House of Commons, 29 April 1988.

36/   Foreign Broadcast Information Service, Daily Report, Latin America, 4 February 1988.

37/   Financial Times (London), 28 April 1988.

38/   Penguin News (Stanley), 23 October 1987 and 25 December 1987.

Annex 48: P. Beck, The Falkland Islands as an International
Problem (1988), p. 49-55.

CHANGING BRITISH PERCEPTIONS

The continuing Argentine challenge, in conjunction with changing international political and legal considerations, caused successive British governments to reappraise the nature and validity of their claim to the islands. Although research is hindered by the extended closure and unavailability of files, a relatively complete picture of British perceptions can be reconstructed in order to indicate that the public image of certainty offered by British governments was qualified in private by a series of doubts.[30] Considerable attention was devoted to the precise legal status of the Falklands in 1833 at a time when Britain presented Onslow's action as a re-occupation based upon pre-existing rights; subsequently Britain, treating sovereignty as non-negotiable and conscious of its power advantage, devoted little thought to either the topic or the alternative version advanced by its rival. During the 1900s the Foreign Office, noting a renewed Argentine challenge, instructed de Bernhardt to prepare a detailed study of the nature and development of the dispute. The resulting 49-page memorandum of 7 December 1910 was based upon an in-depth study of official files and other relevant sources — de Bernhardt confessed possible gaps in his account — and henceforth this paper, revised in 1928 and 1946, became an accepted British point of reference.[31]

De Bernhardt, concentrating upon the facts, refrained from comment upon the merits of British title. But to the reader, his history indicated various weaknesses in the traditional British case. There appeared no certainty about initial British discovery; there was no prior British settlement; there were only seven or eight years of British occupation before 1833; there were grounds for believing that any rights preserved by the 1774 plaque had lapsed through the passage of time; there existed evidence that prior to 1833 Argentina was in effective occupation of the islands; and there was the implication that in 1833 Britain seized control of a legitimate Argentine possession. In practice, the memorandum cast the seeds of doubt and shook official confidence in the strength of a case taken for granted, indeed accepted uncritically, for a long time, even if occasional doubts had been voiced (the Duke of Wellington in 1829, and the British Minister in Buenos Aires in 1885).[32] The contents of the study were not revealed to the outside world, and doubts were confined to a relatively small group of people, even within the Foreign Office. The memorandum was not sent to the Governor of the Falklands — indeed, W. A. Allardyce, the Governor, repeated the traditional history in his *The Story of the Falkland Islands* published in 1911 — while the British embassy in Argentina did not receive a copy until 1927. In public, there appeared no change in Britain's policy of non-negotiation on sovereignty.[83]

The impact of the 1910 memorandum upon official perceptions can be shown most effectively by reference to specific examples. In June 1910, for example, Gerald Spicer, head of the American department, minuted that the British claim to the Falklands 'cannot be seriously contested'.[84] But by 12 December his earlier confidence had evaporated: 'from a perusal of this memo it is difficult to avoid the conclusion that the Argentine government's attitude is not altogether unjustified, and that our action has been somewhat high-handed'. Then, in 1911 Ronald Campbell, an assistant secretary in the American department, demonstrated the manner in which Foreign Office thinking was moving away from an uncritical acceptance of the traditional view:

> The only question is who did have the best claim at the time when we finally annexed the islands. I think undoubtedly the United Provinces of Buenos Ayres . . . Spain had occupied the islands for about 30 years after our evacuation of Port Egmont. The subsequent Spanish evacuation was followed by a period of about ten years during which the islands were uninhabited before the United Provinces turned their attention to them and occupied them in some form or another for about ten years before they were ejected by us . . . We cannot easily make out a good claim, and we have very wisely done everything to avoid discussing the subject with Argentina.[85]

There is also the case of Sir Malcolm Robertson, the British ambassador in Buenos Aires, who informed the Falklands Governor in October 1927 that 'the feeling of the Argentines on the subject of the Falkland Islands is very strong, though they have not even a little toe on which to stand they maintain their claim'.[86] Then, a series of Anglo-Argentine difficulties caused the Foreign Office to send Robertson a copy of de Bernhardt's paper for information, and his next letter to the Governor reflected a transformation.

> If you have read with care the Foreign Office memorandum of 7 December 1910, you must surely have realised that the Argentine attitude is neither 'ridiculous' nor 'childish', as you describe it and I myself had thought it to be. I confess that,

until I received that memorandum myself a few weeks ago, I had no idea of the strength of the Argentine case nor of the weakness of ours . . . I freely admit that my attitude has changed since I wrote to you on 5 October. This has been caused by the Foreign Office memorandum. I had assumed that our right to the Falkland Islands was unassailable. This is very far from being the case.[87]

The year 1927 witnessed also the publication of *The Struggle for the Falkland Islands* by Julius Goebel, whose pro-Argentine, anti-British thesis challenged the traditional British case to title. Perhaps, this was true as far as the dispute's public dimension was concerned but, in reality, Goebel merely confirmed and reinforced existing British doubts about title. Robertson concluded that 'there does not appear to be anything new about the book which does not make our case any weaker than the Foreign Office Memorandum of 1910'. The book came to be interpreted as a respectable source capable of either elaborating points or covering gaps in de Bernhardt's paper, as shown in February 1928, when a revised Foreign Office history of the dispute made considerable use of Goebel's book; in fact, according to the memorandum's bibliography, this appeared to be the only source added since 1910.[88]

During the late 1920s and early 1930s, pre-existing official doubts about British title, the apparent escalation of Argentina's campaign to regain the islands, and Goebel's critique provided both the stimulus and the framework for a series of inter-departmental exchanges on sovereignty, a debate guided by the Foreign Office's legal advisers and partially obscured still by archival closures. In the meantime, the British government proved anxious in public to reaffirm the unchanging nature of its rationale, as implied in the critical review of Goebel's book written anonymously by Sir Cecil Hurst, the Foreign Office's chief legal adviser, for the 1928 *British Yearbook of International Law*.[89] These inter-departmental discussions concluded that previous arguments, centred upon prior discovery and settlement, appeared relatively weak and inappropriate as compared to those emphasising the length and peaceful nature of British occupation, a point accentuated by the 1933 centenary celebrations of British rule.[90] In 1934 one diplomat minuted that 'our best title is of prescription', while two years later Anthony Eden, the foreign minister, emphasised an approach based mainly upon post-1833 rather than pre-1833 criteria.[91]

One hundred years' possession, whether disputed or not, should found a perfectly sound title to sovereignty in international law. Meanwhile, each year that passes, and in addition the celebrations of the centenary of Britain's occupation, strengthens His Majesty's Government's case.

Beckett and Gerald Fitzmaurice, the Foreign Office's legal advisers, exerted a major influence over the inter-departmental discussions. Influenced by the Palmas judgement (1928) on prescriptive title and by Herbert Smith's preference (1935) for the length of occupation rather than 'the dubious claim' derived from the plaque, Beckett glossed over any doubts.

During this period of debate, the British government attempted to conceal any weaknesses in its case. In October 1936, for example, the Royal Institute of International Affairs (RIIA) reflected the sensitivity of the issue when it decided to consult the Foreign Office about the draft of its forthcoming volume on South America. In response, the Foreign Office urged textual changes of sections likely to be exploited by Argentina as emanating from a respected and 'semi-official source'. The RIIA agreed to replace two phrases — these stated that 'Great Britain annexed the Falkland Islands from Argentina in 1833' and 'annexed them by force in 1833' — with a more neutral form of words; thus, *The Republics of South America*, published in 1937, indicated that 'in 1833 HMS *Clio* took the opportunity of occupying the islands in the name of His Britannic Majesty and struck the Argentine flag'.

The Falklands problem re-emerged after the Second World War, and in September 1946 the Foreign Office, having earlier reaffirmed that 'continuous possession for over a century must now be held to constitute the best British title', codified the state of British thinking on the subject in a manner offering a revealing insight into British attitudes of contemporary relevance:

Discovery — The evidence for British priority of discovery is unsatisfactory, but irrelevant.

Occupation — The British case for priority of occupation over the French (1764) is untenable, since the British occupation was not made effective until 1766 . . .

The Secret Understanding of 1770 — There is no evidence to support the belief that a verbal pledge to withdraw from the Falklands was given by Lord North in November 1770. It cannot, however, be wholly proven . . . To accept the fact of a secret pledge is definitely to demolish the British case prior to 1833.

The leaden plaque of 1774 — . . . the British did not return to the Falkland Islands for 60 years, during which their claim may be deemed to have lapsed.

Spanish Withdrawal 1811 — in 1811 . . . the Falkland Islands

> ... in the British view, became *terra nullius* ... Regarding state succession, His Majesty's Government have consistently denied the right whereby the insurgent South American republics accepted among themselves the territorial delimitations of the Spanish Vice-royalties ...
>
> *Non-effective occupation by Argentina* — The Falkland Islands were unoccupied between 1811 and 1826, apart from a brief interval in 1824. In 1823 'a Governor' of the Islands was appointed, but no formal act of possession was carried out ... In their decree of the 10th June 1829 the Buenos Aires Government admitted that 'circumstances' had hitherto prevented any real exercise of sovereignty ... Louis Vernet ... was appointed Governor by a further decree of 1829. This title carried no more weight than did the appointment made in 1823 ...
>
> *Prescription 1833–1946* — Great Britain has been in formal possession and effective occupation of the Falklands since 1833; at that date the Islands were ineffectively occupied by the Buenos Aires Government, and it may be argued that they were thus open to acquisition by the first effectively occupying Power. In this sense, the British occupation of 1833 was, at the time, an act of unjustifiable aggression which has now acquired the backing of the rights of prescription.

The Foreign Office, conceding the confusing nature of the evidence on the early period, concluded that 'the respective positions of Britain and Argentina are best considered as from 1811', that is, the date when Spain was considered to have evacuated the islands. Although the memorandum mentioned the 'entirely British' nature of the population, there was as yet no reference to self-determination.

In this manner, the period between the two World Wars witnessed a significant transformation in the nature of the British rationale employed to support its title, since the case altered from the initial stress upon pre-1833 criteria towards one based upon post-1833 factors, a transformation prompted by changing perceptions of the legal and historical circumstances. However, according to the Foreign Office:

> It would be misleading to attach any particular significance to what appear to be shifts in the factors which at any particular time carried most weight in the Government's thinking. Our case is based on *all* the facts and circumstances both before and after 1833. For example, the right of self determination, which is now an important part of our case, has emerged only relatively recently as a principle of international law ... With a subject as complicated as the history of the Falklands and

the conclusions that may be drawn from that history for sovereignty, it is inevitable that there will be differing and, in some cases, conflicting views.[93]

Annex 49: Joint British and Argentine Statement, Madrid,
October 19, 1989 (Resumption of Relations)

MADRID, 19 OCTOBER 1989

1. DELEGATIONS OF THE BRITISH AND ARGENTINE GOVERNMENTS MET
IN MADRID FROM 17 TO 19 OCTOBER 1989. THE BRITISH DELEGATION
WAS LED BY SIR CRISPIN TICKELL, UNITED KINGDOM PERMANENT
REPRESENTATIVE TO THE UNITED NATIONS, AND THE ARGENTINE
DELEGATION BY AMBASSADOR LUCIO GARCIA DEL SOLAR, SPECIAL
REPRESENTATIVE OF THE GOVERNMENT OF ARGENTINA. THE PURPOSE OF
THEIR MEETING WAS TO DISCUSS THE TOPICS AGREED AT THEIR FIRST
MEETING IN NEW YORK IN AUGUST,VIZ

"(I)   INTRODUCTORY STATEMENTS

(II)   FORMULA ON SOVEREIGNTY

(III)   ORGANIZATION OF WORK

(IV)   BRITISH/ARGENTINE RELATIONS (INCLUDING THE FUTURE
        OF DIPLOMATIC AND CONSULAR RELATIONS):

        (A) MEASURES TO BUILD CONFIDENCE AND AVOID
            INCIDENTS IN THE MILITARY SPHERE

        (B) TRADE AND FINANCIAL RELATIONS

        (C) COMMUNICATIONS LINKS: AIR AND SEA

        (D) FISHERY CONSERVATION AND FUTURE CO-OPERATION
            ON FISHERIES

        (E) CONTACTS BETWEEN THE FALKLAND ISLANDS AND THE
            CONTINENTAL MAINLAND

        (F) CULTURAL, SCIENTIFIC AND SPORTING RELATIONS

        (G) OTHER BILATERAL MATTERS."

2. BOTH GOVERNMENTS AGREED THAT:

    "(1) NOTHING IN THE CONDUCT OR CONTENT OF THE PRESENT
MEETING OR OF ANY SIMILAR SUBSEQUENT MEETINGS SHALL BE
INTERPRETED AS:
                (A) A CHANGE IN THE POSITION OF THE UNITED
                    KINGDOM WITH REGARD TO SOVEREIGNTY OR
                    TERRITORIAL AND MARITIME JURISDICTION
                    OVER THE FALKLAND ISLANDS, SOUTH GEORGIA
                    AND THE SOUTH SANDWICH ISLANDS AND THE
                    SURROUNDING MARITIME AEREAS;

TEL: 03.07.91 16:01 No.003 P.

(B) A CHANGE IN THE POSITION OF THE ARGENTINE
    REPUBLIC WITH REGARD TO SOVEREIGNTY OR
    TERRITORIAL AND MARITIME JURISDICTION
    OVER THE FALKLAND ISLANDS, SOUTH GEORGIA
    AND THE SOUTH SANDWICH ISLANDS AND THE
    SURROUNDING MARITIME AEREAS;

(C) RECONGNITION OF OR SUPPORT FOR THE
    POSITION OF THE UNITED KINGDOM OR THE
    ARGENTINE REPUBLIC WITH REGARD TO
    SOVEREIGNTY OR TERRITORIAL AND
    MARITIME JURISDICTION OVER THE
    FALKLAND ISLANDS, SOUTH GEORGIA AND
    THE SOUTH SANDWICH ISLANDS AND THE
    SURROUNDING MARITIME AEREAS.

(2) NO ACT OR ACTIVITY CARRIED OUT BY THE UNITED
KINGDOM, THE ARGENTINE REPUBLIC OR THIRD PARTIES AS A
CONSEQUENCE AND IN IMPLEMENTATION OF ANYTHING AGREED TO IN
THE PRESENT MEETING OR IN ANY SIMILAR SUBSEQUENT MEETINGS
SHALL CONSTITUTE A BASIS FOR AFFIRMING, SUPPORTING, OR
DENYING THE POSITION OF THE UNITED KINGDOM OR THE ARGENTINE
REPUBLIC REGARDING THE SOVEREIGNTY OR TERRITORIAL AND
MARITIME JURISDICTION OVER THE FALKALND ISLANDS, SOUTH
GEORGIA AND THE SOUTH SANDWICH ISLANDS AND THE SURROUNDING
MARITIME AEREAS."

3. THE TWO GOVERNMENTS CONFIRMED THEIR COMMITMENT TO RESPECT
FULLY THE PRINCIPLES OF THE CHARTER OF THE UNITED NATIONS, IN
PARTICULAR:

- THE OBLIGATION TO SETTLE DISPUTES EXCLUSIVELY BY PEACEFUL
MEANS; AND

- THE OBLIGATION TO REFRAIN FROM THE THREAT OR USE OF FORCE.

THE TWO GOVERNMENTS NOTED THAT ALL HOSTILITIES BETWEEN THEM
HAD CEASED. EACH GOVERNMENT UNDERTOOK NOT TO PURSUE ANY CLAIM
AGAINST THE OTHER, INCLUDING NATIONALS OF THE OTHER, IN
RESPECT OF LOSS OR DAMAGE ARISING FROM THE HOSTILITIES AND
ALL OTHER ACTIONS IN AND AROUND THE FALKLAND ISLANDS, SOUTH
GEORGIA AND THE SOUTH SANDWICH ISLANDS BEFORE 1989.

4. BOTH GOVERNMENTS AGREED, FOLLOWING NOTIFICATION OF THE TWO
PROTECTING POWERS, TO RE-ESTABLISH CONSULAR RELATIONS AT THE
LEVEL OF CONSUL GENERAL.

5. BOTH GOVERNMENTS REAFFIRMED THEIR WISH TO NORMALIZE
RELATIONS BETWEEN THEIR TWO COUNTRIES WITH A VIEW TO RESUMING
DIPLOMATIC RELATIONS, AND AGREED TO INCLUDE THE QUESTION OF
DIPLOMATIC RELATIONS ON THE AGENDA FOR THEIR NEXT MEETING.

6. THE DELEGATIONS EXCHANGED VIEWS AND PROPOSALS ABOUT MEASURES TO BUILD CONFIDENCE AND AVOID INCIDENTS IN THE MILITARY SPHERE. AS A RESULT OF THESE EXCHANGES THEY AGREED TO SET UP A WORKING GROUP TO CONSIDER THESE VIEWS AND PROPOSALS, AND TO REPORT TO THEIR RESPECTIVE GOVERNMENTS WITH THE AIM OF PURSUING THE ISSUE AT THE NEXT SUBSTANTIVE MEETING.

MEANWHILE, WITH THE AIM OF STRENGTHENING MUTUAL CONFIDENCE, THE BRITISH DELEGATION ANNUNCED THE BRITISH GOVERNMENT'S DECISIONS:

- TO DISPENSE WITH THE CURRENT REQUIREMENT OF PRIOR AGREEMENT FOR ARGENTINE MERCHANT SHIPPING TO ENTER THE PROTECTION ZONE.

- TO ALIGN THE LIMITS OF THE PROTECTION ZONE WITH THOSE OF THE CONSERVATION ZONE.

THESE CHANGES WILL COME INTO EFFECT AT AN EARLY DATE TO BE ANNOUNCED.

THE ARGENTINE DELEGATION TOOK NOTE OF THIS ANNOUNCEMENT.

7. EACH DELEGATION AFFIRMED THE WISH OF ITS GOVERNMENT TO PROMOTE COMMERCIAL AND FINANCIAL RELATIONS. BOTH GOVERNMENTS AGREED TO LIFT ALL REMAINING RESTRICTIONS AND RESTRICTIVE PRACTICES IMPOSE SINCE 1982. IN THE LIGHT OF THIS AGREEMENT, THE BRITISH GOVERNMENT AGREED TO FACILITATE THE ESTABLISHMENT OF COOPERATIVE LINKS BETWEEN ARGENTINA AND THE EUROPEAN COMMUNITY.

8. THE BRITISH DELEGATION ANNOUNCED THAT THE EXPORT CREDIT GUARANTEE DEPARTMENT WOULD MAKE AVAILABLE SHORT-TERM COVER FOR BRITISH EXPORTERS TO ARGENTINA UNDER IRREVOCABLE LETTERS OF CREDIT FROM ARGENTINE BANKS. THE BRITISH DELEGATION ALSO ANNOUNCED THAT A TRADE MISSION ORGANIZED BY THE LATIN AMERICAN TRADE ADVISORY GROUP OF THE BRITISH OVERSEAS TRADE BOARD WOULD VISIT ARGENTINA FROM 27 NOVEMBER TO 1 DECEMBER 1989 WITH THE FINANCIAL SUPPORT OF THE DEPARTMENT OF TRADE AND INDUSTRY. THE ARGENTINE DELEGATION WELCOMED THIS PROPOSED VISIT.

9. BOTH GOVERNMENTS AGREED TO THE RESUMPTION OF AIR AND MARITIME COMMUNICATIONS BETWEEN THE TWO COUNTRIES. THEY WILL INVITE THEIR RESPECTIVE CIVIL AVIATION AUTHORITIES TO OPEN APPROPRIATE NEGOTIATIONS.

10. AS REGARDS FISHERIES, BOTH DELEGATIONS PUT FORWARD THEIR RESPECTIVE POSITIONS. THEY AGREED TO SET UP A WORKING GROUP

TEL: 03.07.91 16:01 No.005 P.05

WITH A VIEW TO MAKING PROPOSALS FOR EXCHANGES OF INFORMATION, FOR MEASURES OF COOPERATION AND FOR CONSERVATION MEASURES, TO BE REPORTED TO A FUTURE MEETING.

11. THE TWO DELEGATIONS EXCHANGED VIEWS ON CONTACTS BETWEEN THE FALKLAND ISLANDS AND THE CONTINENTAL MAINLAND, AND AGREED ON THE BENEFIT OF DEVELOPING SUCH LINKS AND TO KEEP THE MATTER UNDER REVIEW.

12. BOTH DELEGATIONS EXPRESSED THEIR SUPPORT FOR THE CULTURAL, SCIENTIFIC AND SPORTING RELATIONS WHICH ALREADY EXISTED AND LOOKED FORWARD TO THEIR FURTHER DEVELOPMENT. THEY EXPRESSED THEIR HOPE THAT AS NORMALIZATION ADVANCED MORE FORMAL RELATIONS IN THESE FIELDS WOULD BE RESUMED, FOR EXAMPLE THROUGH A NEW CULTURAL AGREEMENT.

13. IT WAS AGREED THAT BOTH GOVERNMENTS WOULD JOINTLY SEND THE TEXT OF THE PRESENT STATEMENT TO THE SECRETARY GENERAL OF THE UNITED NATIONS FOR DISTRIBUTION AS AN OFFICIAL DOCUMENT OF THE GENERAL ASSEMBLY, UNDER ITEM 35 OF THE AGENDA OF THE CURRENT SESSION, AND OF THE SECURITY COUNCIL. THE UNITED KINGDOM WILL TRANSMIT THIS JOINT STATEMENT TO THE COMMISSION OF THE EUROPEAN COMMUNITY, AND, FOR ITS PART, THE REPUBLIC OF ARGENTINA WILL DO LIKEWISE TO THE ORGANIZATION OF AMERICAN STATES.

14. BOTH DELEGATIONS AGREED TO HOLD THEIR NEXT SUBSTANTIVE MEETING IN MADRID ON 14 AND 15 FEBRUARY 1990.

15. IN CONCLUSION BOTH DELEGATIONS EXPRESSED THEIR THANKS TO THE SPANISH GOVERNMENT FOR ITS GENEROUS HOSPITALITY AND SUPPORT.

MADRID, 19 OCTOBER 1989.

Ministerio de Relaciones Exteriores y Culto
Dirección General de Prensa

JOINT STATEMENT BY THE BRITISH AND ARGENTINE DELEGATIONS
MADRID - 15 FEBRUARY 1990

1. Delegations of the British and Argentine Governments, as agreed at their meeting in Madrid in October 1989, met again in Madrid on 14 and 15 February 1990. The British delegation was led by Sir Crispin Tickell, United Kingdom Permanent Representative to the United Nations, and the Argentine delegation by Ambassador Lucio Garcia del Solar, Special Representative of the Government of Argentina.

2. Both delegations reaffirmed that the formula on sovereignty over the Falkland Islands (Islas Malvinas), South Georgia and the South Sandwich Islands and the surrounding maritime areas, recorded in paragraph 2 of the Joint Statement of 19 October 1989, applied to this meeting and its consequences.

3. Both Governments, wishing to develop further friendship and cooperation between their two peoples, agreed to re-establish diplomatic relations following notification of the Protecting Powers. Embassies will be re-opened shortly and Ambassadors appointed in accordance with international practice.

4. The British delegation announced the decision of the British Government to lift the Protection Zone established around the Falkland Islands (Islas Malvinas).

5. Both Governments approved with satisfaction the final report of the "British-Argentine Working Group about measures to build confidence and avoid incidents in the military sphere" and decided, under the terms of the formula on sovereignty referred to in paragraph 2 of this Joint Statement, the following:

   (a) To establish an "Interim reciprocal information and consultation system" for movements of units of their armed forces

in areas of the South West Atlantic. The aims of this system are
to increase confidence between the United Kingdom and Argentina
and to contribute to achieving a more normal situation in the
region without unnecessary delay. (The text of this agreement is
included as Annex I to this Joint Statement.)

(b)   To establish a direct communication link between the
Falkland Islands (Islas Malvinas) and the mainland in order to
reduce the possibility of incidents, to limit their consequences
in the case of occurrence, and to increase common knowledge of
military activities in the South West Atlantic. (See Annex I)

(c)   To agree on a set of rules of reciprocal behaviour for naval
and air units of their armed forces when operating in proximity.
(See Annex II).

(d)   To agree on a mechanism for emergencies aimed at
facilitating air and maritime search and rescue operations in the
South-West Atlantic. (See Annex III).

(e)   To establish a system of exchange of information on the
safety and control of air and maritime navigation. (See Annex
IV).

(f)   To continue bilateral consideration of these matters and to
review the measures agreed upon within one year from their coming
into force.

6.   The agreements described in paragraph 5 will enter into force on
the 31st of March 1990. On the same day the decision mentioned in
paragraph 4 will be implemented.

7.   Both delegations expressed the satisfaction of their governments
with the report of the Working Group on fisheries which met in Paris
on 18 and 19 December 1989. It was agreed that both governments
should proceed - through their respective Foreign Ministries - to
exchange available information on the operations of the fishing
fleets, appropriate catch and effort statistics and analyses of the
status of the stocks of the most significant off-shore species in the

maritime area of the Atlantic Ocean between latitude 45 degrees S and latitude 60 degrees S. They also agreed to assess jointly such information, and to explore bilaterally the possibilities for cooperation and conservation.

8. Both governments decided to set up a Working Group on South Atlantic Affairs with the mandate to continue consideration of the issues entrusted to the two working groups mentioned in paragraphs 5 and 7 of this Joint Statement. The Working Group will meet as frequently as the parties consider necessary; its first meeting will be held within one year of the date of this Joint Statement.

9. Both delegations considered the situation regarding contacts between the Falkland Islands (Islas Malvinas) and the mainland and agreed to continue considering this matter. The British delegation recognised the Argentine readiness to facilitate communications and trading opportunities between the Islands and the mainland.

10. Both delegations expressed their agreement to a visit to the cemetery on the Falkland Islands (Islas Malvinas) by close relatives of Argentine nationals buried there. The visit - based on humanitarian considerations - will take place under the auspices of the International Committee of the Red Cross (ICRC). Both governments will seek the good offices of the ICRC and agree, through diplomatic channels, on the arrangements for and timing of the visit.

11. Both delegations agreed that the feasibility and desirability of a general cooperation agreement should be examined through diplomatic channels.

12. Both governments, recognising that the promotion and reciprocal protection of investments should encourage private initiative and increase prosperity in both states, agreed to begin, through diplomatic channels, the negotiation of an Investment Promotion and Protection Agreement.

13. Both delegations agreed that it would be appropriate to abolish

the requirement for visas for nationals of each country wishing to
visit the other. This measure would become effective once
negotiations had been concluded through diplomatic channels.

14.   Both governments, conscious of the need to increase efforts to
protect the environment, will work to ensure bilateral consultation and
cooperation, including within the international institutions.

15.   Both governments, recognising the threat which illicit drugs and
drug abuse have created for all countries, agreed to explore ways of
collaborating in this field, including exchanges of information,
control of trafficking and an agreement to trace, freeze and
confiscate the proceeds of drug trafficking. The Argentine
delegation announced that its government would be represented at the
world conference on "Demand Reduction and the Cocaine Threat" to be
held in London in April 1990.

16.   Both delegations, noting the importance of current international
trends towards greater political and economic interdependence and
integration, agreed to consult through diplomatic channels on these
trends, particularly those concerning the European Community and
Latin America.

17.   It was agreed that both Governments would jointly send the text
of the present statement and its annexes to the Secretary General of
the United Nations for distribution as an official document of the
General Assembly, under Item 35 of the Agenda of the 44th regular
session, and of the Security Council. The United Kingdom will
transmit this Joint Statement to the Presidency and Commission of the
European Community, and the Government of Argentina will do likewise
to the Organisation of American States.

18.   In conclusion, both delegations expressed their thanks to the
Spanish government for its generous hospitality and support.

INTERIM RECIPROCAL INFORMATION AND CONSULTATION SYSTEM

Both parties agree to establish an Interim Reciprocal Information
and Consultation System for movements of units of their Armed
Forces in areas of the South West Atlantic. The aims of this
system are to increase confidence between the United Kingdom and
Argentina and to contribute to achieving a more normal situation
in the region without unnecessary delay. The system consists of
the following provisions:

I.   Direct Communication Link

A.   A direct communication link will be established between the
respective military authorities - under the supervision of both
Foreign Ministries - in order to:

    - Reduce the possibility of incidents and limit their
       consequences if they should occur;

    - Increase common knowledge of military activities in the
       South West Atlantic.

B.   The respective military authorities will be:

        Argentine Naval Authority: Comandante del Area Naval
        Austral (Ushuaia).

        Argentine Air Authority: Jefe de la Novena Brigada Aérea
        (Comodoro Rivadavia).

British Authority: Commander British Forces Falkland
Islands (Malvinas).

C.   It is agreed to establish a direct radio link between the
respective authorities which will include voice and/or telex
transmissions. The link will be manned on a 24 hour basis and
will be tested at least once a week. Technical information
relating to equipment, frequencies and modalities of use will be
exchanged through diplomatic channels.

D.   It is agreed to establish a communications plan for radio
links between units and stations of the parties. Technical
information will be exchanged through diplomatic channels.

II.   Definition of Units

A.   Ship

Any ship belonging to the naval forces of the parties bearing the
external marks distinguishing warships of its nationality, under
the command of an officer duly commissioned by the government and
whose name appears in the naval list, and manned by a crew who are
under regular naval discipline, and British Fleet Auxiliaries.

B.   Aircraft

Any aircraft belonging to the Armed Forces of the parties, manned
by a military crew who are under regular Armed Forces discipline.

C.   Combatant Units

Any ship or aircraft equipped with weapons systems or means of
offensive power or offensive projection capabilities (naval
examples: aircraft carriers, cruisers, destroyers, frigates,
corvettes, submarines, fast patrol boats, amphibious ships or
ships carrying troops; aircraft examples: strike aircraft,
fighters, bombers, missile or troop-carrying aircraft).

III.   Reciprocal Information about Military Movements

1.   Reciprocal written information will be provided through
diplomatic channels, not less than 25 days in advance, about:

   A. Movements of naval forces involving four or more ships;

   B. Movements of aerial forces involving four or more
      aircraft;

   C. Exercises involving more than 1000 men or more than 20
      sorties by aircraft;

   D. Amphibious or airborne exercises involving more than 500
      men or more than 20 sorties by aircraft.

The areas of application of this measure are:

   For Argentine Forces: within rhumb lines joining the
   following geographical coordinates in the specified order:
   46S 63W, 50S 63W, 50S 64W, 53S 64W, 53S 63W, 60S 63W,
   60S 20W, 46S 20W, 46S 63W

   For British Forces: the area south of parallel 40°S and west of meridian 20°W and north of 60°S.

Each party will accept the presence of an observer ship from the other party in the vicinity of naval forces involving four or more ships engaged in manoeuvres within the relevant area of application.

2.   Reciprocal notification of identity, intended track and purpose will be given, not less than 48 hours in advance, of a ship or an aircraft that intends to approach closer to coasts than 50 nautical miles by sea or 70 nautical miles by air.

When specific movements of the kind described in this paragraph are intended to be carried out by combatant units and might cause political or military difficulty to the Argentine Government or to the British Government, the notifying party will be informed immediately and mutual agreement will be necessary to proceed.

IV.   <u>Verification</u>

Verification of compliance with the reciprocal information arrangements in provision III above will be by national means, by observer ships (as provided for in III.1), and by consultations through the direct communication link. If disagreement should arise, the parties would have recourse to the diplomatic channel.

V.   <u>Reciprocal Visits</u>

Reciprocal visits to military bases and naval units may be agreed through the diplomatic channel on a case by case basis.

VI.   Applicability of International Practice

In situations not specifically covered in this system, it is
understood that normal international practice will be applied on a
reciprocal basis.

VII.   Duration

This system, including the reciprocal information measures, will
be reviewed at regular diplomatic-technical meetings.   The first
of these meetings will take place within one year after the entry
into force of the system and will be convened at a date to be
agreed through the diplomatic channel.

SAFETY MEASURES FOR NAVAL AND AIR UNITS WHEN OPERATING
IN PROXIMITY

When operating in proximity, Naval and Air units of the parties
will comply with the following general regulations and rules:

   a)   Naval and Air units of the parties shall avoid any
        movement or action that might be interpreted as a
        hostile act or an act carried out with hostile intent.

   b)   Naval units of the parties shall manoeuvre in a manner
        that clearly show their intentions and shall strictly
        observe the letter and spirit of the international
        regulations for preventing collisions at sea of 1972.

   c)   Air units shall use the greatest caution and prudence
        when manoeuvring in proximity to units of the other

party, in order to contribute to safety and avoid
mutual interference.

d)   Naval and air units of the parties shall not simulate
attacks nor aim guns, missile launchers, torpedo tubes,
other weapons or fire control radars in the direction
of units of the other party.

e)   Naval and air units of the parties shall not launch any
object in the direction of passing ships or aircraft of
the other party, nor use searchlights or other powerful
illumination devices to illuminate their navigation
bridges.

f)   Naval and Air units of the parties operating in
proximity shall avoid the darkening of lights and, in
this respect, shall comply with the International
Regulations for Preventing Collisions at Sea of 1972
and the provisions of Annex VI of the Convention on
International Civil Aviation of 1944.

g)   On no account shall the communication and detection
systems of units of the other party be interfered with
or disrupted.

h)   A prompt exchange of information shall be conducted in
the event of any occurrence which might cause concern
to the other party.

MARITIME AND AIR SEARCH AND RESCUE

When communication or coordination is required in relation to

maritime and air search and rescue (SAR), the following
procedures will apply:

a)   The headquarters of the British Forces in the Falkland
     Islands (Islas Malvinas) shall inform the regional SAR
     Coordination Centres of the Southwest Atlantic Area:

     Maritime SAR: Ushuaia Maritime SAR Coordination Centre

     Air SAR: Comodoro Rivadavia Air SAR Coordination
                     Centre

b)   Maritime SAR operations shall be conducted in
     accordance with the SAR manual of the International
     Maritime Organisation and the SAR manual for Merchant
     Ships.   Air SAR operations shall be conducted in
     accordance with the provisions of Annex XII to the
     Convention on International Civil Aviation and its
     amendments.

c)   In the event that joint participation in a SAR incident
     becomes necessary, the headquarters of the British
     Forces in the Falkland Islands (Islas Malvinas) and the
     appropriate Argentine SAR Coordination Centre will
     coordinate their activities.

SAFETY OF NAVIGATION

1.   The parties will exchange all relevant information so that
Argentina, the Regional Coordinator of Navarea VI, as defined by
the International Maritime Organisation, may issue the

appropriate notices to mariners for that area.

2. In order to enhance flight safety, the parties agreed:

a) to facilitate the operation of Argentine Flight
Information Centres by supplying the information
necessary for Argentina to provide the Air Traffic
Control, Warning, Search and Rescue, Communication and
Meteorological Services within the Argentine Flight
Information Regions (FIR);

b) to exchange information between the Falkland Islands
(Islas Malvinas) and Comodoro Rivadavia (CRV) Flight
Information Centre for identification of aircraft in
flight in the FIRs, in particular on flights in the
vicinity of coastal areas;

c) to respond positively in an emergency to requests to
provide alternative landing facilities at their
airfields for each other's aircraft and aircraft of
third parties; and

d) to exchange aeronautical information about the
airfields of both parties (navigation, approach and
surface facilities).

Annex 50: Joint British and Argentine Statement of
February 15, 1990 (concerning further development
of relations)

GENERAL ASSEMBLY   SECURITY COUNCIL
Forty-fifth session   Forty-fifth year
Item 37 of the preliminary list*
QUESTION OF THE FALKLAND ISLANDS (MALVINAS)

   Letter dated 21 February 1990 from the Permanent Representatives
   of Argentina and the United Kingdom of Great Britain and Northern
   Ireland to the United Nations addressed to the Secretary-General

   We have the honour to convey to Your Excellency the text of the joint
statement and its attachments (see annex) issued at the conclusion of a meeting
between representatives of the Governments of Argentina and the United Kingdom of
Great Britain and Northern Ireland, held in Madrid on 14 and 15 February 1990.

   We request that the present note and its annex be circulated as an official
document of the General Assembly, under item 37 of the preliminary list, and of the
Security Council.

   (Signed) Crispin TICKELL   (Signed) Jorge VAZQUEZ

---

   *   A/45/50.

90-04434 1430e (E)   /...

A/45/136
S/21159
English
Page 2

ANNEX

Joint statement by the British and Argentine delegations

(Madrid - 15 February 1990)

1.   Delegations of the British and Argentine Governments, as agreed at their
meeting in Madrid in October 1989, met again in Madrid on 14 and 15 February 1990.
The British delegation was led by Sir Crispin Tickell, Permanent Representative of
the United Kingdom of Great Britain and Northern Ireland to the United Nations, and
the Argentine delegation by Ambassador Lucio García del Solar, Special
Representative of the Government of Argentina.

2.   Both delegations reaffirmed that the formula on sovereignty over the Falkland
Islands (Islas Malvinas), South Georgia and the South Sandwich Islands and the
surrounding maritime areas, recorded in paragraph 2 of the joint statement of
19 October 1989, applied to this meeting and its consequences.

3.   Both Governments, wishing to develop further friendship and co-operation
between their two peoples, agreed to re-establish diplomatic relations following
notification of the Protecting Powers. Embassies will be reopened shortly and
Ambassadors appointed in accordance with international practice.

4.   The British delegation announced the decision of the British Government to
lift the Protection Zone established around the Falkland Islands (Islas Malvinas).

5.   Both Governments approved with satisfaction the final report of the
"British-Argentine Working Group about measures to build confidence and avoid
incidents in the military sphere" and decided, under the terms of the formula on
sovereignty referred to in paragraph 2 of the present joint statement, the
following:

      (a) To establish an "Interim reciprocal information and consultation system"
for movements of units of their armed forces in areas of the south-west Atlantic.
The aims of this system are to increase confidence between the United Kingdom and
Argentina and to contribute to achieving a more normal situation in the region
without unnecessary delay (the text of this agreement is included as appendix I to
the present joint statement);

      (b) To establish a direct communication link between the Falkland Islands
(Islas Malvinas) and the mainland in order to reduce the possibility of incidents,
to limit their consequences in the case of occurrence, and to increase common
knowledge of military activities in the south-west Atlantic (see appendix I);

      (c) To agree on a set of rules of reciprocal behaviour for naval and air
units of their armed forces when operating in proximity (see appendix II);

      (d) To agree on a mechanism for emergencies aimed at facilitating air and
maritime search and rescue operations in the south-west Atlantic (see appendix III);

/...

A/45/136
S/21159
English
Page 3

(e) To establish a system of exchange of information on the safety and control of air and maritime navigation (see appendix IV);

(f) To continue bilateral consideration of these matters and to review the measures agreed upon within one year from their coming into force.

6.   The agreements described in paragraph 5 above will enter into force on 31 March 1990. On the same day, the decision mentioned in paragraph 4 above will be implemented.

7.   Both delegations expressed the satisfaction of their Governments with the report of the Working Group on Fisheries, which met in Paris on 18 and 19 December 1989. It was agreed that both Governments should proceed - through their respective Foreign Ministries - to exchange available information on the operations of the fishing fleets, appropriate catch and effort statistics and analyses of the status of the stocks of the most significant offshore species in the maritime area of the Atlantic Ocean between latitude 45 degrees S and latitude 60 degrees S. They also agreed to assess jointly such information, and to explore bilaterally the possibilities for co-operation and conservation.

8.   Both Governments decided to set up a Working Group on South Atlantic Affairs with the mandate to continue consideration of the issues entrusted to the two working groups mentioned in paragraphs 5 and 7 of the present joint statement. The Working Group will meet as frequently as the parties consider necessary; its first meeting will be held within one year of the date of this joint statement.

9.   Both delegations considered the situation regarding contacts between the Falkland Islands (Islas Malvinas) and the mainland and agreed to continue considering this matter. The British delegation recognized the Argentine readiness to facilitate communications and trading opportunities between the Islands and the mainland.

10.   Both delegations expressed their agreement to a visit to the cemetery on the Falkland Islands (Islas Malvinas) by close relatives of Argentine nationals buried there. The visit - based on humanitarian considerations - will take place under the auspices of the International Committee of the Red Cross (ICRC). Both Governments will seek the good offices of the ICRC and agree, through diplomatic channels, on the arrangements for and timing of the visit.

11.   Both delegations agreed that the feasibility and desirability of a general co-operation agreement should be examined through diplomatic channels.

12.   Both Governments, recognizing that the promotion and reciprocal protection of investments should encourage private initiative and increase prosperity in both States, agreed to begin, through diplomatic channels, the negotiation of an Investment Promotion and Protection Agreement.

13.   Both delegations agreed that it would be appropriate to abolish the requirement for visas for nationals of each country wishing to visit the other.

/...

A/45/136
S/21159
English
Page 4

This measure would become effective once negotiations had been concluded through diplomatic channels.

14.   Both Governments, conscious of the need to increase efforts to protect the environment, will work to ensure bilateral consultation and co-operation, including within the international institutions.

15.   Both Governments, recognizing the threat that illicit drugs and drug abuse have created for all countries, agreed to explore ways of collaborating in this field, including exchanges of information, control of trafficking and an agreement to trace, freeze and confiscate the proceeds of drug trafficking. The Argentine delegation announced that its Government would be represented at the world conference on "Demand Reduction and the Cocaine Threat" to be held in London in April 1990.

16.   Both delegations, noting the importance of current international trends towards greater political and economic interdependence and integration, agreed to consult through diplomatic channels on these trends, particularly those concerning the European Community and Latin America.

17.   It was agreed that both Governments would jointly send the text of the present statement and its appendices to the Secretary-General of the United Nations for distribution as an official document of the General Assembly, under agenda item 37, and of the Security Council. The United Kingdom will transmit the present joint statement to the Presidency and Commission of the European Community, and the Government of Argentina will do likewise to the Organization of American States.

18.   In conclusion, both delegations expressed their thanks to the Spanish Government for its generous hospitality and support.

APPENDIX I

Interim reciprocal information and consultation system

Both parties agree to establish an Interim Reciprocal Information and Consultation System for movements of units of their armed forces in areas of the south-west Atlantic. The aims of this system are to increase confidence between the United Kingdom of Great Britain and Northern Ireland and Argentina and to contribute to achieving a more normal situation in the region without unnecessary delay. The system consists of the following provisions:

I. DIRECT COMMUNICATION LINK

A.   A direct communication link will be established between the respective military authorities - under the supervision of both Foreign Ministries, in order to:

     (a) Reduce the possibility of incidents and limit their consequences if they should occur;

     (b) Increase common knowledge of military activities in the south-west Atlantic.

B.   The respective military authorities will be:

A/45/136
S/21159
English
Page 5

(a) Argentine Naval Authority: Comandante del Area Naval Austral (Ushuaia);

(b) Argentine Air Authority: Jefe de la Novena Brigada Aerea (Comodoro Rivadavia);

(c) British Authority: Commander British Forces Falkland Islands (Malvinas).

C. It is agreed to establish a direct radio link between the respective authorities, which will include voice and/or telex transmissions. The link will be manned on a 24-hour basis and will be tested at least once a week. Technical information relating to equipment, frequencies and modalities of use will be exchanged through diplomatic channels.

D. It is agreed to establish a communications plan for radio links between units and stations of the parties. Technical information will be exchanged through diplomatic channels.

II. DEFINITION OF UNITS

A. Ship

Any ship belonging to the naval forces of the parties bearing the external marks distinguishing warships of its nationality, under the command of an officer duly commissioned by the Government and whose name appears in the naval list, and manned by a crew who are under regular naval discipline, and British Fleet Auxiliaries.

B. Aircraft

Any aircraft belonging to the armed forces of the parties, manned by a military crew who are under regular armed forces discipline.

C. Combatant units

Any ship or aircraft equipped with weapons systems or means of offensive power or offensive projection capabilities (naval examples: aircraft carriers, cruisers, destroyers, frigates, corvettes, submarines, fast patrol boats, amphibious ships or ships carrying troops; aircraft examples: strike aircraft, fighters, bombers, missile or troop-carrying aircraft).

III. RECIPROCAL INFORMATION ABOUT MILITARY MOVEMENTS

1. Reciprocal written information will be provided through diplomatic channels, not less than 25 days in advance, about:

(a) Movements of naval forces involving four or more ships;

A/45/136
S/21159
English
Page 6

  (b) Movements of aerial forces involving four or more aircraft;

  (c) Exercises involving more than 1,000 men or more than 20 sorties by aircraft;

  (d) Amphibious or airborne exercises involving more than 500 men or more than 20 sorties by aircraft.

The areas of application of this measure are:

  For Argentine Forces: within rhumb lines joining the following geographical co-ordinates in the specified order: 46S 63W, 50S 63W, 50S 64W, 53S 64W, 53S 63W, 60S 63W, 60S 20W, 46S 20W, 46S 63W.

  For British Forces: the area south of parallel 40°S and west of meridian 20°W and north of 60°S.

Each party will accept the presence of an observer ship from the other party in the vicinity of naval forces involving four or more ships engaged in manoeuvres within the relevant area of application.

2.   Reciprocal notification of identity, intended track and purpose will be given, not less than 48 hours in advance, of a ship or an aircraft that intends to approach closer to coasts than 50 nautical miles by sea or 70 nautical miles by air.

  When specific movements of the kind described in this paragraph are intended to be carried out by combatant units and might cause political or military difficulty to the Argentine Government or to the British Government, the notifying party will be informed immediately and mutual agreement will be necessary to proceed.

IV. VERIFICATION

  Verification of compliance with the reciprocal information arrangements in provision III above will be by national means, by observer ships (as provided for in III.1), and by consultations through the direct communication link. If disagreement should arise, the parties would have recourse to the diplomatic channel.

V. RECIPROCAL VISITS

  Reciprocal visits to military bases and naval units may be agreed through the diplomatic channel on a case-by-case basis.

VI. APPLICABILITY OF INTERNATIONAL PRACTICE

  In situations not specifically covered in this system, it is understood that normal international practice will be applied on a reciprocal basis.

A/45/136
S/21159
English
Page 7

VII. DURATION

This system, including the reciprocal information measures, will be reviewed at regular diplomatic-technical meetings. The first of these meetings will take place within one year after the entry into force of the system and will be convened at a date to be agreed through the diplomatic channel.

APPENDIX II

Safety measures for naval and air units when operating in proximity

When operating in proximity, naval and air units of the parties will comply with the following general regulations and rules:

(a) Naval and air units of the parties shall avoid any movement or action that might be interpreted as a hostile act or an act carried out with hostile intent;

(b) Naval units of the parties shall manoeuvre in a manner that clearly shows their intentions and shall strictly observe the letter and spirit of the international regulations for preventing collisions at sea of 1972;

(c) Air units shall use the greatest caution and prudence when manoeuvring in proximity to units of the other party, in order to contribute to safety and avoid mutual interference;

(d) Naval and air units of the parties shall not simulate attacks nor aim guns, missile launchers, torpedo tubes, other weapons or fire control radars in the direction of units of the other party;

(e) Naval and air units of the parties shall not launch any object in the direction of passing ships or aircraft of the other party, nor use searchlights or other powerful illumination devices to illuminate their navigation bridges;

(f) Naval and air units of the parties operating in proximity shall avoid the darkening of lights and, in this respect, shall comply with the International Regulations for Preventing Collisions at Sea of 1972 and the provisions of annex VI of the Convention on International Civil Aviation of 1944;

(g) On no account shall the communication and detection systems of units of the other party be interfered with or disrupted;

(h) A prompt exchange of information shall be conducted in the event of any occurrence that might cause concern to the other party.

A/45/136
S/21159
English
Page 8

APPENDIX III

Maritime and air search and rescue

When communication or co-ordination is required in relation to maritime and air search and rescue (SAR), the following procedures will apply:

(a) The headquarters of the British Forces in the Falkland Islands (Islas Malvinas) shall inform the regional SAR co-ordination centres of the South-West Atlantic Area:

Maritime SAR: Ushuaia Maritime SAR Co-ordination Centre

Air SAR: Comodoro Rivadavia Air SAR Co-ordination Centre

(b) Maritime SAR operations shall be conducted in accordance with the SAR manual of the International Maritime Organization and the SAR manual for merchant ships. Air SAR operations shall be conducted in accordance with the provisions of annex XII to the Convention on International Civil Aviation and its amendments;

(c) In the event that joint participation in a SAR incident becomes necessary, the headquarters of the British Forces in the Falkland Islands (Islas Malvinas) and the appropriate Argentine SAR Co-ordination Centre will co-ordinate their activities.

APPENDIX IV

Safety of navigation

1.   The parties will exchange all relevant information so that Argentina, the Regional Co-ordinator of Navarea VI, as defined by the International Maritime Organization, may issue the appropriate notices to mariners for that area.

2.   In order to enhance flight safety, the parties agreed:

(a) To facilitate the operation of Argentine Flight Information Centres by supplying the information necessary for Argentina to provide the Air Traffic Control, Warning, Search and Rescue, Communication and Meteorological Services within the Argentine Flight Information Regions (FIR);

(b) To exchange information between the Falkland Islands (Islas Malvinas) and Comodoro Rivadavia (CRV) Flight Information Centre for identification of aircraft in flight in the FIRs, in particular on flights in the vicinity of coastal areas;

(c) To respond positively in an emergency to requests to provide alternative landing facilities at their airfields for each other's aircraft and aircraft of third parties; and

(d) To exchange aeronautical information about the airfields of both parties (navigation, approach and surface facilities).

Annex 51: Joint British and Argentine Statement of
November 28, 1990 (concerning conservation of
fisheries)

JOINT STATEMENT ON THE CONSERVATION OF FISHERIES

1.   The Government of the Argentine Republic and the
Government of the United Kingdom of Great Britain and
Northern Ireland agreed that the following formula on
sovereignty, contained in the Joint Statement issued at
Madrid on 19 October 1989, applies to this Statement and its
results:

"(1) Nothing in the conduct or content of the present
      meeting or of any similar subsequent meetings shall be
      interpreted as:

      (a) a change in the position of the United Kingdom
           with regard to sovereignty or territorial and
           maritime jurisdiction over the Falkland Islands,
           South Georgia and the South Sandwich Islands and
           the surrounding maritime areas;

      (b) a change in the position of the Argentine
           Republic with regard to sovereignty or
           territorial and maritime jurisdiction over the
           Falkland Islands, South Georgia and the South
           Sandwich Islands and the surrounding maritime
           areas;

      (c) recognition of or support for the position of the
           United Kingdom or the Argentine Republic with
           regard to sovereignty or territorial and maritime
           jurisdiction over the Falkland Islands, South
           Georgia and the South Sandwich Islands and the
           surrounding maritime areas.

 (2) No act of activity carried out by the United Kingdom,
      the Argentine Republic or third parties as a
      consequence and in implementation of anything agreed
      to in the present meeting or in any similar subsequent
      meetings shall constitute a basis for affirming,
      supporting, or denying the position of the United
      Kingdom or Argentine Republic regarding the
      sovereignty or territorial and maritime jurisdiction
      over the Falkland Islands, South Georgia and the South
      Sandwich Islands and the surrounding maritime areas."

2.   In order to contribute to the conservation of fish
stocks, the two Governments agreed to open the way for
cooperation in this field on an ad-hoc basis; this will be
done:

   a)   by means of the establishment of the "South
      Atlantic Fisheries Commission", composed of
      delegations from both states, to assess the state
      of fish stocks in the South Atlantic in accordance
      with paragraph 7 of the Joint Statement issued at
      Madrid on 15 February 1990;

   b)   by means of the temporary total prohibition of
      commercial fishing by vessels of any flag in the
      maritime area defined in the Annex to this Joint
      Statement, for conservation purposes.

The two Governments further agreed to review this Joint
Statement annually, in particular the duration of the total
prohibition.

3.   The Commission will be composed of a delegation from
each of the two states, and will meet at least twice a year,
alternately in Buenos Aires and London. Recommendations
shall be reached by mutual agreement. In accordance with
paragraph 7 of the Madrid Joint Statement of 15 February
1990, the maritime area which the Commission will consider
in relation to the conservation of the most significant
off-shore species will be waters between latitude 45°S and
latitude 60°S.

4.   The Commission will have the following
functions:

   a)   In accordance with paragraph 7 of the Joint
      Statement issued at Madrid on 15 February 1990, to
      receive from both States the available information
      on the operations of the fishing fleets, appropriate
      catch and effort statistics and analyses of the
      status of the stocks of the most significant
      off-shore species. Both governments will provide
      such information in the form recommended by the
      Commission.

   b)   To assess the information received and to submit to
      both Governments recommendations for the
      conservation of the most significant off-shore
      species in the area.

   c)   To propose to both Governments joint scientific
      research work on the most significant off-shore
      species.

d) In accordance with international law, to recommend
to both Governments possible actions for the
conservation in international waters of migratory and
straddling stocks and species related to them.

e) To monitor the implementation of the prohibition and
make recommendations in this regard to both
Governments.

5. The prohibition in paragraph 2(b) will take effect on 26
December 1990; both Governments agreed to cooperate in order
to implement it.

6. Each Government will take the appropriately related
administrative measures in accordance with this Joint
Statement.

A N N E X

The area referred to in paragraph 2 (b) is the one
encompassed by the lines of the type specified in the
second column, joining points in the first column defined
to the nearest minute of arc on WGS 72 Datum by
coordinates of Latitude and Longitude in the order given.

Coordinates of Latitude and Longitude	Line Type
1. 47'42'S, 60'41'W	
	1-2 rhumb line along meridian.
2. 49'00'S, 60'41'W	
	2-3 parallel of latitude.
3. 49'00'S, 60'55'W	
	3-4 rhumb line along meridian.

4. 49°20'S, 60°55'W

> 4-5 arc of the circle which has a radius of 150 nautical miles and its centre at Latitude 51°40'S, Longitude 59°30'W, moving clockwise.

5. 54°02'S, 58°13'W

> 5-6 rhumb line.

6. 54°38'S, 58°02'W

> 6-7 meridian.

7. 55°30'S, 58°02'W

> 7-8 rhumb line

8. 56°14'S, 58°31W

> 8-9 a line drawn anti-clockwise along the maximum limit of jurisdiction over fisheries in accordance with international law.

9. 47°42'S, 60°41'W

The area mentioned above is described for the sole purpose of the total prohibition   in paragraph 2 (b) of this Joint Statement and, in particular, the formula on sovereignty in paragraph 1 of this Joint Statement applies to it.